G000146457

About The Author

Ian Wishart is an award-winning journalist and author, with a 25 year career in radio, television and magazines, a #1 talk radio show and two #1 bestselling books to his credit. Together with his wife Heidi, they edit and publish the news magazine *Investigate*

For Joshua & Isabella

Eve's Bite

Ian Wishart

Howling At The Moon Publishing Ltd

First edition published 2007
Howling At The Moon Publishing Ltd
PO Box 302-188
North Harbour
North Shore 0751
NEW ZEALAND

www.evesbite.com
email: editorial@investigatemagazine.com

ISBN 978-0-9582401-1-6

Typeset in Adobe Garamond
Cover concept: Ian Wishart, Heidi Wishart, Bozidar Jokanovic
Cover photo: Joe Klune

To get another copy of this book airmailed to you anywhere in the world, or to purchase a fully text-searchable digital edition, visit our website:

www.evesbite.com

CONTENTS

Prologue

Read Me First
The End of the Golden Weather

"The Trojans wondered why the great Wooden Horse had been left behind. And there were some who considered that it had been left there as an offering to the goddess, Pallas Athene, and they thought it should be brought within the city. Others were wiser and would have left the Wooden Horse alone. But those who considered that it should be brought within prevailed; and, as the Horse was too great to bring through the gate, they flung down Part of the wall that they might bring it through. The Wooden Horse was brought within the walls and left upon the streets of the city and the darkness of the night fell."
Homer, The Odyssey

The call came some time just after 2am. I'd been late to bed after finishing my national talk radio slot the previous evening, then killing a couple of hours on last minute deadline prep for our magazine, *Investigate*, due to go to press later that week. And so, when the phone trilled annoyingly beside my ear in the early hours of September 12, 2001, New Zealand time, it took a while to shake the fog of the night's deepest slumber. So much so, in fact, that the first time it rang I dozily hung up on the caller without either listening or saying anything.

Seconds later, it rang again.

Fumbling for the receiver, the perfunctory greeting muttered, I was shaken into a sudden mental clarity by the familiar but this time urgent tones of Shayne Kavanagh, *Investigate's* London-based photo-journalist. There was an edge to his voice that made me sit up this time, and pay attention.

"Listen you dumb bastard! It's Shayne. New York's been attacked. It's been bombed!"

Nah. At two in the morning, with just an hour of sleep under my belt, that particular concept was refusing to register in any coherent way. Kavanagh probably guessed as much from my silence.

"Are you there? America is under attack! Planes have hit the World Trade

Centre, New York's burning, the Pentagon's been hit, I'm watching it here in London on CNN. Do you want me to fly there?"

As a news magazine editor right on deadline, there are sometimes instant decisions you have to make. As a human being faced with the enormity of events like 9/11, sometimes there are instant decisions you simply can't make. I remember pretty much dropping the phone with a vague promise to call Kavanagh back, and then scrabbling for the TV remote. That was the last sleep I got that night.

As a front-line news and current affairs journalist with a quarter century of reportage under my belt, I've seen some sights. I've witnessed the carnage of head-on road collisions and grisly murders, I've survived two near-miss air incidents, I've been inside a TV news chopper being shot at by a psychopathic gunman on the ground below. I've helped tackle an armed bank robber who'd just wounded two people (admittedly I only realized he was armed when I came face to face with the weapon as a group of us wrestled him to the ground) I've even had to break the news (inadvertently, thanks to police forgetting to notify the next of kin) to a mother and child that their airline pilot husband and father has just been killed after ploughing his commercial flight straight into the side of a mountain, with the loss of all on board.

I have experienced much, but nothing came close to preparing me for the gut-wrenching anguish of what flickered live across the TV screen from New York early that morning: the twin towers collapsing, the office workers jumping to certain death rather than waiting to be burned or crushed, the then-unaccounted-for Flight 93. In short, like millions of others across the world in those moments, I sat transfixed as the cathode ray tube in the corner balefully bombarded me with images of destruction, death and malevolent evil on a scale truly hard to fathom.

For an earlier generation, this sense of innocence lost was perhaps best exemplified by the fall of Camelot – John F. Kennedy's assassination in November 1963 at the height of the US/Soviet cold war. Whilst it is true that those presidential gunshots continue to ricochet through history even to this very day, what happened on September 11 will be writ large in history textbooks of the future - probably in Arabic - as the beginning of the end of the West, the straw that broke a civilization's back.

Of course, the story of the death of the West isn't quite that simple – its roots go back a century or more – but there can be little doubt that 9/11 marked the point of no return.

As the tears streamed down my face in the reflected glow of the TV screen on that September morn six years ago, I grieved not just for those whose murders I was watching live on screen. I wept, too, in the realization that this was a new kind of war that the West was unlikely to win.

No matter what President Bush, or Hillary or Obama or Kerry or anyone else tells you, the West is ultimately dead in the water on this one unless the citizens of the United States, Canada, Britain, Australia and New Zealand wake up one morning and smell the smoke from their civilization's engine room. No amount of superior weapons technology, no amount of "surgical" air strikes, no amount of "dialogue" is going to make a blind bit of difference to Islamofascism's inexorable advance across the surface of the planet.

The reason for this is simple, but many in the news media and politics apparently don't want you to hear it – largely, I venture, because telling you would first involve having to admit that their own view of how the world should run is fundamentally and irretrievably wrong. And after all, pride comes before a fall – especially the fall of a civilization.

As you read this book, I hope you'll join the dots and start to realize what you, your family and your friends are facing. The West will lose, unless we can end the poison that is now weakening our civilization by the day. It is our kryptonite, and until we neutralize it we cannot save the planet, let alone ourselves.

In one sense, this book is not really about Islamofascism at all. In another sense, it all is. The rise of radical Islam is merely the opportunistic or parasitic infection that sets in because of the victim's weakened state. Rome fell to the barbarians not because the Goths truly were superior to Rome, but because they were one parasite too many on a civilization already weakened by its own depravity and introspection.

Likewise, if the West's internal problems are not dealt with, it won't matter whether it's mad mullahs or members of a resurgent Pygmy tribe out of Africa – someone, somewhere, sometime will deal the West its death blow.

In terms of being in the right place at the right time, Islamofascists have become 'catch of the day' pretty much by default, which is why I've paid them due care and attention in the conclusion. But never lose sight of the underlying plot: the cancer afflicting the West is the real story of *Eve's Bite*, a story of seductive and destructive philosophies and social engineering that within the space of a generation have intellectually crippled the greatest civilization the world has ever seen.

My thesis is simple, that three intellectual forces over the past 150 years have converged and come to dominate Western society: Darwinism, Marxism and, to a lesser but nonetheless significant extent, Eugenics – Darwinism's illegitimate child beloved of the Nazis and scientists. While public opinion polls show a majority of people don't believe Darwin's Theory of Evolution, and even fewer would describe themselves as Marxists, nonetheless much of the education curriculum in state schools is consistent with Marxist education theory and belief. Most students who've been through the state system have never heard the phrase "Marxist" used in class and could not even tell you what it is, yet if you examine their beliefs you'll find they have been heavily influenced by what their parents would once have called communism.

American philosopher Peter Kreeft set out 17 years ago how Marxism works for change:[1]

> THERE IS NO OBJECTIVELY permanent moral law [and] no subjectively permanent moral law; that human nature is malleable and that *conscience can be shaped, reshaped, or eradicated by social engineering*. This is the position of Marx and of Behaviorism. [emphasis added]

Is there anyone reading this who doesn't think efforts are being made to socially engineer people by manipulating issues of conscience? Given that our students are now either voting or about to join the voting class, their indoctrination poses a major threat to democracy and the destiny of the West, and here's why: civilizations can turn on a dime or, in sociological-speak, in a generation or two. That's because ultimately a civilization put to the test must be able to physically and mentally defend itself. Traditionally, when push comes to shove, that means men aged 16 to 45. But if you create a culture where military service is scorned, where defence forces are not maintained, and where a Marxist state education system drums into kids that there is nothing worth fighting for, then firstly you have a morale problem. Secondly, you have a reality problem because large portions of the map don't see the world the way you do and are increasingly excited about having a whack at an emasculated West. Thirdly, you have a bums-on-seats problem because birthrates in the West are so low that "our" next generation of potential combatants is much smaller than "theirs" - those cultures with birthrates 600% higher.

Which leaves the West relying on the only differential left on the board – technology, in the form of nuclear weapons. Given the speed at which Islamic countries are going nuclear, that differential won't last much longer either.

It was clear Marxist policy, written decades ago, to strip the West of the will to resist. Congratulations, they've pretty much done it.

None of this is to argue that the problem is two-dimensional; that I am suggesting a grand conspiracy has somehow re-created Invasion of the Body Snatchers and everyone who attends a public school or votes for a left-wing government is automatically a vacuous robot. What I *am* arguing is that the political correctness and Marxist indoctrination taking place makes people more *likely* to see the world through those eyes, and makes it harder for any sustained defence of Western culture before the poison weakens resolve again.

---

1   http://www.catholiceducation.org/articles/apologetics/ap0100.html

To argue otherwise is to suggest Advertising doesn't work and Propaganda has no effect on the human mind which, as you'll see from the evidence in this book, is an utterly ridiculous assertion.

The State-directed brainwashing/re-programming/thought control (whatever you want to call it) of the public doesn't prevent individuals from breaking free, but it does make it harder for individuals to do so. The biggest danger however is that it creates a mass bloc of voters who have been educated to believe in the same things that a socialist State believes in, and you end up in a self-perpetuating cycle of Marxism. As Soviet dictator Vladimir Lenin once boasted, capitalists will sell Marxism the rope that Marxism will use to hang capitalists with. This is where the West currently teeters. Contrary views are being excluded from the education system, and increasingly from the news media, and conservative politicians who attempt to articulate their views are often gently ridiculed by the media or, if it looks like their views may be getting public support, aggressively targeted.

Marxists frequently rely on ridicule and name-calling to deflect attention from their agenda. For example, they'll describe books like this one as pushing the "reds under the beds conspiracy theory", or "Islamophobia". They rely on the fact that most people won't bother to read the book; the public usually rely on media coverage of the book to apprise them of the debate, so they won't be exposed to the coherent, fully-documented evidence in here.

My critics will be begging and fervently praying to whatever Deity they *don't* believe in, that none of you read this book, and none of you talk about it with your kids, friends and workmates.

So it is up to you, the readers, to slip below the radar of the State and in some cases a brain-dead media, to tell your friends what you've read and to encourage them to get hold of a copy of *Eve's Bite* and assess the evidence for themselves, without being distracted by negative media spin.

The biggest problem, as I see it, is that since the mid-1800s the West has been in spiritual and cultural decline, even allowing for the American century, and that the twin vultures of Marxism and Islamofascism are now orbiting in ever-decreasing circles.

Can we survive? Only if we rediscover our core beliefs, rediscover what it means to be a Westerner – for all its faults the greatest civilization in history – and only if we re-educate ourselves and our children about the psychological techniques of persuasion being used against us, and vote in new political administrations who'll take a blow-torch to Marxism and Islamofascism in our communities wherever they show up.

As Mark Steyn remarked soon after 9/11: we hand-wringing and soft liberals of the West are "sleepwalking towards national suicide" because we're either too frightened or too stupid to wake up and do something about it.

Bored with our own history and achievements, we let our attention turn towards philosophical baubles and alluring ideas from other lands that washed up on our shores. And, like the naïve Trojans admiring a magnificent wooden horse on their city's doorstep some 29 centuries ago, we too have welcomed modern day wooden horses into our homes, our cities and our lives. It is too late to shut the gate, the horsemen in this latter-day apocalypse are well and truly on the loose.

1

School Daze
The Dumbing Down of a Generation

"The National Socialist state, growing out of a revolution, had the task of centrally leading both propaganda and education, uniting two concepts that are related but not identical, molding them into a unity that in the long term can serve the government and people."
Josef Goebbels, Nazi Propaganda Minister, Nuremberg, 1934

I n a Los Angeles school classroom, a teacher is stunned when her high school class has no idea what the Holocaust was. Across the Atlantic, in a British school, a survey reveals some students think the D-Day invasion in World War 2 was "against New Zealand". The survey, taken for the 60th anniversary of D-Day in 2004, showed massive levels of generational memory loss about the biggest conflict in recorded world history.[2] Some high school students believed D-Day happened in 1066 (the date of William the Conqueror's invasion of England, or 1776 (the US Declaration of Independence).

One student, who correctly guessed D-Day was the date the Allies landed on the beaches of Normandy to begin the push against the Nazis, nonetheless incorrectly wrote that D-Day was led by Private Ryan, the fictitious character in Steven Spielberg's WW2 blockbuster *Saving Private Ryan*.

In all, only 28% of the students knew what D-Day actually was. The survey asked a range of other questions about the World War 2 event, most of which the students were unable to answer. Reuters news agency quoted experts saying "British pupils' ignorance about the basic facts of D-Day probably reflected recent educational trends to move away from 'dates and battles' in teaching history".

As you'll discover later in this book, history has been replaced in many cases by "Queer Studies", "Women's Studies", and "Tolerance Studies", reflecting recent educational trends to move away from knowledge-based learning in favour of social conditioning.

2   http://www.telegraph.co.uk/news/main.jhtml;sessionid=OCP2Z2YM22UTZQFIQMFCM5WA VCBQYJVC?xml=/news/2004/05/30/ndday30.xml

One child, however, scored a perfect 100% in the D-Day exam, stunning his teacher. "I asked him how he knew material which we had not covered in school," the teacher said, "He told me he had picked it up from a D-Day game he played on his computer."

Thank God for capitalist endeavours!

How is it that one of the most significant events of the 20th century could slip so soon into mythology for children undergoing a state education? Well, if you think the kids are rough, try their parents. Another survey of 2,000 British adults found a staggering 11% believe Adolf Hitler is a fictional character, and one in every 20 people (that's nearly equivalent to the number of people who voted for the Greens in the last election) think that Conan the Barbarian is a real figure from early Nordic history.

Nearly 33% don't believe the Cold War – between the West and the communist Soviet Union – was a real event, yet more than 6% believe that the *War of the Worlds*, H.G. Wells' science fiction tale about an invasion by Martians, is real.

New Zealanders will be pleased to know that one in every 30 British adults thinks "the Battle of Helm's Deep in the *Lord of the Rings* trilogy, featuring slavering Orcs, actually took place," reported Britain's *Independent* newspaper.[3]

There is an oft-quoted saying from early 20th century philosopher George Santayana, "Those who cannot remember the past are condemned to repeat it."

But what about those who aren't even taught about the past in any meaningful sense? Because that's where our current generation of school students are at. A search of the entire NZ school curriculum for history and social studies, which can be done online[4] at the Ministry of Education's website, reveals the weighting given to various study topics.

Unless a student is optionally taking History in years 11 or 12, they won't find the Nazis on the formal curriculum during their entire time in school. The MoE offers one NCEA paper, which briefly explores how the Nazis rose to power in the years 1933 and 1934, and another on the Munich Crisis and the attempts to appease Hitler to gain peace. That's it. Additionally, approved optional classroom resources include a sprinkling of other external websites, one of which profiles Nancy Wake, the New Zealander known as "the White Mouse", who helped lead the French Resistance; another tells the story of escapes from Colditz prison camp; the third provides information about the holocaust and the fourth discusses "victims of National Socialism in Germany and right-wing extreme movements".

Presumably we might find "left wing extreme movements" being studied in the NZ curriculum, but they're not described as such. On closer inspection, the only negative portrayal of a left wing extreme movement is the Pol Pot

3   *NZ Herald*, April 6, 2004, "Hitler mythical but Conan real"
4   http://www.tki.org.nz/e/search/

regime in Cambodia, but students are left feeling happy and validated because the good guys – in the form of the left-wing communist Vietnamese Army - came to the rescue and defeated Pot. In the subject list under social sciences, social studies or history, there is no heading for Socialism, nor Marxism, and no study of Soviet dictator Josef Stalin's purges that killed tens of millions.

There is a compulsory social studies unit on the Vietnam War which takes an anti-war perspective, and an optional History unit on the same where students are encouraged to convince their class why the communist liberation of Vietnam from the corrupt South Vietnamese and the Americans was a good thing.

There are however 101 items listed under the heading "Social Justice", 157 under "Women in History" including a large number of compulsory units, 29 results on Women's Suffrage, 96 on Diversity, 63 on Racism, 0 on the US Constitution, 0 on the Magna Carta…I think you probably get the picture.

It is amazing to see how far education has sunk since the State took over the curriculum, and in the spirit of the title of this chapter, it is worth looking at some of the history currently being rapidly forgotten. After all, an education system that does not teach honestly about the major events of Western civilization is doomed to turn out dull-witted, uninformed people – in other words, the gene pool of left-wing voters.

How can a student recognize Marxism in government policy if their education entirely overlooks it? How can a student recognize they're being played like a piano by state propaganda if they've never studied Propaganda's elite concert pianists, the Nazis?

In writing this book, it became self-evident that I would need to spell out some lessons of history before I could show how they're being repeated.

The journey begins in the mid 1800s. Three major forces are at work in Western civilization at the time, all of which have played a major role in the events we examine in this book. The first - Charles Darwin's *On The Origin of Species* better known as the Theory of Evolution – was scientific but massively religious in scope, and we'll explore it elsewhere in this book.

The second of these forces, Marxism, was political. The emergence of the modern Republic – the United States of America – on the back of a popular uprising against the tyranny of monarchial rule, heralded a new kind of politics in the late 18th century. Citizens started flexing their muscles against centuries of direct rule by either Kings or their parliaments. France was the next to catch the revolution bug when its King and Queen were beheaded, and the republican movement sent shockwaves throughout the ruling classes in Europe.

Monarchies had traditionally ruled via a chain of command that nominally began with God, then the King, then his subjects. The Republicans, on the other hand, saw it as God, then the People, then the Government. The idea was that only individuals could have a personal relationship with God, and that truly free individuals were answerable first to God, rather than as "subjects" or chattels of a King. The People, being sovereign themselves under the Republican system, then collectively delegated their sovereignty to a Government and empowered it to act in their name for the common good of their country. The government was supposed to be the servant of the people.

But although the idea of revolution caught on, not everyone had the same view on the chain of command, or the values that the new nation-states should adhere to, and amidst the death throes of empires in Europe, there rose up a philosopher by the name of Karl Marx, the man whose name is synonymous with Communism, Marxism and Socialism.

Marx, for example, didn't share any Christian values with the American revolutionaries half a century earlier.

"Religion is the sigh of the oppressed creature, the heart of a heartless world, and the soul of soulless conditions," he wrote. "It is the opium of the people…The first requisite for the happiness of the people is the abolition of religion."

In Christianity, which was the only major religion in Europe at the time, Marx knew he had a substantial foe. In Marx's ideal world, the people would cease to believe in God and believe only in the state. Eventually, he figured, once the world had converted to socialism, individual states wouldn't matter any longer either, and the people would simply believe in socialist ideals. Picking up on the Biblical warning that mankind cannot serve two masters, Marx figured outlawing one master was the only solution.[5]

> "WHEN ENGELS AND I first joined the secret Communist Society we made it a condition that everything tending to encourage superstitious belief in authority was to be removed from the statutes. Law, morality, religion, are to him so many bourgeois prejudices, behind which lurk in ambush just as many bourgeois interests.
>
> "Communism abolishes eternal truths, it abolishes all religion, and all morality."

Let that message sink in, for a moment, and consider the society in which you now live. Is it closer to Christendom now, or Communism? How many of you still believe in "eternal truths", as opposed to "that may be true for you but not for me"?

Marx *hated* Christianity, and had done since his youth. He was six when his German-Jewish family converted to Christianity, and evidently he wrestled

5   http://en.wikiquote.org/wiki/Karl_Marx

with it. In a letter written at the age of 17, Marx expressed the Christian message in a nutshell:

"Union with Christ bestows inner exaltation, consolation in suffering, calm assurance, and a heart which is open to love of mankind, to all that is noble, to all that is great, not out of ambition, not through the desire of fame, but only because of Christ."

Yet just three months later a letter of advice from his father suggests the teenager was starting to stray:

"Faith [in God] is a real [requirement] of man sooner or later, and there are moments in life when even the atheist is involuntarily drawn to worship the Almighty."

Just two years later, Karl Marx's atheism and ideas of transforming society led his father to write to the 19 year old:

"Since [your] heart is obviously animated and governed by a demon not granted to all men, is that demon heavenly or Faustian?"[6]

During his university years, Marx wrote that "criticism of religion is the foundation of all criticism". He was heavily influenced by another German thinker, Ludwig Feuerbach, who wrote in *Essence of Christianity* three key principles that Marx picked up on: firstly, that "Man is the highest essence for man", which meant he should bow to no god; secondly, that "Man makes religion, religion does not make man"; and thirdly that religion is simply man's way of explaining terrestrial phenomena that seem supernatural to him.

How many times have you heard atheists and callers on talkback radio relying on these arguments to ridicule Christianity?

Marx knew that to achieve his aims of pushing Christianity out of Europe and eventually the world, he first had to brainwash his "proletariat" – to re-educate them with Marxist principles – and then give them the vote.

"Democracy is the road to socialism…The meaning of peace is the absence of opposition to socialism."

Funnily enough, Islam has a similar definition of peace.

Marx was one of the first to call for a free state education for all children, although of course his motives were ulterior. Later socialists like Italy's Antonio Gramsci and France's Louis Althusser developed more detailed plans for education, noting that the ruling class, whatever it might be, determines the definition of "knowledge" or "truth" – which gels with the curriculum priorities I alluded to a few pages back: the current 'ruling class' in Western bureaucracies, being Marxist-leaning, have determined that studying "isms" is more important than studying history and the foundations of Western civilization. Marx, Gramsci and Althusser would approve. They saw Marxist capture of education as imperative.

There is an interesting discourse in Althusser's *Lenin and Philosophy and*

Other Essays, where he describes the two branches of "State Apparatus", the first being institutions of enforcement like Police or the Army, and the second being what he calls Ideological State Apparatuses, which are organizations or groups that determine how we think. Intriguingly, Althusser describes schools as a "*Religious* Ideological State Apparatus" [emphasis added], a clear hat-tip to the idea that schools are there to fashion children's *beliefs*, not teach them objective facts, and he states that the "dominant ideological State apparatus, is the educational apparatus, which has in fact replaced in its functions the previously dominant ideological State apparatus, the Church".

Hopefully you have begun to see why they don't teach NZ school students the facts about Marxism – the brighter kids might realize they're guinea-pigs in a Marxist ideological experiment. Socialists don't really see schools as learning institutions, but more as Churches of the State, with your children as their congregation. They *do* teach religion in schools, just not the one you think!

Marxist thought came to dominate the young intellectual classes, and found an ally in Darwinism.

"Darwin, who I am now reading, is splendid," wrote Friedrich Engels in a letter[7] to Marx soon after *On The Origin of Species* was published in 1859. Both communists could identify with "survival of the fittest", and saw that the biological ideas advanced by Darwin could equally be imposed on society at large.

The theme was later elaborated on by Soviet revolutionary Leon Trotsky, who first of all explained why atheism was crucial in the education system[8]:

> "RELIGIOUSNESS IS IRRECONCILABLE with the Marxian standpoint. We are of the opinion that atheism, as an inseparable element of the materialist view of life, is a necessary condition for the theoretical education of the revolutionist. He who believes in another world is not capable of concentrating all his passion on the transformation of this one."

Trotsky then wrote that Darwin's Theory of Evolution must be taught in state schools, not because it is a good theory but because it makes belief in God impossible – and that was the supreme aim of Marxism:

> "DARWINISM ITSELF IS … entirely irreconcilable with this belief. In this, as in other respects, Darwinism is a forerunner, a preparation for Marxism. Taken in a broadly materialist and dialectic sense, Marxism is the application of Darwinism to human society."

7   http://mmcconeghy.com/students/supsocialdarwinism.html
8   http://www.marxists.org/history/international/comintern/sections/britain/periodicals/communist_review/1923/7/com_ed.htm

Karl Marx, meanwhile, was so enamoured of Darwin that he offered to dedicate his thesis *Das Kapital* to the biologist, but Darwin turned down the offer, saying that endorsing the open attacks on religion that Marx was making could leave Darwin open to flak from members of his own family.

Not that other members of Darwin's family were shy of jumping on the evolution, triumph-of-science bandwagon. One of these was Francis Galton, a cousin of Charles Darwin and now widely recognized as the father of the Eugenics movement, our third major ideology we're exploring.

Galton believed that Darwin's Theory of Evolution, natural selection and survival of the fittest all meant that science could and should intervene to improve the makeup of human society. Why leave it to nature, when the superior intellect of Man could alter nature's course and speed things up. To wit, Eugenics entailed selective breeding of the rich and bright, whilst preventing the poor and dullwitted from breeding.

Galton's Eugenics Society hosted guest speakers like Professor Karl Pearson:

> "WE ARE CEASING AS A NATION to breed intelligence as we did fifty to a hundred years ago. The mentally better stock in the nation is not reproducing itself at the same rate as it did of old; the less able and the less energetic are more fertile than the better stocks. No scheme of wider or more thorough education will bring up, in the scale of intelligence, hereditary weakness to the level of hereditary strength. The only remedy, if one be possible at all, is to alter the relative fertility of the good and bad stocks in the community."[9]

It is important to remember that these advocates were the leading scientific lights of their time, early in the 20th century. Galton himself wrote of the need to worm eugenics into popular culture with an early form of propaganda:[10]

> "THERE ARE THREE STAGES to be passed through. Firstly, it must be made familiar as an academic question, until its exact importance has been understood and accepted as a fact. Secondly, it must be recognized as a subject whose practical development deserves serious consideration. And thirdly, *it must be introduced into the national conscience, like a new religion.*" [emphasis added]

---

9   http://galton.org/browse/galton/search/books/essays-on-eugenics/pages/essays-eugenics_0086.htm

10   http://galton.org/cgi-bin/searchImages/galton/search/books/essays-on-eugenics/pages/essays-eugenics_0049.htm

What is it with these whacky 19th century philosophers and their obsession with creating new religions based on evolutionary theory? Anyway, Galton continues:

> "IT HAS, INDEED, strong claims to become an orthodox religious tenet of the future, for Eugenics cooperates with the workings of Nature by securing that humanity shall be represented by the fittest races. What Nature does blindly, slowly, and ruthlessly, man may do providently, quickly, and kindly. As it lies within his power, so it becomes his duty to work in that direction… the improvement of our stock seems to me one of the highest objects that we can reasonably attempt."

I'll return to Eugenics later in the book, because it has re-surfaced in modern times as genetic modification, stem cell research, euthanasia and selective screening and culling of fetuses. But suffice to say that by the early 20th century, these three major ideologies were trying to achieve major social change in different ways: Marxism, through what philosopher Steven Pinker calls "social engineering", Darwinism by inspiring the "death of God" movement across society, and Eugenics – applied Darwinism – leading to a brave new world based on selective breeding, killing of "inferior stock", and the creation of "a master race" by science.

All three doctrines are founded on atheism. These doctrines caused more bloodshed in the 20th century than had been spilt in all the recorded wars of human history combined, and two of these doctrines (Darwinism has been politically strong throughout) – albeit in modified form - are making a comeback today in Western education and popular media.

To understand why they are so dangerous, however, first requires a return to what many students apparently now believe is a fictional event: World War 2.

2

PR Stormtroopers
The Legacy of the Nazis

"If the day should ever come when we [the Nazis] must go, if some day we are compelled to leave the scene of history, we will slam the door so hard that the universe will shake and mankind will stand back in stupefaction…"
Josef Goebbels, Nazi Minister of Propaganda, 1944

Goebbels is long dead, but there is some truth to his provocative challenge. The echoes of Nazism continue to reverberate around the planet, six decades after its disappearance. Like Marxism, not everything the Nazis did has been bad for humanity in the long run. Where Marx made us aware of the worst excesses of capitalist greed and their impact on working conditions, and where he provided the impetus for free education (albeit that his supporters have recently managed to capture our education and social policy), the Nazis have given us rocket science, the jet engine, Volkswagen, BMW, Porsche and freeway systems.

But the legacy not so frequently talked about is the secret weapon that helped them gain power: propaganda – the ability to tailor their policies to hit the hearts and minds of ordinary Germans and gently lead them to Hell without virtually a murmur of protestation. Scholars, politicians and PR strategists are still "stupefied" to this day at the sheer animal cunning and Orwellian "thought re-programming" techniques that Hitler and his administration employed to soundly thrash the average German - whilst making the victim believe it was good for him! The reason it isn't talked about much is because everyone in positions of power has studied Nazi propaganda techniques and they're now used on a daily basis in every country in the West as the basis of political spin, PR and advertising.

One of the first weak points that the Nazis exploited to gain power was Germany's young people. Hitler, and more importantly Goebbels, knew that getting control of children and teenagers, harnessing their natural anti-establishment rebellious streak and taking advantage of youthful idealism, was a way to control their parents.

The Nazis had started youth organizations in the early 1920s, a decade *before* they came to power and long before anyone took them seriously as a threat. But while Establishment Germany slept – occasionally waking long enough to snigger at the ranting Adolf Hitler and his rag-tag band of followers - the Nazi party worked hard. In that decade, they built the foundations for their future secret police, the Gestapo, with some of those early graduates of the Nazi youth movement.

"From the time a boy entered the Hitler Youth until he became a soldier or a member of the SS, he received a total education in Nazi ideology," records one Holocaust website.[11] "Loyalty to the Hitler Youth took precedence over loyalty to one's family."

Swept up in loyalty to the greater cause, children were encouraged to become informers on the views, opinions and actions of their parents and neighbours – for the good of the country and for the good of their families, they were told.

Of course, in the early days, Hitler's team only *collected* the intelligence, more as an exercise in seeing how far they could push loyalty than anything else, because they had no powers to do anything with it. But they quickly saw how propaganda used on teenagers turned them into ideological robots.

Adolf Hitler would later boast of his success in swinging teens behind "the cause".[12]

"WHEN AN OPPONENT DECLARES, 'I will not come over to your side', I calmly say, 'Your child belongs to us already. A people lives forever. What are you? You will pass on. Your descendants, however, now stand in the new camp. In a short time they will know nothing else but this new community."

He would later add:

"THIS NEW REICH will give its youth to no one, but will itself take youth and give to youth its education and its own upbringing."[13]

American Nazi war crimes prosecutor Major Wallis told the Nuremberg hearings that one of the reasons the Nazis were able to become so totalitarian

11   http://www.flholocaustmuseum.org/history_wing/thirdreich/hitler_youth.cfm
12   http://www.nizkor.org/hweb/imt/tgmwc/tgmwc-01/tgmwc-01-04-01.html
13   ibid

was their control of the school curriculum:

"THE NATION WAS BEING psychologically prepared...One of the most important steps was the re-shaping of the educational system so as to educate the German youth to be amenable to their will."[14]

Something to think about as modern teenagers embrace modern propaganda and the "isms" they're required to learn about in state schools.

Hitler's policy was that "youth should be led by youth" – that children were more likely to absorb propaganda from peers just a few years older, than middle-aged balding men. In this sense the Nazis were way ahead of their time in figuring out peer pressure. Children from the age of 10 were recruited to the Hitler Youth and its sub-organisations, where they met weekly to learn all about the problems in the world and how Nazism was the only fair and just solution, while propaganda officials like Berlin's Schulze Wechsungen rubbed their hands together with glee.

"We had to destroy our airplanes, tanks, guns and the like," he said of Germany's forced disarmament in the years after the World War 1 defeat, "but not the weapon of propaganda. How could we not have used it, who is foolish enough to underestimate its power? We owe our rise to it and will have to depend on it even more in the future. It is a powerful tool in molding the nature and the thinking of the new, the modern man."

By the time the war broke out, membership had grown from only a thousand in the mid 1920s to more than eight million.

As the online encyclopedia, Wikipedia, reports, the Boy Scout movement – currently under sustained attack in the West from gay activist groups – was similarly hounded by the Nazis.

"After outlawing the Boy Scouts in all the lands Germany controlled, the Hitler Youth appropriated many of the Scouts' activities, though changed in content and intention. A limited amount of cruelty of the older boys toward the younger was tolerated and even encouraged, since it was believed this would weed out the unfit and harden the rest."

And hard they were. Again, this from Wikipedia:

"During the Battle of Berlin, Axmann's Hitler Youth formed a major part of the last line of German defense, and were reportedly among the fiercest German soldiers."

The frontline troops, fighting to save Berlin in the final days of the war, were boys as young as 11, still battling long after their adult colleagues had dropped their weapons and fled.

These were the children of parents who, fearful that the children they had

---

14   ibid

originally cheerfully volunteered for Hitler Youth would betray them, wittingly or unwittingly, had reluctantly signed up to join the Nazi Party lest their lack of enthusiasm for "the cause" became a talking point. Those who didn't accept that Germany had a 'Jewish problem' were initially laughed at and ridiculed by the Nazis as 'deniers' – in much the same way that scientists trying to argue that global warming is *not* man-made are currently being labeled "climate change deniers" by politicians like Al Gore or New Zealand's David Parker. In Nazi Germany, of course, the penalty for continuing to "deny" was death.

The key role of propaganda, however, was to minimize the occurrence of "deniers" by making their positions seem utterly ridiculous and unpatriotic to the average German.

"Propaganda is a means to an end," said Josef Goebbels at the 1934 Nuremberg Rally. "Its purpose is to lead the people to an understanding that will allow it to willingly and *without internal resistance* [emphasis added] devote itself to the tasks and goals of a superior leadership.

"It is not only a matter of doing the right thing; the people must understand that the right thing *is* the right thing. Propaganda includes everything that helps the people to realize this."

Are you recognizing any modern political spin in this? Smacking? Kyoto?

"Propaganda often has particular importance in that it speaks to the emotions rather than to pure understanding," wrote Berlin-based propaganda official Wechsungen, also in 1934. "The individual as well as the masses are subject to "attitudes"; their emotions determine their condition. The politician may not coldly ignore these emotions; he must recognize and understand them if he is to choose the proper of propaganda to reach his goals."[15]

And if you've ever wondered why, like a Hydra, some issues just refuse to die over the years and keep coming back no matter how many times the public reject them, it is because the Nazis taught stamina, when it comes to waging the battle, and the need to keep wearing down resistance:

"Propaganda strives for long term effects," emphasized Wechsungen. "Only occasionally does it need to aim for momentary successes. Truly effective propaganda must achieve a continuing understanding of the masses. It must use effective suggestion, which I define as an idea transformed into reality through the subconscious.

"The essential task of propaganda is to use psychological skill to create a favorable atmosphere. As Schopenhauer says: 'When the heart resists, the mind will not accept.'

"We are on the attack, on the march. There is no turning back, no wavering. The propagandists must think subjectively. Absolutely subjectively, one-sidedly! He has under all circumstances to avoid the notorious and dangerous

15   http://www.calvin.edu/academic/cas/gpa/polprop.htm

German objectivism! He need not weigh right and wrong, he does not need to worry if there might be some slight truth on the enemy's side. Propaganda is concerned only with *its* goal, with *its* justice, *its* truth. All else is half truth. The more consistently, the more uniformly propaganda is applied, the greater will be its success — and the sooner success will come."

This is a message applied virtually every hour in the Western world: Forget the facts, lie like a flatfish and as long as you sound sincere the public will buy it. What the Nazis realized, and modern political spindoctors likewise, is that to continue in power they have to get money out of the public either by way of taxes, donations, contributions of labour or force. If the money supply dries up, ultimately the ruling class is out on its ear. But the ruling classes also regard taxpayers as fundamentally stupid and easily led, as Wechsungen himself admits.

"The masses are mostly extraordinarily forgetful, and their understanding less than that of the learned. Propaganda had to be made not to please the learned, but rather to reach the masses. We wanted to appeal to the intuitive world of the great masses, not the understanding of the intellectuals. The significance of events and facts must be presented over and over again, until after a long time indeed the masses recognize the necessity of a fundamental change, until they demand it."

The ultimate purpose of propaganda, then, is not just to gain acceptance of "the Big Lie" but to make the public feel so committed to the ideal that they feel good paying for it. The Nazis – like modern governments trying to pitch "carbon taxes" – need cash and acquiescence.

Goebbels also recognized, very early on, the critical need to have the media on your side in terms of their worldview – a situation largely the case now for liberals in NZ, the US, Australia and Britain – as well as the incredible power of radio and TV in particular to influence the emotions of the masses:[16]

"THE EFFECTIVE PROPAGANDIST must be a master of the art of speech, of writing, of journalism, of the poster, and of the leaflet. He must have the gift to use the major methods of influencing public opinion such as the press, film, and radio to serve his ideas and goals.

"This is particularly necessary in a day when technology is advancing. Radio is already an invention of the past, since television will probably soon arrive. On the one hand successful propaganda must be a master of these methods of political opinion, but on the other it may not become stale in using them. It must find new ways and methods every day to reach success.

"The nature of propaganda remains the same, but the means provided by advancing technology are becoming ever broader and far-reaching. One need only consider the revolutionary impact of the invention of radio, which gave the spoken word true mass effectiveness. The technology of propaganda has changed greatly in recent years, but the art of propaganda has remained the same."

And you couldn't find a better example of propaganda remaining the same than the example you're about to read. It is "dog-whistle politics" in action, which means propaganda designed to hit people at a subconscious, emotional level.

It was Emperor Charles V who talked of "ruling with an iron fist in a velvet glove". Translated, it means governments should attempt to do things softly at first, so as not to scare the cattle, but never forget that the State has the power and should use it if necessary; hence, "the gloves are off". A pure example of this in action emerged late 2006 in New Zealand when the country's left-wing government lashed out at a minority religious sect, the Exclusive Brethren. The Brethren, who keep largely to themselves and generally don't vote on the grounds that it would be casting a vote for the devil you don't know instead of the one that's already in place, incurred the wrath of the Labour administration by funding anti-government leaflets in the lead-up to New Zealand's 2005 general election. Labour was incensed, and even more so when it discovered a Brethren member had hired private investigators to sniff out rumoured "dirt" on the government.

It should be noted for the sake of completeness and context that the group did nothing illegal. Its pre-election pamphlets accurately summed up a range of concerns about left-wing policy, and the political intrigue over the private investigators was more hot air than anything else – such events being routine in many other western jurisdictions.

But the New Zealand Labour Government suddenly became extremely vindictive, vilifying the religious sect repeatedly under the protection of parliamentary privilege. It wasn't until *Investigate* magazine ran a side by side comparison of statements by Labour politicians, against Nazi propaganda, that the full extent of the power of that propaganda was revealed:

David Benson-Pope (22 Nov 05): "[National] tried to buy the election with its tax cuts and its underhand campaigns, financed by strange sects and shady deals with industry in return for favours that the voters were never supposed to know about."

Hanns Oberlindober, Nazi propagandist, 1937: For decades, you controlled so-called statesmen like puppets, keeping yourself in the background despite your native Jewish vanity. Between you and the peoples, there hung the mystic curtain of your lodges, your so-called religious mission, and your obvious cowardice.

Hon Dr Michael Cullen (23 Nov 05): "…it was a particularly sick sight to see the way in which the National Party was bought and paid for by a small religious sect."
Adolf Hitler, 1942: This conspiracy of Jews and capitalists…of that time, we wanted to do away with.

Hon Trevor Mallard (23 May 06): "We all thought, and we knew, that they had their hands in the Brethren's pockets for $500,000, but it is clear they actually had their hand in their (pockets) for $1.2 million"
Adolf Hitler, 1919: Today's leaders fully realized the danger of Jewry, they (seeking their own advantage) accepted the readily proffered support of the Jews and also returned the favor.

Georgina Beyer (23 May 06): "The National members rave on about Australia so much…by the way, could he drag the Exclusive Brethren off with him? In fact, why do the Exclusive Brethren not pay for the airfares of all the Opposition?"
Adolf Hitler, 1933: "Why does the world shed crocodile's tears over the richly merited fate of a small Jewish minority? … I ask Roosevelt, I ask the American people: Are you prepared to receive in your midst these well-poisoners of the German people? We would willingly give everyone of them a free steamer-ticket and a thousand-mark note for travelling expenses, if we could get rid of them."

Hon Phil Goff (14 June 06): "…National was richly and secretly funded by a clandestine group, the Exclusive Brethren. It is an extremist religious group…I want to know right now from the National Party what it promised this extremist group in order to get that sort of money."
Adolf Hitler, 1919: His [The Jew's] method of battle is that public opinion which is never expressed in the press but which is nonetheless managed and falsified by it. His power is the power of money.

Hon Pete Hodgson (20 June 06): "…a very strange group of white men who do not even vote, who put a million dollars on the table to help the National Party…that is a very strange group of people"
Adolf Hitler, 1939: We are resolved to prevent the settlement in our country of a strange people which was capable of snatching for itself all the leading positions in the land, and to oust it.

Jill Pettis (21 June 06): "I suggest that he (Don Brash) is already in cahoots with the Devil, and it is called the Exclusive Brethren."
Julius Streicher, Nazi propagandist, 1941: The war the German people are fighting today is a holy war. It is a war against the Devil. The German people must win this war if the Devil is to die and humanity is to live.

Hon Dr Michael Cullen (22 June 06): "Members opposite should wear scarves saying "Exclusive Brethren" because they have already been sponsored."
Max Eisen, Holocaust survivor: "I had a friend across the street who always walked with me to school. The first day here we had to march to school wearing the yellow star. I looked around and I couldn't see him. I realized he didn't want to be seen with someone wearing the yellow star."

Hon Chris Carter (2 August 06): "...a group that does not share core New Zealand values. The Exclusive Brethren do not believe in voting and do not believe in equal rights for women, but are well prepared to give a million dollars to the National Party...Dr Brash raises the question of some New Zealanders not sharing core values, and he therefore says they should not come to this country...If he is talking about the Exclusive Brethren I agree with him.
Adolf Hitler, 1919: This thinking and striving after money and power, and the feelings that go along with it, serve the purposes of the Jew who is unscrupulous in the choice of methods and pitiless in their employment. In autocratically ruled states he whines for the favor of "His Majesty" and misuses it like a leech fastened upon the nations. In democracies he vies for the favor of the masses, cringes before the "majesty of the people," and recognizes only the majesty of money.

Hon Dr Michael Cullen (23 August 06): "Did he (Dr Brash) tell the Exclusive Brethren that? Did he tell them that he would work with the Devil to get rid of this government?
Adolf Hitler, 1925: The goal then was clear and simple: fight against the devilish power which has pushed Germany into this misery.

Hon Steve Maharey: (23 August 06): "The big embarrassment for the National Party is of course the Exclusive Brethren...We are also told by people that he (Don Brash) went as far to make sure those appointments were taken out of his diary so that no one could discover them...why does he not tell us the truth about the Exclusive Brethren?
Tip-offs to the Gestapo, 1935: Hamm and Opfen (Sieg!): The rolling mill master **Gustav Hütt** should be ashamed. From pure greed, he took the Jewish rabbi **Kurt Schreiner** into his house. He even said that he liked the Jew as much as any German.

Hon Pete Hodgson: (23 August 06): "And then, finally, he (Don Brash) confessed he knew the Exclusive Brethren were bankrolling his campaign."
Tip-offs to the Gestapo, 1935: Berleberg in W.: It is a disgrace that hereditary farmers Georg Heinrich Saßmannshausen and Heinrich Dreisbach, both from Birkenfeld, do business with the notorious Talmud Jew and Nazi-hater Simon from Erndtebrück. That is how these Jewish lackeys thank their Führer Adolf Hitler for freeing them from Jewish serfdom!

Rt Hon Helen Clark (29 August 06): "I know what a cover-up looks like when Dr Brash commissions support from the Exclusive Brethren and then will not tell the truth about it."
Tip-offs to the Gestapo, 1935: It is disgraceful that a group of officials and businessmen in Jülich still get together with Jews and go bowling. Look into it, Mr. County Inspector!

Hon Trevor Mallard (5 September 06): "…chinless scarf wearers…"
Adolf Hitler, Sept 1919: Through thousands of years of the closest kind of inbreeding, Jews in general have maintained their race and their peculiarities far more distinctly than many of the peoples among whom they have lived.

The tone of the vilification was clear, and designed to create in the hearts of ordinary people an absolute fear and loathing of the Exclusive Brethren, and a mental association that anyone who mingles or meets with the Brethren must be corrupt. Has the world learnt lessons from the Holocaust? Apparently not. The left-wing party that preaches "tolerance" is itself utterly intolerant of any who dare to criticize it.

As we all know, the Nazis, despite the best propaganda in the world, couldn't match the military forces raised against them. They did, however, leave behind a legacy of hate, and examples – in their medical and scientific "research" programmes, of what happens when scientists are allowed to experiment on humans.

The Nazis did this by largely convincing themselves that Jews were sub-human, and therefore their lives were of no spiritual or practical consequence. Later in this book, you'll see how modern science is now making similar arguments to justify new experiments to create half-human/half animal hybrids, or in defending the millions of abortions annually.

For his part, although Josef Goebbels could not see the darkness in his own work, he did recognize the looming threat of Marxism in this essay published in early 1945, just weeks before the fall of Berlin:[17]

"NO ONE CAN PREDICT the distant future, but there are some

___
17   http://www.calvin.edu/academic/cas/gpa/goeb49.htm

facts and possibilities that are clear over the coming fifty years. For example, … that the events of this war will have sunk into myth."

Based on the number of people who now believe Adolf Hitler didn't exist, Goebbels was certainly right on that point.

> "ONE CAN ALSO PREDICT with a high degree of certainty that Europe will be a united continent in the year 2000. One will fly from Berlin to Paris for breakfast in fifteen minutes, and our most modern weapons will be seen as antiques, and much more. Germany, however, will still be under military occupation according to the plans of the Yalta Conference, and the English and Americans will be training its people in democracy."

Goebbels was right on all these, as well – American bases remain in Germany to this day. But it was his predictions in regard to the spread of Marxism that bear thinking about:

> "STALIN, FOLLOWS MUCH more far-reaching goals… He sees a future in which the entire world is subjected to the dictatorship of the Moscow Internationale, which means the Kremlin. His dream may seem fantastic and absurd, but if we Germans do not stop him, it will undoubtedly become reality.
>
> "An iron curtain would fall over this enormous territory controlled by the Soviet Union, behind which nations would be slaughtered. All that would be left is human raw material, a stupid, fermenting mass of millions of desperate proletarianized working animals who would only know what the Kremlin wanted them to know about the rest of the world…
>
> "The remainder of Europe would fall into chaotic political and social confusion that would prepare the way for the Bolshevization that will follow. Life and existence in these nations would become hell, which was after all the point of the exercise.

Most of the European democracies are socialist in nature, and by all accounts life is already "hell" for many Europeans. But in case you are wondering how the greatest propagandist in the world ended up, the website everything2.com records:

BEFORE HITLER'S SUICIDE on April 30, 1945, Goebbels was named the Reich chancellor. One day later, as Soviet troops storm Berlin, Goebbels orders an SS doctor to euthanize his six children, aged 4 to 12, via lethal injection. He then orders an SS orderly to shoot him and his wife. Before taking his last breath, Goebbels muttered these last words: "We shall go down in history as the greatest statesmen of all time, or as the greatest criminals."

In murdering his own children, Goebbels at least had an inkling, right at the end, of the evil that his propaganda had become, and the heart-ripping pain and agony and blood he had cost the world.

3

Media Bias 101
Mainstream Media as a Propaganda Tool

"People shouldn't expect the mass media to do investigative stories. That job belongs to the 'fringe' media."
Ted Koppel, former ABC Nightline host

Mass communication has, as Goebbels predicted, come a long way since World War 2. Television was indeed "the next big thing", and played a massive role in the dumbing down of the West in the latter party of the 20th century. While there are signs that network TV's days as a major public influence are numbered, thanks to the internet, it is TV that best illustrates how the brainwashing has played out.

I came to NZ's TV3 network, then an NBC affiliate, in 1989, from a career as a radio news journalist rising to metro-market news director for the number one FM station in New Zealand's largest city, Auckland. In radio, particularly with so much competition, we learned to tailor our news content and presentation style with what we perceived our audience to be. This was at the behest of American news "consultants".

While there was some merit in altering your presentation style to suit the demographic, the idea of dropping important stories simply because they were "boring" to under 35s was a mistake. Instead of demanding better newswriting to make "boring" stories interesting, radio simply ditched a lot of coverage of significant issues, to concentrate on more light-hearted, entertainment-type news.

I, along with nearly all my colleagues, bought the pension plan on this – although I did make an attempt to make the serious stuff interesting. Across America, New Zealand, Canada and Australia this dumbing down of the broadcast media was taking place throughout the 1980s.

So when I joined TV3, initially the new medium resonated with me. TV news, you see, is predicated first and foremost on pictures. "If it bleeds, it leads", was the accepted ethos. Important and worthy stories that are not highly visual will generally be bumped down the bulletin, or not run at all. As police and crime reporter for the network, working with plenty of blood, I massaged my stories into lead stories 90% of the time. When you see a picture on television, you are not seeing everything else taking place outside the frame. The anti-whatever demonstration that sounds so big and looks so shocking on the nightly news may be, and in fact sometimes is, only a handful of people that the news producer has rounded up and made them squeeze together for visual effect while they chant loudly in an otherwise deserted town square. They stop chanting when the cameras are turned off.

Why doesn't the network show the real picture – a wide shot of the pitiful demonstration in context? Because every morning when stories are assigned in the daily production meeting, network producers want guaranteed coverage of the angles they are seeking. "Failing to deliver", which means either not getting the story to air at all or not portraying the story the way the bulletin producers wanted, is a cardinal offence in TV newsrooms. It is embarrassing to the network to admit to viewers that the stories they're presenting are not widely supported or all that major.

The whole point of the network news is "importance". Telling the truth about news manipulation would undermine the credibility of a network's own news judgement, as in, why are they clearly covering non-stories? TV news is about making a silk purse from a pig's ear. It is also symbiotic, in the sense that politicians and lobbyists need TV, but TV equally needs them, and the telegenic ones who most closely match the prevailing newsroom worldview will get the easiest rides.

So TV journalists, if they want the big pay packets and clothing allowances, learn early that they must toe the line and give the bosses what they want. I was very good at this. Admittedly, in my assignment to homicides, air crashes, disasters and the like, it usually did not involve any worldview clash. I selected the most heart-wrenching footage and sound bites I could find, strung them together and created news symphonies that left viewers moved to tears and myself with a string of accolades. In other words, I rode that pony for all it was worth. TV was about raw, guttural emotion, just as Nazi Josef Goebbels had predicted in highlighting the medium as perfect for propaganda. Emotion on TV got attention.

There were times when one would cover a stage-managed protest on some worthy liberal issue, with barely anyone there, but the point of the story was to give favourable publicity to the worthy liberal issue, so you shot the story to make it fill the screen and be much larger than life.

Had I turned around and delivered shots of the empty halls and the pitiful turnout, I'd have been criticised for not getting with the programme. Later in my TV career, as I became more cynical about the manipulation I was privy to, I did start to do this, and consequently got accused of far more "FTDs" – failure to deliver.

In the final three years of my TV news career, I had the choice of promotion to network Chief of Staff, or continuing to work on a major investigative story on big business and political corruption that the network didn't want. I chose the big story, jumped networks, produced a major award-winning documentary, the subject of my first bestselling book *The Paradise Conspiracy*, and basically ended my TV career as a result.

I say all of this not to blow my own trumpet, but to illustrate my intimate association with "the Beast" - I bring to this issue the knowledge of The Insider. TV news is heavily manipulated – not overtly but by the social views of the journalists themselves – and presents liberal views as orthodox, and conservative views as quaint or outdated.

When TV covers a conservative protest or meeting, you will indeed see pictures of empty seats and wide open spaces (if they exist), because the journalists themselves are cynical about conservatives and cover such stories with the blessing of their producers.

Several years ago, at the height of a debate about mass immigration into New Zealand, *Investigate* magazine ran video recorders across the main network news channels for a week. The object of the exercise[18] was to prove just how biased the news broadcasts are.

On One's *Late Edition*, anchor Peter Williams opened with this:

> "Winston Peters is unrepentant in the wake of a new poll which suggests many New Zealanders think he's increasing division in the community."

Let's pause there for a moment and search for liberal-loaded newspeak. We're told Peters is "unrepentant". Unrepentant for what? Who elected *One News* to be judge and jury on what politicians should be repentant for? If *One News* wants to editorialise, it should broadcast editorials and state clearly that's what they are.

But it gets better. *Late Edition* then tells us there's a new poll suggesting many New Zealanders think Peters was increasing division in the community.

> "The *One News* Colmar-Brunton poll shows the majority believe his comments on Asian immigration raise tensions.
>
> "Auckland is home to one in three people born in another country. It's often portrayed as the start of what will be an

increasingly changing face of New Zealand. Changes Winston Peters warns will lead to a divided and mutually exclusive society.

"But in a *One News* Colmar-Brunton poll, it's Winston Peters who's being called divisive. Seventy-one percent of those polled say his views increase tension between Asian immigrants and the rest of New Zealand. Only 23% disagree."

The facts were presented as if Moses had just held up stone tablets and read from them, and on the face of it they appeared damning of Peters.

But, again, was it really that simple? Once again, no.

You see, opinion polling is an art form. I know. I worked in the industry for a year. The answer you get in a poll is almost 100% dependent on what question you ask and how you tilt it. In a truly objective poll, questions are phrased as neutrally as possible so as not to skew the results. But in polls designed by news organisations, the questions are often far more obtuse.

The value of this *One News* poll on immigration was about to be defined by whether or not its questions were horribly biased. Let's take a look:

QUESTION 1: "Winston Peters' views and statements increase tension and division between Asian immigrants and the rest of New Zealand... Agree...Disagree...Don't Know."

As you can see, it's not a question. It's a political statement and it could have been drafted by the Prime Minister's office for all the objectivity it displayed.

One News is *telling* survey respondents that Peters is being divisive. In polling terms, *One News* has loaded the dice for what some may believe are political reasons. By making a firm statement portraying a negative image, *One News* is inviting respondents to see it that way before they've even opened their mouths to respond. This is called "framing the debate", and is compulsory in any PR campaign. In the abortion debate, "framing" often centres on victims of rape or incest, even though only 1% of abortions fall into that category. Yet by making the public see it that way, they lead debate by the nose.

QUESTION 2: "Asian immigration is a good thing. It makes the country more multicultural and the economy stronger...Agree... Disagree...Don't know."

Again, a political statement rather than a polling question. *One News* is telling those surveyed that they should believe immigration is a good thing. The final 'question' in the poll asked whether the Government should stop any further Asian immigration (given that we've now established Peters is being unkind to Asians and that Asian immigration is good for our economy and good for multiculturalism), to which 71% disagreed and said the Government should not stop Asian immigration.

Having set up their straw-man, *One News* then tries to set him alight.

> "THE GOVERNMENT SAYS the poll is proof Winston Peters has read it wrong.
>
> "I think this is a very telling poll indeed," Labour's Immigration Minister Lianne Dalziel is quoted as saying.

The liberal prejudice running through the report - that Peters is being divisive and causing tension by daring to comment on the issue, that he should shut up because immigration is a good thing and multiculturalism is a good thing - these are the prejudices of staff in the news organisation, not scientifically-tested facts.

Ironically, the reporter and producers who worked on the story, and the person who dreamt up the poll 'questions', may not even realize they have the biases - the attitudes are so ingrained they are accepted as "the way it is".

But *One News* hadn't finished the hatchet-job. Anchor Peter Williams came back after the break to interview sociologist Paul Spoonley from Massey University.

"Is Winston Peters' reading of the issue all wrong? Is he the one actually out of touch with what New Zealand is thinking? Are you surprised Paul that New Zealanders, at least according to this poll, appear to have a pretty liberal attitude towards Asian immigration?"

"No, not really," replied Spoonley. "I think what they're beginning to realize is that our economic future is very much with Asia, and we're beginning to accept that Asians coming here is part of that future."

What *One News* never declared in their coverage was that Paul Spoonley has been highly critical of NZ First leader Winston Peters on his immigration stand in the past, and that Spoonley is funded by the United Nations to help the UN plan for immigration.

"Embracing cultural diversity and demonstrating a tolerance of others is surely one of the most significant challenges of this period of our history," Spoonley told an audience in 1996, before getting stuck into people whipping up hysteria about migrants:

> "SOME NATIONAL POLITICIANS, notably Winston Peters of the New Zealand First party, have articulated these concerns. These politics reflect the beliefs held by significant numbers that 'at the

economic level, the nation-state is threatened by globalisation; at the cultural level (so it is thought), it is threatened by immigration'. Racist politics are one result.

"Peters has always denied any racist intent…but, inevitably, his rhetoric is seen as an endorsement of certain racist views in the wider community. It is reinforced by an increased and declared interest by the New Zealand police in the involvement of Asians in various criminal activities, and especially the possibility that Triad gangs are operating in New Zealand.

"This is an irony because one of the post-war myths was that Chinese migrants were law-abiding and had a strong work ethic. In fact, the statistics for those charged with drug offences in 1965 show that 103 of the 113 involved were Chinese. Few knew about the statistics and the popular mythology that prevailed in a post-war era meant that Chinese were viewed benignly. But with the racialisation of Asian migrants in the 1990s, the mythology has been discarded and one of the stereotypes which sustains this racialisation of Asian involvement is organised crime. It contributes to the generally negative perceptions held towards Asians by New Zealanders.

"These negative and hostile reactions have been articulated in a variety of ways. In its most extreme form, they result in racist and neo-fascist politics as expressed by skinhead and motorbike gangs…The most significant expression of the anti-Asian sentiments are provided by New Zealand First, and specifically its leader Winston Peters, whose statements encapsulate the guarded racism of middle (and typically elderly) New Zealand."

In other words, Paul Spoonley is hardly an "independent" academic in the immigration debate. Politically, from his speeches at least, he appears to be a globalist and is certainly happy to take funding from UNESCO whilst pushing multiculturalism as a cure-all for the world. In addition, he's not a Peters fan, and he won't like this book.

Meanwhile, across on *3 News* they were running this:

"PROOF TODAY THAT Winston Peters has been mining a very popular prejudice. A TV3/NFO poll has surveyed feelings about levels of immigration, and Asian migrants stand out.

"Asians were the only ethnic grouping to attract a majority disapproval rating among those surveyed.

"53% said they felt too many Asians were coming here."

Different TV channels, different polling companies, and diametrically-opposed poll results. TV1 saying 71% favour Asian immigration. TV3 saying 53% disapprove of Asian immigration. Both polls had a margin of error of plus or minus 3.4%.

Even so, TV3 still labelled Peters' comments as prejudiced. Who says so? How can one possibly "pre-judge" the immigration issue? Surely it's a simple question of whether New Zealanders want new immigrants or not, end of story. How can there be a moral side to this that one could pass pre-judgement on?

Yet both news organisations pitched the story as if to say that people who questioned immigration levels were "prejudiced".

There are many more examples, but the above should illustrate how journalists write stories that begin with a presumption. They presume feminism, multiculturalism, gay rights, the United Nations, gun control are all good things, things that any sane and rational person would support. But they have never sat down and done the "says who?" test. As you're about to see, that weakness in the Fourth Estate has enabled massive rifts in the tectonic plates of culture, and the results have been catastrophic.

4

The Beagle Boys
Darwinism's Last Stand

"Liberals' creation myth is Charles Darwin's theory of evolution, which is about one notch above Scientology in scientific rigour. It's a make-believe story, based on a theory that is a tautology, with no proof in the scientist's laboratory or the fossil record – and that's after 150 years of very determined looking. We wouldn't still be talking about it but for the fact that liberals think evolution disproves God."

Ann Coulter, Godless

Darwin would be impressed, were he alive to witness it: two great beasts grunting and snarling at each other across a clearing in what will clearly be a battle to the death – survival of the fittest. One of the creatures is a gnarly 148 years old, but the other is much, much more ancient – a sleeping giant awakened by the noise of the younger leviathan in the forests of public opinion.

Yes, if Charles Darwin were alive today (and one of the Galapagos tortoises he picked up on his voyage in *The Beagle* still is) he would no doubt appreciate the irony of the fact that his very own Theory of Evolution is fighting for its own life against the older theory that Darwin claimed to have done away with in 1859 – the belief that the earth, and life, was created by a divine designer.

After 148 years of evolution-based science and, following the infamous Scopes "monkey trial", teaching in schools, the tide has begun to turn on the Darwinists and the battlegrounds are schools in the US, Canada, Australia, New Zealand and now Britain, as school boards and even state education authorities debate whether the latest scientific discoveries that undermine Darwinism should be allowed into the classroom. Naturally, the naturalists are up in arms.

The dangerous new theory is called "Intelligent Design", and there's a very good chance you've heard about it. The reason it is making fundamentalist atheist scientists froth at the mouth is because it uses science to refute some current core scientific beliefs.

Like a stake through the heart of a vampire, naturalist and explorer Charles Darwin believed his *Origin of Species* thesis in 1859 would spell the end of a superstitious belief in a "young earth" or, even, God. By studying animal species and documenting similarities and differences, Darwin was sure he could prove that plants and animals had evolved from a common ancestor, perhaps a one-celled amoeba. Given that humans and the great apes shared many characteristics, Darwin speculated that humans had descended from apes. Darwin's Theory suggested that random mutations, generated by chance or environmental pressures, not God, had caused and guided the development of all life.

In an age increasingly dominated by science and reason, and after a millennium of religious dogma, witch-trials, inquisitions and persecution of scientists, the chance for science to lash out at religion was more than appealing. It was, in a way, a sociological example of one of Newton's Laws of Physics: for every action (supernatural religious dogma) there is an equal and opposite reaction (rationalistic scientific attack).

For the best part of a century, the idea of creation has been publicly regarded as dead and buried by science, so why, in the past couple of years, has Darwin's Theory come under such heavy fire not just from religious groups but from scientists as well?

Firstly, a bit of housekeeping: when it comes to Design, there are two different groups involved. There are Biblical Creationists who maintain that creation took place exactly as it is written in the Bible's Book of Genesis and that the Earth, therefore, must be only roughly 10,000 years old based on their own interpretation of the biblical timeframe. They point to references in the Old Testament, particularly the Book of Job, which appear to describe dinosaur-like creatures encountered by the Israelites as proof of human/dinosaur interaction. This group believes that archaeological evidence of a great flood and legends of such a disaster in virtually every culture from Hawaii to Europe point to the authenticity of the Bible, and that such a massive deluge of water and sediment would explain fossilization.

The other group - the one this chapter focuses on - is called the Intelligent Design movement, and comprises a growing number of scientists who disagree with Biblical Creationists on the so-called "young earth" theory, but who believe there is now overwhelming scientific evidence that the current theory of evolution cannot explain life on this planet.

You will note through this chapter I am extensively quoting various eminent biologists in support of my argument. These people are hostile witnesses, which in many respects are the best to have. Their admissions, in their own science journals, of the massive weaknesses of Darwinism, are, frankly, compelling reading. They are not taken out of context. The disputes are real.

In New Zealand, the US and elsewhere, media coverage has been fairly superficial. The Intelligent Design vs Evolution debate has been portrayed by axe-grinding liberals as orthodox scientists up against well-meaning religious buffoons who shouldn't be allowed anywhere near a classroom. But while such coverage has been entertaining, it hasn't tackled the deeper scientific issues that are causing major schisms in the scientific community.

Put another way, the scientists behind the Intelligent Design movement are now mounting a major attack on Evolutionists, and it is this debate that I'm focusing on.

The basic issues are these: there is ample evidence to support one element of Darwin's theory – microevolution. This means examples of change *within* a species. But there is virtually no evidence for macroevolution – the claim that one species can mutate into something else.

Evolutionists often deliberately distort the two issues, using the evidence of change within a species (moth colourations/finch beak sizes/bacterial resistance to antibiotics) to argue that evolution as the wider public understands it (pond-slime to space traveler) is therefore true.

The problem with their argument is this. A moth that changes colour is still a …? A bird that has a bigger beak remains a…? A bacteria that becomes resistant to an antibiotic remains a…? A human who becomes immune to a bacteria remains a…?

You know the answers.

And the reason Darwinists desperately want you to sign up to the whole package is because the religious aspect of their package only kicks in if you believe macroevolution – that a monkey can become a man, or a 10 tonne Triceratops can become a turkey.

If you believe that, then you'll believe life is not special, and Mankind is the master of all he surveys. You'll believe there is no God (the Darwinists hope), and free yourself and your family from any moral code.

This, then, is why they push for evolution to be taught in schools, because acceptance of the philosophy undermines religion, and religion in the eyes of Marxists and Darwinists is a bad thing that prevents Marxism and scientism (a belief that atheistic science can and should replace religion and philosophy as mankind's ultimate doctrine) from dominating human society.

So let's examine macro-evolution. Darwinists believe, for example, that modern whales originally evolved from a carnivorous cow-like creature about the size of a wolf.

Is it possible, asks Intelligent Design, for something so small to mutate in a short period of geological time into a 100 tonne monster? While there are many scientists who would argue yes, there are a growing number of scientists who say 'No'.

Few journalists who've covered the controversy and swallowed the Pennsylvania court ruling[19] that ID is "not science", for example, are aware of how contemptuous many of the world's leading scientists are of current Darwinian theory.

Lynn Margulis is a world-renowned biologist responsible for crucial work on mitochondria – the energy source for plant and animal cells. She currently holds the position Distinguished University Professor of Biology at the University of Massachusetts, yet she challenged a conference of molecular biologists in the USA to come up with "one, single, unambiguous example" of the formation of a new species via an accumulation of mutations to an original species, and none have so far been able to meet the challenge.

Adding salt to the scientific wound, Margulis claims[20] Darwinism will ultimately be regarded by history as "a minor twentieth century religious sect within the sprawling religious persuasion of Anglo-Saxon biology."

Darwinists, she goads, "wallow in their zoological, capitalistic, competitive, cost-benefit interpretation of Darwin…Neo-Darwinism, which insists on [the slow accrual of mutations] is in a complete funk."

Now to be fair, Margulis is no fan of Intelligent Design either, but she does make a strong case that traditional textbook evolution, as taught in schools, is effectively a crock. Margulis isn't the only scientist to accuse her colleagues of turning Darwinism into a religion – a belief system that must be accepted at the risk of excommunication from the scientific brotherhood. Harvard-trained law professor Phillip Johnson waded into the evolution debate with a provocative series of books attacking Darwinists for being big on persuasive courtroom-style rhetoric, but short on substance and evidence in their arguments.

In his book *Darwin on Trial*, Johnson recounts how in one scientific conference debate with Darwinist Michael Ruse, author of *Darwinism Defended*, he argued that Darwinism was essentially a front for "naturalistic metaphysics" – the worship of nature and science as an actual religion in itself. Ruse vehemently disagreed on stage, but a year later made a surprising

---

19   The judge in the Dover case based his decision on the narrow interpretation that science must, by definition, confine itself *only* to evidence that leads to a natural, rather than supernatural, conclusion. Smart readers will note however that science should go wherever the evidence leads: if God actually did create life, then what use to taxpayers is a science system that spends all your money searching only for a natural cause that actually doesn't exist? Surely science should simply remain open-minded. A scientific system that rules out avenues of inquiry in advance is nothing more than a paid religion itself where the priests wear white coats and the news media sing hymns to them. Under the Dover ruling, if God suddenly appeared in the clouds one Tuesday afternoon and announced his return, scientists would be duty bound to pretend it hadn't happened and instead to continue their routine inquiries into the breeding pattern of the rare Patagonian swamp warbler, or some such bird. I mean, really, the judge's ruling goes beyond honest skepticism and well into Three Wise Monkeys territory. Justice, as a New Zealand Appeal Court judge once remarked, "should be blind, not stupid".
20   http://en.wikipedia.org/wiki/Lynn_Margulis

concession in a very controversial address to fellow Darwinist scientists in 1993:

> "I MUST SAY THAT I've been coming to this kind of position myself...the science side has certain metaphysical [religious] assumptions built into doing science, which – it may not be a good thing to admit in a court of law – but I think in all honesty that we should recognise."

His remarks were greeted by stunned silence from fellow Darwinists, and followed up with an article in a peer magazine headlined "Did Michael Ruse Give Away The Store?".

In New Zealand, one man well placed to observe the theological side of the evolution debate is Dr Bill Peddie, head of science at a major New Zealand high school. Although a state school, a large percentage of its board is Christian, as are many of Peddie's students, yet he himself is an avid evolutionist. In a 2002 interview with *Investigate* magazine, Peddie admits a religious fervour has overtaken both sides of the debate.

"An Exclusive Brethren person knows that there are certain beliefs they must adhere to. Evolution is not one of them. It's a non-negotiable starting point. By the same token, people who take science courses at college and university may not learn any genetics, but they will still be fervent believers that evolution is the way to go because they know that the majority of scientists who've studied this have come out in favour of evolution."

Not that the truth of a matter can ever be decided by a popular vote. As Peddie would himself concede, there was a time when the majority of scientists believed the earth was flat.

Richard Dawkins, author of *The Blind Watchmaker* and one of the world's leading proponents of Darwinism, is a fundamentalist follower of the atheism religion, and insists that evolution can prove the non-existence of Christianity's God. Another effectively in the same camp was the late Carl Sagan. It is this driving force of atheism, a theological position that is in itself religious, that permeates science and fuels much of the creation/evolution debate.

At the centenary celebration of Darwin's Theory in 1959, world famous biologist Sir Julian Huxley – the brother of well known atheist Aldous Huxley - told the prestigious scientific gathering in Chicago that:

> "IN THE EVOLUTIONARY PATTERN of thought there is no longer either need or room for the supernatural. The earth was not created, it evolved. So did all the plants and animals that inhabit it, including our human selves, mind and soul as well as brain

and body…the evolutionary vision is enabling us to discern, however incompletely, the lineaments of the *new religion* that we can be sure will arise to serve the needs of the coming era." [emphasis added]

Huxley's comments may come as a shock to parents who thought that their kids were not being taught religion in schools.

The Huxley family, particularly Aldous, have been instrumental in turning atheism into an unofficial religion over the past hundred years. But despite apparently "pure" scientific motives for doing so, Aldous Huxley later admitted his opposition to creation was philosophically motivated:

"I HAD MOTIVES for not wanting the world to have a meaning; consequently assumed that it had none, and was able without any difficulty to find satisfying reasons for this assumption. The philosopher who finds no meaning in the world is not concerned exclusively with a problem in pure metaphysics, he is also concerned to prove that there is no valid reason why he personally should not do as he wants to do, or why his friends should not seize political power and govern in the way that they find most advantageous to themselves.

"For myself, the philosophy of meaninglessness was essentially an instrument of liberation, sexual and political."

In other words, Darwin's survival of the fittest theory lent itself ideally to both atheists and free-market capitalists as a replacement for the moral structure of orthodox religion. Not only has evolution become the cornerstone of modern economic theory and legitimised control of governments by big business, it has had a profound effect on the generations of children who have been taught about it. Some critics, yours truly included, blame much of modern societal breakdown on the atheistic, "every man for himself" foundation of Darwinism.

In essence, argues Phillip Johnson, scientists are pushing their own religion in schools and universities – disguised as "objective scientific fact". Statements are made to students that all life descended from a one-celled amoeba, created randomly by a lightning strike in an ancient puddle on the new planet Earth, when no hard evidence exists to prove the truth of such statements and much of the evidence points the other way.

The struggle for survival between Darwinism and Christianity, says Johnson, is not really a struggle between science *and* religion, it is a battle *between two religions* for control of the hearts, minds and financial donations of the public.

"Prejudice is a major problem, however, because the leaders of science see themselves as locked in a desperate battle against religious fundamentalists, a label which they tend to apply broadly to anyone who believes in a Creator who plays an active role in worldly affairs," argues Johnson.

"These fundamentalists are seen as a threat to liberal freedom, and especially as a threat to public support for scientific research.

"As the creation myth of scientific naturalism, Darwinism plays an indispensable ideological role in the war against [Christianity]. For that reason, the scientific organisations are devoted to protecting Darwinism rather than testing it, and the rules of scientific investigation have been shaped to help them succeed… scientists themselves become fanatics."

That fanaticism has meant some spectacular gymnastic feats as scientists try to make Darwinism fit emerging evidence that conflicts with the theory of evolution. Evidence like the lack of fossil support.

"No wonder paleontologists shied away from evolution for so long," writes paleontologist and Darwinist Niles Eldredge.[21] "It never seems to happen. Assiduous collecting up cliff faces yields [evolutionary] zig-zags, minor oscillations, and the very occasional slight accumulation of change – over millions of years, at a rate too slow to account for all the prodigious change that has occurred in evolutionary history.

"When we do see the introduction of evolutionary novelty, it usually shows up with a bang, and often with no firm evidence that the fossils did not evolve elsewhere!

"Evolution cannot forever be going on 'somewhere else'. Yet that's how the fossil record has struck many a forlorn paleontologist looking to learn something about evolution."

And this from a prominent Darwinist! Eldredge's complaints are not isolated. More than 250,000 fossil species are now identified and catalogued, and arguably none of them include any of the "thousands" of transitional species that Darwin believed must have existed if his theory of evolution were true. Nowhere are there fossils that show a weasel-cat, or a deer-giraffe, or any other of the alleged half-breed species said to have existed. In fact, a search of the literature on giraffe evolution has failed to find a single example of a short-necked giraffe at all. The long ones just suddenly appeared.

While it is true that there are millions more fossils waiting to be exhumed from ancient rocks by paleontologists, it is also true that evolutionists are caught in a trap of their own making: in a non-created world, where everything evolves by random chance, the rules of mathematical probability theory come into play. Under those rules, it is considered statistically likely that the fossils we have recovered from all corners of the globe are enough to be representative

21   Niles Eldredge - Chairman and Curator of Invertebrates, American Museum of Natural History. "Reinventing Darwin: The Great Evolutionary Debate," (1995), Phoenix: London, 1996, p. 95

of the main species that once walked the earth, and conversely that small, still undiscovered, species confined to isolated geographic areas are unlikely to have played a major part in evolution towards modern life-forms.

Paleontologists have recovered plant and animal and bacteria fossils dating back 3.8 billion years from a range of rock strata throughout the world. Despite all of that, it is accepted that hard evidence of trans-species evolution is hard to find.

The traditional evolutionary position cannot easily explain away discoveries like 2002's Australian announcement of worm or snail tracks discovered in sandstone that's been dated up to two billion years old. Evolutionists have previously claimed that only one-celled bacteria and amoeba existed up until around 600 million years ago, yet photos have now been published by the University of Western Australia of a lifeform that was much bigger, moving, and complex enough to generate trails.

If you search the science curriculum in New Zealand schools online, the word "Cambrian" turns up zero results. Which is strange, when you consider that almost every type of creature alive on the planet today, whether animal or vegetable, owes its existence to what paleontologists call "the Cambrian Explosion", and which evolutionists try not to talk about in public. In a world previously inhabited only by the aforementioned worms and a few sea sponges, something happened 500 million years ago that has been unrepeated on earth since: let there be life.

In the blink of a geological eye, as little as five million years and a maximum of ten, virtually every single animal phyla that exists or has ever existed on earth – including the 30 or so groups of them still around today - came apparently miraculously to life. There is no evidence of evolution. One day it was just worms. The next, trilobites, insects, fish – you name it, they appeared.

One sudden appearance every so often, spaced out at regular intervals, you could put down to chance. But the entire menagerie appearing on earth at once? It sounds spookily close to Genesis. So much so, that evolutionary theorist Jeffrey Schwartz prefers to invoke the Greek gods instead, saying the major animal groups "appear in the fossil record as Athena did from the head of Zeus – full blown and raring to go."

Nor has the search for mankind's elusive "missing link" back to the apes come up with any evidence – leading anthropologists around the world are privately more frustrated than ever at the lack of evidence for human evolution. Dr Richard Leakey, the world famous evolutionist and discoverer of pre-human remains in Africa's Great Rift Valley, is reported to have shrugged and drawn a large questionmark on a blackboard when asked by students several years ago whether science was any closer to proving the origins of humanity.

Indeed, recent studies of human mitochondrial DNA show that all modern humans can trace their ancestry back to *one* woman in Africa around 200,000 years ago. That woman was as human as anyone on the streets of New York today. Scientists have, probably only half-jokingly, nicknamed her 'Eve'.

Nor is there evidence that Eve descended from ancient apes. Intelligent Design advocates say this, too, indicates a sudden appearance of modern humans.

Another example is modern birds: there is no evolutionary trail illustrating what they evolved from. While many evolutionists long believed that ancient reptilian birds like Archaeopteryx, Hesperornis or Icthyornis were possible ancestors of modern birds, recent discoveries have shown that modern birds existed pretty much "as is" during the time of the dinosaurs. Even the oldest fossil bats appear in the fossil record with the same sophisticated echo-locating sonar system that modern bats have, meaning that complex sonar seems to have appeared overnight, rather than via gradual evolution.

The suggestion that dinosaurs might have been feathered – still not widely accepted – doesn't automatically mean they are related to modern birds. Convergent evolution, where the same feature has supposedly evolved simultaneously in totally unrelated species (birds and bats' wings, for example, or sonar in bats and dolphins), provide problems, not explanations, for Darwinism. Convergent evolution shows you don't need to hold to "common ancestor theory" to account for the rise of various features, meaning biologists may simply be guessing when they assume apes and humans, or birds and dinosaurs, share a common ancestor.

Writing in the *Journal of Theoretical Biology*,[22] scientists Mae-Wan Ho and Peter Saunders said in 1979:

> "IT IS NOW APPROXIMATELY half a century since the neo-Darwinian synthesis was formulated. A great deal of research has been carried on within the paradigm it defines. Yet the successes of this theory are limited to the minutiae of evolution, such as the adaptive change in colouration of moths; while it has remarkably little to say on the questions which interest us most, such as how there came to be moths in the first place."

And even the colouration of moths theory, hailed by Richard Dawkins as proof, has had some fairly significant doubts raised over it.[23]

Another scientist tackling the sacred cow is British biologist Brian Goodwin:

> "NEO-DARWINISM HAS FAILED as an evolutionary theory that can explain the origin of species, understood as organisms of

22   *Beyond neo-Darwinism - An Epigenetic Approach to Evolution*, Journal of Theoretical Biology, Vol. 78, pp.573- 591, 1979
23   *Icons of Evolution*, Jonathan Wells, Chapter 7

distinctive form and behaviour. In other words, it is not an adequate theory of evolution. What it does provide is a partial theory of adaptation, or microevolution (small-scale adaptive changes in organisms)."[24]

Chicago University's Department of Ecology and Evolution has also been critical of Darwinism:[25]

"WE CONCLUDE – UNEXPECTEDLY – that there is little evidence for the neo-Darwinian view: its theoretical foundations and the experimental evidence supporting it are weak."

To get around the lack of fossil evidence for evolution, Niles Eldredge joined another of Darwinism's "high priests" – Harvard University's Stephen Jay Gould (now deceased) – in proposing an alternative theory: "punctuated equilibrium". According to their scenario, the sudden appearance of new species in the fossil record, without any evidence of evolution, meant that evolution must happen extremely rapidly in isolated populations of creatures who then mutate rapidly into a new species. The rate of evolution then drops to virtually zero until, millions of years later, that species mutates into another new species by the same instant process.

Such a scenario flies directly in the face of Darwin's belief that mutations had to be random, numerous, small, and occurring all the time.

The Punctuated Equilibrium theory is similar to what became dubbed "the hopeful monster theory" of the 1940s, where top geneticist Richard Goldschmidt suggested that perhaps an overnight massive mutation occurred, whereby a dinosaur laid an egg and out of it hatched a bird. Which, of course, is tantamount to admitting a miracle – divine intervention – according to Creationists.

The problem for Eldredge, Gould and Goldschmidt is that if a random, chance mutation can indeed create a new species – what does the sole representative of that new species mate with to create offspring? The scientific definition of a species is that it cannot mate with members of another species.

And, given the problems faced in keeping endangered species alive today where perhaps 80 breeding pairs survive, what about the risk of a new species arising in ancient times with just one breeding pair – one partner of which gets eaten by a marauding predator? Or the first bird hatches from what should have been a dinosaur egg, only to get trampled by a passing brontosaurus – the ancient equivalent of road-kill.

24   *Neo-Darwinism has failed as an evolutionary theory*, The Times Higher Education Supplement, May 19, 1995
25   *The Genetics of Adaptation: A Reassessment*, The American Naturalist, Vol. 140, No. 5, November 1992

Remember, the mitochondrial DNA research on modern humans indicates we're all descended from just one woman. One "Eve". Where did this mother of all humanity suddenly come from? Why her? Why aren't we descended from her own mother?

Gould and Eldredge's theory, disparagingly referred to as 'punk eek' by critics, has become one of the dominant Darwinist doctrines, but like the original Darwinism it is still haunted by a lack of fossil evidence, and certainly nothing that proves one species became something else.

In the 1980s Britain's Museum of Natural History provoked a storm of outrage in the hallowed halls of academia when its scientists took the position that evolution was an unproven theory, and put display signs up, saying as much. The prestigious journal *Nature* recorded comments by one of the Museum's senior scientists that featured in a video for public display at the museum:

> "THE SURVIVAL OF THE FITTEST is an empty phrase; it is a play on words. For this reason, many critics feel that not only is the idea of evolution unscientific, but the idea of natural selection also.
>
> "The idea of evolution by natural selection is a matter of logic, not science, and it follows that the concept of evolution by natural selection is not, strictly speaking, scientific..."

One of the Museum's exhibits on "Man's Place in Evolution" rejected the idea that Homo erectus was a direct ancestor of modern humans, Homo sapiens.

"What the Creationists have insisted on for years," seethed Darwinist L B Halstead in *Nature*, "is now being openly advertised by the Natural History Museum."

Interestingly, Halstead's biggest criticism wasn't the position being taken by the Museum, but the fact it was "going public" with doubts about Darwinism that had previously been confined to scientific conferences and professional journals.

But when *Nature's* editors then waxed lyrical about whether the scientists in charge of "the nearest thing to a citadel of Darwinism" had lost their senses in questioning the theory of evolution, around two dozen of the world's top biologists wrote in to back up the Museum, saying they were "astonished" that *Nature* would "advocate that theory be presented as fact".

The Museum was eventually pressured however, thanks in no small part to criticism by atheist and Darwinist Anthony Flew (whom you will hear more of soon because of his recent conversion to Intelligent Design theory) who called the affair a "breach of trust" by civil servants, to back down on its public questioning of evolution, and by 1987 had removed the controversial signs and video clips.

Nonetheless, the fury of the debate lurks just underneath the surface.

Naturalist Brian Leith posed one of the fundamental questions – is it possible that evolutionists have become so hung up on propping up Darwin's failing theory that they're clinging to a theory that just doesn't make sense anymore? [26]

> "CAN WE BE CERTAIN that a particular fossil, which may appear to be intermediate between other creatures, is really an ancestor? With the growing sophistication of taxonomy there is a feeling that many of the neo-Darwinian assumptions about fossils and ancestry may be scientifically unfounded, and should be dropped.
>
> "This realization, that the theory may be incapable of helping taxonomy, and may even be a hindrance to it, has led to a rejection of Darwinian ideas among some taxonomists who feel that we should be finding out more about the pattern before we become dogmatic about the process which is supposed to explain it."

Nor has the destruction of evolution focused solely on the fossil record. Molecular biochemist Michael Behe, of Lehigh University in Pennsylvania, put the cat-bird among the pigeon-dinosaurs with his book *Darwin's Black Box*, in which he argues that evolution is unsustainable given what we now know about molecular biology.

Behe's basic argument, illustrated with various examples from nature, is that even one-celled organisms can be more complex in their structure than a modern car-factory. Some tasks carried out within a cell, he says, involve interlinking molecular components, each of which has a unique task to perform and without which the entire organism would die.

Is it possible, on the Darwinian thesis of small, random mutations over a long period of time, that a complex cell structure involving nine crucial components working together to perform one operation could evolve? If so, how would the organism have survived during the millions of years it took for each random mutation to come about before it could be fully functional? And if mutations are just random chance, how did the organism end up with nine interdependent components, instead of nine useless ones?

Behe, and other scientists who support him, argue that the odds of *random* mutations accounting for such feats are equivalent to a tornado whizzing through a scrap-metal yard and accidentally assembling a Boeing 747 in the process. Mathematicians working on probability theory have long had

26   *The Descent of Darwin: A Handbook of Doubts about Darwinism*, Collins: London, 1982

serious reservations about the claimed ability of evolution to account for the enormous complexity of life on earth.

Behe's arguments remain hotly debated in scientific and atheist circles, but even renowned chemistry professor and Darwinist Robert Shapiro of New York University – author of *Origins: A Skeptic's Guide to the Creation of Life on Earth* – acknowledges their importance:

"Michael Behe has done a top-notch job of explaining and illuminating one of the most vexing problems in biology: the origin of the complexity that permeates all of life on this planet…this book should be on the essential reading list of all those who are interested in the question of where we came from, as it presents the most thorough and clever presentation of the design argument that I have seen."

Another expert to weigh in against Darwin is Dr William Bradley, a consultant to Boeing Aerospace and Shell Oil, among others, an expert on polymers and thermodynamics – both of which are critical to the origin of life issue – and the recently retired head of Texas A&M University's mechanical engineering department.

Bradley has extensively researched the chemical issues central to where life came from, and his 1984 book *The Mystery of Life's Origin* prompted Darwinist biologist Dean Kenyon to state publicly that Bradley's work was "cogent, original and compelling", and "the authors believe, and I now concur, that there is a fundamental flaw in all current theories of the chemical origins of life".

Kenyon has now abandoned Darwinism.

Where did life come from? Darwin speculated that a lightning strike on a primitive pond, in a conducive atmosphere of certain gases, might have done the trick, *a la* Frankenstein's Monster. Trying to repeat the feat, scientists shunted massive electrical charges into a sealed container of ammonia, methane and hydrogen – gases that scientists believed represented earth's early atmosphere. They were delighted to discover that the experiment created amino acids, essential building blocks for life.

Although the experiment was recounted in school textbooks for decades as proof of the ease with which life could theoretically be created, the theory and the "proof" fell apart in the 1980s when NASA discovered that earth never had an atmosphere composed of those gases, but nitrogen and carbon dioxide which don't react in the same way.

In other words, the life from a puddle idea is dead – despite what you may have learned in school or on the news.

But even though scientists can create amino acids in lab experiments, no scientist has ever been able to go the next step and create real life. This, despite billions of dollars in research and the best brains that humankind can offer. If humans have tried and failed to intelligently design life, say critics, how strong is the theory that nature fluked it?

While nature has had a lot of time, its work must be random. It could just as easily mutate a good gene into a useless one. In contrast, human scientists working with powerful computers and bright minds who can speed up the process in lab tests and stimulate exactly the genes they need, still can't achieve it.

In an interview[27] with former *Chicago Tribune* journalist, now Christian author, Lee Strobel, William Bradley set out the difficulties evolutionists face in asserting life came from non-life.

"There are an equal number of amino acids that are right and left-handed, and only left-handed ones work in living matter. Now you've got to get only these select ones to link together in the right sequence. And you also need the correct kind of chemical bonds – namely peptide bonds – in the correct places in order for the protein to be able to fold in a specific, three dimensional way. Otherwise it won't function.

"It's sort of like a printer taking letters out of a basket and setting type the way they used to do it by hand. If you guide it with your intelligence, it's no problem. But if you choose letters at random and put them together haphazardly – including upside down and backwards – then what are the chances that you'd get words, sentences and paragraphs that would make sense? It's extremely unlikely.

"In the same way, perhaps 100 amino acids have to be put together in just the right manner to make a protein molecule. And remember, that's just the first step. Creating one protein molecule doesn't mean you've created life. Now you have to bring together a collection of protein molecules – maybe two hundred of them – with just the right functions, to get a living cell."

And even then, what made that first ever cell reproduce? If its entire existence was down to chance, what was the chance it would realize a need to reproduce and find a way to do it?

Almost every year you hear TV newsreaders confidently revealing that scientists have discovered amino acids - "the building blocks of life" – in meteorite fragments, but the phrase is misleading. It is the scientific equivalent of finding a nail, and announcing that you have found the building blocks of a skyscraper.

So difficult is the task of creating life that the late Nobel laureate Sir Francis Crick, the co-discoverer of DNA, has speculated that life probably arose on earth as a result of an alien civilization deliberately seeding earth with its first life forms.

"When a scientist of Crick's calibre feels he has to invoke undetectable spacemen," notes Phillip Johnson, "it is time to consider whether the field of prebiological evolution has come to a dead end."

And if life cannot arise naturally on the one planet that teems with life, where else could it have arisen?

Molecular scientists in particular have been flocking to the Intelligent Design

27   *The Case For Faith* by Lee Strobel, Zondervan

side of the debate. One such is nanoscientist James Tour, a professor at the Department of Chemistry and Centre for Nanoscale Science and Technology at Houston's Rice University. Tour holds a doctorate in organic chemistry from Purdue University, did post-doctoral work at Stanford, has written more than 140 technical research articles and holds seventeen United States patents.

"I build molecules for a living," he said in an interview for Lee Strobel's book. *The Case for Faith*. "I can't begin to tell you how difficult that job is."

Like the others, James Tour is absolutely convinced, after years of molecular work, that life on earth was created by an Intelligent Designer. He says the "fingerprints of God" are everywhere.

"Only a rookie who knows nothing about science would say science takes away from faith. If you really study science, it will bring you closer to God."

Nobel prize-winning biologist Professor Christian Anfinsen is another to stick his oar in on current evolutionary theory, labelling one of the best anti-Darwin offerings – *Not By Chance* by biophysicist Lee Spetner – as "extremely thorough and compelling". Spetner says no evolutionary scientist has so far been able to refute his research and findings.

Geneticists already know, for example, that our genetic code, our DNA, contains 99% of the same information as a chimpanzee. Humans, on the same measure, are around 60% the same as daffodils. Spetner argues, among other things, that the genome of each creature includes vast numbers of dormant genetic switches which, were they turned on in the right sequence, might give us vastly different traits and appearances – yet the code has been within us since the dawn of time.

Spetner points to experiments on the embryos of rats and other animals that show identical embryos can develop different features given a simulated environment change in the lab.

"If a population of rodents were to shift their diet abruptly to a large hard seed, the phenotype [loose translation: appearance or characteristics] of the next generation would change abruptly. The phenotype [how it looks] would change, but the genotype [overall genetic code of the animal] would not.

"The fossil record of these rodents would show an abrupt change in the jaw and tooth structure. Yet there would have been *no mutation and no selection* [Spetner's emphasis]. The entire population would have changed together with the environment."

Yet, notes Spetner, a change in appearance in fossils has traditionally been recognised as evolution by Darwinists. Have they failed to see the wood for the trees?

But perhaps some of Spetner's most devastating criticism of Darwinism centres on the mathematical probability theory argument. Remember that question about whether a mutant new species could avoid being trampled by a brontosaurus? Well, believe it or not evolutionists have indeed calculated the odds of just such an event happening.

Sir Ronald Fisher was a brilliant British mathematician whose calculations on probability were applied to the theory of natural selection, and he became one of the leading supporters of Darwin's theories. After years of studying genetics and biology, as well as the fossil record, Fisher concluded that the average random mutation that occurs in an organism – when such a mutation actually takes place - gives it an advantage of about 0.1% against its fellow, un-mutated animals. But the odds against such a mutated creature (or indeed any individual member of a species) surviving to pass on its new gene are about 500 to 1, because of random environmental factors like predators, weather or famine, to name a few. The actual number of mutants in a group of 100,000 cows, for example, would need to be nearly 2,500 in order for a guarantee that any mutant gene would survive to be passed on to a new generation.

Dr Spetner says that for evolution to work, Fisher's results show there have to be a large number of mutations taking place in a population at any one time in order for just one of them to take hold in the species genome.

Another top evolutionist, scientist G Ledyard Stebbins, established in research published in the 1960s that the average number of positive random mutations needed to turn an organism into a new species was 500. Work since then has centred on how often random mutations actually occur in nature and whether they are of a kind sufficient to be positive, rather than negative or useless, to a species. Spetner's calculations show that *the chance of random evolution succeeding against nature's odds are about 1 in 10 to the power to 2,738 against*, which is 1 followed by 2,738 zeroes.

To put that into some kind of perspective, imagine having 150 people standing in a line tossing a coin at exactly the same moment, and in every case it comes up heads. The odds against that happening are just 10 to the power of 45. If you could flip the coins once every second, it would take somewhere in the region of 74 *trillion* years before such a result could be assured. That's 1500 times longer than the earth has been in existence. In other words, although it is technically possible, it is regarded as impossible. And that's just 1 followed by 45 zeroes, not the higher threshold of 1 followed by 2,738 zeroes.

The earth's 4.5 billion year lifespan may seem like an incredibly long time to comprehend, but Spetner is adamant that a non-created universe, governed only by natural laws, has to comply with those natural laws. And those laws, he says, include the law of probability.

Spetner concludes that as mutations are obviously happening, they're not happening by chance but by design in the form of built in plans in the genes. A random universe, he says, simply can't account for the odds not just against life but against the survival of life.

Interestingly, more than one evolutionist has found themselves, when trying to argue against Michael Behe's irreducible complexity theory, for example, suggesting that complex cells with interlinking components can "spontaneously arise" within evolution because the blueprint may be written in the genes. Which, responds Behe, sounds a lot like "intelligent design".

And don't get Intelligent Design biologists started on debating the complexity of DNA and the human genome. All scientists are agreed that DNA is a messaging system that carries within it the plans for the entire lifeform. Surprisingly, unlike wartime military codes that can take the best supercomputers years to crack, DNA is structured in a logical form, much like a book, making it easy for scientists to read the messages. Yet if all of the DNA in just *your* body alone was taken and laid end to end, it would stretch 50 *billion* kilometres – that's a straight line that would stretch from the sun to beyond the edge of the solar system. Just in one human body.

And if that is mind-boggling, try breaking it down to just one human blood cell. Surely that can't be too complex? In fact, each *single* cell in our bodies contains more information than the entire 30-volume set of the *Encyclopedia Britannica*.

But evolutionists still have other problems too: there is no way of telling whether a fossil animal is truly a new species or whether it is simply a larger or smaller specimen of the same fossil found elsewhere. Darwinists like to talk of the "classic example" of finches on the Galapagos Islands – a drought in 1977 caused a shortage of the small seeds that the birds normally eat, which in turn caused the smaller finches to die off because they couldn't eat the larger seeds left. Within a generation, scientists discovered the average size of the finches, and their beaks, had increased markedly. This, they said, was proof of evolution by natural selection.

Except, it wasn't. As soon as food supplies returned to normal, so did the survival rate of the smaller finches and the finch population soon returned to birds of pre-drought size. This, say Intelligent Design biologists, is simply evidence that animals have sufficient variation in their existing genetic code that enables them to adapt to changing conditions. *A la* Lee Spetner's thesis.

Whales are another classic example. There is plenty of evidence to show variations in whales over the ages, but the missing link is just as missing here as it is for humans.

"I've never found anything that's convinced me that evolution is not occurring," says New Zealand science teacher Bill Peddie.

"The fact is that we have plenty of evidence of new species arising, sometimes by human intervention to show it can be done, but then you've also got things like new species of cichlid fishes and so on in lakes – there's a famous lake in Africa where a bit got cut off and they got the new fish appearing within the space of about a couple of hundred years. It can be quite a rapid process if you get a change of environment."

The true test of whether something is a new species though is the degree of difference between it and its alleged parent, and whether it can interbreed with the original species. If it cannot, it is said to be a different species. The problem for scientists is that there is no way of knowing whether fossil animals could interbreed or not – the soft parts of the animal and its DNA are no longer available for study. What we, in modern science, presume are different species may well have simply been regional or micro-evolved variants of the same animal, in the same way that Great Danes and Dachshunds are still just dogs, not dog/cat crosses.

So do we know for sure that those cichlid fish in Africa were not capable of mating with their ancestors?

"Well, no, we don't," admits Peddie. "One of our problems is that the definitions of species are human-made and often just for convenience. How many differences do you have to make before you say it is a new species?"

Another example Peddie cites to prove evolution is the development of marine life on the Central American coast. North and South America used to be separate island continents – there was no Mexico to act as a land bridge between them. At that stage, says Peddie, fossil records show similar marine life on both the Pacific side and the Atlantic side.

But after the land bridge formed, the marine life changed.

"When there was an actual land barrier, the marine species developed separately and began looking different on either side. That's a radical change."

But again, Spetner and others would argue, are we really looking at different species, or just the development of different races within a species?

What would paleontologists make, 10,000 years from now, of the huge numbers of what we know are different-looking types of genetically-identical dog? Imagine digging up the skeleton of a massive Newfoundland or St Bernard, and also the skeletons of a Chihuahua and a Dachshund: is it possible that school students 10,000 years in the future might be forced to pass exams by describing how Chihuahuas evolved into Newfoundlands over a long period of time?

If Darwin's Theory of Evolution is on such shaky ground in the upper reaches of science, why are New Zealand high school students still being taught the subject without any reference to the many controversies now dogging it?

New Zealand's biology syllabus book for Year 12 students includes evolution and says: "Evolution is the process by which new species of plants and animals develop from earlier forms. The process of evolution normally occurs slowly, most often in response to a change in a species' environment…life is thought to have evolved from just a few original unicellular organisms some three billion years ago to the complex array of millions of species we see today."

All of which is beginning to look decidedly old-fashioned when measured against what scientists are currently arguing.

The textbook continues: "New Zealand has two closely related large native parrots: the kea that inhabits mountainous regions of the South Island and the kaka that inhabits bush in the North Island. It is thought that these two species share a common ancestor."

The book then goes on to explain to students how some birds got used to the cold and adapted, while the other parrots fled to the warmer north. This makes them new species, it says. Yet if school science teachers were to tell students that humans with black skin were a different *species* from those with white skin, simply because they'd adapted to hot climates, they'd be shot down in flames.

"You can't prove those sorts of theories," admits Ministry of Education science curriculum advisor Chris Arcus when confronted with the kea/kaka example, "because you can't replicate them in a laboratory. But that's the nature of science. In science we avoid use of the word 'fact', because fact sounds like it's absolutely set in concrete. We talk more about probability, weight of evidence, and the cohesiveness of theories that support this sort of thing."

Curricula notes for a seventh form bursary level biology course show an extensive role being played by evolutionary theory, yet debate about evolution theories – at least in the notes - is limited to "Darwin vs Lamarck". Lamarck was an evolutionist like Darwin with a slightly different spin on the process. He wasn't a Design advocate. In modern terms, it would be like limiting debate on Iraq policy to a comparison between George Bush and Donald Rumsfeld.

Lamarck's prominence in the New Zealand curriculum is unmatched in the international war of the experts: barely more than two paragraphs about him in Spetner's *Not By Chance*, nothing in Behe's *Darwin's Black Box*, nothing in Johnson's *Darwin on Trial*, and nothing in J P Moreland's *The Creation Hypothesis*.

Meanwhile, fresh from discussing the views of an obscure Darwinian predecessor, NZ students are again taught that evolution creates new species, and are invited to "provide NZ examples, e.g. blue penguins, protokaka and divaricating shrubs", while later on in the course they are again told to study "the evolution of New Zealand flora and fauna", with the instruction that "mammals, insects and legumes are well documented".

The claim in a New Zealand high school biology textbook that trans-species evolution by way of "slow accumulated mutations" is so "well documented" in this country that students can readily provide exam-winning projects showing this, would undoubtedly come as news to scientists like Lynn Margulis at the cutting edge of the debate, seeing as a conference of the world's top molecular biologists failed to produce "one unambiguous example" resulting from the slow accumulation of mutations.

While New Zealand college students are earnestly studying "evidence for human evolution", including "humans and their recent ancestors", the world's leading anthropologists and paleontologists are banging their heads against walls at the complete lack of evidence for human evolution.

The total world fossil collection of ancient apes and humans – all the bones recovered in the world from all the alleged different species, would fit in a small cardboard box that you could sit on the front seat of your car. Is that really enough evidence to even begin to speculate on human evolution?

Perhaps the most frustrating part of the debate for ordinary people is that Intelligent Design scientists and Evolutionists are all working from the same basic data, but drawing entirely different conclusions. Case in point? NZ's seventh form textbooks state "all organisms are made of cells, and the complex processes occurring in all cells are so similar that this strongly suggests a common ancestor. The genetic code is the same for all species and is estimated to be 3.8 billion years old!"

This, say the Darwinists, proves evolution.

This, says the Intelligent Design movement, proves a designer crafted all life from the same DNA building blocks, but turned on different genetic switches to create different species.

Whatever the rights or wrongs of the debate, it goes well beyond the scope of this chapter to highlight all the technical arguments in different areas. But there is certainly enough evidence to show that science itself is by no means united on the reality of evolution.

Is there room for the *real* scientific debate to be aired in our classrooms?

Strangely enough, Darwinists are dead against it. Scientific atheist Ian Plimer is a geology professor at Melbourne University who told the *NZ Listener* that allowing the debate "into schools is just about the worst thing that you can do."

Nor does New Zealand's Bill Peddie like the idea.

"It would not be helpful, the sort of detail you're talking, it wouldn't be helpful to have it aired in the junior [high] school. Bits of it are already aired in the senior school. For example, a Year 13 Biology student doing scholarship biology would be expected to be reading in these areas and be aware that everything is not as cut and dried as they were led to believe earlier.

"This is helpful, useful and sensible. It isn't helpful for somebody who's barely aware that there's a difference between an atom and a molecule to be discussing different binding theories for atoms. When you're starting math you learn your two-times table, you don't get into imaginary numbers at that level."

But as we've already seen, the level of debate at Year 13 level is actually slim. The Ministry of Education appears more conciliatory, but relies on science teachers to decide.

"At no stage do we say that this is *the* theory that should be taught," says Chris

Arcus, "but the syllabus does recognise that there are a range of theoretical positions and a range of evidences supporting those positions. As an aside it does recognise the role that Maori knowledge plays in an understanding of scientific phenomena."

Interestingly, New Zealand's education syllabus contains a large, officially-mandated coverage of Maori creation myths, and there would be few schoolchildren today who could not recount the story of Maui, or Rangi and Papa-nui. The number of children, on the other hand, who could say they learnt about Intelligent Design's scientific objections to Darwinism in a New Zealand state school, as part of the Government curricula, would be non-existent.

"The reason why people question the advisability of debating evolution publicly," explains Peddie, "is because people will misunderstand what is being said. They'll use it as an example of boosting the Creation vs Evolution debate, one side or the other, instead of understanding what the scientific models are saying. The model itself [Darwinism, neo-Darwinism for example] might only be transitory, and it could even be based on a wrong-headed idea, but if it causes you to make new observations and notice some relationships you didn't notice before well then we would say, in terms of science, that yes, we're really making progress."

But the problem with Peddie's analysis is a philosophical one: by teaching only a select few top students the truth (or, more accurately, giving them just the barest hint) about the major problems emerging with Darwin's Theory of Evolution, and leaving everyone else with a school curricula that says the Theory is scientifically sound, Western schools are turning out millions of students with what may turn out to be false beliefs about life and their place in it.

When those beliefs go to the heart of spiritual issues like the existence of a Creator or whether humanity is governed by a moral code, the societal damage could be severe from awarding such widespread credibility to what even supporters of evolution admit could be a "wrong-headed" idea.

Molecular biologist Michael Denton, another top scientist with serious doubts about evolution, describes just how high the stakes are in his book *Evolution: A Theory In Crisis*.

"The twentieth century would be incomprehensible without the Darwinian revolution. The social and political currents which have swept the world in the past eighty years would have been impossible without its intellectual sanction…

"The influence of evolutionary theory on fields far removed from biology is one of the most spectacular examples in history of how a highly speculative idea for which there is no really hard scientific evidence can come to fashion the thinking of a whole society and dominate the outlook of an age.

"Today it is perhaps the Darwinian view of nature more than any other that is responsible for the agnostic and skeptical outlook of the twentieth century…a theory that literally changed the world.

"The decline in religious belief can probably be attributed more to the propagation and advocacy by the intellectual and scientific community of the Darwinian version of evolution than to any other single factor."

And just in case there are still lingering doubts about the religious aspects of Darwinism, British atheist Richard Dawkins wrote in *The Blind Watchmaker* that Darwin "made it possible to be an intellectually-fulfilled atheist". Expressed another way – take away the crutch of evolution and atheism once again loses any claim to have an intelligent or intellectual basis.[28]

Cornell University's William Provine, another prominent evolutionist and atheist, went even further in print by saying that if Darwinism is true, then there are five inescapable conclusions: there's no evidence for God; there's no life after death; there's no absolute foundation for right and wrong; there's no ultimate meaning for life; and people don't really have free will.

When biological evolutionists go beyond the theory to argue the metaphysical, they then invite a full on, knock-em-down-drag-em-out debate with Intelligent Design about other aspects of the argument like Big Bang Cosmology – the discovery that the Universe burst into being within literally a split second 14 billion years ago and had never existed before that moment. Eminent scientist Stephen Hawking has calculated that the creation of the Universe was so precise that if the Universe's rate of expansion during the first second of its existence had deviated by as little as 1/100,000,000,000,000,00 0th of a second, the Universe would have collapsed into a fireball.

More than one scientific atheist has ditched atheism after studying Big Bang Cosmology – among them Harvard-trained Patrick Glynn who says he became an atheist because of Darwin but has now embraced what he calls "the God hypothesis".

"Ironically, the picture of the Universe bequeathed to us by the most advanced twentieth-century science is closer in spirit to the vision presented in the Book of Genesis than anything offered by science since Copernicus."

Back here in New Zealand, our school curriculum is in no shape to handle broad-spectrum debate about the origins of life or cosmology. Indeed, the rapid pace of development overseas appears to be leaving our schools behind.

Chris Arcus, like many teachers, is aware of the life from a puddle experiment in the fifties. Also like many teachers, he was unaware it had been shot down by NASA in the eighties. And because the science curricula is effectively set by

28   In *The God Delusion*, p100, Dawkins quotes surveys of American scientists revealing 93% do *not* believe in a personal God, and British & Commonwealth scientists where around 95% don't believe. This contrasts sharply to the 90% of the US general public who do believe in God. Dawkins expresses surprise that the public don't match "the atheism of the intellectual elite". When the elite have such a strong vested interest in protecting their own belief system, it does raise questions about scientific integrity.

a committee of science teachers, setting the record straight would depend on how up to speed those teachers are on international research.

But there are obviously a large number of science teachers who are up to speed, because a *Listener* article in 2000 quoted Darwinists bemoaning the growing number of science teachers who were "Creationists or Creationism-prone". Anthropology researcher Margaret Scott, who interviewed science teachers for an MA thesis entitled *The Resurgence of Creationism*, said some told her that evidence for evolution was "very suspect", and that given the shakiness of evolutionary theory, perhaps alternatives needed to be debated. Scott was aghast but, then again, is she herself academically equipped to argue the toss with US scientists who've been grappling with evolution for their entire careers and found it wanting?

And therein lies the rub – has Darwinism with its religious atheistic doctrine and demand for total adherence to its teachings become so dominant that, like an educational black hole, good students with an inkling that things are not right get sucked into it, never to emerge again as independent thinkers? At the upper levels of the Darwinist side you are almost guaranteed to find a staunch atheist at every turn. How much does that metaphysical world-view impact on the way they teach the subject and produce university graduates?

In America, students and lecturers who reject the atheistic doctrine but nonetheless pass their exams are still being persecuted by atheists in positions of power, as the case of geosciences doctoral graduate Marcus Ross in March 2007 shows.

Ross hit the headlines because, despite passing his doctorate with flying colours, he's a "young earth" creationist. That annoyed some American scientists who felt he should be stripped of his doctorate because of his beliefs, as the *New York Times* reported in an interview with atheist fundamentalist Eugenie Scott:[29]

> DR. SCOTT, A FORMER professor of physical anthropology at the University of Colorado, said in an interview that graduate admissions committees were entitled to consider the difficulties that would arise from admitting a doctoral candidate with views "so at variance with what we consider standard science." She said such students "would require so much remedial instruction it would not be worth my time".
>
> Dr. Dini, of Texas Tech, agreed. Scientists "ought to make certain the people they are conferring advanced degrees on understand the philosophy of science and are indeed philosophers of science," he said.

---

29   http://briefingroom.typepad.com/the_briefing_room/2007/02/scientists_seek.html

The case was covered, both on *Investigate* magazine's TBR.cc blog, and also at a US blog[30] where the host raised further examples of good scientists being harangued for their beliefs:

> In March 2006 Dr. Francis Beckwith was nearly denied tenure at Baylor University. As that link explains, his academic credentials are so outstanding that his support for discussion of intelligent design is the most likely reason for the controversy. (Further discussion at *World Magazine*.) - Also check out this transcript from a 2005 NPR segment on intelligent design, in which they interview several IDers/creationists who feel they have been discriminated against by the establishment. Most notable is Dr. Richard Sternberg, who experienced hostile retaliation from the Smithsonian Institute after allowing the publication of an article favorable to intelligent design in a peer-reviewed biology publication. In the NPR transcript, note where the journalist doing the piece explains that she tried to contact numerous intelligent design supporters, who mostly refused to speak to her, saying it would be as much as their career was worth to be so publicly identified prior to receiving their tenure.

The blogger, a medical student, then raises another interesting point in response to a critic:

> To take up your third section second here: You say, "Patently ridiculous nonsense such as global floods is junk science." Well, that kind of begs the question. We are trying to discuss whether a global flood is a better explanation of the fossil record than Darwin's theory. It would explain how you have trees and giant animals (whales, dinosaurs) crossing multiple layers of sediment, which according to evolutionary geology ought to have been laid down over millions of years. It would explain the frequent occurrence of more "advanced" animals in the same strata as their much earlier "ancestors." It would explain how fossils of sea creatures have been found on the tops of high mountains, as in the Himalayas. And of course, it would explain the observation that fossils were formed with great rapidity during disasters like the Mt. St. Helen's eruption, but all carcasses which have been left lying around or in bogs of mud have been observed to rot to bits, rather than fossilizing. Which kind of

messes up the whole evolutionary scenario.

If I leave a dead bird in my yard, it doesn't become a fossil. But if there's a dead bird lying on the bank as a river undergoes a tremendous flood, it might fossilize.

It is precisely the refusal of evolutionists to even allow the discussion of other reasonable explanations which leads IDers and creationists to level charges of witch-hunting and modern inquisitions.

And that's the wider problem. You can see the intricate debates taking place on the merits of Darwinian theory, yet school textbooks and exam papers scratch only the "evolution for dummies" bits and none of the controversy. If you don't buy into the whole doctrine you flunk the course. And why should high school students be made to sit pass/fail exams on a topic that even the experts don't agree on?

More significantly, and this perhaps is where the international battle over teaching evolution in schools needs to go, is why are we teaching evolution at all? Does the Theory of Evolution, as taught in schools, have any relevance to future lawyers, accountants, office workers, parents? I suggest it is only of relevance to those who intend a career in the biological sciences.

The fact that virtually all the leading lights involved in trying to protect Darwin's monopoly on school science classes are atheists, indicates to me that schools have been captured by what is effectively a rival religion.

Strong evidence of this is supported by the late Harvard Zoologist Ernst Mayr, one of Darwinism's most respected defenders, who confesses that when evolutionists all come together to ridicule Intelligent Design, they do so primarily for a religious reason:[31]

"THERE IS INDEED one belief that all true original Darwinians held in common, and that was their rejection of creationism, their rejection of special creation. This was the flag around which they assembled and under which they marched. When Hull claimed that "the Darwinians did not totally agree with each other, even over essentials" (1985:785), he overlooked one essential on which all these Darwinians agreed.

"*Nothing was more essential for them than to decide whether evolution is a natural phenomenon or something controlled by God.* [emphasis added] The conviction that the diversity of the natural world was the result of natural processes and not

---

31   Emeritus Professor of Zoology, Harvard University, Ernst Mayr, *One Long Argument: Charles Darwin and the Genesis of Modern Evolutionary Thought*, Harvard University Press, 1991, p.99

the work of God was the idea that brought all the so-called Darwinians together in spite of their disagreements on other of Darwin's theories..."

Does that sound like balanced science of the kind you'd find in a biology class, or the transcript of discussion at the annual Satanists Picnic? I would have thought that "Nothing was more essential than finding the truth." Apparently not. The real aim of Darwinism in science is to promote the "death of God" movement. Are you comfortable that you received an honest science education, or that your kids are receiving one, when these are the confessions of what motivates "scientists"?

If there is no overwhelming scientific reason to teach Darwinism in schools, then the motivation for some of these people must indeed be religious: Dawkins and others are already on the public record linking Darwinism as a foundation pillar of their faith in the non-existence of God. Ernst Mayr agrees that Darwinism is the key to social change in the Western world:

> "THE TRUTH OF THE MATTER is that unless a person is still an adherent of creationism and believes in the literal truth of every word in the Bible, every modern thinker - any modern person who has a worldview - is in the last analysis a Darwinian. The rejection of special creation, the inclusion of man into the realm of the living world (the elimination of the special position of man versus the animals), and various other beliefs of every enlightened modern person are ultimately all based on the consequences of the theories contained in the *Origin of Species*."

In other words, by teaching what Ann Coulter calls "the Liberals' creation myth" in schools, scientists reckon they have successfully brainwashed an entire generation of Westerners. And scientists have the cheek to complain about religion?

Atheism, along with its cousins rationalism and secular humanism, *is* a religion. The existence or non-existence of God cannot be proven on current knowledge scientifically, therefore belief or disbelief are flipsides of the same religious coin. They are "faith" decisions.

If Dawkins, Eugenie Scott and others wish to keep preaching what they see as the historical evidence for their personal religious faith in public schools, perhaps Christianity should be entitled to stop pussy-footing around and be allowed to teach school students the considerable historical and archaeological evidence in support of Christ's Resurrection and the historical accuracy of the New Testament. Because there's far more hard evidence for that than there is of macroevolution.

My recommendation to some of those who feel strongly in the US is to consider – if fundamentalist atheists keep refusing to allow Darwinism's weaknesses to be debated in class in the interests of scientific balance – assessing whether any theory of evolution or origins is relevant to general schooling or whether such courses should be challenged as primarily "establishment of religion" by the State, especially as the Association of Rationalists and Humanists' New Zealand branch has recently conceded in submissions to the New Zealand government that rationalism and secular humanism are indeed a "belief system".[32]

The comments of atheist fundamentalist Eugenie Scott, of the National Centre for Science Education, suggesting students who graduate with secular educations should be prevented from getting jobs, if they are Christian, would again be solid evidence that those promoting evolution in schools have a religious motivation for doing so.

Even skeptics are concerned about this trend.

In a stunning piece of editorial commentary, a 2002 edition of *Scientific American* acknowledges the rise of the cargo-cult worship of men in white coats - epitomised by the ultimate high priest, Stephen Hawking.

"What is it about Hawking that draws us to him as a scientific saint?" asks columnist and skeptic Michael Shermer. "He is, I believe, the embodiment of a larger social phenomenon known as scientism. Scientism is a scientific worldview that encompasses natural explanations for all phenomena, eschews supernatural and paranormal speculations, and embraces empiricism and reason as the twin pillars of a philosophy of life appropriate for an Age of Science."

You can almost hear the drums roll to the majestic accompaniment of a cathedral organ, as Shermer continues.

"First, cosmology and evolutionary theory ask the ultimate origin questions that have traditionally been the province of religion and theology.

"Scientism is courageously proffering naturalistic answers that supplant supernaturalistic ones and in the process is providing spiritual sustenance for those whose needs are not being met by these ancient cultural traditions.

"Second, we are, at base, a socially hierarchical primate species. We show deference to our leaders, pay respect to our elders and follow the dictates of our shamans [witchdoctors]; this being the Age of Science, it is scientism's shamans who command our veneration.

"Third, because of language, we are also storytelling, mythmaking primates, with scientism as the foundational stratum of our story and scientists as the premier mythmakers of our time."

In other words, everyone, even *Scientific American*, is now acknowledging that when we learn science at school we are being baptised in a new religion, with a deliberate religious agenda of its own.

The problem is a fundamental one for the biological sciences: evolution is the only theory, barring the supernatural, that remotely explains the diversity of life on our planet. Science abhors a vacuum, and debunking evolution without offering a rational, non-supernatural alternative, is anathema to science.

Scientific American quoted a public lecture given by Hawking where he was asked "the biggest question of all: 'Is there a God?'

"Asked this ultimately unanswerable question...a wry smile formed and the Delphic oracle spoke: 'I do not answer God questions'."

If it sounds a little like the old adage: 'don't go looking for trouble and you won't find it', you could be right.

The only other option on offer – admitting an intelligent Creator is responsible for life, the universe and everything – would undermine the importance of science and heighten the importance of religious study, clearly an outcome so horrific in its implications that science would rather stick with the Devil they know than the Deity they don't.

Which brings us to Professor Antony Flew, one of the world's leading atheist philosophers and authors, who famously argued that the burden of proof for design in the world fell on Christians to prove, not atheists to rebut. Every time you come across some spotty-faced little atheist in an internet chatroom who can't spell but insists "it is up to Christians to prove God exists, because all the natural evidence says he doesn't" – you're dealing with someone using Antony Flew's argument, even if young Mr Spotty Face has never heard of Flew.

In late 2004, after a series of debates via correspondence with biblical scholar Gary Habermas, Flew shocked many academics by publicly renouncing atheism, because of the strength of the evidence of Intelligent Design.

Flew was quoted as saying his confidence in atheism began to falter because evolutionary science still cannot "produce a plausible conjecture as to how any of these complex molecules might have evolved from simple entities." Flew added that, taken as a whole, the relatively recent scientific developments in "Big Bang Cosmology, fine tuning [the discovery that the laws of the universe appear deliberately fine-tuned for the existence of life on this particular planet] and Intelligent Design arguments" finally convinced him it was no longer possible to be an intellectually-fulfilled atheist, regardless of Darwin.

"I think that the most impressive arguments for God's existence are those that are supported by recent scientific discoveries. I think the argument to Intelligent Design is enormously stronger that it was when I first met it."

Flew says he now believes his prominent fellow atheist, Richard Dawkins, is getting it wrong when he tries to use Darwinism to deny the existence of God.

"Darwin himself pointed out that his whole argument began with a being which already possessed reproductive powers [the first living cell and alleged common ancestor of all life]. This is the creature the evolution of which a truly comprehensive theory of evolution must give some account. Darwin himself was well aware that he had not produced such an account.

"It now seems to me that the findings of more than fifty years of DNA research have provided materials for a new and enormously powerful argument to design."

Flew is not a Christian, and he is not arguing that the Christian God exists. But he does now accept that atheism is no longer an *intellectual* position in the market place of ideas.

As you read through *Eve's Bite*, you'll discover it's a blow-by-blow counterpoint to Richard Dawkins latest book, *The God Delusion*. It wasn't intentional; knowing Dawkins' work I really couldn't be bothered buying a copy of *Delusion*, and only picked one up after 290 of the pages of *Eve's Bite* had already been written. The irony of coming at many of the same issues from precisely opposite positions amused me, and seeing as *Eve's Bite* destroys the social premises of *The God Delusion* I hope you'll bear with me for just a few more pages so I can tackle Dawkins specifically on some of his outrageously misleading writing.

5

The Dawkins Delusion
Atheism's High Priest

"While the rest of the species is descended from apes, redheads are descended from cats."

Mark Twain

The title of atheist Richard Dawkin's latest book, *The God Delusion*, was well chosen. Dawkins is, indeed, deluded in his understanding of religion and the nature of God. Whilst yours truly must wade through papers published in scientific journals in order to comment on the truth or falsity of evolution, Dawkins – judging from his book – does little to no homework on religion. And boasts of his ignorance:[33]

"The notion that religion is a proper *field*, in which one might claim *expertise*, is not one that should go unquestioned," he chortles in his tome, before adding, "Why shouldn't we comment on God, as scientists?" He doesn't waste time illustrating why it was unwise when, as a demonstration of his wisdom, he leaves a name-drop reference to that flavour of the month way back in 1993, *The Gospel of Thomas*.[34]

"*THE GOSPEL OF THOMAS*, for example, has numerous anecdotes about the child Jesus abusing his magical powers in the manner of a mischievous fairy, impishly transforming his playmates into goats, or turning mud into sparrows...It will be said that nobody believes crude miracle stories such as those in *The Gospel of Thomas* anyway."

Here's a test that you can do at home: go to your computer, right now, and enter the Google search phrase "The Gospel of Thomas" (and putting it in

---

33 *The God Delusion*, Richard Dawkins, Bantam Press, p16
34 Ibid, p96

quote marks will find it faster). Read through *The Gospel of Thomas*, and judge for yourself if the world's leading fundamentalist atheist – one of the planet's "top three intellectuals" according to the blurb on his book - has a blind clue what he's talking about.

I'll give you a hint. There do exist some apocryphal fictional tales written perhaps a hundred and 30 years after the death of Christ about miracles in his youth, but they're not in the Gospel he proudly quoted in his bestselling book.

To put the scale of Dawkins' fumbling in perspective, it would be equivalent to me criticizing him for the claims in his book *The Magic Faraway Tree* – oh, that's right, he didn't author that title even though it does sound like one of his. Would Dawkins cut Intelligent Design scientists slack if they published a book demolishing the evolution of the fruit fly but accidentally using the genome of the hippopotamus to do it? No, it'd be a credibility slam-dunk, over and out, and we'd never hear the end of it.

Those of us around the world who have studied the historical basis of the Christian religion shake our heads sadly every time Dawkins gets up to speak, as do many of the more intelligent atheists who find the evolutionary zoologist embarrassing to their cause because of the errors he makes and his frothing-at-the-mouth fundamentalism.

"He's a fanatic," muttered the guy behind the counter at the bookstore when I purchased my copy of *The God Delusion*.

"He's a *Macroglossus sobrinus*," I smiled. Or perhaps I used the vernacular, "long-tongued fruit bat". Whatever. Dawkins, for his part, reckons he can disprove God using science:[35]

> "GOD'S EXISTENCE or non-existence is a scientific fact about the universe, discoverable in principle if not in practice…and even if God's existence is never proved or disproved with certainty one way or the other, available evidence and reasoning may yield an estimate of probability far from 50%."

Sounds like a challenge to me. I'm up for it. Game on. By the end of this chapter, let's see whether I can push the probability of God's existence higher than 50%.

Dawkins reckons the four main gospels are all fairy stories:[36]

Dawkins Claim 1:
"ALL HAVE THE STATUS of legends, as factually dubious as the stories of King Arthur and his Knights of the Round Table."

---

35   Ibid, p50
36   Ibid, p96

Really? Given that we don't yet have definite proof of the existence of the legendary King Arthur, or any other contemporaneous writings about him, that's a pretty wild call from Dawkins. Because in contrast, there are more than 5,600 hand-transcribed copies[37] of the original New Testament, or fragments thereof, dating back to around 70 years after the death of Christ. These ancient documents, collected from all around the Mediterranean, were considered so important by the first Christians that they were painstakingly hand-copied, word for word as the number of church communities grew like wildfire in the years after the crucifixion.

These documents, unlike the mythical King Arthur, stare archaeologists, historians and biblical scholars in the face. They can and have been carbon-dated, they are accurate to within 99.5% of each other across the entire 5,686 copies, and they are identical on all key aspects of Christian doctrine. They are packed with substantiated historical facts that have proven a treasure trove to historians and archaeologists in shedding light on the ancient Near East.

In fact, we have more copies of the ancient New Testament in universities, museums and libraries than any other ancient book.[38] The next closest is Homer's *Illiad*, of which only 643 manuscripts survive. Julius Caesar's *Gallic Wars* provides us with only 10 copies, of which the earliest of those was written one thousand years after the events in question. Of Plato's writings – a staple of classical educations and universities – only 7 copies exist, the earliest of which was still written 1,300 years after the event.

Dawkins would regard it absurd that we don't believe in Plato, or the details of Caesar's wars, yet there is far less evidence for them.

So as to the first claim, I'd say the gospels beat the legend of King Arthur as matters of historical fact.

Dawkins 0.

Dawkins Claim 2:[39]

"EVER SINCE THE 19TH CENTURY, scholarly theologians have made an overwhelming case that the gospels are not reliable accounts of what happened in the history of the real world. All were written long after the death of Jesus, and also after the epistles of Paul, which mention almost none of the alleged facts of Jesus' life. All were then copied and recopied, through many different 'Chinese Whispers generations' by fallible scribes who, in any case, had their own religious agendas."

Are you rolling on the floor laughing yet? Would this be the same Dawkins

---

37   *New Evidence That Demands A Verdict*, Josh McDowell, Nelson, p36
38   Ibid, p38
39   *The God Delusion*, p92-93

who denied there could be any "expertise" or even a field of study, who is now approvingly quoting "scholarly theologians" and an "overwhelming" case?

Dawkins appeals, however, to a kind of circular argument. The publication of Darwin's theory in 1859 sent shockwaves through liberal Christianity (the ones who secretly don't believe in God anyway but lack the courage to admit it), and particularly through a couple of theological seminaries, Tubingen in Germany being one of them. The boys at Tubingen spent the next few decades trying to reconcile what little faith they had with the new star on the block, "science", and basically became default priests of scientism (the religion of science). If scientists said miracles could not exist, then hey, the miracle stories in the Bible must be made up. If scientists said we were all descended from apes, then Genesis must be a lie, and so too the New Testament which references Adam, Eve and the Flood.

So his argument is circular, in that Darwin spooked the horses and Dawkins now approvingly quotes the spooked horses in broad support of his Darwinian materialist position.

Back in the 19th century, however, they did not have radiocarbon dating, they didn't have 5,600 early manuscript copies and they certainly didn't have all the archaeological evidence that now exists. In recent times, Christianity has become more "muscular", as Dawkins calls it elsewhere, because the latest research by "scholarly theologians" is overturning what Tubingen's intimidated fossils were saying.

Let's look at some of those for a moment. Firstly, the idea that the gospels were written as late as 150 AD (120 years after the crucifixion) was certainly a popular one prior to radiocarbon dating. If true, then Dawkins would be correct when he claims elsewhere that the gospel writers never knew Jesus.

But in the past 160 years there's been a major shift in thinking because new evidence was discovered, and even liberal theologians like John A. T. Robinson now believe the entire New Testament was written and published within about three decades of the crucifixion.[40] That means everything in the NT was out there by 70AD, available for challenge and criticism from other eyewitnesses to the events in question. Two of the gospels, Matthew and John, appear to be written by the apostles concerned, and John certainly claims this. Luke was a companion of Paul's, and Mark is recorded as an assistant to the apostle Peter. Mark's gospel, the earliest, is in fact the gospel of Peter.

The apostle Paul, whom Dawkins claims in his book knew virtually nothing of Christ, says in 1.Cor 15:3-6:

> "FOR WHAT I RECEIVED I passed on to you as of first importance: that Christ died for our sins according to the Scriptures, that

---

40   *Redating the New Testament,* Dr John A. T. Robinson, Westminster, 1976

he was buried, that he was raised on the third day, according to the Scriptures, and that he appeared to Peter, and then to the Twelve. After that he appeared to more than 500 of the brothers at the same time, most of whom are still living, though some have fallen asleep [died]. Then he appeared to James, then to all the apostles, and last of all to me also."

Paul's first letter to the Corinthians was written around 55AD, but this particular verse contains the earliest and most fundamental of Christian creeds, and it is widely accepted in both liberal and conservative scholarship that Paul "received" the creed when he met Peter and James, the brother of Jesus, in Jerusalem soon after his road to Damascus conversion, within two years of the death of Christ. We know Paul went to this meeting because it is recorded in Acts 9:27, written by Luke. And we know Paul only met Peter and James, because he says so himself in Gal. 1:18. It is seen as no coincidence that the fundamental creed above names the only two apostles who could have relayed the teaching to him.

No matter how you look at the passage though, you have evidence of Christ portrayed publicly as a resurrected God, almost immediately after the event in question – and that portrayal coming from the apostles, not from Paul in the first instance.

I've already covered the error of his "Chinese Whispers…fallible scribes" comment. If it were true you'd see major variations in the manuscripts, not a 99.5% match-up.[41]

Dawkins can rely on 160 year old theological opinions if he likes (he does with his science, and boasts about that, too), but it's a bit like favourably quoting a 160 year old medical paper on the value of bloodletting as a cure for haemophilia.

Still no points on the board for Dawkins.

Perhaps the central thesis of *The God Delusion*, however, is the idea that something complex (the Universe) needs a more complex Designer, and a complex Designer had to have evolved from something less complex, therefore he can't exist.

Dawkins Claim 3:[42]

"DESIGN IS NOT A REAL alternative at all, because it raises an even bigger problem than it solves: who designed the designer?"

Bring on Inspector Morse, I say. Clearly every common or garden

41   *A General Introduction to the Bible*, Geisler & Nix, Moody Press, 1986
42   *The God Delusion*, p121

fundamentalist atheist is reading Dawkins, because this is the question they keep hitting me with. The great man wastes more processed trees trying to prove this particular point than I can bear to conceptualise. His contribution to Greenhouse emissions on this one misguided topic alone is probably equivalent to Al Gore's power bill, and that's saying something! Especially when I can relieve Dawkins of his schoolboy atheist construction of the argument in just a few short paragraphs.

I know Richard won't listen. He'll sit there raving on and on about "Flying Spaghetti Monsterism", like some B-grade actor in a bad British comedy – *Blackadder* series one comes to mind, or perhaps *Root of all Evil*. But for intelligent and discerning readers, here's how Christian theology frees Dawkins from a mousetrap of his own making:

He poses the idea that someone must have designed the designer, otherwise when the universe began the designer would have been unevolved and very simple, and simple things cannot create universes. In this little paradox he sets up, Dawkins believes he has delivered the coup de grace to theistic religion. He forgets one very important little fact. TIME.

As his good friend Stephen Hawking would have told him, had Dawkins only asked, Time only exists *within* the four walls of our universe. It does not exist outside the universe. Dawkins, sitting inside the universe, assumes that the rules and laws of physics, chemistry, biology and time must apply to God as well. But if he reads *A Brief History Of Time*, or any other major works on Big Bang Cosmology, Dawkins would have found out that all those laws only exist on the *inside* of our universe. When we talk of "natural" laws, they apply only *inside* the natural universe. Outside the universe is a timeless realm, something we humans simply cannot conceive. It has no past, no future, only an enduring present. Gravity doesn't exist there, electromagnetic force does not exist there, $E=mc^2$ doesn't exist there. We know this because we know all the laws we take for granted came into existence for the purposes of this particular universe. That is what the best scientific brains on the planet now believe.

The idea of a God in a timeless realm "evolving" is about as rational as talking about a square circle or Dawkins' spaghetti monster. It is a contradiction in terms. Evolution takes place only in the natural realm, according to natural laws, and with large doses of Time thrown in for good measure. Why would an eternal being, with no natural environmental pressures, "evolve"? As Dawkins defines it, Evolution is a linear concept, implying change over a progression of time. If there is no progression of time, however, there can be no evolution.

Naturalism, materialistic science, call it what you will, is only valid as a form of investigation *inside* the universe, because all the laws it measures things against came into existence moments after the Big Bang.

Now to the nature of God. If Dawkins had bothered to read the Bible, he'd discover that God introduces himself to Moses in Ex. 3:14 – not as Yahweh but as "I AM". What a concept! The Bible is replete with the theology of God as a timeless eternal entity, and when God refers to himself in the Bible he does so in the everlasting present tense. Jesus Christ, in the New Testament, is recorded at John 8:58:

> "I TELL YOU THE TRUTH," Jesus answered, "before Abraham was born, I AM!"

Christ's comment is utterly bizarre. It makes no coherent grammatical sense, *unless* he is naming himself the eternal God who dwells outside time. Clearly the Jews of the day recognised this because they picked up rocks and tried to stone Christ for blasphemy. Only someone with no beginning or ending could refer to themselves as "I AM". From a time-locked human perspective, the phrase makes no sense at all.

Yet here is a primitive tribe of wandering nomads who manage to conceptualise and express the natural boundaries of Time and the supernatural dominion of Eternity, roughly 3,500 years before cosmologists could scientifically verify that Time was indeed created.

The biological laws that Dawkins rabbits on about, the increasing complexity he rabbits on about, and his linear mental block about the Designer needing to have a beginning – all of these things are the product of a mind that hasn't read either 1) the cosmology papers or 2) the Bible but 3) considers himself an expert on both.

Dawkins' entire book essentially tries to judge God from the perspective of Dawkins' comprehension. Arguably, it should have been a much shorter book – a page would have done it. But the analogy I would draw is this: imagine two giant deep sea squid having a debate about whether the city of New York existed, and whether they could ride in the elevator to the top of the Empire State Building. The two squid had heard about the rumoured existence of a place called New York from a friend of a friend of a fish they'd once eaten. Both squid decided the city had to be fictitious, because the whole idea of living on land was preposterous and inconceivable.

Dawkins is one of those squid. Trapped by his own intellectual limitations, he insists on dragging half of the rest of us with him.

No one created the Designer, because creation is a chronological construct applicable only to objects subject to the natural laws of the universe. The universe has a timeline, hence each person reading this can point roughly to a time they themselves were created. How can anything be "created" inside a timeless realm? It simply "is".

Our universe, in contrast, does not exist in timelessness. It ticks. The clock started when the bang started. When you get to the edge of the natural universe, you also reach the limits of natural science. What lies beyond? A void of some unimaginable description probably, to separate the Time-bound from the Timeless, and beyond that, that realm of eternity that we struggle to describe with words like "heaven" or "paradise". It is not a place you can travel to using spacecraft or any natural force. You cannot somehow bridge the void with a natural phenomenon like a wormhole. It is a barrier we transcend only in death.

Science has established the boundary of natural: the edge of the universe. That's where natural laws end. By science's own definition, anything beyond the boundaries of the natural is *super*natural.

Points on the board for Dawkins? Still zip.

Dawkins claims natural selection is not driven by random chance, which seems to me to be an odd statement to make. Nonetheless, let's examine his logic momentarily:

Dawkins Claim 4:[43]

"WHAT IS IT THAT MAKES natural selection succeed as a solution to the problem of improbability, where chance and design both fail at the starting gate? The answer is that natural selection is a cumulative process, which breaks the problem of improbability up into small pieces. Each of the small pieces is slightly improbable, but not prohibitively so. When large numbers of these slightly improbable events are stacked up in series, the end product of the accumulation is very very improbable indeed."

It is this thesis, he argues, that counters Intelligent Design's "irreducible complexity". Dawkins believes organisms can accumulate changes and lug them around for generations until they turn into something useful.[44]

"IN *CLIMBING MOUNT IMPROBABLE*, I expressed the point in a parable. One side of the mountain is a sheer cliff, impossible to climb, but on the other side is a gentle slope to the summit. On the summit sits a complex device such as an eye or a bacterial flagellar motor. The absurd notion that such complexity could spontaneously self-assemble is symbolized by leaping from the foot of the cliff to the top in one bound. Evolution, in contrast, goes around the back of the mountain and creeps up the gentle slope to the summit: easy!"

43   *The God Delusion*, p121
44   Ibid, p121-122

Or is it? The bacterial flagellum motor is an inbuilt machine – which even Dawkins admits is virtually identical to a Mazda RX7 engine in the way it works - that powers a long flagellum, like a propeller. The principle of accumulation, or what others call "co-option", would suggest that the bacteria picked up the useful bits during its leisurely journey up the gentle side of the mountain, then hey presto, got to the top and found it had a fully operational motor. Here's my response to Dawkins: ever tried carrying heavy baggage up a hill?

Because that's what he's asking you to believe in his "just so" story. He wants you to believe that the bacteria, and other organisms, can carry around useless junk components that may in fact weigh them down and make them uncompetitive, for hundreds or even millions of generations, until finally they can be turned into something useful. The problem with the flagellum example is that the entire thing is a motor. If all the components are not in place and working, the motor doesn't work, and your bacteria doesn't actually climb the hill at all. That's what Intelligent Design means by irreducible complexity. Something that is so critical that it needs to work as a complete package or the organism is unlikely to survive. Human bloodclotting is another good example – it has an incredibly complex molecular reaction behind it, but the human race would not have lasted long if we had to wait millions of years for bloodclotting to evolve (and it doesn't matter which presumed "ancestor" you push it back to – immediate wound repair is crucial to all living things, or the species dies out on the spot).

What Dawkins is simplistically really asking you to believe is that if you take your pet horse out into the paddock, hang 5kg weights off its ears, park it under a tree with juicy leaves at the top and wait long enough, you'll see your horse turn into a giraffe by growing its neck despite the extra baggage weighing it down.

Darwin's theory is supposed to favour organisms that travel light and efficiently, that can evade predators, but predate well, and which survive long enough to breed. That's natural selection in a nutshell. It doesn't generally favour useless baggage.

Dawkins also makes a fatal error in assembling his theory of accumulation. He assumes that an organism, with no ability to "wish" new evolutionary features into existence, nonetheless magically knows in advance that it needs eight key molecular structures to build its eventual flagellum motor (it actually has around 200 components, but I'll stick to eight for laughs); as if the organism is following instructions from a Meccano set or has a shopping list. It doesn't have this advantage, of course.

Imagine the analogy of a one-armed-bandit slot machine with eight barrels, rather than three, and the gambler needs eight bananas in a row to score the jackpot.

In the Dawkins version, the first barrel locks into place – a minor improbability – and he waits for the second barrel to lock, and so on until all eight barrels magically display bananas as a collective accumulation of minor improbabilities.

But in real life, it doesn't work that way. An organism that mutates, or picks up a junk gene or molecule, may or may not hold onto it long enough to lock it into place with the next piece of junk that's relevant, and so on. In our gambling analogy, it's like getting four barrels with bananas in a row when suddenly the first two barrels unlock and roll over to lemons, because the organism has just jettisoned two still-useless components.

Imagine if, halfway through your weekly lotto draw, you had five balls in order and the sixth drops down the chute, when suddenly the machine spits your first five balls back out again and selects something entirely different. You'd hate it, but that's how purposeless evolution is: it's random, it's nature, it's chance. It's Toyota's infamous swearing dog ad.

Dawkins continually uses the example of the evolution of the eye in his books, admitting in the quote about Mount Improbable above that the idea of a fully-functioning eye evolving at once is as absurd as leaping up a cliff in one bound. Again, he argues the eye went around the back way, slowly but surely climbing the mountain, picking up functionality along the way. Other academics, however, see the weakness in his arguments the same way I do.

"The existence of viable stages on the way does not explain how it was possible that many very unlikely genes came along in the right order to direct all the details," wrote Stanford University's noted scholar Robert Wesson, "while at the same time an immensely larger number of continually occurring deleterious mutations were continually being eliminated."[45]

Nor, as another scientist noted, does it explain how a highly complex thing like a light-sensitive cell evolved in the first place.

Richard Dawkins tries to gloss over fatal problems like this by suggesting "half a wing" is still better than no wing. But he's fudging, and preaching to his converted – people who'd believe the Moon was inhabited by a giant purple bunny if high priest Richard Dawkins told them so. We're not talking about the end result of the process, we're talking about the molecular and genetic coding and reactions – the software, if you like - that allow you to have any kind of wing, period. If all the chemicals and molecules are not in place, you are not even going to have $1/64^{th}$ of a wing. Not even a stump. A cocktail is not "half a cocktail" if its constituent fluids are sitting in their own separate containers, unmixed, on the bench, the ice is in the freezer still and nobody has even purchased the vodka yet!

Except maybe Dawkins, who probably needs a drink.

If you look carefully at Dawkins' work - and he's touted as Britain's best

45   *Beyond Natural Selection*, 1991, MIT Press

evolutionary thinker - you'll find he waffles, evades, ducks, weaves and does his best to blind with scientific rhetoric. In calculating the likelihood of life on other planets, for example, he simply bases his entire line of reasoning on a wild guess. After a passable - not stellar, just passable - rundown of the cosmological anthropic principle, which shows Earth appears to have been placed in just the right spot in the universe to sustain life, he then calculates there are a billion billion, or 1000,000,000,000,000,000 planets in the universe. Now watch his next statement closely:[46]

> "SUPPOSE [LIFE] WAS SO improbable as to occur on only one in a billion planets...we are talking about odds of one in a billion."

Now *where* did he pluck that "Suppose...one in a billion" figure from? Nowhere. It is merely a figure that makes his argument sound plausible. So far, science has been unable to find *any* evidence that life originated on Earth naturally. As you saw in the previous chapter, it now appears impossible, which is why Nobel laureates like the late Sir Francis Crick were invoking "invisible spacemen" as a possible agent in bringing life to Earth. Science knows of only one planet in the universe containing life, and you're on it. Science has only discovered a hundred and fifty or so other planets, and none of them are capable of sustaining life. So where does Dawkins get the chutzpah to invent this "one in a billion" chance of life originating, and then extrapolating it out like this:[47]

> "EVEN WITH SUCH ABSURDLY long odds, life will still have arisen on a billion planets - of which Earth, of course, is one."

Because Dawkins is clearly ignorant of the work mathematicians and astrobiologists have done on this exact issue, I'll remind you of the bits of the anthropic principle he left out of his book. There are not just one or two "Goldilocks" requirements for life to exist on Earth. At last count there were something like 128, which all had to line up like one-armed bandit barrels. Astrophysicist Dr Hugh Ross calculates the odds thus:[48]

> "WITH CONSIDERABLE SECURITY, therefore, we can draw the conclusion that even with a hundred billion trillion stars in the observable universe, the probability of finding...a single planet capable of supporting physical life is much less than one

46   *The God Delusion*, p138
47   Ibid
48   *The Creator and the Cosmos*, Hugh Ross, Ph.D. Navpress, 2001

in a trillion, trillion, trillion, trillion, trillion, trillion, trillion, trillion, trillion, trillion, trillion. The odds actually are higher that the reader will be killed by a sudden reversal in the second law of thermodynamics."

Just to put those odds in perspective against the Dawkins guess, the calculated (rather than merely "supposed") figure is one chance in 1,000,000, 000,000,000,000,000,000,000,000,000,000,000,000,000,000,000,000 ,000,000,000,000,000,000,000,000,000,000,000,000,000,000,000,00 0,000,000,000,000,000,000,000,000.

Just for the record, Dawkins' estimate of there being a billion billion planets in the universe looks like this: 1,000,000,000,000,000,000. Even if there were a trillion billion planets, it would only add three zeros to the end of the Dawkins list.

The deluded Dawkins, on the basis of his dodgy probability calculations, then exclaims, "I think it is definitely worth spending money on trying to duplicate the event in the lab and - by the same token - on SETI, because I think it is likely that there is intelligent life elsewhere."

As long as it's his money being spent, not the rest of ours. Dawkins, and other atheists, are forever appealing to "Science of the Gaps", an appeal to the public to keep holding the faith, because an evolutionary breakthrough is "just around the corner". How many corners and dead-ends have they taken us down using generous dollops of taxpayer funding, and very little to show for it? An alternative construction of the argument: "Just because we don't have an answer yet doesn't mean science won't find one in the next 200 years". Why don't they simply acknowledge the problem: "we don't have the answers...we can't find any aliens...we've repeatedly failed to create genuine life despite throwing the national debt of several African nations at it...we don't actually know how macroevolution works...we haven't really found any slam-dunk hard evidence of thousands of transitional species...we can't explain the Cambrian explosion of fully operational and apparently non-evolved animals...and we don't know why when we open the tiniest living organisms we found molecular rotary engines that far exceed anything humans have ever designed...please don't hurt us, we're atheists".

Dawkins' book, *The God Delusion*, is riddled throughout with erroneous assumptions and bogus factual constructions. It should be reclassified as "science fiction".

6

The Church/State Debate
Why Full Church/State Separation is a Myth

"Upon this rock I will build my church; and the gates of Hell shall
not prevail against it."
Jesus Christ, Matt 16:18

To understand the battle raging over Church/State separation, you first
have to understand how and why the term first arose, and what its
implications are. Make no mistake – the fight is really about preventing
an all-powerful secular state from establishing Secularism as a compulsory
national religion.

When the American Republic was born, its founding fathers drafted a
Constitution and Declaration of Independence designed to protect the
individual states of the colony from a central government over-reaching
its powers. Unlike the other British colonies - New Zealand, Australia and
Canada – whose provincial governments still looked ultimately to England
as the centre of power, the Americans had seen the abusive powers of big,
central government first hand. So upon gaining independence, they had no
intention of creating another big monster to rule over them. Instead, the vast
bulk of power in the new Republic was deliberately vested in the individual
state governments, not the federal administration in Washington D.C.

Despite the constitutional twists and turns in the US over the past century,
much real power remains vested in those states. In some matters New Zealand,
for example, has negotiated formal international treaties directly with the
Government of California, not the Bush administration.

The first amendment clause of the US Constitution is the one dealing with
the balance between church and federal government:

"CONGRESS SHALL MAKE no law respecting an establishment of
religion or prohibiting the free exercise thereof ..."

How difficult is that to understand? The federal congress had no powers to make law establishing an official religion, nor could it make a law restricting religion in any way. So how is it that we have moved in the West from the clause above, to the concept now springing up in debates and blogsites from Washington to Sydney to Auckland, that the default position of democracy requires a "separation of Church and State"?

The so-called "wall of separation" between Church and State is not ancient and revered. In fact, it is barely 200 years old. Thomas Jefferson, one of those who helped draft the US Constitution, coined that particular phrase in 1802 as part of a letter to members of the Danbury Baptist congregation in Connecticut who'd written to congratulate him on becoming President that year.

There was a reason for the Danbury Baptists writing that transcended mere congratulations, however. In their home state they were a religious minority – Congregationalism was the "established" religion in Connecticut, meaning it was the official religion of the state. All citizens, whether they were Congregationalists or not, paid a small tax towards the cost of running the church. With memories still fresh of the heavy hand first of Catholicism and latterly Anglicanism as the official religion back in England, the Baptists wanted to know whether the federal constitution could protect minority churches in the individual states.

For those who don't understand the US system, it can be summed up thus: each of the states is itself a sovereign government. Legislation of affairs within Connecticut, then, is the responsibility of the State Government of Connecticut and under the US Constitution the federal government has little power to intervene. The federal administration was there to look after the defense of the realm and to handle the foreign affairs of the collective states.

"Religion is at all times and places a Matter between God and Individuals -- that no man ought to suffer in Name, person or affects on account of his religious Opinions... That the legitimate Power of civil government extends no further than to punish the man who works ill to his neighbor...." wrote the Danbury Baptists to President Jefferson.

Analysing the correspondence, Liberty Counsel's Mathew Staver writes:[49]

> "THE DANBURY BAPTISTS believed that religion was an unalienable right and they hoped that Jefferson would raise the consciousness of the people to recognize religious freedom as unalienable. However, the Danbury Baptists acknowledged that the President of the United States was not a "national Legislator" and they also understood that the "national government cannot destroy the Laws of each State." In other words, they recognized Jefferson's limited

49   http://www.lc.org/Resources/separation.html

influence as the federal executive on the individual states."

For his part, Jefferson wrote an initial draft response to the Baptists:

> BELIEVING WITH YOU that religion is a matter which lies solely between man & his god, that he owes account to none other for his faith or his worship, that legitimate powers of government reach actions only and not opinions, I contemplate with sovereign reverence that act of the whole American people which declared that their legislature should make no law respecting an establishment of religion, or prohibiting the free exercise thereof; thus building a wall of separation between church and state. Congress thus inhibited from acts respecting religion, and the Executive authorized only to execute their acts, I have refrained from prescribing even occasional performances of devotion...

Jefferson had been trying to explain why – unlike the first two US Presidents – he would not be proclaiming "national fastings and thanksgivings, as my predecessors did". He was dissuaded, however, from including the final sentence about prescribing national days of prayer, on the advice of federal Attorney-General Levi Lincoln, who said it would "give great offense to the New England clergy". Lincoln pointed out that the five New England states had become used to "observing fasts and thanksgivings in performance of proclamations from the respective Executives…[and the] custom is venerable, being handed down from our ancestors."

Lincoln struck out the final sentence in the first draft of Jefferson's letter,[50] and a margin note on the document in Jefferson's handwriting confirms he omitted the line because "it might give uneasiness to some of our republican [in the sense of citizens of the new republic] friends in the eastern states where the proclamation of thanksgivings by their [state government] Executive is an ancient habit, and well respected."

This is a point that needs to be explained in the context of the US federal system. Jefferson recognized that the individual states had authority in regards to how closely they linked themselves to a particular church. The First Amendment clause was inserted at the request of those very states, who had official state churches and no wish for the federal government to suddenly start telling them how and what to worship. Six of the founding 13 states, in fact, refused to ratify the Constitution unless it specifically included the First Amendment. They figured that clause would protect them from bureaucrats in Washington D.C.

As a result, it continued to be within the constitutional powers of

---

50   http://www.loc.gov/loc/lcib/9806/danpre.html

Connecticut to proclaim state days of prayer. It was not within the powers of the US federal government, and Jefferson was trying to say that the first two federal presidents had overstepped the mark, albeit with good intentions, when they issued such proclamations out of Washington.

After excising that sentence, Jefferson's reply was sent, and the "wall of separation between church and state" line entered modern usage.

It is worth noting the flip side of Jefferson's letter to the Danbury Baptists: if the Left take the wall of separation as being a real wall applicable to all governments, then the other part of Jefferson's same letter should not be ignored by the Left either:

> "[T]HAT LEGITIMATE powers of government reach actions only *and not opinions.*"

As masters of indoctrination, brainwashing and propaganda designed to change the opinions of the public, in some cases enforced by law, a strong legal case can be made that secular governments are in fact establishing their own religion and enforcing it on their citizens, by attempting to alter their beliefs.

This fundamental belief that governments have no constitutional right to meddle in what people think is apparent throughout Thomas Jefferson's writings, such as this from 1779: "The opinions of men are not the object of civil government, nor under its jurisdiction."[51]

Those who argue that Jefferson was a total secularist who wanted Christianity out of government are mistaken. While he was probably a Deist (believing in a remote God who didn't interact with humans) leaning towards agnosticism, it didn't prevent Jefferson from promoting Christianity on occasion. Prohibited by the constitution from promoting a particular religion to the individual states, there was no such "wall of separation" preventing the US federal government from preaching to the native Indian tribes because they fell under federal, not state, authority; and President Jefferson actually approved treaties with those tribes that allowed "propagation of the Gospel among the Heathen."

Why would you do that if you genuinely believed there was no place for government and religion to work together?

Instead, Jefferson was at heart a republican who believed governments should at all times remain servants of the people, not their masters.

"It had become a universal and almost uncontroverted position in the several States that the purposes of society do *not* require a surrender of all our rights to our ordinary governors," wrote Jefferson in a letter to Noah Webster, "and which experience has nevertheless proved they [the government] will be constantly encroaching on if submitted to them."

---

51   http://etext.virginia.edu/jefferson/quotations/jeff0750.htm

One of the constant targets of government interference, continued Jefferson, was freedom of religion:[52]

> "THERE ARE ALSO CERTAIN fences which experience has proved peculiarly efficacious [effective] against wrong, and rarely obstructive of right, which yet the governing powers have ever shown a disposition to weaken and remove. Of the first kind, for instance, is freedom of religion."

Another constitutional founding father, James Madison, also explained the purpose behind the First Amendment:[53]

> "THE PEOPLE FEARED one sect might obtain a preeminence [with the State], or two combine together, and establish a religion to which they would compel others to conform."

Jefferson makes the same point in a letter to Benjamin Franklin, explaining that he wanted to ensure the federal government did not take sides in the ongoing turf wars between the Episcopalians [Anglicans] and the Congregationalists. It wasn't Christianity itself that he was against, but the "establishment of a particular form of Christianity" as the national denomination.

Jefferson underlined the importance of man's "natural rights", rights which did not emerge from thin air or a conference of ethicists, but were instead "that which the Books of the Law [Old Testament] and the Gospel do contain."

So firmly did Jefferson – the man who coined the phrase "a wall of separation between Church and State" – believe in the supremacy of Church that he feared for the safety of American citizens if any government ever tried to take the place of God as the source of rights:[54]

> "CAN THE LIBERTIES OF a nation be thought secure if we have lost the only firm basis, a conviction in the minds of the people that these liberties are the gift of God? That they are not to be violated but with His wrath?"

New Zealand Herald columnist John Roughan echoed this warning in early 2007, when analyzing a call made by atheist former teacher Ernie Barrington for New Zealand's political leaders to stop sitting on the fence and admit what most of them already truly believe, that 'there is no God'. Barrington said he was looking forward to the time when a public figure says, "I don't believe in

---

52   http://etext.virginia.edu/jefferson/quotations/jeff0950.htm
53   http://dentonfoundation.org/onenation_trueintent.htm
54   Excerpt from notes on State of Virginia, 1781

the existence of God. I am an atheist."

Roughan, however, finds that prospect frightening.[55]

> MR BARRINGTON WILL be looking forward for a long time. Atheism is scary, as is religious dogma in someone who wants to be entrusted with power. But atheism is more scary, I suspect, in its sheer conceit.
>
> Political leaders understand, I think, that though we are as secular as Mr Barrington says - most people don't admire or even like religion and turn away from its display - we find atheism just as repellent.
>
> Atheism, humanism, rationalism, call it what you like, is a conviction that offers nothing beyond the reach of human knowledge, when there plainly are such things. Not just the obvious: the boggling infinity of the universe and its density that suggests matter we still cannot see. Or the apparently random behaviour of subatomic particles that comprises everything we see. Quantum physics sounds like metaphysics to me.
>
> Our very brain remains largely unexplained. How do thoughts happen? Physically, what is going on in there? How do neurons compose a symphony? What makes us love?
>
> I like mysteries in existence. I'm not religious about it but there are things I sense spiritually, for want of a better word. I want to be awed by infinite possibilities.
>
> A politician who admitted he or she was an atheist would be denying these possibilities. Worse, they would be declaring a fearful conceit that no power is beyond them.
>
> I think the answer to Mr Barrington's question is right there.

The New Zealand Parliament opens its sessions each day with a prayer beginning, "Almighty God," and ending "in the name of our Lord Jesus Christ, Amen". It has been this way for 153 years, since the very first sitting of the Parliament back on 16 June, 1854.[56]

"Those who drafted the New Zealand constitution were emphatic that it should guarantee strict equality for all," records a government history site. "That was accepted as an axiom. Members met therefore in a watchful mood ready to scotch any infringement of the principle.

"The question arose almost at once. A South Island Scot, James Macandrew, moved that the first act of the House of Representatives should

55   http://www.nzherald.co.nz/section/466/story.cfm?c_id=466&objectid=10418878
56   http://nzhistory.net.nz/Gallery/parlt-hist/sounds/prayer.html

be a public acknowledgment of the divine being and a supplication for his favour on its future labours. Seconded by a Scot from Nelson, this was at once challenged by a Roman Catholic from Auckland, who protested against converting the House into a conventicle. An Aucklander said that he too felt deeply grateful to providence for having brought him to New Zealand but as members were of various denominations he would not care to see a clergyman of any particular sect brought in to say prayer."

As debate raged between Catholic and Protestant, between Anglican and Presbyterian, one Catholic member of Parliament, Frederick Weld, "begged that nothing should be done to impair the perfect religious equality of members. His amendment affirming the principle of religious equality was lost by 20 to 10 and Macandrew's motion was carried. Prayers were read by the Reverend F.J. Lloyd, Church of England, who it was said to be was the first clergyman to be found. The House then saw no harm in giving the assurance Weld had asked."

In other words, right from the get-go, New Zealand's parliament rejected any formal break with religion. Indeed, the issue being debated was not so much whether prayer itself was a bad thing, so much as whether any denomination was going to get the upper hand.

Was New Zealand a nation founded on Christianity? In many respects, yes. Like America before it, many of the first European residents in New Zealand were Christian missionaries whose goal was conversion of the native Maori population. It was only because of Christianity's influence that the Maori people decided to allow British settlements in New Zealand. At one of the biggest ever gatherings of Maori chiefs, held in 1860, New Zealand's Governor, Thomas Gore Browne, spelt out how far they'd come:[57]

> FINALLY, I MUST CONGRATULATE you on the vast progress in civilization which your people have made under the protection of the Queen. Cannibalism has been exchanged for Christianity; Slavery has been abolished; War has become more rare; prisoners taken in war are not slain; European habits are gradually replacing those of your ancestors of which all Christians are necessarily ashamed. The old have reason to be thankful that their sunset is brighter than their dawn, and the young may be grateful that their life did not begin until the darkness of the heathen night had been dispelled by that Light which is the glory of all civilised nations.
>
> Earnestly praying that God may grant his blessing on your deliberations and guide you on the right path, I leave you to the free discussion of the subjects I have indicated, and of any

57   *Investigate* August 04, www.thebriefingroom.com

others you may think likely to promote the welfare of your race. Signed Thomas Gore Browne, Governor.

That was the official State position. It was further underlined by colonial Secretary Donald Maclean:

> It is not intended to hide from you what you may hear from other sources, namely the fact that the English in former times often invaded other countries. Their ancestors, when they took possession of a place, frequently destroyed its inhabitants. But when Christianity obtained a greater influence amongst them, Wise men began to reflect on the sin of destroying human beings created by God to live on the earth. The Queen directed the Parliament to consider the subject, when it was proved that wrongs had been committed. The evidence adduced confirmed the fact that aboriginal subjects had been ill treated. This occasioned much shame to many good people in England, and it was determined in Parliament that such proceedings should not be permitted in future. About this period attention was directed to New Zealand as a field for European settlement, and it was decided by the Queen and her ministers, that in occupying the country, the New Zealanders should be treated with kindness, and a humane policy pursued towards them, with a view to their becoming a prosperous people, and united with the English.
>
> There is no desire to conceal from you the wrongs being committed elsewhere, but Christian principles have ruled the conduct of the British government in these Islands. The policy pursued has been one of uniform kindness, and in accordance with the precepts of Christianity.

It is impossible to read that statement of position from the New Zealand government in 1860 as anything less than an admission of the central role Christianity played in the establishment of the colony and its government. But to remove any doubts, here is the response from some of the chiefs, giving their reasons for signing the Treaty of Waitangi, the document that allowed the nation of New Zealand to exist and grow (the tribal name is in capitals, followed by the name of the chief):

> NGATITOA, Porirua; Te Ahukaramu: first, God; second, the Queen; third, the Governor. Let there be one Queen for us. Make known to us all the laws, that we may all dwell under one law.

TE TAWERA; Tamati Hapimana: I have but one law, the law of God. It was through the missionaries that I came to know what was right. It was like God's command to John," Go and prepare the path," for the missionaries came first and cleared the way, and afterwards the Lord came.

NGATIWHAKAUE, Rotorua; Te Amohau: let there be only one road. In former times it was evil; now Christianity has come among us, and we live in peace. In former times we were lost in the dark, but the gospel has come, and now we live.

NGAPUHI, Bay of Islands; Thomas Walker Nene: Who knows the mind of the Americans, or that of the French? Therefore, I say let us have the English to protect us. When the Governor came here, he brought with him the word of God by which we live; and it is through the teaching of that word that we are able to meet together this day, under one roof. Therefore, I say, I know no sovereign but the Queen, and I shall never know any other. I am walking by the side of the Pakeha.

PUKAKI, Manukau; Ihaka, chief of Pukaki: The former wars and jealousies disappeared, when the light of Christianity shone forth. My friends, the native chiefs, my desire is this: that religion, goodwill and peace should prevail throughout the land. If you approve, accept these things. Be strong to suppress the evil, that confusion may not grow. If confusion should spring up in any particular part, let the chiefs hasten there, to put it down, and let the European chiefs do the same, who are of the same mind. Let them both go together for the purpose of putting down evil and confusion. My own desire as this, that peace may prevail throughout the land for ever, and that our warfare should be directed towards the increase of schools, and the promotion of religion.

Did you note the first comment from Ngatitoa's Te Ahukaramu? "First, God; second, the Queen; third, the Governor."

The chief knew, better than most politicians alive today, the correct pecking order. Under God, he knew, all men and women were equal and called to obey laws laid out for the good of all humankind. God's laws, being unchangeable, were a yardstick that all – even Maori – could agree on, whereas the laws of men tended to favour one group or the other. Once you elevate State above

God, the rulers feel beholden to nothing, and democracy suffers. Maori would not have trusted the British, had both cultures not been Christian. New Zealand as we know it would not exist.

These then, were the predominant views of both partners, Maori and British, to the Treaty of Waitangi. This was the New Zealand they envisaged. So how is it then that from this auspicious beginning, bureaucrats and liberal politicians a hundred and fifty years later are rewriting history and writing Christianity out of both the history books and the pomp and ceremony of State?

The first concerted push began in 2003, when far Left liberal MP Matt Robson tired to get cross-party support to either ditch the prayer at the start of Parliament, or at least water it down to something Sikhs, Hindus, Muslims, atheists and cat-fanciers could live with.

"I had previously taken soundings with religious leaders of the major faiths," wrote Robson in an *NZ Herald* opinion piece.[58] Those I spoke to agreed that Parliament should adopt an inclusive statement. They had long moved to such a position in their inter-faith meetings. Rationalists, too, wanted to be included in Parliament's thoughts when it opened each day."

It's at this point that Robson displays a major misunderstanding about the reason for the prayer. The prayer, correctly, acknowledges that the Parliament works under a higher authority and "humbly" asks for God's "guidance" in the affairs of state. But the way Robson writes, "Rationalists, too, wanted to be included in Parliament's thoughts…", you'd think the prayer was some kind of spell being uttered by a beneficent Parliament usurping the role of "god", spreading its blessings on its followers. The prayer *isn't* about mentioning the various disparate groups in New Zealand to let them know their kindly masters are thinking of them!

I believe Robson when he says he took advice from "religious leaders of the major faiths…[who] had long moved to such a position in their interfaith meetings." I believe him, because I know who these "religious leaders" are – the theological flotsam, jetsam and detritus who no longer believe in the Christian God, but keep taking the wages every week.

The Dean of Auckland's Holy Trinity Cathedral, the Right Reverend Richard Randerson, may have been one of Robson's misguided advisors. Randerson hit the headlines in January this year by unexpectedly "outing" himself, after enthusiastically siding with an atheist about the apparent non-existence of God:[59]

> "THREE CHEERS FOR Ernie Barrington in his call for respect for atheists. I would go further and seek to remove the word from

58   http://www.nzherald.co.nz/search/story.cfm?storyid=27892200-39E0-11DA-8E1B-A5B353C55561
59   http://www.nzherald.co.nz/search/story.cfm?storyid=00064373-7387-15A0-800E83027AF1010E

our vocabulary. Far better that people be defined in terms of what they do believe rather than what they do not. Humanist is a better word for those who believe in human wellbeing but do not source their commitment from a religious base.

"Atheism is understood to mean a denial of belief in a particular image of God as supernatural creator. Richard Dawkins' thesis that there is no proof of such a being as a scientifically verifiable entity is quite correct.

"In terms of the existence of such a being, an atheist is construed as a non-believer, an agnostic as one who feels it cannot be proved one way or the other. By that measure, I regard myself as an agnostic.

"The issue of the parliamentary prayer is also under review, as is the nature of the prayers used at Anzac Day services.

"As a church leader I feel uncomfortable leading prayers in public that have an exclusively Christian ending, thus excluding people of other faiths."

At the end of his agnostic epistle, having now also admitted that, as assistant Anglican Bishop of Auckland he felt "uncomfortable" reciting Christian prayers, Randerson proudly declared his credentials, including that he "is a member of the drafting group of the proposed National Diversity Statement." More on that "Diversity Statement" shortly. You may well wonder which religion he was representing on that group. I'm not sure he knows himself.

You may have noticed his agreement with Richard Dawkins' suggestion that God can be scientifically disproved. If an Assistant Bishop can be taken in by Dawkins' ridiculous caterwauling, God help the rest of us.

Little wonder that the New Zealand Government is shouting "church/state separation" from the rooftops when the leadership of New Zealand's largest church is pushing a doctrine of Christ/church separation!

And that's the kind of advice liberal MP Matt Robson was getting – from reverends who are lucky if they get three parishioners in their "mainstream" liberal churches of a Sunday. I'll bet Robson didn't bother to ask those pesky evangelical types whose Sunday services draw thousands of people to their auditoriums.

"The fact that Parliament was opened each sitting day with an Anglican prayer introduced in 1854 surprised me," continued Robson. "It struck me that MPs were declaring that not all religions and beliefs were equal."

Well, hello? Here's a piece of news: no one except a secular humanist would say something as daft as that. Every religion on the planet believes *it* alone has the essential truth. No religious people anywhere genuinely believe that "religions and beliefs are equal". Only halfwits who don't know a thing about religion, and can't be bothered finding out, make claims like that. Those of us with faith can tolerate and accept that other religions believe different things, but we don't for a moment believe them to be equally valid.

"I also noticed that the great majority of MPs did not swear their allegiance on the Bible but affirmed," said Robson.

Yeah, well, that explains a lot.

"In my parliamentary office in South Auckland various people raised, ever so gently and politely, the fact that they felt excluded by the opening prayer, which talked of "true religion ... through Jesus Christ our Lord Amen". "One day I was visited by leaders of the Sikh faith. Sikhs have been here since the early 19th century. A number of my visitors, unlike me, had been born in New Zealand. I had the radio on as Parliament began. The words "true religion ... through Jesus Christ our Lord Amen" seemed to boom out. "We discussed how my visitors, knowledgeable and respectful of the Christian religion, felt as though the words of the prayer were not for them. I decided that I would seek cross-party support at the next all-party meeting to adopt an all-inclusive opening of Parliament for New Zealanders of all beliefs. "The response was vitriolic. "No way," said the National Party representative. "We will not agree to a change. If 'they' come here, they can accept our ways." "Other parties, apart from the Greens, thought the same. I reminded the National MP that many of the "they" were born here, and that there was no state religion.

"Moreover, the Bill of Rights Act upheld freedom of belief and I thought Parliament should do the same. I submitted a proposal to review the prayer to Parliament's standing orders committee. This was heard last week. But all the parties, except the Greens, held to the same position."

That was in 2003, but Robson has kept on pushing, and the future of Parliament's prayer is now "under review", whilst the secular state flexes its muscles. In early 2007, a Draft National Statement on Religious Diversity was released for public discussion in New Zealand, calling for "tolerance" of different religions, and suggesting that "New Zealand has no state religion".

Representatives of migrant religious communities – Buddhists, Hindus and Muslims – immediately protested that "tolerance" wasn't good enough, they demanded "respect".

Christian groups, on the other hand, were furious that the left wing government and a small group of liberal Christians had drafted a statement saying New Zealand has "no state religion".

It may not have a "state religion" codified by law, and in comparison with some European nations this is a good thing. But New Zealand, with a national anthem entitled "God Defend New Zealand", inherited its constitutional arrangements lock stock and barrel from England, and given that its politicians, judiciary, and other public servants are required to swear oaths of allegiance to Queen Elizabeth II, who is also the titular head of the Anglican Church, I suspect the Labour government is simply trying its luck to once again alter the Constitution by Prime Ministerial decree, rather than due process. And, given the track record of the Left, that's no great surprise. Christianity is the majority religion, the one that our society was built on. To simply shove it aside as one among many is not only insulting to Maori and Pakeha, but it is also dangerous in the expectations that it delivers followers of faiths like Islam, for example.

The clear message is, "we're abdicating the throne, potentially it could now be yours". And Islam, as a political religion, will fill the vacuum left by vacuous liberal Christians and secularists, if given a chance.

The Draft National Statement also, controversially, requires that children be taught about the diversity of religious belief, "impartially". Let's examine that little minefield for a moment. Given that, in a predominantly Christian country, the vast majority of teachers don't have a clue about the core principles of the Christian faith, exactly what are these kids going to be taught, and who is going to teach them?

When national public schools were established in 1877, they were forbidden under an Act of Parliament from including any religious instruction or observances during school hours or services. The reason for this was not because New Zealand's founding fathers were atheists – we have already seen they were not – but because of the potential for sectarian disagreement between Protestants and Catholics. Thus it was deemed more appropriate to leave religion out of schools entirely. After all, nearly every family attended church services on a Sunday anyway, so religious instruction was correctly left to parents and their churches to handle.

Schools were, however, permitted to allow religious teaching or observances outside school hours, which in practice meant that a school might voluntarily open 15 minutes earlier to allow for a prayer and perhaps a flag raising ceremony each day. This meant local communities continued to have an informal say with their local schools.

This practice continues right to the present day. In nearly every New Zealand primary school, despite the official banning of religion from the classroom, children gather once a week for a class known as "Bible in Schools", where biblical stories with morals, values, and the groundings of faith are taught. Officially, the school is closed for that hour session each week, and parents are given the option of withdrawing their children from the Bible in Schools class if they wish. Few do. Most, even parents from other religious faiths, prefer to see some kind of morality and values taught in school rather than none, and they prefer Christian values to secular ones.

But naturally this hasn't gone down well with liberal educationalists and the Government. In August last year draft guidelines were released threatening to end even the Christian prayers said in Maori, the karakia, which are traditional in school cultural activities.

The reaction from Maori leaders, proud of their Christian heritage despite the godless wonders infesting the Beehive, was thunderous.[60]

NEW GUIDELINES TO CLARIFY the role of religion in schools, are an example of Political Correctness gone berserk says Maori Party Co-leader, Dr Pita Sharples.

"If this is such an issue at this time, then the Maori Party suggests that the community must be involved in the discussion…This is a fascinating discussion, which must involve us all, in our own settings, and should not be dealt to by way of Ministry guidelines.

"The Maori Party does not see any value in schools being obliged to respect artificial divisions between what is considered 'secular' and 'non-secular'. Our emphasis has always been on schools doing what they can to develop a nourishing environment which reflects a unified and holistic approach to life.

"We believe there is a spiritual existence alongside the physical" stated Dr Sharples. "We also respect the right for communities to follow religious practices and uphold cultural values without discrimination or bias. While we appreciate that a religious world view is clearly available through the integration of a religious school into the state system, this does not resolve issues for parents who want their children to have access to religious or spiritual values in general stream education" said Dr Sharples.

"Avoiding any religious allusion in schooling seems to me, to limit the very concept of knowledge and learning that we expect in education" said Dr Sharples. "Indeed, having some understanding of the ethics and morals that are wrapped up in our social mores, is a key factor in our nationhood.

"How could one possibly describe the process of colonisation in the history of Aotearoa, without discussing the impact of missionaries? How can one discuss the signing of the Treaty of Waitangi, our foundation as a nation, without reference to the role of Anglican, Wesleyan and Roman Catholics clergy within the negotiations, and Anglican and Wesleyan missionaries?

"If we carry out this blatant censorship and revisionist history, our children will miss out on the significance of tradition and the lasting impacts it has had our way of life as a country" said Dr Sharples.

"If we carry this brainwashing programme to its logical extreme, we will see the dismantling of many institutions - the prayer at the start of Parliament; the playing of our national anthem at Olympic sporting events; the observance of national days such as Easter or Christmas; the practise of 'swearing on the Bible' undertaken in sessions of the Court.

"Does one get rid of Christmas? Does one get rid of Easter? Does one instruct the Speaker of the House to desist from starting each session with a Parliamentary Prayer? Where does it all stop?

"Every culture has a spiritual reference which is exhibited in a diversity of beliefs, behaviours and values" said Dr Sharples. "Threatening schools that they will set the spiritual police on them, to punish 'law-breakers' for practising 'religious karakia' is just another example of the PC brigade out of control".

Amen to that, Brother! Sharples may have thought he was joking when he asked if they were going to get rid of Christmas and Easter. The reality is, some people are trying.

Each year the newspapers feature stories about a school or daycare centre somewhere that has banned Christ, and Christian carols, purportedly so as "not to offend Muslims". To their credit, most Muslims in New Zealand simply scratch their heads sadly at the ignorance of secular educators: Jesus, you see, is a revered prophet in Islam. In truth, the educators use Muslims and Hindus to hide behind; they're really taking Christ out of Christmas because they themselves are atheist or New Age, and *they* don't like it.

This past Christmas, an increasing number of large retailers instructed staff to say "Happy Holidays" instead of "Merry Christmas", and nativity scenes were conspicuously absent from the large malls.

In America, the war against Christianity is even hotter. A murderer who had clubbed a 71 year old woman to death with an axe handle in order to rob her, had his sentence quashed because the prosecutor briefly (for less than five seconds according to author David Kupelian) referred to a Bible verse in the courtroom.

The modern US Supreme Court, largely staffed by secularists in recent times, interprets the First Amendment to mean that Christianity cannot, in any way, be associated with anything in the government or public sector. Yet as dissenting Supreme Court judge William Rehnquist reminded his colleagues in a 1985 case,[61] the idea that this was the aim of the men who drafted the US

61   http://www.belcherfoundation.org/wallace_v_jaffree_dissent.htm

Constitution 200 years ago is laughable. He quoted Supreme Court justice Joseph Story, a man appointed to the bench by President Madison and who served on the Court for 34 years between 1811 and 1845.

During that time, Story was also a noted professor at the Harvard Law School, and wrote what Rehnquist describes as "by far the most comprehensive treatise on the United States Constitution that had then appeared."

Volume 2 of Story's *Commentaries on the Constitution of the United States* 630-632 (5th ed. 1891) discussed the meaning of the Establishment Clause of the First Amendment this way:

> "PROBABLY AT THE TIME of the adoption of the Constitution, and of the amendment to it now under consideration [First Amendment], the general if not the universal sentiment in America was, that Christianity ought to receive encouragement from the State so far as was not incompatible with the private rights of conscience and the freedom of religious worship. An attempt to level all religions, and to make it a matter of state policy to hold all in utter indifference, would have created universal disapprobation, if not universal indignation.
>
> . . . .
>
> "The real object of the [First] [A]mendment was not to countenance, much less to advance, Mahometanism, or Judaism, or infidelity, by prostrating Christianity; but to exclude all rivalry among Christian sects, and to prevent any national ecclesiastical establishment which should give to a hierarchy the exclusive patronage of the national government. It thus cut off the means of religious persecution (the vice and pest of former ages), and of the subversion of the rights of conscience in matters of religion, which had been trampled upon almost from the days of the Apostles to the present age. . . ." (Footnotes omitted.)

Got the message yet? The separation of Church and State has nothing to do with making all religions equal, nor with banning prayer from public places. Rehnquist cites another senior jurist, Thomas Cooley, whose "eminence as a legal authority rivaled that of Story." Cooley stated in his treatise entitled Constitutional Limitations that aid to a particular religious sect was prohibited by the United States Constitution, but he went on to say:

> "BUT WHILE THUS CAREFUL to establish, protect, and defend religious freedom and equality, *the American constitutions contain no provisions which prohibit the authorities from such*

solemn recognition of a superintending Providence in public transactions and exercises as the general religious sentiment of mankind inspires, [my emphasis] and as seems meet and proper in finite and dependent beings. Whatever may be the shades of religious belief, all must acknowledge the fitness of recognizing in important human affairs the superintending care and control of the Great Governor of the Universe, and of acknowledging with thanksgiving his boundless favors, or bowing in contrition when visited with the penalties of his broken laws.

No principle of constitutional law is violated when thanksgiving or fast days are appointed; when chaplains are designated for the army and navy; when legislative sessions are opened with prayer or the reading of the Scriptures, or when religious teaching is encouraged by a general exemption of the houses of religious worship from taxation for the support of State government. Undoubtedly the spirit of the Constitution will require, in all these cases, that care be taken to avoid discrimination in favor of or against any one religious denomination or sect; but the power to do any of these things does not become unconstitutional simply because of its susceptibility to abuse. . . ." *Id.,* at * 470--* 471.

Cooley added that:

"[T]HIS PUBLIC RECOGNITION of religious worship, however, is not based entirely, perhaps not even mainly, upon a sense of what is due to the Supreme Being himself as the author of all good and of all law; but the same reasons of state policy which induce the government to aid institutions of charity and seminaries of instruction will incline it also to foster religious worship and religious institutions, as conservators of the public morals and valuable, if not indispensable, assistants to the preservation of the public order." *Id.,* at *470.

On the basis of this, and the transcripts of debates among the founders about their intentions for the First Amendment clause, Justice Rehnquist issued a dissenting ruling in 1985 that:

THE GREATEST INJURY of the "wall" notion is its mischievous diversion of judges from the actual intentions of the drafters of the Bill of Rights. The "crucible of litigation," *ante,* at 2487, is well adapted to adjudicating factual disputes on the basis of testimony presented in court, but no amount of repetition of historical errors in judicial opinions can make the errors true. The "wall of separation between church and State" is a metaphor based on bad history, a metaphor which has proved useless as a guide to judging. It should be frankly and explicitly abandoned.

So how do we view this battle over the separation of church and state, and why should we care? After all, as supporters of separation correctly argue, "You cannot legislate for faith". In other words, you cannot pass laws to force people to worship or believe. They're dead right. But the argument is actually far deeper and more complex than that. The real question is "what sort of society do we want to become?" Christianity has been the engine room of modern democracy and civilization. Societies modeled on Christian values became the most successful in the world.

Christianity has safeguarded the rights of secularists and other religions because of its own firm internal belief that you cannot make faith compulsory – people must be left to choose for themselves. Indeed, secularism and pluralism have flourished in Christian countries, in sharp contrast to societies dominated by other religions.

The point I am making is this: if it ain't broke, don't try to fix it.

What is the inherent, urgent need for the West to shake off Christian values and observances? Is this going to lead to genuine increased "freedoms", or is it going to lead to a new Dark Ages? Because if you examine the evidence in this book, secularism is far less tolerant of dissent than Christianity. Secularism wants the right to brainwash kids far more than Christianity does. Christianity tolerates secularism, but secularism does not tolerate Christianity. So if secularists get their way, how soon before we all live under a new form of totalitarianism where no dissent is tolerated?

Secularists cannot handle any scientific challenge to evolutionary theory. They refuse to allow debate. Secularists cannot handle any public display of religion. As this book discloses, secularists want to go further and ban religion at home so that children are not exposed to it.

Ask yourself the question, which religion poses the bigger danger to society as we know it: Christianity or secular humanism?

So regardless of whether you are Christian or just of no religious belief at all, your best interests are actually served by supporting continued reflection of Christian values, because rabid secular humanists can just as easily mop up smaller pockets of opposition once they get rid of Christianity. And who will look after your interests then?

As I mentioned earlier, the Government is looking to require schools to teach "impartially" about a number of religions. I asked if you could trust them. Now I'll give you the evidence that says you cannot, because our education system, and in fact much of the social bureaucracy, has been 'captured' by people who are not neutral, but who actually hate Christianity and everything it stands for. These people are using their positions to push their own ideologies – beliefs that flow automatically out of the Big-3 themes: Eugenics, Darwinism and Marxism.

This next section of the book is where the rubber hits the road, where I offer some serious examples of what happens when these ideologies are put into practice in our modern world. What you are about to read will chill you.

7

Buying The 'Big Lie'
Yes, Virginia, There is an Agenda

"If you tell a lie big enough and keep repeating it, people will eventually come to believe it. The lie can be maintained only for such time as the State can shield the people from the political, economic and/or military consequences of the lie. It thus becomes vitally important for the State to use all of its powers to repress dissent, for the truth is the mortal enemy of the lie, and thus by extension, the truth is the greatest enemy of the State."
Josef Goebbels, Nazi Propaganda Minister, WW2

For those of us old enough to remember the early 1980s, there were two standout events that did for casual sex what the movie *Jaws* had for swimming a few summers earlier. The first of these socioquakes was a cover story in *Time* magazine about the horror new sexually-transmitted disease, Herpes. It was August 1982, and for many people around the world it was the first they had heard of the incurable infection with its nasty sores and reproductive implications. Everybody, and I do mean everybody, was talking about it: the first major knock to the confidence of the "free love" generation.

The second socioquake struck only months later, with confirmation of a deadly new disease scientists were calling AIDS – also sexually transmitted, spreading rapidly and with no cure.

For people whose previous notions of sexually transmitted diseases – once quaintly titled Venereal Disease, or VD, after the Roman goddess of 'love' – were confined to syphilis, gonorrhea or lice, these new nasties took the risks of sexual freedom to a whole new level. Suddenly, every potential boyfriend or girlfriend was also capable of signing your death warrant in an act of lust.

And for a few months there, people thought long and hard about who they slept with.

Then along came the "Safe Sex" campaign. Instead of urging caution, monogamy and a host of other sensible measures, liberals figured they could bluff their way through the sexual disease scares by pitching the use of condoms: after all, if they protected against pregnancy chances are they might provide a protective barrier to stop the exchange of bodily fluids, which science had pretty much figured out was the primary method of transmitting the HIV virus from one victim to another.

Early studies were promising, in theory condoms could work to slow down the spread of AIDS, but there were two issues clouding the horizon. One was the growing public realization - epitomized in a joke that did the rounds about the new AIDS victim who was having trouble convincing his parents he was Haitian - that AIDS was a disease targeting homosexual men and, yes, residents of the Caribbean island of Haiti. The second issue was figuring out how to prevent a public backlash against homosexuals.

The Haitian connection proved in the end to be just a sub-branch of the gay/dirty needle arm of the disease. But as the AIDS roll call began increasingly to resemble the membership list of a San Francisco bathhouse (and in fact was in many cases), both medical researchers and the gay community panicked. The medics were worried that lucrative and necessary government funding for research would dry up if the public became bored with "the gay plague", and the gay community feared that everything it had worked to achieve in terms of acceptability would disappear out the window if there was a moral backlash against "dirty homosexuals".

The trail of the disease wasn't helping their cause in any way, especially with revelations that many gay men had not just multiple sexual partners but *hundreds* of sexual partners. A 1978 study[62] by gay doctors Alan Bell and Martin Weinburg found that nearly half the male homosexuals surveyed had more than 500 sexual partners during their lifetimes.

There are stories on every street corner about the kind of gay promiscuity that, frankly, you'd be lucky to see in a warren of rabbits. One police officer assigned to vice squad as a young cop in the seventies recalls a sting operation in a public toilet, where his task was to sit in a cubicle and wait – his superiors hadn't told him all the nitty gritty details but said he'd figure it out as it developed. Inside the cubicle was a hole in one of the partitions, just below waist height. Sure enough, after a few minutes someone entered the cubicle next to him and the next thing the newbie officer saw was something being poked through the hole a few inches from where he sat. Like a coiled spring, the officer acted on reflex, grabbing his beat truncheon and bringing it crashing down on the intruding appendage. Its owner, now shrieking in pain, had simply been cruising for anonymous gay sex in a public restroom,

62   Bell, Alan, and Weinberg, Martin (1978). *Homosexualities: A Study of Diversity Among Men and Women*. New York: Simon & Shuster.

George Michael-style. Random, irresponsible, meaningless sex. The last thing he expected that night was the possibility that someone in an adjacent cubicle would be offended at his obscene act in a public place.

As former lesbian activist Tammy Bruce tells it in *The Death of Right and Wrong*, "The fact that promiscuous sex has been the essence of gay male liberation is an important point. This promiscuity is truly a gay *male* phenomenon and not characteristic of homosexuality per se – or you would find lesbians in bathhouses looking for easy sex with scores of partners. That's not happening."

Somehow, there had to be some kind of PR spin to swing attention away from the gay community and make AIDS an "inclusive", not "exclusive" disease.

In his bestselling book, *The Marketing of Evil*, journalist David Kupelian from online news portal *WorldNetDaily* recounts how gay activists and pop-psychology whizzkids Marshall Kirk and Hunter Madsen hatched a plan in the mid-80s for a PR fightback on behalf of the gay community that culminated in a radical new book, *After the Ball: How America Will Conquer Its Fear and Hatred of Gays in the '90s*.

Gay leaders from groups across America had gathered for a 1988 'think tank' on how to spin American society on its axis in a make or break, do or die brainwashing/re-programming campaign. As a result of the think tank, Kirk and Madsen's book emerged.

"As cynical as it may seem," wrote Kirk and Madsen, "AIDS gives us a chance, however brief, to establish ourselves as a victimized minority legitimately deserving of America's special protection and care."

But Kirk and Madsen had no intentions of playing fair: this was a fight to the death, about death, and they urged their colleagues in the gay community to use every dirty trick in the book.

"The campaign we outline in this book, though complex, depends centrally upon a programme of unabashed propaganda, firmly grounded in long-established principles of psychology and advertising."

Propaganda can sometimes be true, but Kirk and Madsen weren't keen on the facts getting in the way of a good story.

"Our effect is achieved without reference to facts, logic or proof," they wrote, "the person's beliefs can be altered whether he is conscious of the attack or not."

Make a note of that: the masters of gay persuasion boasting that they can re-programme you without you even realizing they've done it. One method was to "mainstream" gays into major media using gay or gay-friendly journalists and producers:

"The visual media, film and television, are plainly the most powerful image makers in Western civilization. The average American watches over seven hours of TV daily. Those hours open up a gateway into the private world of straights, through which a Trojan Horse might be passed," wrote Kirk and Madsen in *After the Ball*. "As far as desensitization is concerned, the medium is the message—of normalcy. So far, gay Hollywood has provided our best covert weapon in the battle to desensitize the mainstream."

Ever wondered why there are so many TV shows every day and movies with strong gay themes, when the biggest population studies ever

❝ The Nazi Position:

"Many a one laughed at the propaganda of the [Nazi Party] in the past from a position of superiority. It is true that we had only one thing to say, and we yelled and screamed and propagandized it again and again with a stubbornness that drove the "wise" to desperation. We proclaimed it with such simplicity that they thought it absurd and almost childish. They did not understand that repetition is the precursor to success and simplicity is the key to the emotional and mental world of the masses." –
Schulze Wechsungen, German Propaganda Ministry, 1934 ❞

undertaken have shown homosexuality running at less than one percent in the population?[63]

When you turn on the TV this week, keep a mental note of every gay character you see on the screen, then measure it against the one percent yardstick. Then ask yourself if homosexuality is over-represented in primetime, and then ask yourself, "Why?"

The authors of *After the Ball* had a grand plan, summed up largely in a three-keyword pitch: "Desensitize, jam and convert".

The "Desensitization" phase involved shoving homosexuality in the faces of the public, a "continuous flood of gay-related advertising, presented in the least offensive fashion possible. If straights can't shut off the shower, they may at least eventually get used to being wet."

By "advertising", however, they weren't talking about a 30 second spot in *The Simpsons*, they were talking about soaking Western culture in homosexuality

---

63   *Sexual Behaviour in Britain*, Wellings, Field, Johnson & Wadsworth, published in 1994 and based on interviews with 20,000 men and women. It found that core homosexual orientation was limited to 0.6% in men, and a staggeringly low 0.1% in women. *Ninety percent* of people claiming to be gay, the study found, are actually just uninhibited bisexuals when push comes to shove

and turning up the heat so slowly the public never even realized they were being cooked:

> "THE MAIN THING is to talk about gayness until the issue becomes thoroughly tiresome. You can forget about trying right up front to persuade folks that homosexuality is a 'good' thing. But if you can get straights to think homosexuality is just *another* thing – meriting no more than a shrug of the shoulders – then your battle for legal and social rights is virtually won."

Again, think of *Brokeback Mountain*, *Will and Grace*, New Zealand's *Shortland Street*, *Queer Nation*, any number of shows, and think of how it is second nature to you these days compared with, say, 15 years ago. What's changed? Nothing except the marketing spin.

The public, they pitched, needs to:

> "…VIEW HOMOSEXUALITY with indifference instead of keen emotion. Ideally we would have the 'straight' register differences in sexual preference the way they register different tastes for icecream…Talk about gays and gayness as loudly and as often as possible…almost any behaviour begins to look normal if you are exposed to enough of it at close quarters and among your acquaintances."

This aspect, incidentally, closely follows the Nazi propaganda technique of "The Big Lie".

"Each sign will tap patriotic sentiment; each message will drill a seemingly agreeable position into mainstream heads," Kirk and Madsen wrote.

The "Jamming" phase follows desensitization. Recognising that conservatives would not fall for the spin (well, not all of them), Kirk and Madsen urged gay activists around the world to target their opponents with personal abuse and carefully chosen phrases to make conservatives look like bigots:

> "JAM HOMOHATRED by linking it to Nazi horror…Most contemporary hate groups on the Religious Right will bitterly resent the implied connection between homohatred and Nazi fascism. But since they can't defend the latter, they'll end up having to distance themselves by insisting that they would never go to such extremes. Such declarations of civility toward gays, of course, set our worst detractors on the slippery slope toward recognition of fundamental gay rights.

"The public should be shown images of ranting homophobes whose secondary traits and beliefs disgust middle America…the Ku Klux Klan demanding that gays be burned alive or castrated; bigoted southern ministers drooling with hysterical hatred to a degree that looks both comical and deranged; menacing punks, thugs and convicts…"

Getting the feeling you've been played for suckers? It is a total campaign of behaviour modification. If police road safety campaigns were this effective, the roads would be free of drink-drivers.

"THESE IMAGES (of anyone opposed to homosexual behavior) should be combined with those of their gay victims by a method propagandists call the 'bracket technique'. For example, for a few seconds an unctuous beady-eyed Southern preacher is seen pounding the pulpit in rage about 'those sick, abominable creatures'. While his tirade continues over the soundtrack, the picture switches to pathetic photos of gays who look decent, harmless, and likable; and then we cut back to the poisonous face of the preacher, and so forth. The contrast speaks for itself. The effect is devastating."

Ads like this did indeed run in the United States. But pause for a moment. What effect would such ads have had if, instead of "decent, harmless and likable" gays, the shots used had been taken in the San Francisco bathhouse detailed here, and later on page 134 of this book in their full context (*be warned, the following paragraph is explicit*):

"[M]Y EYES TOOK A MOMENT to adjust. I was in a large space filled with small wooden cubicles, like cupboards, in which men were apparently expected to kneel and give head. Glory holes were drilled into these closets, and other men came by, hoisted out their dicks, and inserted them into the holes in the cubicles. In another part of the room, men stepped up on a raised platform and other men stood below, eager to suck them off in a standing position…"

The contrast between a pastor talking about "sick" sexual behaviour, interposed with shots of the gay lifestyle in all its trappings, would engender a very different response from the version of the ad that actually went to air. And that, dear jury, shows you how TV can be and is used to manipulate the way you think.

The "hysterical" backwoods preachers analogy was a particular favourite, because the gay persuaders realized their biggest opposition would come from churches. Their solution was to drive a wedge into Christianity's already growing rift between liberal and conservative wings.

> "WHILE PUBLIC OPINION is one primary source of mainstream values, religious authority is the other. When conservative churches condemn gays, there are only two things we can do to confound the homophobia of true believers.
>
> "First, we can use talk to muddy the moral waters. This means publicizing support for gays by more moderate churches, raising theological objections of our own about conservative interpretations of biblical teachings.
>
> "Second, we can undermine the moral authority of homophobic churches by portraying them as antiquated backwaters, badly out of step with the times and with the latest findings of psychology. Against the mighty pull of Old Time Religion one must set the mightier draw of Science and Public Opinion.
>
> "Such an unholy alliance has worked well against churches before, on such topics as divorce and abortion. With enough talk about the prevalence and acceptability of homosexuality, that alliance can work again here."

It wasn't the only unholy alliance they struck. As part of "Jamming", their book recommended working with gay journalists in the news media to get slanted, gay-positive stories into the news as often as possible. Within a year of their book being published, the National Lesbian and Gay Journalists Association of America was formed. Kirk and Madsen urged gays to "not demand direct support for homosexual practices, but…instead take anti-discrimination as its theme."

In other words, turn homosexuality into a "human rights" issue rather than a debate about homosexuality itself. The new buzzwords, said Kirk and Madsen, should be "homophobe…tolerance…diversity" and, they added, drop references to "homosexual" in favour of the word "gay", which was seen as more "cheerful". This was back in 1988. How many times a year do we now hear all these buzzwords?

> "PORTRAY GAYS AS VICTIMS, not as aggressive challengers…make gays look good…make the victimizers look bad."

The gay persuaders' logic was that gays "be cast as victims in need of protection so that straights will be inclined by reflex to assume the role of protector. If gays are presented, instead, as a strong and prideful tribe promoting a rigidly non-conformist and deviant lifestyle, they are more likely to be seen as a public menace that justifies resistance and oppression."

News stories, they suggested, should publicize "brutalized gays, dramatizations of job and housing insecurity" – cue the 1993 movie *Philadelphia* – or other issues like "loss of child custody", all of this to portray gays as victims of heterosexual society.

> "IN ORDER TO MAKE A GAY VICTIM sympathetic to straights, you have to portray him as Everyman…completely unexceptional in appearance…in a word they should be indistinguishable from the straights we would like to reach.
> "*The masses should not be shocked and repelled by premature exposure to homosexual behaviour itself…the imagery of sex should be downplayed…make use of symbols which reduce the mainstream's sense of threat, [to] lower its guard…*Replace the mainstream's self-righteous pride about its homophobia with shame and guilt." [emphasis added]

As part of pushing the "prevalence" of homosexuality in the media, they pushed out false figures based on outdated research by the pedophile Alfred Kinsey, suggesting up to ten percent of the population are gay. This despite major recent studies showing fewer than one percent are. Additionally, Kirk and Madsen strongly argued that gays needed to claim heroes of history as their own.

"Paint gay men and lesbians as superior – veritable pillars of society. Famous historical figures are considered especially useful to us," they noted, not just because of the prestige but because they're "invariably dead as a doornail, hence in no position to deny the truth and sue for libel."

Cue the movie *Alexander*, anyone?

If there is any opposition left after this gay blitzkrieg, they write, silence it once and for all.

> "LONG AFTER GAY [RIGHTS] have become commonplace, it will be time to get tough with remaining opponents. To be blunt, they must be vilified. We intend to make the anti-gays look so nasty that average Americans will want to dissociate themselves from such types."

They're right, they were blunt. Vilification of their opponents, making them look "nasty" even if they weren't. The "We intend" refers, by the way, to that previously-mentioned group of nearly 200 core activists from across the US who met to strategize in 1988, just in case you are wondering how two authors could plot 'world domination' on their own.

I would also add, however, before we go any further, that references in these chapters to the gay activists/gay propagandists/gay elite are specific to the radical wing of the movement. Every movement or organization has its chiefs and its Indians. Please don't sit there thinking your gay friend or colleague is part of some vast queer global conspiracy – there definitely is one, but it was strategized by people far higher up the PR food chain than "Tristan" in accounts. Tristan, and other gay mates, are as much victims of the PR spin as the rest of us are.

" The Nazi Position:

[Propaganda] is the proclaimer of an idea, it undermines the positions of the enemy with all the means and forces at its disposal. It stands in the middle of life, in the middle of events, and draws the necessary consequences. Whether the means of propaganda are proper or whether it serves the facts or ideas is entirely irrelevant. It would be inexcusable weakness if propaganda did not use every means at its disposal to bring down as rapidly as possible the rotten system it faces." – **Schulze Wechsungen, German Ministry of Propaganda, 1934** **"**

One example of the vilification the propagandists talked of was the murder of homosexual teenager Matthew Shepard, killed by two men (who were not Christians) in 1998. Despite that inconvenient little fact, the radical gay movement pitched it as a Christian "hate crime". Entire websites have been created by the gay rights movement expressing hate for Christians, this despite a major new investigation by ABC 20/20 in 2004 which found Shepard was probably not killed because he was gay, but simply because the offenders wanted to rob him.

But then again, as Kirk and Madsen wrote, never let the facts get in the way of a good story.

So that's jamming, what did "Conversion" entail?

"WE MEAN CONVERSION of the average American's emotions, mind and will, through a planned psychological attack, in the form of propaganda fed to the nation via the media. We mean 'subverting' the mechanism of prejudice to our own ends – using the very processes that made America hate us to turn their hatred into warm regard – whether they like it or not.

"In Conversion, we mimic the natural process of stereotype-learning, with the following effect: we take the bigot's good feelings about all-right guys, and attach them to the label 'gay', either weakening or, eventually, replacing his bad feelings toward the label and the prior stereotype…

"Whereas in Jamming the target is shown a bigot being rejected by his crowd for his prejudice against gays, in Conversion the target is shown his crowd actually associating with gays in good fellowship. Once again, it's very difficult for the average person, who, by nature and training, almost invariably feels what he sees his fellows feeling, not to respond in this knee-jerk fashion to a sufficiently-calculated advertisement.

"It makes no difference that the ads are lies," write Kirk and Madsen, because the end justifies the means.

If you haven't recognized classic re-programming, or "brainwashing", by now, you are probably brain dead. Yet the effect on a generation of children and young adults has been nothing less than stunning.

As David Kupelian points out in *The Marketing of Evil*, a reader poll in the popular teen magazine *Seventeen* in 1991 found only 17% of readers supported homosexuality. Taken again in 1999, after eight years of "persuasion", support for gay rights had tripled to 54%, a majority. What changed? Nothing but the marketing spin. And those results are replicated everywhere.

In another example, a Pew research poll in 1996 found 65% of Americans opposed to gay marriage, and only 27% in favour. Up until 2004 there was no major media push for gay marriage, so unsurprisingly the figures for and against remained relatively static – another Pew poll in February 2004 showed 63% opposed and 30% in favour.

Then came a massive worldwide PR push for gay marriage in 2004, with New Zealand becoming one of the first countries in the world to legalise a form of civil union that was, in fact, gay marriage, and many American states holding gay marriage ceremonies until the courts ruled them out of order.

Although there was no change in the preceding eight years, the last two years have seen the gay desensitization agenda working on the minds of the public like magic mushrooms: a Pew poll in 2006 found opposition to gay marriage had dropped to only 51%, a slide of 12 percentage points in just two years.

What's changed? Again, nothing in substance, just a battle-weary "give-them-what-they-want-and-maybe-they'll-shut-up-and-go-away" resignation.

Pew centre's Michael Dimock echoes the point. "A lot of people who opposed it [in 2004] were in an intense environment and either feel less strongly [in 2006] or feel that people can do what they want to do."

And "what they want to do" is growing in scale every year as well. To give you an idea of just how far Kirk and Madsen's original propaganda pitch has come and how much it has conditioned how we think, here's some advice from a New Zealand government sexual health website, hubba.co.nz:

> "WHO WE 'LIKE' or are 'attracted to', or who we fall 'in love' with depends on our sexual orientation. This is something each of us has to discover for ourselves as we experience friendships and relationships with different people. People who are attracted to the opposite sex (e.g. girl/boy relationships) are described as being 'straight' or preferring 'heterosexual' relationships.
>
> "People who are attracted to people of the same sex as they are (e.g. boy/boy or girl/girl relationships) are described as being 'gay' or 'lesbian' (if you're a girl) or preferring "homosexual" relationships. Some people have always felt this way, while other people recognize these feelings later on in life. Being attracted to people the same sex as you is OK.
>
> "Some people like both guys and girls and can have relationships with men or women. This is called being 'bisexual' or 'bisexuality'."

Remember, this is pure PR spin aimed at adolescent teens. The next paragraph is an absolute howler.

> "IT DOESN'T MATTER WHO you are attracted to, have relationships with or what label you put on it. People love different people and for different reasons. Some people get worried or confused if they are attracted to someone who is the same sex as they are, because it's not the 'norm'. That doesn't mean it's not normal though. Lots of people are gay, lesbian and bisexual (i.e. that girl down the road, my bro, your doctor, Ellen Degeneres, your friend, that super spunk on TV, the waitress in that café) – all of them are happy, strong, on to it people who have the right to love."

Examine the underlying message in that quote: "It doesn't matter who you are attracted to, have relationships with or what label you put on it". Today, it is homosexuality and bisexuality, but tomorrow it will be incest, pedophilia and bestiality.

Don't believe me? Here's some advice for students on the goaskalice. com website, a "health question and answer service" run by the prestigious Columbia University's Health Education Programme. The advice was in response to a question about having sex with a sheep:

> "STDs (SEXUALLY TRANSMITTED DISEASES), including HIV, cannot be transmitted through sexual contact between humans and animals because they are species-specific. If you remain concerned about potential disease risk in general, follow safer-sex guidelines – such as wearing a condom – in all of your sexual encounters."

Why not go the whole hog and tell the questioner to make sure he wears his winter woollies? There's another advantage to sex with animals, advises "Alice", they won't secretly video your encounter and plaster it all over the internet:

> "As WITH OTHER UNCOMMON, taboo, and/or illegal activities, sexual contacts with animals might be stimulating for some people because they are secretive, forbidden and dangerous. An animal doesn't 'kiss and tell', nor do his or her expectations 'get in the way'."

Heck no! I'm sure the last thing Daisy the cow expected was to star in "Barnyard Adventures With A Pre-Med Student".

It would be humorous – just maybe – if it were not so heart-achingly tragic. There are people out there in our society who do, actually, do this stuff. They are so dysfunctional as human beings that a relationship with their pet – wait a minute, now I'm falling into the trap of political correctness - that raping their pet is preferable to finding a fellow human to settle down with and have kids.

In the Australian state of New South Wales, just before Christmas 2006, a woman was found naked in a paddock *in flagrante delicto* with a horse. In 25 years as a network news reporter, I have never written a sentence like that one until now, and never thought I would.

In New Zealand, a man with a collection of thousands of child rape and bestiality videos and images was given a slap on the hand with a wet bus ticket:

"A man who amassed thousands of images of child porn and bestiality was sentenced today to community service," reported the *NZ Press Association* in early February this year.

> "GEOFFREY HUNT, 22, earlier pleaded guilty to 15 charges of possessing objectionable material -- including images of sexual abuse involving children as young as three years old.
>
> "Hunt was charged after he took his computer to a repair firm, where staff found the material and alerted police.
>
> "An investigation showed the former information technology professional had been collecting the images from early 2004, and perhaps earlier.
>
> "At least 12,000 images and about 60 videos were found, featuring sexual abuse of children as young as three, with the majority aged between seven and 15, as well as images of bestiality and other sexual fetish material.
>
> "In Wellington District Court Judge Denys Barry sentenced Hunt to 250 hours of community service."

Take a look at the politically correct phrasing of the lead paragraph in that story: "child porn". Is the rape and sexual abuse of a three year old really "pornography"? Once again, it's a value-laden term that plays on society's growing acceptance of "porn".

Although liberals use the "slope" phrase themselves, they like to snort and sneer derisively when conservatives talk about a "slippery slope" – that when you start letting little things slide pretty soon the whole hillside is caving away underneath you. It's analogous to that other wonderful saying: "give 'em an inch and they'll take a mile". These sayings don't arise in a vacuum. They resonate with the public because they have more than just a core of truth to them. We like sayings like these because they reflect human nature, yet liberals live in a state of absolute denial. It's almost as if the academics and journalists and sociologists who've helped create this mess have been the victims of DIY frontal lobotomies. You can't actually debate with them because they skitter and evade and conflate and spout weasel words like there's no tomorrow (as you'll see in the next chapter).

Yet the case of Geoffrey Hunt above is an obvious one of slippery slopes. I'd bet good money it began with "standard" internet porn sites and, when these no longer titillated, graduated to child rape and then bestiality. For heaven's sake – he's only 22 years old! Why is he being turned on by raping children and small furry animals?

Why has our society become so sick that people no longer feel any inhibitions with their fantasies, and consequently those fantasies are getting darker and more evil by the year?

This was something that Kirk and Madsen knew all about: within the ranks of the gay community are pedophiles who prefer to call themselves the North American Man Boy Love Association.

"We're not judging you," the authors told the pedophiles.

You and I both know there's a "but" in there somewhere, however I couldn't resist interjecting. Madsen, an architect of the most comprehensive gay PR strategy ever published and a senior partner at the world headquarters of one of the planet's biggest advertising agencies, JWT, is telling pedophiles, "We're not judging you."

There's a perfect example of a moral compass gone south! Madsen and Kirk *should* have been judging pedophiles. But the truth is, the gay agenda includes legalized pedophilia, as former gay activists like Tammy Bruce have also warned.[64]

"We're not judging you, but others do, and very harshly; please keep a low profile," Kirk and Madsen told NAMBLA.[65] Elsewhere in their book, they explained why they didn't want homosexuality's dirty little secrets coming out during the desensitizing and jamming phases:

> "FIRST YOU GET YOUR FOOT in the door, by being as similar as possible; then, and only then – *when your one little difference [sexual orientation] is finally accepted – can you start dragging in your other peculiarities, one by one. You hammer in the wedge narrow end first.* As the saying goes, allow the camel's nose beneath your tent, and his whole body will soon follow."
> [emphasis added]

And don't even begin to speculate on the whole camel thing! But the key point is this: hiding from you, the public, the worst excesses of the gay, lesbian, bisexual and transgender community was a deliberate and carefully strategized move in the chess game to ultimately legalise a whole range of "philias". Clearly, by their own words, gay activists like Kirk and advertising guru Madsen, had no intention of "judging" or excommunicating child rapists from the gay rights movement, they simply wanted them to stay hidden until the coast was clear.

Now it would be wrong for anyone to infer from this that every homosexual is a closet pedophile or a supporter of pedophilia. Far from it. Many, probably by far the majority, gays are as disgusted by it as heterosexuals are. However,

64   Tammy Bruce, *The Death of Right & Wrong*, Prima, 2003,p.193
65   http://www.leaderu.com/socialsciences/sellinghomosexuality.html

the Kirk/Madsen plan recognizes child rapists as fellow travelers in the gay rights movement, and that is a serious indictment on the morality of Kirk and Madsen and their agenda.

The gay-rights movement is the clean-cut, cowboy-next-door. NAMBLA is his in-bred, half-shaven, pot-bellied and drooling imbecile cousin whose knuckles drag on the ground, Darwinian-style, and who only gets dragged out for special "in house" occasions. But they're part of the same family. NAMBLA has a little brother down-under that he plays with, the Australasian Man-Boy Love Association.[66]

"AMBLA is a regular attendant at the annual IPCE (International Paedophile and Child Emancipation) Conference," begins an entry on a pedophile website.

Child emancipation? These gay men think that by raping children they are freeing them? At least the gay Catholic priests who sexually abused young people knew they were doing something evil, but NAMBLA and AMBLA have long since lost any vestige of conscience.

> "AMBLA IS NOT AN exclusively paedophile organisation, but it is supportive of paedophiles. Amongst boy-lovers, paedophiles are clearly the most oppressed group (in the West), and are probably second only to children themselves in the extent of the oppression. We consider other subordination equally important; none of us are free unless all of us are free.
>
> "We are committed to the principles of an open, liberal-democratic society as our only legitimate means of redress. As citizens of a liberal democracy, boy-lovers have the right to organise for the purpose, firstly (and given the lies most importantly) to know ourselves. To know ourselves spiritually as well as personally, and to represent our conscience. Secondly, we have the right in a liberal democracy to organise for interest-articulation and interest representation."

AMBLA, incidentally, is officially "defunct", but of course any organization is only a reflection of its members, and its members continue to molest children. Except these days they call it "intergenerational love". How sweet.

Make no bones about it, gay marriage and civil unions are simply a bridgehead for the eventual legalizing of sex with children, animals and polygamy.

Denmark, incidentally, is on track to licence animal "brothels" where paying customers can buy sex with the beast of their choice. Even more

---

stunningly, only one person on a 12 member government ethics panel that included numerous animal rights organizations voted against this horrendous development late last year.[67]

Have you been "desensitized" to the liberalization of gay "rights" and sexual behaviour? To answer that question, consider this. In 2005, a senior left-wing NZ Labour government cabinet minister (and former schoolteacher) in charge of the portolios of Social Development policy and Child Protection hit the headlines when students he'd taught back in 1982 came forward to reveal he used to bind and gag students as a form of classroom discipline. Questioned in Parliament about this, the politician made the mistake of lying about the incident in the debating chamber, which resulted in a police investigation.

The police found prima facie evidence (although they 'chose' not to prosecute) that assaults had taken place, and also found evidence that the politician had forced young 13 and 14 year old schoolgirls to strip to their nighties and panties and stand outside in near freezing conditions at night on school camps whilst he spotlighted them with a torch for an hour – again, a form of "discipline". The children were not allowed to move, regardless of medical conditions or pain.

Then in November 2006, as a result of further inquiries, *Investigate* magazine published an online-only special report detailing the politician's involvement in extreme sado-masochism and bondage sex sessions, including alleged adult-child sex torture fetishes (acted out between the politician in the role of "child" and a bondage mistress dressed as a school teacher) and "puppy play". Now remember, this politician was in charge of New Zealand's national child protection agencies, and also in charge of the government department that implements social policy. As the politician responsible for legalizing "gay marriage-lite", or civil unions, in New Zealand in 2004, this man had also been previously accused of treating schoolchildren in a way that closely resembled sexual bondage and discipline.

You would think that a story like this would create major headlines. But despite the politician expressly refusing to issue any categorical denial whatsoever, the story was largely ignored by the mainstream media. Although one TV network showed interest, the attitude of its parliamentary journalist was, "So what? What happens between consenting adults in private is their business, not ours."

So presumably, if a left-wing politician was found in bed with a goat, that story would also be ignored on the presumption that the goat consented!

Now *that* is desensitization. In the space of less than 20 years, the public no longer bat an eyelid at the extremes. What was previously seen as abhorrent, bizarre and a form of mental illness is now treated with that "shrug of the

67   http://www.metro.co.uk/weird/article.html?in_article_id=27524&in_page_id=2

shoulders" that Kirk and Madsen had been hoping for.

In *The Death of Right and Wrong*, Tammy Bruce recounts her own brush with the bondage and discipline fetish movement.

"During my activism in the feminist and gay communities, the conditioning was nonstop. The effort, using the mass media primarily, was and is to brainwash the public into believing that certain sexual practices are merely 'alternative lifestyles'. I had my first shock during a meeting for an AIDS action group in 1990. We were planning a protest geared to gaining more media awareness of the need for AIDS research funding when the discussion suddenly shifted to the need to show more support for our sisters involved in sadomasochism. One participant, a young lesbian dressed in leather and with virtually every visible part of her body pierced, demanded that the AIDS action include 'S&M visibility'.

"I said that the desire to inflict pain on someone was sick; that S&M had absolutely nothing to do with homosexuality; and the fact that no one else had spoken up to challenge what was being said, was in itself very disturbing. Well, you can imagine how that room erupted. It actually became a shouting match. I was predictably condemned as intolerant and self-loathing and as a danger to the community. I was told that my describing S&M as a sickness put gay people at risk. Why? Because if any 'alternative' sexual practice was condemned, there would be the 'slippery slope', and no gays would be safe from all those maniacal Christian fundamentalists. By default, it was argued, we had a responsibility to embrace and support anyone who challenged the sexual and social status quo.

"The idea took hold, and now all manner of sexual perversion enjoys the protection and support of what was once a legitimate civil rights effort for decent people. The real slippery slope has been the one leading into the Left's moral vacuum. It is a singular attitude that prohibits any judgement about obvious moral decay because of the paranoid belief that judgement of any sort would destroy the gay lifestyle, whatever that is. You see one very public display of this 'big tent' approach when you watch news coverage of any of the major gay pride marches. Have you ever noticed how big the parade banner is?

"In the old days, the banners declared the parades were for Gay and Lesbian Rights. That is rather straightforward. Today, reflective of the any-perversion-is-our-perversion mentality, the banners read Gay, Lesbian, Bisexual and Transgendered Rights. I think the only reason the words 'And Women Who Love Their Cocker Spaniels Too Much' haven't appeared yet is that the organisers simply ran out of room," concludes Tammy Bruce.

Allowing the creeping moral cancer of sadomasochism to enter the sexual mainstream under the guise of "private behaviour between consenting adults" is a step towards social anarchy, and even legitimizing sexual cannibalism.

After all, that is precisely the argument raised by German computer geek Armin Meiwes who lured a 43 year old Berlin man to his death by posting an ad, and asked his victim if he was prepared to be killed and eaten as part of Meiwes' sexual fantasy.

Incredibly, or perhaps not so in godless Europe, the victim agreed, as this report from Britain's *Guardian* newspaper makes clear:

> ...GERMAN PROSECUTORS DESCRIBED how Meiwes had fantasised about killing and devouring someone, including his classmates, from the age of eight.
>
> The desire grew stronger after the death of his mother in 1999, prosecutor Marcus Köhler said.
>
> In March 2001 Meiwes advertised on the internet for a "young well-built man, who wanted to be eaten". Brandes replied.
>
> On the evening of March 9, the two men went up to the bedroom in Meiwes' rambling timbered farmhouse. Mr Brandes swallowed 20 sleeping tablets and half a bottle of schnapps before Meiwes cut off Brandes' penis, with his agreement, and fried it for both of them to eat.
>
> Brandes - by this stage bleeding heavily - then took a bath, while Meiwes read a *Star Trek* novel.
>
> In the early hours of the morning, he finished off his victim by stabbing him in the neck with a large kitchen knife, kissing him first.
>
> The cannibal then chopped Mr Brandes into pieces and put several bits of him in his freezer, next to a takeaway pizza, and buried the skull in his garden.
>
> Over the next few weeks, he defrosted and cooked parts of Mr Brandes in olive oil and garlic, eventually consuming 20kg of human flesh before police finally turned up at his door.
>
> "With every bite, my memory of him grew stronger," he said.
>
> Behind bars, Meiwes told detectives that he had consumed his victim with a bottle of South African red wine, had got out his best cutlery and decorated his dinner table with candles. He tasted of pork, he added.
>
> The unprecedented case has proved problematic for German lawyers who discovered that cannibalism is not illegal in Germany.
>
> Instead, they have charged Meiwes with murder for the purposes of sexual pleasure and with "disturbing the peace of the dead".

The accused, however, has a unique defence: that his victim actually agreed to be killed and eaten.

Crucial to the case is a gruesome videotape made by Meiwes of the entire evening, during which Brandes apparently makes clear his consent.

Before setting off on his one-way journey to Rotenburg, Brandes was, outwardly at least, a successful, financially secure professional, with a live-in girlfriend.

The girlfriend, Bettina L, told German TV that she had enjoyed a healthy sex life with Brandes but they had split up after he revealed that he also liked men.

In fact, prosecutors said yesterday, Brandes was suffering from a severe psychiatric disorder and "a strong desire for self-destruction".

After killing Brandes, the German cannibal met five other men who responded to his internet advert, including one from London.

He did not, however, kill them. In July 2001 a student stumbled on Meiwes' chat-room and alerted the German authorities, who arrested him last December. Yesterday Meiwes told the court that he had felt lonely and neglected as a child after his father walked out on the family. He had fantasised about having a blond "younger brother", who he could keep forever by "consuming him".

The German court hearing the case dropped the murder charge to one of "manslaughter" because it determined Meiwes had "no base motives". He was sentenced 2004 to eight years' jail.

But this case of two mental and spiritual trainwrecks – Meiwes and Brandes - colliding is a perfect example of the "slippery slope" argument. If the current push in the West to introduce Euthanasia is approved, the mindset of the public, police and courts will shift to regarding sexual cannibalism as "just" a form of voluntary euthanasia between consenting adults.

Desensitization, again.

There is another aspect to this that is often overlooked. What two "consenting" adults do behind closed doors may nonetheless have a major flow-on impact on other people – family members, emergency service workers, taxpayers. In the next chapter, you'll see just how the next phase in selling gay rights is set to impact the wider community.

8

The Trophy Child
"I Want a Human Pet"

"The family unit-spawning ground of lies, betrayals, mediocrity, hypocrisy and violence--will be abolished. The family unit, which only dampens imagination and curbs free will, must be eliminated. Perfect boys will be conceived and grown in the genetic laboratory. They will be bonded together in communal setting, under the control and instruction of homosexual savants."
Michael Swift, Gay Community News, 1987

I t is easy to frame a debate in terms of individual freedoms, but are such "freedoms" absolute, or do they only exist within the context of what society as a whole is prepared to support? Gay adoption being a perfect example. It can only take place with the acquiescence of society, because babies don't just drop out of trees. And how do we balance out the right of a child whose life is already starting out behind the eight ball – without either of his or her biological parents – to be placed in the most stable and genuinely loving environment possible?

Gay surrogacy, where a lesbian or heterosexual woman gives birth to the biological child of a gay person, has been around for a long time. At least in those cases the children maintain a connection with a biological parent who genuinely has their best interests at heart.

But a total gay adoption is a different kettle of fish. It goes kicking and screaming against the whole definition of "gay". If being homosexual means only being attracted to members of the same sex, then procreation as a "natural" outcome of such a relationship goes out the window. In the "wild", two gay men cannot produce a baby without either doing what they claim they cannot – sleeping with a woman – or seeking artificial intervention.

But gay activists have been exceedingly cunning. By framing the gay marriage debate in the way they have – the very word "marriage" carries with it the same emotional loadings as a heterosexual relationship – the activists have created another false image to fool the general public, 99% of whom are not gay and not privy to the darker activities of gay relationships. Thus, if you sell a message that resonates with a heterosexual couple's own emotional cues – "we're just two guys who love each other, who want a committed relationship in the form of marriage so we can settle down and bring up children, just like everybody else" – it becomes really hard for heterosexuals to see beyond the smokescreen.

In 2003, one US newspaper carried a story headlined "Married and Gay Couples Not All That Different", which, as the headline suggested, told readers how normal gay couples are.

"We're the couple next door," said one. "We have a dog and a cat. I drive a Volvo. I'm boring."

And out in suburbia, everyone nodded their heads in sympathy while tut-tutting, "They're just like us".

Perhaps that's why the same Pew poll last year revealed a massive boost in support for gay adoption as well, with only 48% opposed, compared with 57% opposition in a 1999 poll.

But what is a gay relationship *really* like? When gays talk about "committed relationships", what do they *really* mean? And are gay relationships a suitable environment for bringing up children?

Let's look at some hard evidence.

First there's Kirk and Madsen's take on the average gay male relationship.

"Gay men aren't very good at having and holding lovers…gay men tire of their partners [sexually] more rapidly than straight men."

Heterosexual women often make the mistake, thanks to the carefully sanitized TV shows, of presuming that gay men are really women trapped in men's bodies, and therefore that these men act and think more like women than men. They're wrong. To truly pigeon-hole the average gay male, take an extreme tomcat straight male, multiply his libido by a factor of ten, throw in a mega-dose of narcissism, and also sprinkle in heavy drug use and a willingness to deliberately engage in life-threatening sexual behaviour. If that sounds like your average Western female I'd be highly surprised.

On the website GayNZ.com, staff writers last November discussed a refusal by a major internet dating site to accept Gay-targeted advertising about safe sex. The dating site refused on the grounds that most New Zealanders using the dating site were looking for friendship or maybe a date, and flooding the site with sexual health advertising would change the tone of the site. To which GayNZ replied:

> "FRIENDSHIP AND DATING may be the norm for some users of dating websites *but for gay men, hooking up for sex is clearly prevalent, as just a couple of minutes trawling through dating sites will reveal*." [emphasis added].

In the same 2006 GayNZ article[68] they reported up to 83% of gay men they surveyed online were prepared to have sex without condoms with strangers.

In other words, as even gay websites are forced to concede, the primal drive for gay men is trawling for sex.

And unlike most who will undoubtedly criticize me for this book, I do speak with some personal experience. At the age of 20 when I first moved to Auckland I spent six months living in a house with several gay flatmates – two of them were a couple. They were all nice enough guys but I did not envy their lifestyles, which involved literally a revolving door of sex sessions with numerous different men, and the associated emotional baggage and drug use that came with the territory. Throughout my career in broadcasting I worked closely on a daily basis with gay and lesbian colleagues, some of whom were social colleagues as well.

If anyone had suggested to me in 1984 that gay couples were monogamous I'd have laughed until Christmas.

But in that same year, 1984, two gay medical researchers, David McWhirter and Andrew Mattison, themselves a "couple", interviewed 156 male couples about monogamy.[69] They found "fidelity is not defined in terms of sexual behaviour, but rather by their emotional commitment to one another." In other words, unlike heterosexuals, gay men did not define sleeping around as unfaithfulness, unless one of those outside encounters became a threat to the core relationship.

The researchers found that although more than 60% of couples began their relationships expecting to be monogamous, those relationships quickly began to include outside liaisons. Given those statistics mentioned earlier that nearly half of all gay men end up with more than 500 sexual partners, this all ties in.

McWhirter and Mattison found that *all* couples who had been together for five years – 100% of them – had brought extra males into the "marriage bed". In fact, they wrote:

> "THE SINGLE MOST IMPORTANT factor that keeps couples together past the ten-year mark is the lack of possessiveness they feel. Many couples learn very early in their relationship that ownership of each other sexually can become the greatest internal threat to their staying together."

Of the 156 couples surveyed, only 7 had managed to achieve monogamy, and none of those relationships had existed longer than 5 years.

68   http://www.gaynz.com/aarticles/anmviewer.asp?a=1556
69   *Textbook of Homosexuality and Mental Health*, ed. Robert P Cabaj and Terry S. Stein; American Psychiatric Press, 1996

Do we really want to put orphan children into homes like this?

But that's not the only study. In 1991 German "sexologist" and homosexual Dr Martin Dannecker published a study of 900 gay males which found 83% of men in "steady relationships" were taking part in numerous sexual encounters outside the relationship over a one year period.[70]

In fact Dannecker's work paints an even bleaker picture: gay men in "committed" relationships averaged more sexual partners per year than single gay men. For gay men in steady partnerships, he said, "the average number of homosexual contacts per person was 115 in the past year." In contrast, single gay men had only 45 sexual contacts.

What sort of message would that send to adopted children growing up in a gay household? They would grow up viewing extreme promiscuity as "normal".

A recent study of gay men published in the medical journal *AIDS* in 2003 found most "steady partnerships" lasted 18 months at most, and in that time of "monogamy" each partner still managed to chalk up a further 12 conquests on average outside the relationship.

And please don't assume that my data is one-sided. Most of these surveys were published by gay researchers, and even leading gay magazines like *Advocate* in the US routinely discuss these issues. It is the politically-correct mainstream media who don't tell the wider public. While it is true that the homosexual community hates the idea of airing its dirty laundry in public, it has dirty laundry by the truckload. An *Advocate* study in 1994 for example, found 52% of respondents claimed to be "monogamous", yet 85% of those same respondents reported the biggest problem in their relationships was fights caused when partners cheated. You try and do the math on that one!

Gay activists Kirk and Madsen, like the other gay researchers behind some of those studies above, are clear on why gay men cannot get over their promiscuity.

> "[THE AVERAGE GAY MALE] seeks [sexual] novelty in partners, rather than practices, and becomes massively promiscuous; [but] eventually all bodies become boring, and only new practices will thrill."

Translated into plain English: gay men seek sexual novelty in numbers of conquests. It is only later, when they are older and jaded, that the thought of a fresh young body no longer turns them on and instead the quest is for ever more deviant sexual practices.

"The cheating ratio of 'married' [committed] gay males, given enough time, approaches 100%," conclude Kirk and Madsen.

So one is forced to ask the question again: why in Heaven's name are we

70   Martin Dannecker, *Theories of Homosexuality*, Gay Men's Press, 1991

in the West even remotely considering legalizing gay adoption of children? It is not as if the figures above have been plucked out of thin air – they are the sum total of all studies of gay male behaviour, carried out by gay researchers for the most part.

Whose "rights" are more important here – the men who wish to play happy families for a little while, or the children who need stable and committed parenting for a lifetime?

Because the statistics just don't stack up. While the news media can always find a handsome couple who epitomize everything good about gay adoption, and contrast them on TV with halfwit hillbilly white trash heterosexuals, and while there are always exceptions and there may indeed be some gay couples who would make suitable long term parents, the weight of the scientific evidence, as opposed to the media-spun anecdotal reports, is overwhelming. Gay men would not make good parents, compared with the average heterosexual couple.

And let's face it, I find it highly doubtful that many gay men really and truly fancy the idea of being parents – it wouldn't fit the lifestyle. A child is not a Bichon-Frise. But the danger is that in opening up adoption we'll get situations where gay couples go in with the best of intentions and find the stress of bringing up children not related to them drives a nail into their already shaky "committed" relationship. Where then for the child or children, while two highly-charged gay parents go through a messy break-up by throwing themselves back into the gay singles scene with party drugs and random, anonymous sexual encounters? Are we to ignore the many studies on the damage divorce causes to kids?

Then there's the psychological damage. Recent studies indicate the big increase of suicides involving young males in the West could be directly related to homosexuality. Ironically, only 4.9% of gay men reported youth suicide attempts in the repressive 1950s. Now that being gay is tolerated and even welcomed in popular culture, young gays are trying to kill themselves at rates never before witnessed:

> THE LIFETIME INCIDENCE OF "SUICIDE ATTEMPTS" for homosexually oriented male adolescents has increased about 6-fold since 1950, from about 5 to 30 percent. Of significant interest are the YRBS study result producing a "suicide attempt" average of about 30 percent for a 12-month period."[71]

Will social workers tasked with assessing the merits of gay couples wanting to

---

71   http://fsw.ucalgary.ca/ramsay/homosexuality-suicide/construction/b0-male-youth-suicide-increase.htm

adopt be briefed on the intimate workings of the gay community, or will they only have the sanitized, politically-correct version? Can heterosexual social workers, who have only experienced ordinary opposite sex relationships, ever truly understand what a gay relationship really is? And can gay social workers ever truly be objective enough when dealing with gay adoption applications?

The criticisms here are based not on the mere *fact* that someone is gay, but on the gay *lifestyle*. I would likewise be appalled if adoption was opened up to include a couple of heterosexual, party animal bachelor boys.

Liberal Newstalk ZB talk host Oliver Driver says he's in favour of gay adoption because the only issue is whether they're good parents. "Clearly, if they're the kind of gay people who are out there having sex with everyone, then they wouldn't be good parents," he concedes. Driver is dead right and deserves some credit for recognizing the real issue, but the real problem is, how the heck are we supposed to determine which gay couple is highly promiscuous, and which one isn't? What do liberals propose? Some kind of secret police force to tail prospective adoptive gay parents for weeks to check on their morality? That's never going to happen, so we're still left with the gay adoption issue turning into Russian Roulette with babies instead of bullets.

The sociological and scientific studies carried out are overwhelming: something like 98% of gay men live and breathe the gay lifestyle, and the gay lifestyle is no place for kids of any age. Ironically, the people who will shout loudest against my conclusions here are the same ones who day in and day out hail the "triumph of science over religion", yet they are prepared to totally gloss over the science on this particular issue. Are we all supposed to ignore the science for the sake of political correctness and not offending the gay community?

How many sexually or otherwise abused children do we already have to deal with, without adding to it by artificially creating unnatural families just for the sake of political correctness? Surely, it is time for the madness to stop, if we truly value the rights of children.

Speaking of offending the gay community, how's this for an example of Kirk and Madsen's "Conversion" idea in action in 2007, carried on David Farrar's Kiwiblog:

> THE NATIONAL HEALTH SERVICE in Scotland has told doctors and nurses to avoid using the terms 'mom' and 'dad' as the terms could be offensive to homosexual couples with children!!!
>
> As part of their "zero-tolerance policy to discriminatory language" they recommend when talking to children to consider using 'parents', 'carers' or 'guardians' rather than 'mother' or 'father'.
>
> They also rule as unacceptable the terms 'husband', 'wife' and 'marriage' as they exclude lesbian, gay and bisexual people.

Instead, health care workers should use the terms 'partners' and 'next of kin'.

How long until someone tries this on here?[72]

Hat Tip: Family First

Then there's another side to the argument that is totally ignored. Gay adoption is not the same as heterosexual adoption. Two men can *never* provide the intimate female nurturing role that a mother provides. Gays argue that they can balance this by ensuring there are women in the children's lives, but those women at best will be mimicking the role of aunts, if that. Why should an orphaned child be deprived of a genuine mother figure just because we've become politically correct?

Likewise, two lesbian women bringing up a child cannot provide the positive masculine influence that a father brings to a family.

Sure, sociologists will try and quote studies purporting to show no major side effects. But sociology is a field riddled with both Marxism, where it sprang from, and sexual and social liberalism. In other words, sociologists are sometimes guilty of trying to find the evidence to fit their preconceptions. Some work is not as loaded, and therefore not as prone to bias, but you can bet that when someone has been paid to do a study on gay parenting, that there is a reason for that study being commissioned in the first place. The idea that children don't need biological mothers, or biological fathers, and can be raised by anyone, goes against all commonsense and every instinct known to humankind. Children are statistically at far more risk of being physically and sexually abused by non-biological "caregivers", and there is no reason to expect, given the evidence I've just laid out, that the homosexual community could do a better job at parenting than nature's choice – the real parents.

Yet you are about to be bombarded by precisely this propaganda.

New Zealand Green Party MP Sue Bradford, the woman behind the anti-smacking legislation, gave a speech in New Zealand's Parliament on March 1st 2007, highlighted by the lobby group Family First, protesting about a proposed law requiring the biological father of all children to be named on birth registration forms.

According to Bradford, "this aspect of the Bill is nothing short of draconian - it makes criminals out of women who wish to make choices to raise their children without the involvement of their biological father."

What about a child's right to know its biological father, to know its gene pool? According to Bradford, these rights are secondary to "a woman's choice":

72   http://www.kiwiblog.co.nz/2007/02/mom_and_dad_now_homophobic_ter.html. also http://www.lgbthealthscotland.org.uk/documents/Good_LGBT_Practice_NHS.pdf

"THERE ARE A RANGE OF … situations where women may not wish to have the father of their child's name registered.

"One is where the woman is in a same-sex relationship, wants her partner to share parental responsibilities, but wants to conceive naturally rather than by assisted reproductive technology.

"Another is where the woman has a partner of the opposite sex who is infertile, but chooses to conceive naturally to another man.

"A third is where the woman simply wants to raise a child on her own without any involvement financially or emotionally from another parent.

"These are all reasonable choices for women to want to make, and choices that some women do make. Yet with the new section 9 proposed by this Bill, they are not choices that women will be lawfully permitted to make."

So obsessed with the rights of adults and accommodating their sexual choices, but not a whisper in there of the genuine heart-rights of the child to ultimately know his or her father. And while we're at it, let's lay to rest the myth being promulgated by gay groups, including the NZ AIDS Foundation, that heterosexuals can't make marriages work either. While there is plenty of evidence to suggest that heterosexual de-facto relationships are not very stable, proper marriage remains on surprisingly solid ground.

A survey of more than two thousand men and women published in the *Journal of Sex Research* in 1997 found 77% of married men and 88% of married women had remained faithful to their marriage vows.

Another 1997 survey, published in *The Social Organisation of Sexuality: Sexual Practices in the United States*, mirrored the first with a finding that 75% of married men and 85% of women had not strayed beyond the marriage bed.

A 1994 US survey of 1,049 adults found 81% of men and 85% of women had remained true to their marriage vows.[73]

Why the massive difference between the faithfulness of heterosexual marriage partners, and that of male homosexuals? Partly because gay men don't value monogamy much, if at all. They do value relationships, but they also enjoy random sex with strangers, and lots of it. Some gay activists have written that homosexual marriage is only a stepping stone to introducing a much wider range of marriage possibilities, including polygamy.

"Being queer is more than setting up house, sleeping with a person of the same gender, and seeking state approval for doing so," writes Paula Ettelbrick, the former legal director of the gay Lambda Legal Defense and Education Fund.

"Being queer means pushing the parameters of sex, sexuality, and family, and in the process transforming the very fabric of society."

As we're about to see, what gay academics and activists are discussing privately about their sexual orientation and its meaning casts this entire debate in a whole new light, one that you won't see in the daily media.

9

Born Or Made?
The Myth of Sexual Orientation

"[HIV] may even have occurred, though rarely, for centuries. It now seems likely that the primary reason the epidemic began when it did was not because a microbe jumped from animals to people, but because large scale changes in human behavior provided HIV with radically new opportunities to spread."

Gabriel Rotello, gay activist, Sexual Ecology

Ever since the AIDS crisis arose in the 80's, and the push to be "inclusive", it has been a catch-cry of the gay rights movement that "people don't 'choose' to be gay, we're born that way." This single slogan has been the most effective public relations sword the movement has. It silences critics who previously argued homosexuality was a lifestyle choice. It induces empathy from the wider public who say "why should these people be penalized for something that isn't their fault?" And it undercuts the implication in the Bible that homosexuality, again, was a choice, not an inherited condition. It makes it possible for gay activists to say, "God made me this way, but he must be evil to then condemn me for it".

There is no doubt that the "born gay" concept is high-explosive weaponry, impacting on a range of different fronts.

As slogans go, it is simple, easily understood – even by young schoolchildren – and leaves no room for further debate. Which is why this same slogan now appears throughout the Western world in school health and sexual education literature. In the space of 23 years, an entire generation has been brainwashed into accepting this "fact" just as readily as the fact that the Earth is round.

To reinforce it, researchers (again, some of them gay), have set out to "prove" some kind of genetic reason for homosexuality. They have failed to find one, and leaving aside the problems in specifically identifying a hereditary cause for homosexuality, there are some very logical reasons as to why this is unlikely as well. According to that other icon in the liberal bible, Evolutionary theory, species evolve according to their reproductive capabilities. Survival comes down to who can produce offspring. So how exactly does a gene for genuine homosexuality survive in the human gene pool? Why didn't it disappear thousands of years ago? Even without "survival of the fittest" thrown in, it still seems to me impossible that an "inherited" condition can be passed on via people who, by and large, don't have kids.

So logic, combined with the failure of science to actually find an inheritable cause for homosexuality, rules out natural genetics: people are not, in a natural way, born gay.

But what about genetic damage? What about some kind of environmental factor that may affect babies *in utero* and mess with their hormones at a crucial stage of fetal or even post-natal development?

On this score, there is indeed some supportive evidence. It is possible that in humankind's rush for progress we have created chemicals and pollution that are harming us and our unborn children – even the children we haven't even conceived yet. Dioxin is one such chemical, best known as a by-product of the Agent Orange herbicide used in the Vietnam War which was then repacked commercially as a scrub dessicant for farms and rural areas. Exposure to dioxins during pregnancy has lead to babies being born without brains, as well as strange tumours and other defects.

Other chemicals, estrogen compounds that are similar to the female hormone, have been found in scientific studies to cause sexual defects and a change in sexual orientation of animals like seagulls and fish that are exposed to them. These estrogen compounds can also be found in agricultural products, which may explain some of the mystery about so-called gay behaviour in sheep. Similar compounds are found in soy milk and products like tofu. The science on this is not yet conclusive in regards to the effects on humans, but a baby boy fed soy infant formula receives five times the estrogen dose contained in the contraceptive pill.

Is it possible that human scientific error has caused an apparent upsurge in "gayness" during the 20th century? The evidence suggests there might (and I do stress *might*) be an arguable case.

Gay activists don't like this line of research. While they're desperate for a genetic cause to emerge, they want it to be natural for the reasons outlined at the top of this chapter, not the result of toxic pollution causing genetic damage.

So, for example, when I first wrote a glancing reference to the estrogenic pollution debate in *Investigate*, gay activists immediately pounced from the woodwork to label me a "gay soy conspiracy theorist", in the true fascist fashion of playing the man, not the ball.

The reason for their opposition to the idea, it turns out, is simple. Homosexuality caused by environmental, man-made toxins, lets God off the hook and by definition re-classifies gays as "victims", rather than proud flag-bearers of a historic natural legacy.

But even if we allow for genetic damage as a cause for those people who genuinely believe and have always felt gay, there are still a much larger number of gay men and women for whom homosexuality is indeed a choice, even if they're not prepared to admit it to themselves.

I suspected as much back in 1984 when I discussed these kinds of issues with my gay housemates. One of them, now prominent in the New Zealand AIDS Foundation, explained how he had always felt gay and the idea of sleeping with a woman was as abhorrent to him as sleeping with a man would be to me. He said he simply could not get aroused by women, end of story. Yet, a few weeks later, after working closely with an attractive network television news reporter on an environmental documentary, he confessed to me that he was attracted to her.

"I'll tell you," he confided, "if any woman could make me heterosexual, Janet* (not her real name) would be the one."

He had formed an emotional connection with Janet, you see, after working on the story for two weeks, and it was the emotional connection that opened him up to viewing her in a different light.

Ironically, he couldn't act on it even if he had wanted to give up the gay lifestyle, as Janet was already in a long term relationship, but it underscored for me – living in that house – a growing suspicion that the gay lifestyle was more about conquering your own sexual inhibitions as part of an addiction to sex, rather than a genuine boy-meets-boy romantic story as it has been latterly portrayed.

Independent surveys have shown that very few "gay" people have only had gay sex – a stunning 91% of gay men and 96% of lesbian women have grazed in the neighbouring paddock at some point in their lives. Gay propagandists Marshall Kirk and Hunter Madsen, whose book *After the Ball* laid out an agenda to brainwash heterosexuals into accepting the whole gay rights package, advised gay groups to continually push the "born gay" slogan, even if they *knew* it wasn't true.

"We argue that, for all practical purposes, gays should be considered to have been born gay, even though sexual orientation, for most humans, seems to be the product of a complex interaction between innate pre-dispositions and environmental factors during childhood and early adolescence."

Environmental factors? I thought you could only talk about that under pain of being labeled a "conspiracy theorist"?

Kirk and Madsen clarify their thinking:

"To suggest *in public* [my emphasis] that homosexuality might be chosen, is to open the can of worms labeled 'moral choices and sin' and give the religious intransigents a stick to beat us with. Straights must be taught that it is as natural for some persons to be homosexual as it is to be heterosexual: wickedness and seduction have nothing to do with it."

In other words, 'maintain the party line at all costs, and keep those dumb straights fooled'.

Kirk and Madsen have given you a clue, but what are some of the other leading lights in gay ideology really saying about homosexuality in their own magazines and professional journals? Take lesbian academic Dr Lillian Faderman, who won the Monette/Horwitz Award from the gay Lambda Literary Foundation. She, like Kirk and Madsen, sees it as imperative to their political struggle for "rights" to continue pushing the public line that sexual preference is built in from birth. But she clearly doesn't believe it herself and says as much:

"I must confess that I am both elated and terrified by the possibilities of 'a bisexual moment'," she told the *Advocate* gay magazine in 1995.[74] "I'm elated because *I truly believe that bisexuality is the natural human condition* [my emphasis]. But I'm much less happy when I think of the possibility of huge numbers of homosexuals (two thirds of women who identify as lesbian, for example) running off to explore the heterosexual side of their bisexual potential and, as a result, decimating our political ranks.

"The concept of gay and lesbian identity may be nothing but a social construct, but it has been crucial, enabling us to become a political movement and demand the rights that are due to us as a minority."

According to Dr Faderman, everything you've heard about gays and lesbians being born that way is nothing more than "a social construct" used as a Trojan Horse to get special recognition of their sexual choices. Her next paragraph is especially telling:

"What becomes of our political movement if we openly acknowledge that sexuality is flexible and fluid, that gay and lesbian does not signify 'a people' but rather 'a sometime behaviour'?"

There are no gay and lesbian people, Dr Faderman is saying, just people who behave that way by choice. "Bisexuality", she says, is the real innate human sexual preference if you can just break down your inhibitions enough.

"And we continue to demand Rights," she says, "ignoring the fact that human sexuality is fluid and flexible, acting as though we are all stuck in our category forever…The narrow categories of identity politics are obviously deceptive."

Nor is Faderman singing that song alone. Dr John de Cecco (pronounced

---

74   *The Advocate*, 9-5-95, p43

Check-o) is a gay psychologist, the Director of the Centre for Research and Education in Sexuality at San Francisco State University, and also the editor of the *Journal of Homosexuality*. He's also written a book entitled, *If You Seduce A Straight Person Can You Make Them Gay?* The answer inside the book is an unequivocal "Yes!"

De Cecco writes of studies by himself and other experts in human sexuality, which proved conclusively that there was such variability in people's lives that the "born gay" idea was a myth. As one book reviewer noted:

> "ONE SUCH MAN who was carefully studied, identified by the code name "D," had heterosexual feelings, fantasies, dreams and sex until age 27 at which time he experimented sexually with a gay man. By four years later, his behavior, feelings, fantasies and dreams were almost exclusively homosexual."[75]
>
> The scientific conclusion reached for such evidence, he said, "…shows that life-long, exclusive homosexuality, as articulated by gay rhetoric, is more a statement about the culture in which it occurs than the 'essence' of homosexuality."

All of which sort of shoots down that other "big lie", that socializing extensively with gay people cannot make you gay. Clearly, according to Dr De Cecco and others, if your inhibitions are lowered enough, you can become "gay" or bisexual.

And if you can choose to be gay, you can equally choose not to be gay or – to couch it in politically-correct liberal-speak – explore your bisexual side, which brings you right back to the religious doctrine of choosing good rather than evil. It would be naïve and grossly insensitive of me to suggest, however, that "choosing" to be straight can occur with a snap of the fingers as if it is no big deal. Sexuality patterns should be treated like an addiction.

This continuum of sexuality could explain why some ex-gays later return to homosexual behaviour – having already imprinted their brains to be attracted by members of the same sex, that arousal pathway may always exist *if* they choose to act on it. Choice, however, remains the operative word.

Other gay academics agree with De Cecco. In her book *Queer by Choice*, lesbian Dr Vera Whisman laments, "The political dangers of a choice discourse go beyond the simple (if controversial) notion that some people genuinely choose their homosexuality. Indeed, my conclusions question some of the fundamental basis upon which the gay and lesbian rights movement has been built. If we cannot make political claims

---

75   *If You Seduce A Straight Person Can You Make Them Gay?*, ed. By Dr. John De Cecco; New York: Harrington Park Press, 1993, pgs. 129-130

based on an essential and shared nature, are we not left once again as individual deviants? Without an essentialist (born that way) foundation, do we [even] have a viable politics?"

"I don't think lesbians are born…I think they are made," says lesbian writer Jennie Ruby in *Off Our Backs*. "The gay rights movement has (for many good practical reasons) adopted largely an identity politics."

Intriguingly, the first long term study[76] of the children of lesbian mothers shows exactly this. Thirty nine children in 27 lesbian families were assessed in a study published in early 1999, which also used a control group of heterosexual families to measure against. The study was hailed by gay marriage and gay adoption advocates as proof that children were at no greater risk of becoming homosexual just because they were raised in lesbian families.

At least, that's what the news headlines around the world trumpeted. But if you read the fine print of the study, you see that simply isn't true. A staggering 15% of the children raised in lesbian families had gone on to have a same sex relationship, compared with *none* of the children raised by heterosexuals. Most of the kids did not identify exclusively as homosexual – hence the headlines proclaiming "no differences" – but in fact they were bisexual. And if homosexuality is, in fact, a lifestyle choice as many gay academics and researchers now claim, then growing up in a gay household clearly influenced these children to experiment with gay sexual behaviour.

Additionally, the study noted even more of the children "from lesbian family backgrounds stated that they had previously considered, or thought it a future possibility, that they might experience same-gender attraction or have a same-gender sexual relationship or both."

So despite what gay activists will tell you via a compliant news media, there is in fact good evidence that growing up in a gay household dramatically increases your risk of venturing into gay sexual behaviour. Leave aside the moral argument, because the more stunning outcome from the study is that it again underlines homosexuality as being a choice, not something you are born with. After all, why would 15% of children in lesbian households enter same sex relationships, when the real proportion of apparently exclusive homosexuality in the community is less than one percent?

Examples of lesbians by choice include actress Anne Heche, star of the recent TV series *Men in Trees*, who left her husband to become the live-in partner of Ellen DeGeneres, then four years later dropped DeGeneres in favour of a new husband. Then there's also this sad case in the American

76   "Do Parents Influence the Sexual Orientation of Their Children? Findings from a Longitudinal Study of Lesbian Families" by Susan Golombok, Ph.D., and Fiona Tasker, Ph.D. in Developmental Psychology, Vol.32, 1999, No. 1, pp 3-11.

state of Utah, which again serves as another good reason to be very wary of gay adoption. In it, the biological mother of the child says she is no longer gay and doesn't want her daughter associating with her former "life partner":[77]

> IN A RULING HANDED DOWN on Friday the Utah Supreme Court denied visitation 'rights' to a non biological 'parent'. Former lesbian and mother of the child, Cheryl Pike Barlow, did not want her ex partner, Keri Lynne Jones to see the girl.
>
> Issuing a split decision in the case of a 5-year-old girl conceived in the context of a lesbian relationship, the justices said Keri Lynne Jones does not have the right to seek visitation with the child - even though Jones and her former partner decided to have her together, raised her together for a time, and gave her both of their surnames.
>
> The girl's biological mother, Cheryl Pike Barlow, says she is no longer gay and doesn't want Jones, who was joined to her in a Vermont civil union, to see the girl.
>
> Jones - who had been traveling to Texas for visitation every other weekend until Barlow refused to allow it last year - said Friday she is devastated.

As *Investigate* magazine's blogsite, TBR.cc reported, "In the context of the American constitutional system with its three branches of Government this ruling is interesting because of the reasoning behind this decision: "Recognizing a "new class of parents" would "overstep" the bounds of the courts and invade the territory of lawmakers, said the majority of the high court Friday. The *in loco parentis* relationship can be terminated by biological parents like Barlow, they said. However Chief Justice Christine M. Durham dissented, saying the case should be treated like a typical divorce where two parents are quarreling over child custody and visitation. The ultimate issue, Durham said, is what is in the best interest of the girl. *As the nontraditional family becomes more prevalent*, (emphasis added) more children will form parent-child relationships with adults who have no biological or legal connection to them, she said. The child "ought to be protected from losing a relationship with someone who is, as far as the child is concerned, a parent," Durham wrote.

But the evidence in this chapter challenges the very foundations of Chief Justice Durham's assumptions. If these "nontraditional" families are artificially constructed by choice, fluid and unstable by nature and not the result of genuine exclusive sexual attraction, then why should we recognize any artificially defined family?

---

77   http://briefingroom.typepad.com/the_briefing_room/2007/02/utah_ruling_on_.html

In her book, *Apples and Oranges,* lesbian writer Jan Clausen is another who lashes out at the "born gay" propaganda message fooling heterosexuals worldwide.

"What's got to stop is the rigging of history to make the 'either/or' look permanent and universal. I understand why this argument may sound erotic to outsiders for whom the public assertion of a coherent, unchanging lesbian or gay identity has proved an indispensable tactic in the battle against homophobic persecution."

I touched on this aspect in a nationwide radio debate this year with New Zealand actor and talk host Oliver Driver – who in his spare time (purely as an item of interesting trivia) is also the voice of Jenji in the TV series *Power Rangers.* Driver was strongly of the view that gays were gays, straights were straights, and gays should not be persecuted for being born that way. "It's about rights," he explained to me.

But is it? Really? If gays genuinely are not "born that way", but are simply sexually uninhibited, then it's a lifestyle choice, and he's really saying that a gay lifestyle choice is just as valid in parenting terms as a heterosexual nuclear family lifestyle choice. Yet Driver has already publicly conceded in the last chapter that the promiscuous gay lifestyle is no place for children.

The problem is, I tried to reinforce, it isn't about the technicality of whether one is "gay" or not (which in my view is a personal matter between the individual and their Maker), it is really about the associated lifestyle that goes with it. Driver is a genuine, intelligent and compassionate social liberal and, like most Gen-Xers, assumes that gay relationships mirror heterosexual ones. "I have many gay friends, and the only difference between them and anyone else is that they're gay".

But is it that simple, or is that simply the message Gen-X has been conditioned to accept? You'll recall Kirk and Madsen's PR pitch was designed to foster reactions exactly like Driver's:

"Gays must be cast as victims in need of protection so that straights will be inclined by reflex to assume the role of protector."

On the other hand, what if all these gay academics, researchers and writers are correct, and there is in fact no such entity as a "gay" person, only someone who indulges in "gay" behaviour? Where does that leave the "gay rights" pitch? Are we really asking for rights for *people*, or are we in fact seeking rights for a particular lifestyle choice? Because if it's the latter, if we as a society are really being asked to approve a lifestyle choice and a type of sexual behaviour, then let's get it clear, let's get it on the table and talk about it.

Another well-known media liberal in New Zealand, *Listener* columnist and blogger Russell Brown, takes a similar line to Oliver Driver's, expressing absolute umbrage at what he sees as conservative lies and paranoia designed to "depict gay men as sex-crazed timebombs". Those conservatives who dare to suggest within Brown's hearing that gay men are promiscuous or in any way different from heterosexual males, are described as "gay conspiracy theorists" fit for ridicule in his various blog contributions.

So again, let's put the "they're just like us" liberal myth to the test.

In his 1996 book, *Reviving the Tribe*, gay sociologist Eric Rofes reinforced the need for the gay community to continue seeking pleasure, despite AIDS and despite conservatives. As self-described 'kinky' journalist Benjamin Shepard describes it, Rofes was railing "against those who suggested gay men should just 'grow up' and reject public sexual culture."

"Even a cursory look at the histories of our movement," says Rofes, "will show that sexual liberation has been inextricably bound together with gay liberation, the women's movement, and the emancipation of youth."

There's that reference again: "emancipation of youth", similar to NAMBLA's "child emancipation" goal. Rofes makes it very clear that the gay agenda IS the Left's agenda: "We believe continuing work on sexual liberation is crucial to social justice efforts."

But it is elsewhere in *Reviving the Tribe* that Rofes describes the lusts driving the average gay man when he wrote his book in the late 1990s. ***Be warned, the following excerpt is sexually explicit, but relevant:***

> [M]Y EYES TOOK A MOMENT to adjust. I was in a large space filled with small wooden cubicles, like cupboards, in which men were apparently expected to kneel and give head. Glory holes were drilled into these closets, and other men came by, hoisted out their dicks, and inserted them into the holes in the cubicles. In another part of the room, men stepped up on a raised platform and other men stood below, eager to suck them off in a standing position.
>
> While there may have been thirty men in the room, none were talking. The only slurps,—sounds were the throb of the music and the sounds of sucking, gagging, coughing, moans of relief . . .. . I moved toward the next room and discovered more cupboards, aligned along an elaborate maze filled with several dozen men moving, glancing, stopping, moving, kneeling, sucking, moving, unzipping . . . . As my eyes adjusted, I recognized more and more people colleagues from political work, neighbors from my apartment building, friends from the gym. Everyone seemed plugged into the same intense energy and focused oral sex — on the same thing.
>
> I remained at Blow Buddies until three in the morning. During that time, I gave head to three different men. Seven men sucked my dick. I did not witness a single condom in use

during oral sex. I did not encounter a single man who refused to participate in unprotected oral sex, and four of the men who sucked me asked me to reach orgasm in their mouths. Of the men I sucked, one came in my mouth.

I left Blow Buddies that evening sexually satisfied, and happy with the ability of gay men to create environments which encourage men to enjoy a lot of sex.

If the only difference between those men and Oliver Driver, Russell Brown or even John Kerry is that "they're gay", I'll roll on the floor laughing and you can pick me up some time in 2012, because it'll take that long for me to get over it.

In case any of you are tempted to listen to spin suggesting times have changed and so have gays since the 90s, here's what Eric Rofes wrote in 2005:[78]

"RECENTLY I ATTENDED A DANCE PARTY, one of the many evenings of intense music and cavorting available to thousands of gay men in my city each weekend. I looked over the crowd of primarily twenty-something and thirty-something men, shirtless, gyrating, arms reaching to the heavens. I thought immediately at how the doomsayers criticize this population of young gay men, saying things such as, "I didn't work my ass off during the past 30 years to create a culture of drug use and unprotected sex and self-centered me-me-me attitudes. This is not what the gay movement was all about...."

And then I realized something, something surprising and simple. As someone who has spent the last 30 years working on gay liberation and AIDS activism and sexual liberation, what I saw before me was precisely the world I was trying to create. When we fought during the 1980s and 1990s to prevent gay men's sexual cultures from being destroyed, when we worked to preserve certain values about gender play, friendship, and erotic desire, when we quietly worked behind the scenes to ensure that certain spaces would survive gentrification and public health crackdowns, we were fighting to preserve the ability of new generations of gay men to create worlds of pleasure and desire.

As I looked out over the sea of dancing men, I realized, despite all the battles we've lost in terms of politics and discourse and the media, gay men and gay sexual cultures had managed to survive and, indeed, thrive."

---

78   http://www.tobe.ca/tobe/content.jsp?sid=14237876811649850556196125422&ctid=1000
338&cnid=1000851

And once again the politically incorrect question that no one wants to ask: Are gay men really born with an attraction to men in exactly the same way heterosexuals are attracted to each other? Or are they simply addicted to sex – a recognized psychological disorder?

In the late 1980s, New York University sociologist Dr David Greenberg wrote a massive book, *The Construction of Homosexuality*, published by the University of Chicago Press. It was 635 pages long, and is said to be the most comprehensive, "extensive and thorough" study of homosexuality throughout history ever undertaken. There are a couple of significant things. Firstly, Greenberg is a social liberal, and undertook the study in order to make people more tolerant of homosexuality. However, his study was controversial. Gay rights groups had been hoping Greenberg would put his academic seal of approval on the "born gay" myth. Instead, the overwhelming conclusion of his study is that homosexuality is a lifestyle choice, and always has been. Greenberg is adamant that words like "gay" and "lesbian", used to describe a genuine exclusive sexual orientation, are simply a convenient and totally inaccurate label.

The facts, he points out, are these: from his research into ancient cultures, virtually every culture studied reveals extensive bisexual behaviour right throughout their communities. If you study the ancient religions, he says, virtually all involve gods having sex with humans, and many worship rituals reflected these sexual acts. Here's a selection of what Greenberg found:[79]

EGYPTIAN CULTURE BELIEVED that "homosexual intercourse with a god was auspicious." Having anal intercourse with a god was the sign of a man's mastery over fear of the god. Thus one Egyptian coffin text reads, "Atum [a god] has no power over me, for I copulate between his buttocks." In another coffin text, the deceased person vows, "I will swallow for myself the phallus of [the god] Re."

Greece: Homosexuality was not only a conspicuous feature of life in ancient Greece, it was exalted. The seduction of young boys by older men was expected and honored. Those who could afford, in time and money, to seduce young boys, did so. Graphic pictures of man-boy sex (pederasty) adorn countless Greek vases.

"Sexual intimacy between men was widespread throughout ancient Greek civilization. … What was accepted and practiced among the leading citizens was bisexuality; a man was expected to sire a large number of offspring and to head a family while

---

79   http://vesler.blogspot.com/2006/04/why-judaism-rejected-homos_114634268752564895.html

engaging a male lover. ... The male homosexual act usually involved anal intercourse with a boy."

"The interchangeability of boys and women was widely taken for granted."

But the culture most appreciated boys: "Athenus, for example, remarked that Alexander the Great was indifferent to women but passionate for males. In Euripides' play 'The Cyclops,' Cyclops proclaims, 'I prefer boys to girls.' Plato never married. The philosopher Bion (third century B.C.) advised against marriage and restricted his attention to his (male) pupils. The stoic philosopher Zeno ... was also known for his exclusive interest in boys." And "Plato makes clear in 'Symposium' that it was perfectly acceptable to court a lad, and admirable to win him."

As Greenberg writes, "The Greeks assumed that ordinarily sexual choices were not mutually exclusive, but rather that people were generally capable of responding erotically to beauty in both sexes. Often they could and did."

"Sparta, too, institutionalized homosexual relations between mature men and adolescent boys." In Sparta, homosexuality "seems to have been universal among male citizens."

Rome: Polybius, the Greek historian who visited Rome in the second century CBE, wrote that most young men had male lovers. And Greenberg notes that "Many of the leading figures in Roman literary life in the late Republic – Catullus, Tibullus, Vergil and Horance – wrote homophile poetry." In addition, "male prostitution flourished throughout Italy."

The emperor Trajan was known for his love of boys; his successor, Hadrian, put up sculptures of his male lover and Commodus "kept a little boy, naked except for jewelry, and often slept with him." Tatian, a Christian who lived in Rome in the second century, wrote that the Romans "consider pederasty [Man-boy sex] to be particularly privileged and try to round up herds of boys like herds of grazing mares."

Greenberg's thesis is extensive and highly respected, and argues strongly that bisexuality is the normative human condition and was so in all ancient cultures, except one, which we'll come to shortly. Oh, and by the way: David Greenberg is gay.

Although Greenberg knew his study would be used to undermine the claims of the gay rights movement that people were born gay, he stated his belief that he "had an obligation to the truth".

In a major review of Greenberg's work, Chicago University's Don Browning writes:[80]

> FROM [GREENBERG'S] PERSPECTIVE, the idea of a static homosexual orientation or essence simply does not hold up against the huge variety of homosexual, bisexual and heterosexual patterns. Not only does Greenberg cover Western societies, but he is constantly making excursions to China, Japan and South America as well. Everywhere he finds significant variations in the prevalence of homosexuality, depending on the social logics of different societies. At one point he indulges in a thought-experiment with reference to certain New Guinea tribes where ritual homosexual practices with young boys are normative:
>
> "It is reasonable to suppose that if a bunch of Melanesian infants were to be transported in infancy to the United States and adopted few would seek out the pederastic relationships into which they are inducted in New Guinea, or take younger homosexual partners when they reach maturity. Similarly, American children raised in New Guinea would accommodate themselves to the Melanesian practices."
>
> Greenberg is aware of the comfort that essentialist theories of homosexuality have given the gay and lesbian movements:
>
> "When heterosexual chauvinists have told homosexuals to change, essentialist theories have provided a ready response: I can't. When parents have sought to bar homosexual teachers from the classroom lest their children (horror of horrors) become homosexual, essentialist theories have provided a seemingly authoritative basis for denying the possibility."
>
> In response to these concerns, Greenberg says: "The present study is concerned only with scientific concerns and cannot make concessions to such opportunistic considerations. It should be pointed out, though, that nothing in the social-constructivist position legitimates the denial of rights. Assertive gay liberationists have argued that it may be strategically wiser to concede the possibility that a few students might be influenced to become gay by having an openly gay teacher as a role model, and to say, 'So what?' "
>
> It is clear that this is a stance that Greenberg endorses. In the nooks and crannies of Greenberg's huge study one can discern this outlook: homosexual and bisexual behavior probably is spreading to larger portions of the society.

The implications of that last statement are huge. People are not born gay, they are made gay, and the "making" is done by exposure to the gay lifestyle and gay worldview. So if New Zealand and American schools are selling the myth that "you can't catch homosexuality", yet gay researchers are saying, "yes you can!", don't parents have a right to decide how much their children are exposed to? And shouldn't schools and the Ministry of Education be ordered to cease and desist such indoctrination by stealth? This is something I'll tackle in the next chapter, but I'm flagging it now so you can mull it over.

Intriguingly, Chicago University's Browning highlights in his review how mainstream liberal churches have fallen hook line and sinker for the "born gay" myth.

> NEARLY ALL OFFICIAL STATEMENTS on homosexuality by these churches in recent years have adopted some version of the essentialist view of homosexuality. It is interesting to think how this has happened in view of the fact that there are articulate intellectuals in both the gay and lesbian communities who have published views similar to Greenberg's.
>
> Gay author Dennis Altman has denied the essentialist view and declared that the homosexual movement is a direct continuation of the counterculture's move toward a freer and more inclusive bisexuality (a position similar to the one held by Foucault). This is true, he argues, whether or not individual gays and lesbians recognize it in their own experience. And for some years, certain feminist lesbians have characterized their lesbianism as a political act rather than an orientation. In spite of these testimonies, the churches have for the most part bought variations of the essentialist view put forth by the modern medical and mental health disciplines.

There is one final point Professor Browning concludes with, and it is highly relevant to the current debate. He warns that Greenberg's analysis confirms evangelical Christians' deepest fears:

> "[THAT] HOMOSEXUALITY CAN GROW, and the church's stance against it is essential if the [gay activist] movement is to be contained. Mainline denominations will be thrown into a state of confusion possibly more profound than the one that now besets them.
>
> "Accepting Greenberg's thesis might suggest that the new tolerance of these churches, especially the move toward the ordination of homosexuals, is one more way *modern societies*

help create, not just liberate, individuals with gay and lesbian tendencies." [emphasis added]

Now *that* statement is political dynamite. It flies in the face of everything you and your children are being taught in schools, and in Human Rights and anti-discrimination literature. Yet if true, it means that across the western world gay activist groups have so successfully captured the political system that they are effectively legislating to indoctrinate kids into the gay lifestyle. They are changing the way you think, they are breaking down thousands of years of inhibitions, and they are creating a climate where bisexuality will again be considered the norm, and where the ordinary family will struggle to survive in a sea of hostility and peer pressure to conform.

Many in the heterosexual community would be more tolerant if gays chose to live by the social rules that govern heterosexual families. After all, the central gay activist message has been "we're just like you". If that's true, then monogamy for one should be monogamy for the other. But if in fact that message has been a smokescreen designed simply to hide an ongoing pattern of behaviour that is negative in terms of health, mental health and bringing up children, surely we should be rethinking exactly what it is we've been asked to tolerate. People are already legally free to indulge in pretty much whatever they like in their own homes and society groups, but when those same people demand access to children, surely somebody somewhere has to ask the question: is this the best thing for the child?

American Jewish commentator and talk host Dennis Prager's fascinating analysis of Greenberg's research is worth returning to, for some wider context. Of male lust, he writes:[81]

> HUMAN SEXUALITY, ESPECIALLY male sexuality, is polymorphous, or utterly wild (far more so than animal sexuality). Men have had sex with women and with men; with little girls and young boys; with a single partner and in large groups; with total strangers and immediate family members; and with a variety of domesticated animals.
>
> They have achieved orgasm with inanimate objects such as leather, shoes, and other pieces of clothing, through urinating and defecating on each other (interested readers can see a photograph of the former at select art museums exhibiting the works of the photographer Robert Mapplethorpe); by dressing in women's garments; by watching other human beings being tortured; by fondling children of either sex; by listening to a

81   http://www.orthodoxytoday.org/articles2/PragerHomosexuality.shtml

woman's disembodied voice (e.g., "phone sex"); and, of course, by looking at pictures of bodies or parts of bodies.

There is little, animate or inanimate, that has not excited some men to orgasm. Of course, not all of these practices have been condoned by societies — parent-child incest and seducing another's man's wife have rarely been countenanced — but many have, and all illustrate what the unchanneled, or in Freudian terms, the "un-sublimated," sex drive can lead to.

Prager argues, persuasively, that a highly destructively-sexed society is heading to spiritual doom on a number of levels. Alone among all the ancient cultures, he says, only Judaism forbade homosexual or adulterous behaviour.

AMONG THE CONSEQUENCES of the unchanneled sex drive is the sexualization of everything — including religion. Unless the sex drive is appropriately harnessed (not squelched — which leads to its own destructive consequences), higher religion could not have developed. Thus, the first thing Judaism did was to de-sexualize God: "In the beginning God created the heavens and the earth" by his will, not through any sexual behavior.

This was an utterly radical break with all other religions, and it alone changed human history. The gods of virtually all [other] civilizations engaged in sexual relations. In the Near East, the Babylonian god Ishtar seduced a man, Gilgamesh, the Babylonian hero. In Egyptian religion, the god Osiris had sexual relations with his sister, the goddess Isis, and she conceived the god Horus. In Canaan, El, the chief god, had sex with Asherah. In Hindu belief, the god Krishna was sexually active, having had many wives and pursuing Radha; the god Samba, son of Krishna, seduced mortal women and men. In Greek beliefs, Zeus married Hera, chased women, abducted the beautiful young male, Ganymede, and masturbated at other times; Poseidon married Amphitrite, pursued Demeter, and raped Tantalus. In Rome, the gods sexually pursued both men and women.

Just as an aside, many of these ancient religions had "temple prostitutes" – men, women and children – who worshippers were required to have sex with as part of the worship, in mimicry of the acts of the "gods". The practice was common as recently as 1948 in Hindu temples in India where female and child prostitutes were available. It was outlawed that year.

It is worth contemplating, for a moment, what Greenberg discovered about Aztec society:

> AMONG THE AZTECS, "Sodomy was virtually universal, involving even children as young as six. Cortez also found sodomy to be widespread among the Aztecs, and admonished them to give it up – along with human sacrifice and cannibalism. One of the Aztec gods, Xochipili, was the patron of male homosexuality and male prostitution."

If you wanted a more recent example of the kind of cultures the Jews waged war against when they entered ancient Israel, the Aztecs would be it. A society where human sacrificial victims, some of them children and babies, were sliced open whilst alive and their hearts torn out. The Spanish explorer Cortez wiped out the Aztecs, and is blasted by modern liberal historians and educationists for trying to impose his Catholic beliefs on native cultures. Implicit in such an accusation, however, is the idea that we should "tolerate" the kind of society described above by Greenberg. Is that where we are now heading – that all kinds of genuine evil should now be "tolerated"?

Prager is aware of the argument from some gay activists that while the Bible prescribed the death penalty for homosexuality, it also decreed the same for collecting wood on the Sabbath, therefore neither penalty can be taken seriously any longer. Prager argues the comparison is not valid, because the Bible reserved its strongest possible language for sexual sin, calling it "an abomination", comparable to the similarly described child sacrifice.

Greenberg appears to draw a similar conclusion:

> "WHEN THE WORD TOEVAH ("abomination") does appear in the Hebrew Bible, it is sometimes applied to idolatry, cult prostitution, magic, or divination, and is sometimes used more generally. It *always* conveys great repugnance".

One could argue that modern society's return to pagan sexual practices, and the huge rise in "child sacrifice" in terms of the millions of abortions performed every year, are an unavoidable consequence of the attack on Judeo-Christian values, and the drop in religious faith in the West. If the original state of humankind was depravity, says Prager, we're sinking back into it:

> IT IS JUDAISM'S SEXUAL MORALITY, not homosexuality, that historically has been deviant. Moreover, the Bible lists homosexuality together with child sacrifice among the

"abominations" practiced by the peoples living in the land about to be conquered by the Jews. The two are certainly not morally equatable, but they both characterized a morally primitive world that Judaism set out to destroy. They both characterized a way of life opposite to the one that God demanded of Jews (and even of non-Jew — homosexuality is among the sexual offenses that constitute one of the "seven laws of the children of Noah" that Judaism holds all people must observe). Finally, the Bible adds a unique threat to the Jews if they engage in homosexuality and the other offenses of the Canaanites: "You will be vomited out of the land" just as the non-Jews who practise these things were vomited out of the land. Again, as Greenberg notes, this threat "suggests that the offenses were considered serious indeed."

Such God-decreed penalties and threats would only make sense if being "gay" really is a choice. Think about it: if God really is good, by definition, then how could he condemn people if they were born gay and it was outside the individual's control? But God's opposition to sexual sin makes far more sense once you realize how widespread pedophilia, bestiality and bisexuality were in virtually every ancient culture outside of Judaism. If homosexuality is not so much a statement of "gayness" as a statement of pagan opposition to the Judeo-Christian God - in effect, Man giving God a defiant gesture - then the religious stand-off over homosexuality starts to make sense on a good-vs-evil spiritual level.

Over the past decade, although the debates have rarely if ever made it into the mainstream media thanks to what critics call "the Gay Elite's stranglehold" on publicity, there has been a growing realisation among homosexuals that they can indeed "swing both ways", that uninhibited bisexuality may in fact be the true nature of "gay".

"No wonder lesbians are so nervous," says an article in the May/June 1996 issue of *Girlfriends*, a lesbian magazine in the US. "What makes the lesbian movement strong is the formation of a collective identity, unified behind sexual orientation as a category. If bisexuality undoes that, it kicks the lesbian movement where it really hurts: in the heart and soul of identity politics."

As if to prove the point, soon after that article was published, a major story broke in gay media about JoAnne Loulan, a lesbian psychotherapist on the board of the American Psychiatric Association. The APA had earlier removed homosexuality from its list of mental illnesses after heavy lobbying from The National Centre for Lesbian Rights which argued homosexuality was "innate and unchangeable".

So JoAnne Loulan was a lesbian heavy-hitter. Yet in the February 18, 1997 edition of *The Advocate* gay magazine, she scandalized the gay rights movement with a report that she'd altered her sexual orientation and fallen in love with a man!

Yet in the mainstream media, in the wake of the 1998 murder of Matthew Shepard, NBC's then *Today* show host Katie Couric was able to ask this loaded question of Wyoming Governor Jim Geiringer:

"Some gay rights activists have said that some conservative political organizations like the Christian Coalition, the Family Research Council and Focus on the Family are contributing to this anti-homosexual atmosphere by having an ad campaign saying if you are homosexual you can change your orientation…do you believe that such groups are contributing to this climate?"

Hello? The lights are on but no one is home! How is it that mainstream media can sneer at the idea of changing sexual orientation, at the same time as gay media are reporting that gays are choosing to go straight?

Are we re-living the Mad Hatter's Teaparty? This is where the myths and lies that Kirk and Madsen urged gay activists to promote, regardless of the truth, get dangerous. Because gay activists are telling mainstream media one thing, encouraging journalists to scorn anyone who suggests being gay is a choice, whilst discussing exactly the opposite in their own media.

Commentator Ryan Sorba, interjecting in an online debate[82] on "gay marriage" late last year, got stuck into the hypocrisy of The National Centre for Lesbian Rights.

"Kate Kendall, the actual director of this dishonest organization, who hooted and hollered that sexual orientation was fixed, innate and unchangeable, and commanded the American Psychiatric Association to halt all forms of homoerotic and homosexual reparative therapies for people looking to get help, actually wrote an article for *Frontiers* magazine arguing that sexual orientation is fluid, not fixed!!."[83]

Sorba was angry at the activists who, he said, "had the nerve to go to the American Psychiatric Association and deceptively argue that homosexual reparative therapy was the dangerous equivalent of pouring bleach on a dark person's skin to try and make them lighter…[then] after the fact, one of these 'lesbians' went right out and changed their own sexual orientation, and the other wrote an article that sexuality is changeable!"

At first blush, some people might look at all this and say, "so what, they're bisexual, what's the difference?" Well, for one thing, bisexual is not "gay" – bisexual is uninhibited. If you can swing both ways, you can definitely choose which way you'll swing or how often you swing. I lost count, during the debate over civil unions, of the number of times I saw breathless newspaper

82   www.campusprogress.org/features/1162/infighting-gay-marriage
83   *Frontiers*, 4-19-96, pg31

and TV stories about "gay" men and women who'd only "discovered" they were "gay" after 25 years of marriage and raising four kids! None in the media dared call them what they really were: bisexual.

The other difference is this: using a lie – "we're born gay" – to shut down heterosexual public discussion is one thing, but using that lie to shut down avenues of psychological help and hope for other gay people who don't feel comfortable with their feelings - using a lie to shut them down and force them to conform to the lie – in my opinion that's cruel. Very cruel.

After all, how many men and women remain trapped in gay relationships because they themselves have been brainwashed to believe it is a life sentence, when secretly they wish they could settle down, have kids and a normal life like everyone else?

As you've seen in this chapter, and in the linked article references if you read them, there appears to genuinely be no such thing as a gay person, there is only someone who practices gay behaviour as part of their total sexual repertoire.

If these same people had lived in ancient Greece, Rome, Egypt or among the Aztecs, they would know that they were bisexual, not homosexual and that they could, if they chose, focus on opposite sex attraction. If the very term "Gay" – used to suggest exclusive same sex attraction – is in fact a carefully orchestrated lie created by the gay movement's political wing to give themselves a sense of group identity, then how many millions of gay men and women are themselves victims of the big lie?

Instead, to dull the pain within, they throw themselves further into the abyss of drugs and meaningless sex whilst proclaiming loudly – more to convince themselves than anyone else – how happy they are.

Worse, according to one lesbian activist, some seek to deaden their pain by taking it out on innocent, vulnerable children, as you'll soon see.

10

The War Against Parents
Give Me a Child & I'll Give You the Man

"Propaganda and education prepared the way…It is the absolute right of the State to supervise the formation of public opinion."
Josef Goebbels, Nazi Minister of Propaganda

If you're looking for a canary down the mineshaft when it comes to the lunacy of political correctness indoctrination, look no further than the smallest member of the Anglosphere, Middle Earth, home of the *Lord of the Rings* movies, a.k.a. New Zealand. Unlike America's melting pot migrants, New Zealand's European settlers were almost exclusively the lower middle classes of Victorian England whose superiors, through some admittedly dodgy dealings, managed to steal a lot of land and authority away from the far more numerous native Maori population.

I promise you, there is no more tragic sight in the world than a bunch of guilt-ridden hobbits, which is pretty much what we'd become by the late sixties when a resurgent Maori sovereignty movement, spurred by events in the United States with black Americans, began to stridently challenge Anglocentric cultural assumptions.

Loading that baggage on top of New Zealand's involvement in the Vietnam War, the hippie/drug counterculture that arose alongside, and the growing sport of bra-burning, hairy armpits and "liberation for women", and you end up with a heady mix of fuel to throw on the fire.

The protesting students of the sixties became the schoolteachers of the early seventies, became the school principals of the 1980s and the head honchos of the education system in the 90s. They quickly identified, very early on, that targeting the children was the secret to controlling the future.

Francis Xavier, a 16th century monk and founder of the controversial Jesuit Order of the Roman Catholic Church, coined a phrase that hauntingly echoes down the centuries: "Give me a child until he is seven, and I will give you the man".

The premise of the statement is that a child's formative years, and the information he receives during that time, define how that child will later view the world.

Socialists and the wider Left have long recognized the power of re-programming youth. Which is why in New Zealand, for example, there is a huge push to get a compulsory government-approved early childhood curricula into all pre-school and daycare facilities, even those privately owned.

Should parents be worried? I touched on it earlier in the book, but it needs repeating: The Nazis set up a state education system with precisely this concept of indoctrination in mind, as the Nuremberg trials were told:[84]

> "THE FIRST STEPS TAKEN in making the German schools the tools of the Nazi education system were two decrees in May 1934, whereby the Reich Ministry of Education was established and the control of education by local authorities was replaced by the absolute authority of the Reich in all educational matters. These decrees are set out in documents 2078-PS, 2088-PS, 2992-PS. Thereafter, the curricula and organisation of the German schools and universities were modified by a series of decrees in order to make these schools effective instruments for the teaching of Nazi doctrines."

In modern New Zealand, teacher training is centralised at state facilities, and the influence and policies of the major left-wing teacher unions are significant. Back at Nuremberg, this homogenisation of teachers was also a factor in the rise of Nazism:[85]

> "ALL TEACHERS WERE REQUIRED to belong to the National Socialist Teachers' League, which Organisation was charged with the training of all teachers in the theories and doctrines of the N.S.D.A.P. [Nazi Party]"

That was then. This is now: In his seminal work *Worlds Colliding*, on the clash between our conservative heartland and the permissive worldview pushed by liberal governments in the West, Dr Rex Ahdar of Otago University's Law Faculty writes of the major philosophical divide that separates the liberal State from traditional family values. To illustrate that chasm, he quotes liberal educationist John White.

White, an Emeritus Professor in the Philosophy of Education, whose work

---

84   http://www.nizkor.org/hweb/imt/tgmwc/tgmwc-01/tgmwc-01-04-01.html
85   ibid

is at the core of education systems in the West, argues stridently that parents should *not* be allowed to shape a child's values, they should simply deliver their child as a blank moral canvas to school, where appropriate values can be instilled by *teachers*:

> "If the parent has an obligation to bring up his child as a morally autonomous person," claims White, "he cannot at the same time have the right to indoctrinate him with any beliefs whatsoever, since some beliefs may contradict those on which his educational endeavour should be based.
>
> "It is hard to see, for instance, how a desire for one's child's moral autonomy is compatible with the attempt to make him into a good Christian, Muslim or orthodox Jew…The unavoidable implication seems to be that *parents should not be left with this freedom to indoctrinate*." [my emphasis]

The sheer, unadulterated atheistic *arrogance* is actually hard to comprehend. Since when have parents ever had "an obligation to bring up [a] child as a morally autonomous person"? When was that particular law passed? It hasn't been, of course, but that's the way the Left works, the end – creating a brainwashed socialist child – justifies the means – riding roughshod over the rights of parents regardless of the law.

This is the ideal that state education systems in the West are working towards – not just a ban on religion or values in public or in public schools, but *no religion or values at home either.*

Commenting on this, and similar comments from other liberal educationists, Rex Ahdar suggests the State is now trying to position itself as the de-facto parent to children:

"Notice how there is a direct relationship between the State and the child. The child is a 'creature of the State'. Parents are to the side, and perform a purely facilitative role in fostering future citizens."

This new form of Liberalism, with the State as the supreme arbiter of societal values, is exploding into play throughout the West. English law Lord, Oliver of Aylmerton, reflected these new values in a 1988 judgement:

> "Whatever the position of the parent may be as a matter of law – and it matters not whether he or she is described as having a 'right' in law or a 'claim' by the law of nature or as a matter of common sense – it is perfectly clear that any 'right' vested in him or her must yield to the dictates of the welfare of the child [as determined by the State]."

The US Supreme Court has taken a similar position on the power of the State to decide what is best for children. Arguably, however, it is the United Nations Convention on the Rights of the Child that has become the globalist Trojan Horse on this issue, as *New American* magazine's William Grigg reports:[86]

> BEFORE THE ADVENT OF THE UN, it was understood that treaties were intended to regulate how sovereign nations interact, rather than alter the domestic institutions of a given nation. UN "human rights" treaties are designed to restructure the legal and political systems of signatory nations. The UN's "children's rights" treaty is even more radical since it claims power to regulate relationships within the home.
>
> In an address to the 1997 Second World Congress on Family Law and the Rights of Children and Youth in San Francisco, East Timorese Nobel Peace Prize Laureate Dr. Jose Ramos-Horta explained that the Convention "challenges the dichotomy between the privacy of the family and the public domain of the State and its instrumentalities. The Convention disaggregates the rights of children from the rights of families and constitutes children as independent actors - with respect to both parents and with respect to the State."
>
> Simply put, the Convention fundamentally assumes that the state, not the parents, is the primary custodian of children. "The state is the custodian of the rights of children," declared acting UNICEF director Dr. Richard Jolley at the 1995 UN Social Summit in Copenhagen. "The state is the guardian of the law. Who but the state can enforce the law and protect the rights of individuals, including children?"
>
> If the state is the primary protector of children, it follows that parents are the greatest and most constant threat to the well-being of the state's children. This point was made forcefully in a presentation at the 2001 Special Session on Children at UN headquarters. During a video presentation at that session, a Salvadoran youngster declared: "Parents are the principal violators of our rights!"

Those rights basically treat children as autonomous adults with virtually the same rights as adults; the freedoms in Article 13 of the Convention, for example, to "seek, receive and impart information and ideas of all kinds".

"Strictly applied," reports Grigg, "Article 13 of the Convention would permit

86   Reprinted online at http://www.getusout.org/artman/publish/article_92.shtml

a national government to censor a child's access to 'anti-government' websites, yet authorize action against a parent refusing to let a youngster download cyberporn.

"Article 14 asserts that the child's "freedom of thought, conscience and religion" must be recognized, which - as applied in the home - has troubling implications for parents desiring to pass their religious convictions on to their young (or, for that matter, for parents seeking to discourage involvement in the occult).

"Article 15 refers to a child's right to "freedom of association and to freedom of peaceful assembly" - freedoms that diligent parents concerned about the quality of a child's friends and associates must occasionally infringe upon.

"Parents who practice spanking and other forms of physical discipline run afoul of Article 19, which supposedly protects children from 'all forms of physical or mental violence, injury or abuse....' UNICEF's Dr. Jolley, asked about whether the Convention forbids spanking, replied: 'There are some people, I think, that want to maintain the right of being able to *beat* [emphasis added] their children, which the Convention discourages.'

"Following Britain's ratification of the Convention, reported the January 28, 1995 issue of *The Guardian* of London, the UN's 'children's rights' committee demanded that the British government 'ban corporal punishment in private schools' and outlaw 'chastisement' of children at home," says Grigg.

Sound familiar? New Zealand Green MP Sue Bradford's anti-smacking bill, backed by Labour, is virtually a cut and paste from the United Nations. Is it really about "smacking", or is the real intention what Jose Ramos Horta warned us about – a left wing agenda to smash the nuclear family by progressively introducing new laws in favour of state control of children?

When you look at that thesis, and then look at the social revolution of the sixties and seventies in the West, it is hard to escape the pawprints of Marx and an explicit agenda to adopt communist ideas of child-rearing. Radical feminism in 1973, for example, was drawing up a long term agenda of its own with a series of check-box items in the to-do column.

At a major women's conference in New Zealand that year, the Soviet-backed Socialist Action League mobilised amongst the disaffected women, finding fertile ground with young feminists.[87] These women then drafted an action plan which included infiltrating the left-wing Labour Party in order to influence future policy direction.

This was perhaps one of their most successful moves, resulting in massive social engineering policy on both occasions that Labour has been in government since then.

---

87   http://www.investigatemagazine.com/pdf's/new%20women.pdf

Their primary target was the nuclear family - mum, dad and the kids:

"TODAY, THE NUCLEAR FAMILY unit remains as the base economic cell of class society...the family also serves to perpetuate capitalist rule by inculcating in children the values of the private-property system. Obedience to authority is first learned in the family. With its thrust against the family institution, the women's liberation movement is profoundly revolutionary."

The women's demands also included these gems:

•Abortion to be free and on demand
•Sex education and birth control 'integrated into the education system at all levels' and readily accessible through 'government-financed clincs'
•An end to coercive family laws
•De facto marriage should be considered to have the same status, legally and socially, as marriage by legal contract.
•"The rearing, social welfare and education of children should become the responsibility of society, rather than individual parents...All laws enforcing individual ownership of children should be abolished."
•"All discrimination against homosexual men and women should be outlawed...laws should be repealed."
•"All laws victimizing prostitutes should be abolished".
•"Paid maternity leave of 12 weeks ...should be made available."
•"The government should provide the finance for free child care centres, open to all children from early infancy for 24 hours a day."

Only someone who is brain-dead in New Zealand could fail to notice that all but one of those demands has been met, and that many of the feminists at that 1973 women's conference are now running the country. They may not be as strident about Marxism's economic policies, but the social policies are a complete rip and read from the Politburo. The nascent Marxism of the early 1970s Marxism now holds power in a real, barely veiled sense.

Compare it with Leon Trotsky's affirmation of communist policy in Soviet Russia:[88]

"THE FATHER CAN NO LONGER merely point with his hand to the icon and reinforce this gesture with a slap on the face. The parents must retort to spiritual weapons. The children who base themselves on the official authority of the school show

88   http://www.marxists.org/archive/trotsky/works/1932/1932-family.htm

themselves, however, to be the better armed. The injured amour propre of the parent often turns against the state. This usually happens in those families which are hostile to the new regime in its fundamental tasks. *The majority of proletarian parents reconcile themselves to the loss of part of their parental authority the more readily as the state takes over the greater part of their parental cares.*" [emphasis added]

In other words, as the new smacking ban and a range of other anti-family laws are introduced, parents should "lie back and think of Moscow".

Interestingly, and probably not coincidentally, when Canada ratified the UN Convention, a lobby group calling itself the Foundation for Children, Youth and the Law emerged from the woodwork to mount legal challenges to parental smacking through the Canadian Courts. The legal challenge was underwritten by the Court Challenges Programme, which Grigg reports is "directed by a board of radical human rights activists. One member of that board is Shelagh Day, who headed the 'lesbian caucus' at the 1995 UN World Conference on Women in Beijing."

Even more intriguingly, and again not a coincidence, the Foundation for Children, Youth and the Law successfully lobbied to get the age of sexual consent in Canada lowered to 14 years old. So smacking is "harmful" to children says the Foundation, but a bit of "how's yer father" involving your 14 year old daughter and a 50 year old man is perfectly OK?

This too, was something being promoted back by radical feminism in 1973. Much as they hated men, they hated family units even more, and pushed for policies that would encourage sexual promiscuity - recognising that this in itself would tempt and destroy marriages, and discredit marriage in general:[89]

> "[THE FAMILY] MOULDS the behaviour and character structure of children from infancy and throughout adolescence, disciplining them and teaching submission to established authority. The family represses sexuality, discouraging all sexual activity which is not within marriage.
>
> "Our goal must be to create economic and social institutions that are superior to the present family institution."

Gay and transgendered rights groups have also signaled in conferences in the US that the UN Convention on the Rights of the Child is a "powerful" weapon for gays in their outreach to youth. Of particular note, says the National Centre for Lesbian Rights, are Article 28 with its right to educate,

---

89   http://www.investigatemagazine.com/pdf's/new%20women.pdf

and the right to privacy in Article 16, which can be used, says the NCLR to make schools withhold information about children from their parents. The NCLR has boasted how it used the UN Convention in a successful court case that allowed a "lesbian" teenager to divorce her mother and be "adopted" by a lesbian couple in San Francisco.

As *Investigate* magazine reported in October 2005,[90] a New Zealand girl, statutorily raped by older men at the age of 14 in a public park, was subsequently removed from the care of her parents by the state and encouraged to begin legal proceedings to "divorce" her conservative parents because they had dared to lay a police complaint against the men responsible for sex with a child. The girl's state school cited 'privacy' issues in refusing to even divulge so much as a school report to her parents. The child was placed on an "independent youth" taxpayer-funded benefit, and given government legal aid for her divorce hearings.

New Zealand is a signatory to the United Nations Convention on the Rights Of the Child – the intriguingly-named 'UNCROC' – and what a crock it is. Every couple of years the New Zealand Government is required to report to UNCROC on progress being made implementing United Nations policy in this country.

The full text of UNCROC is proudly displayed on the Child, Youth and Family website[91] of the New Zealand government, and a couple of clauses are worth a closer look:

> **Article 2(2).**
> STATES PARTIES SHALL take all appropriate measures to ensure that the child is protected against all forms of discrimination or punishment on the basis of the status, activities, expressed opinions, or beliefs of the child's parents, legal guardians, or family members.

Expressed one way, this could mean a child should not be discriminated against or punished because of what her parents believe. Expressed another way, if lawyers were to take a child-centric focus, one could argue the child, a citizen of the state, should be protected from her family's belief systems and values if the state doesn't like them. Given the nature of the document, this is the most likely long-term interpretation.

> **Article 3**
> 1. IN ALL ACTIONS concerning children, whether undertaken

---

90   http://www.thebriefingroom.com/archives/2006/03/investigate_oct.html
91   http://www.cyf.govt.nz/432.htm

by public or private social welfare institutions, courts of law, administrative authorities or legislative bodies, the best interests of the child shall be a primary consideration.

2. States Parties undertake to ensure the child such protection and care as is necessary for his or her well-being, taking into account the rights and duties of his or her parents, legal guardians, or other individuals legally responsible for him or her, and, to this end, shall take all appropriate legislative and administrative measures.

It is Article 3 of the UNCROC document that requires governments to begin making traditional parental rights subservient to what the UN calls "the best interests of the child". Again, it is left up to individual states and their courts how and when they exercise these new powers, but a recent UNCROC report on New Zealand, dated June 2003, notes at paragraph 272:

"NEW ZEALAND CONTINUES to affirm the principle of the best interests of the child. However, submissions [to UNCROC] raised concerns that the 'best interests of the child' concept is not driving policy. It is anticipated that developing the Children's Policy and Research Agenda will help to address this.
"Under the Guardianship Act 1968 the welfare of the child must always be the first and paramount consideration in guardianship, custody and access matters. However, while the Act clearly states that the welfare of the child must be the first and paramount consideration, much of the Act focuses on the custody and access rights of the parents.
"The current law relating to custody, access and guardianship is under review," noted UNCROC, "and will consider whether there should be a greater emphasis on children's rights (rather than the rights of parents)."

The "review" UNCROC talked of subsequently materialised and passed into law through the New Zealand Parliament as the highly-controversial Care of Children Act, which removed the supremacy of biological parents and made them equivalent to de-facto partners, gay or straight. The Act also endorsed, with the personal support of New Zealand Prime Minister Helen Clark, the 'right' of a ten year old girl to be given an abortion without her parents' knowledge, let alone consent. This, despite public opinion polls showing 76% of citizens were strongly opposed to this usurpation of parental authority.

As will be noted elsewhere in the book, abortion is a serious surgical procedure with complications that can last a woman's entire life. Under New Zealand law a medic cannot even offer a teaspoon of paracetamol without written parental consent, yet the Government has taken upon itself the right to rip a child from a womb without telling parents.

Unlike the United States, which has to some extent resisted the social engineering "orders" from the United Nations, New Zealand has been eager in most cases to sign up – its leaders and bureaucrats flattered by the attention and the concept of globalism that the UN espouses.

As I've said elsewhere in this book, dangerous ideas don't arise in a vacuum. They have a backstory, a trail you can follow until you reach its genesis. Like so many of the ideas we're tracking here, UNCROC orginates in Marxism, and specifically Marx and Engels' *Communist Manifesto*, published in 1848. In it, the pair argue for the "abolition of the family", claiming children were being exploited by natural families and should instead regard the State as mother and father.

"Do you charge us with wanting to stop the exploitation of children by their parents?" challenged the communists. "To this charge, we plead guilty."

This, incidentally, was the same Karl Marx who coined the phrase, "The road to Hell is paved with good intentions." It is probably fair to say he genuinely believed his ideas were the key to an ideal new world. But his good intentions were misguided.

Marx realized, very early on, that busting the family up and giving all children a free education courtesy of the State was the key to the future of communism:

> "BUT, YOU SAY, WE DESTROY the most hallowed of relations, when we replace home education by social. And your education! Is not that also social, and determined by the social conditions under which you educate, by the intervention direct or indirect, of society, by means of schools, etc.? The Communists have not intended the intervention of society in education; they do but seek to alter the character of that intervention, and to rescue education from the influence of the ruling class."

On the Marxist achievement scorecard you can tick the box that says "Free state education". Not content with re-educating your kids with politically-correct State propaganda, Marx boasted of breaking down the idea of marriage, in favour of open "free love".

BOURGEOIS MARRIAGE IS, in reality, a system of wives in common and thus, at the most, what the Communists might possibly be reproached with is that they desire to introduce, in substitution for a hypocritically concealed, an openly legalized system of free love.

On the Marxist scorecard, busting families through extreme sexualisation of the culture can also be ticked as "achieved". National loyalties would be crushed, he said, as re-educated citizens of the world came to see themselves owing allegiance to one world unifying force.

NATIONAL DIFFERENCES AND ANTAGONISM between peoples are daily more and more vanishing, owing to the development of the bourgeoisie, to freedom of commerce, to the world market, to uniformity in the mode of production and in the conditions of life corresponding thereto. The supremacy of the proletariat will cause them to vanish still faster. United action of the leading civilized countries at least is one of the first conditions for the emancipation of the proletariat.

United Nations and its various conventions, anyone? Tick that box as well. Marxism may never have been formally adopted by any government in the West, but it dominates the universities, the intellectual circles and the teacher training colleges. The writing is on the wall or, as Hunter S. Thompson might say, "the hog is in the tunnel".

Is it ever! Personally, I blame the conservatives. For some reason that I can't quite put my finger on, conservative politicians go to sleep when they get elected to government. They get comfortable in the big fat armchairs and the languid limousine rides, and they forget why they are there. They almost never unwind socialist policies, preferring to manage "the status quo", and they almost never tackle the intelligentsia working against them by cradle-snatching future voters in primary schools. Traditionally, left wing governments install their cronies in positions of power, while conservatives install their cronies in positions of riches. And when conservatives get elected, they generally ignore the rot in the public service and the education system. Like termites eating away at the foundations of a house, generations of Marxist educators have successfully brainwashed our children into swallowing a little bit more of the poison each year.

Consider this for a moment. On the TV news we frequently see parents portrayed in a very bad light, and usually the TV news doesn't tell us whether the parents are genuinely married, or de-facto, or simply a mother with a new boyfriend. And regardless of whether you like Christians or not, when was the last time you saw a positive media portrayal of Christians? We are told, repeatedly by various Government ministers and bureaucrats that collectively our parenting skills are appalling and that the State must step in.

Now read this quote from Marxist revolutionary leader Leon Trotsky, in a 1937 essay on attempts to smash the family in the Soviet Union:[92]

> "WHILE THE HOPE STILL LIVED of concentrating the education of the new generations in the hands of the state, the government was not only unconcerned about supporting the authority of the "elders", and, in particular of the mother and father, but on the contrary tried its best to separate the children from the family, in order thus to protect them from the traditions of a stagnant mode of life. Only a little while ago, in the course of the first five-year plan, the schools and the Communist Youth were using children for the exposure, shaming and in general "re-educating" of their drunken fathers or religious mothers - with what success is another question. At any rate, this method meant a shaking of parental authority to its very foundations."

Trotsky was a huge fan of destroying the family, and believed that the then Soviet leader Josef Stalin had not gone far enough. Worse, argued Trotsky, Stalin was also slacking off in smashing the church, just when he should have hammered home the death blow:

> "THE DENIAL OF GOD, his assistance and his miracles, was the sharpest wedge of all those which the revolutionary power drove between children and parents."

Now, again, you may not agree with religion, but when you view quotes like that it is impossible not to see there is a Marxist agenda permeating Western popular culture today with all the subtlety of a fumescent skunk.

We have, in the West, a groundswell of citizens, 99% of whom would not identify with or think of themselves as Marxists, yet when you examine what they believe, one or more of their core principles is a foundation principle of communism. It is the educational equivalent of "Stockholm Syndrome", where hostages eventually come to adopt the ideals and beliefs of their captors, without really realizing it.

I should add, lest someone takes offence, that we're not talking about some grand conspiracy here involving the average schoolteacher. Although the younger teachers have gone through indoctrination, they are blind to much

92   http://www.marxists.org/archive/trotsky/works/1936-rev/ch07.htm

of it and forced to teach the curriculum they get handed. Die hard socialist change agents, as a rule, don't linger at the coal face, they prefer to serve their careers in the engine rooms of state, in the policy areas of various government agencies. They may comprise only two percent of the education system, but if they're the two percent who happen to run 80% of the Ministry of Education, then they have power regardless of their numbers.

" The Marxist Position:

"The first, primary grade should not last longer than three or four years, and in addition to imparting the first "instrumental" notions of schooling – reading, writing, sums, geography, history – ought in particular to deal with an aspect of education that is now neglected – i.e. with "rights and duties", with the first notions of the State and society as primordial elements of a new conception of the world which challenges the conceptions that are imparted by the various traditional social environments."
– Communist philosopher Antonio Gramsci, 1949 "

11

Garbage In, Garbage Out
The Globalist Indoctrination

"Anyone who knows anything of history knows that great social changes are impossible without feminine upheaval. Social progress can be measured exactly by the social position of the fair sex, the ugly ones included."
Karl Marx

The idea of a transnational world body uniting the nations was a Marxist one. We now, of course, have it and the NZ education curriculum requires compulsory lessons about it. Globalisation, and the overarching supremacy of the United Nations, are strongly emphasised as key points of the education policy:[93]

"STUDENTS WILL DEVELOP understandings of international organisations and global issues that affect New Zealand, of the roles and responsibilities that New Zealanders have within such international organisations as the United Nations."

To reach this endgoal, the policy spells out: "There are five perspectives that are integral to a balanced programme in social studies…bicultural perspectives; multicultural perspectives; gender perspectives; perspectives on current issues; and perspectives on the future."

Under "Values Exploration", the policy sets out how students will be led to the answers the Government wants them to find:[94]

"STUDENTS WILL BE CHALLENGED to think clearly and critically about human behaviour, and to explore different values and

---

93   http://www.tki.org.nz/r/socialscience/curriculum/settings_e.php
94   http://www.tki.org.nz/r/governance/nzcf/ess_learning_e.php

viewpoints. Such learning will help them to clarify their own values and to make informed judgments. Commonly held values, such as concern for social justice and the welfare of others, acceptance of cultural diversity, and respect for the environment will be fostered ...

"Values Exploration usually begins with students identifying and explaining a range of values positions in relation to a concept or issue. By identifying and explaining these values positions, students can critique particular viewpoints and reflect on their own position, re-evaluating it in the light of their findings.

"When students explore values, they are challenged to think about the nature of social justice, the welfare of others, acceptance of cultural diversity, and respect for the environment. They come to recognise that people's values are formed by many influences and that they may change over time. Throughout the process of Values Exploration, students will reflect upon and evaluate their thinking and their findings."

It is clear from the curriculum document that social studies is little more than paint by numbers, using only the colour "red". If you have children in a state school in New Zealand, this is what they are being taught. Their minds are being washed clean and refitted with a secular humanist worldview.

As part of their compulsory studies, primary school pupils will be directed to a website called "Monumental Stories" which contains the biographies of famous and important New Zealand women. Among the women whose lives they'll study are Prime Minister Helen Clark, Governor-General Dame Sylvia Cartwright, Chief Justice Sian Elias, former Labour Governor-General Dame Catherine Tizard, and Labour trade unionist Sonja Davies.

❝ The Marxist Position:
"The Soviet State...openly supports [atheist] propaganda against religious belief.
It is precisely this situation which the Church interprets as religious persecution."
– Leon Trotsky, Soviet revolutionary, 1934 ❞

" **The Nazi Position:**
Hitler Youth syllabus,
Fourth Year, compulsory study:
"Adolf Hitler and his Comrades"
- *Horst Wessel*
- *Herbert Norkus*
- *Rudolf Hess*
- *Hermann Göring*
- *Our Reich Youth Leader*
- *Adolf Hitler*   **"**

As part of their values exploration requirements, ten year olds will be taught the central values of the Confucian religion. The website listed as a teaching resource for the module, the "School of Metaphysics", is an occult website based on New Age and Gnostic teachings,[95] and the specific page recommended for New Zealand schools tells ten year olds that:[96]

> "CONFUCIANISM...DOES NOT RELY on an image of the supernatural. For many common people, an image of the Buddha, or God, is to help them restrain themselves. The Buddha watches over you to see what you do. In so doing, this idea creates a society which is more peaceful, less violent, doing more good things for the common good and less things for the individual greed.
>
> "But if you already know all that, there is no Buddha or God. There is nobody looking over your head. Confucius says that if you can understand the real meaning of society, the people-to-people relationship, you don't need all that.
>
> "The common good is embodied in Confucius' sayings."

The New Zealand Social Studies Curriculum, in its classroom resource kit for this module, tells students to immerse themselves in Confucian values, and states: "Is Confucianism a religion? Confucianism is often called a religion, but it is really a code of behaviour. It tells people how they should act towards each other".

---

95   http://www.som.org/
96   http://www.som.org/8interfaith/confucius.htm

Confucianism, drifting as it does into the meaning of life and denying, as it does, that God exists, is little more than the religion of secular humanism in an earlier time. A religion which all New Zealand school pupils are expected to *compulsorily* spend *three weeks* learning as part of the State's preparation for them to become contributing members of society.

Interestingly, the Education Ministry defines this process as "socialisation – the modification from infancy of an individual's behaviour to conform with the demands of society."

The students will go on to study in a positive way other religions such as Hinduism and Islam – in fact, the Hindu module requires them to make cards and ornaments honouring and praying to a Hindu god. By contrast, when they come to learn about Christianity the syllabus largely confines discussion to the corruption of the Catholic Church in the Middle Ages:

"The Catholic Church was the only church in Europe during the Middle Ages, and it had its own laws and large coffers," begins one study text. "Bishops, who were often wealthy and came from noble families, ruled over groups of parishes called 'diocese'."

In a module called "Turrets and Treachery", students are asked "What were some of the rules that medieval monks and nuns lived by? How important was the church in these times? How did it help the people or did the people help them?"

Little wonder, perhaps, that kids emerge from our schools with the view that Eastern religions are wise and moral, while Christianity is corrupt and ultimately about lining the pockets of the church hierarchy.

And something else to ponder: this religious segment is the supposedly "impartial" way of teaching children about diverse religions. Do you think those courses above were impartial? Would you trust the Ministry of Education to educate your kids?

" The Marxist Position:

"Give me four years to teach the children and the seed I have sown will never be uprooted. Give us the child for 8 years and it will be a Bolshevik forever"
- Vladimir Lenin, first Soviet dictator, c1920   "

In light of New Zealand's UN-ordered responsibilities to accept refugees, there is a four week study on the horrors that refugees face and how they need a welcoming new country to live in. This module falls under the Multicultural; Gender and Current Issues requirements.

Remember, all of the Social Studies curriculum is compulsory.

As 13 and 14 year olds, students will get to transpose their annual lessons on the Treaty of Waitangi against the effects of colonisation on Native Americans and Australia's "Stolen Generation" Aborigines. "How was the West won and who precisely was it won from?," records the syllabus on the US module, while the Australian module addresses the need for a "National Sorry Day" in Australia and "calls for the Government to apologise formally to the Aboriginal community."

From what we could ascertain, these two units were the only direct exposure students will get to the US and Australia, leaving a largely negative taste in their mouths.

To make up for it, schoolchildren will be required to study the "Sunshine Sisters" – New Zealand's suffragette movement. "We want men to stand out of our sunshine," is the voice echoing from the past, in one class resource. Naturally, this module falls under "Gender issues".

More stand-out NZ women are under the spotlight later in the year, Princess Te Puea and another suffragette, Kate Sheppard. Just in case students feel they're having Labour Party wimmins committee policy rammed down their throats, another social studies module reminds them how fortunate they are, by comparing the Government of Helen Clark quite favourably to that of Cambodian despot Pol Pot – the man responsible for the killing fields.

Discrimination suffered by Chinese goldminers back in the nineteenth century forms a massive part of the Social Studies Curricula – details of Helen Clark's apology to the Chinese community are read out, and the class will spend *ten weeks* exploring the racist treatment dealt out to the Chinese in New Zealand, Australia and the United States.

China, which still bases its social policy on Marxism, gets huge positive attention whilst children are taught that New Zealand's two closest allies, the US and Australia, are evil. Little wonder that anti-Americanism is on the rise.

Under the heading "Values Exploration", children are required to recognise "xenophobia" for what it is, and recognise the "consequences of people holding differing values positions about allowing Chinese citizenship rights." They are also required to "consider possible social action that could be taken to address social issues such as racism, bullying and discrimination."

Later, the values they are taught in this module will be reinforced with regard to "the current immigration debate".

Traditional socialist views of big business are reinforced to 14 year olds in their "Greenies versus Greedies" study module.

"Conservationists and environmental groups tend to see large multinational or transnational organisations as the greedies of the world, exploiting resources and ripping off indigenous peoples," begins the class briefing, which then directs pupils to the website of McSpotlight, which targets some of these international pirates. While the curriculum does provide for students to go to the corporate websites of some of the targeted companies, like BP, there's no guarantee that they'll find any response to the McSpotlight claims there.

If they take social studies after the age of 15, students will return to the McDonalds issue to examine the "McDonaldisation" of industry, allegedly driving down wage rates and trapping young people in repetitive mindless roles.

The older students are also encouraged to become Treaty of Waitangi protestors, in a module entitled "We Protest!", and to beware of "institutional racism". Again, little wonder so many high school students join protest marches.

OK, by now you probably get the picture. A complete breakdown of the Social Studies Curriculum can be found on the website, www.tki.org.nz. But what is abundantly clear is that educationists are no longer content to train kids *how* to think, they're telling them *what* to think.

In Britain this year, there is growing outrage over plans by the Labour government to implement recommendations from the Joint Committee on Human Rights (JCHR) that will make it a *crime* for Christian church schools to teach students that sex outside of heterosexual marriage is a sin:[97]

> "WE DO NOT CONSIDER that the right to freedom of conscience and religion requires the school curriculum to be exempted from the scope of the sexual orientation regulations.
> "In our view the Regulations prohibiting sexual orientation discrimination should clearly apply to the curriculum, so that homosexual pupils are not subjected to teaching, as part of the religious education or other curriculum, that their sexual orientation is sinful or morally wrong."

Church schools will be required by law to teach that gay marriage is a positive and valid expression of sexuality and family, and that gay adoption is equally valid.

The idea that Christian schools can be forbidden from teaching the Christian faith by a secular government is a prime example of the State trying to flex its muscles and influence the beliefs of citizens. As you'd recall from our earlier chapter on Church/State separation, this also flies in the face of US President Thomas Jefferson's belief that the State has no right to interfere in the beliefs of citizens, and no power under the US Constitution's Wall of Separation clause to dictate to churches.

The Joint Committee on Human Rights tries to argue that its proposed regulations will still allow church schools to make the bland statement that some religions believe homosexuality is wrong, but church schools will be forbidden by law from suggesting such a position is objectively true:

> "IN OUR VIEW THERE is an important difference between this factual information being imparted in a descriptive way as part of a wide-ranging syllabus about different religions, and a curriculum which teaches a particular religion's doctrinal beliefs as if they were objectively true. The latter is likely to lead to unjustifiable discrimination against homosexual pupils."

So now governments believe they alone have the power to dictate what is "objectively true" and what is not. Again, that is one of the most dangerous threats to democracy to emerge so far this millennium.

The JCHR report declares as "objectively true" this "fact":

> "SEXUAL ORIENTATION, race and sex… are inherent characteristics."

Oh really? You cannot truly change your gender or your race, so those two categories are indeed "inherent" to an individual. But "sexual orientation", based on studies and reports by leading gay academics and scientists, is indeed chosen, not inherent, as you saw in the earlier chapters.

Can you now see how dangerous it has been for Western civilization to allow the "big lie" to circulate in the name of "tolerance"? What began as a gesture of tolerance by the heterosexual community has turned into draconian laws to force you to believe the lie, with criminal penalties if you do not. We gave them an inch, now they're taking our freedom away.

And at its very core, the battle is being fought over children. The British government doesn't really care what parents or adults believe, but it cares deeply about what the next generation will believe, which is why it is making these changes to the school curriculum compulsory.

The JCHR is also behind the British government's attack on Catholic adoption agencies, forcing them to provide babies to gay "couples" wanting to adopt. The Church has indicated it will refuse to handle *any* adoptions, rather than deliver children into gay households, based on what we now know of the gay lifestyle.

Prominent Anglican theologian Tom Wright was among the first to point out the hypocrisy of the Tony Blair government's moves on both fronts:[98]

> This completely fails to take into account the views and beliefs of all those involved. The idea that New Labour - which has got every second thing wrong and is backtracking on extended drinking hours, is in a mess over this cash-for-peerages business, cannot keep all its prisons under control - the idea that New Labour can come up with a new morality which it forces on the Catholic Church after 2,000 years - I am sorry - this is amazing arrogance on the part of the Government.
>
> Legislation for a nouveau morality is deeply unwise. That is not how morality works. At a time when the Government is foundering with so many of its policies - and I haven't even mentioned Iraq - the thought that this Government has the moral credibility to be able tell the Roman Catholic Church how to order one area of its episcopal teaching is frankly laughable. When you think about it like that, it is quite extraordinary.

Yet, again, these things are not happening in a vacuum, nor is Britain alone. Similar moves are afoot in New Zealand, as you're about to read.

12

Track And Trace
Big Sister Comes Calling

"We don't need no education / We dont need no thought control
No dark sarcasm in the classroom/Teachers leave them kids alone
Hey! Teachers! Leave them kids alone!/All in all it's just
Another brick in the wall."
Pink Floyd, Brick In The Wall Part 2, 1979

t's not just education. Marxist ideology dominates social services agencies, in the same way it dominates sociology as a field. Back in the eighties when I worked as a Cabinet press secretary, the theory of political manipulation was simple: manufacture a "crisis" of some kind, whip the public into a fervour with various scare stories, then offer a "solution" and become their saviour.

Now step back and look at the big picture for a moment. Marxists destroy the social fabric of the West, creating family breakdown, rising crime and all the other ills befalling us. Then they offer up "solutions" that we would once have run a million miles from but we're now so conditioned and battered by the "crisis" that we'd sell our souls to the Devil himself just to end the pressure.

One such "solution" is rising up in New Zealand even now, such as the plan by Children's Commissioner, Cindy Kiro, to set up monitoring and state surveillance of every child living in New Zealand. This, she says, is necessary to combat child abuse. But notice how the poison pill is wrapped up in soft, caring language:[99]

"MY VISION IS THAT EVERY CHILD in New Zealand is safe, nurtured, educated, healthy, and has hope for the future," said Dr Kiro. "While we are moving in the right direction with more resources being dedicated to improving the lives and outlook for our children, more needs to be done."

99   http://www.scoop.co.nz/stories/PO0610/S00305.htm

But it's the "more needs to be done" bit you should be worried about. Kiro's plan, outlined just before Christmas 2006, is a state super agency charged with:

> "…MONITORING THE DEVELOPMENT of *every child and young person in New Zealand* [my emphasis] through co-ordinated planned assessment at key life stages and supporting families to make sure children have the opportunity to reach their full potential. The assessments would take into account the whole child: their physical, social, educational, emotional, and psychological development."

The unanswered question in there – measuring the child against whose yardstick? What the parents believe is right for their children, or what the State thinks is best? A clue is in Kiro's next paragraph.

> "ENSURING THAT CHILDREN are safe and nurtured, have the resources to develop to their full potential, and have their views considered in matters that affect them, is a fundamental responsibility of governments and communities."

Notice the phrase, "a fundamental responsibility of governments and communities"? What happened to parents and families? Again, Kiro gives us another clue:

> "THIS ADOPTS A LIFE CYCLE approach, recognising that as children grow there are some key transition times where there is an opportunity to ensure that they have the skills and resources to manage the transition well. Assessment would be at these key life stages. These would include: early childhood focusing on attachment between infant and caregivers and on physical growth and development; primary and secondary school entry focusing on general health, personal identity, school engagement and social wellbeing; and moving to tertiary education or employment and training opportunities and the transition associated with this."

Did you see the word "parents" in there? No. The word the State plans to use is "caregivers", a gender-neutral, biological-relation-neutral piece of Orwellian newspeak designed to subtly recondition people out of thinking about biological parents.

"Individual plans, owned by the child and held by the family, will be developed in partnership with children and families and each child would have a named primary professional responsible for ensuring the child and family have access to services and advice as needed."

How exactly does a child "own" a lifeplan written for them by the government? Why does the family merely "hold" it? Because the Marxists want your children.

Let's stop here for just a moment. Here's how one New Zealand blogger, Liberty Scott, sees it:[100]

> STALIN'S BUREAUCRAT IN WELLINGTON, Dr Cindy Kiro, is persisting with her Orwellian proposal that the state monitor every child from birth religiously to make sure that parents are being good. She has given it a long vapid name (Te Ara Tukutuku Nga Whanaungatanga o Nga Tamariki: Weaving Pathways to Wellbeing) to make it sound so nice and inclusive, instead of "State monitoring of parents and children" which is what it bloody well is.
>
> What if a parent doesn't want a taxpayer funded, state organised plan? How can it be "owned" by the child? What absolute nonsense, the child has no choice and is unable to make these sorts of decisions, which is why it is - a child. The "named primary professional" would for starters want taxpayer funding and, hey, what agency could monitor that? Dr Kiro's one, or one she could help set up (more taxpayer funding). So the state would appoint a Big Brother or Big Sister for your family to "ensure it has access to services and advice as needed". Who decides what is needed? How often do you see this Big Sister? Does she come around uninvited? Does she check you pay your bills? Does she check what food you give the children, what books, TV, internet access is allowed? Does she check what religious/political/ethical beliefs you teach?

And if you are under any illusions that this will be a voluntary thing, forget it:[101]

> "WE NEED TO PLAN AND IMPLEMENT this in a systematic way to ensure that *no child* falls between the cracks. We need to ensure that the services we currently have can work together in a better way. We need to make this investment in resources, structures and systems and in people. We owe it to our children and to our communities."

100   http://libertyscott.blogspot.com/2006/10/big-sister-cindy-stalin-kiro-supported.html
101   http://www.scoop.co.nz/stories/PO0610/S00305.htm

As Liberty Scott says, Kiro and her agency are using the "crisis" of child abuse, which is confined for the most part to a particular section of the community, to impose a "solution" that suddenly entails state surveillance of every single family in the country.

"She talks about 'we' 'investing' in 'resources'," says Liberty Scott, "which means YOU being forced to pay money to keep an eye on other people's kids because of poor parenting...instead of cutting off benefits, law enforcement against abusive parents and teaching parents individual responsibility."

The Children's Commissioner hopes to phase in the whole Big Brother system within ten years, and gives a run-down of how special agents will have access to complete government and, in some cases, private records of all members of a family, held in a giant new database.

> "THE CHILD AND THEIR FAMILY will be integrated through a lead professional, who has responsibility to collate information and co-ordinate service delivery. A common record will include entries from all practitioners involved... Where statutory interventions or specialist intervention [Police or Child Protection agents] are required the integrated service delivery will continue, co-ordinated by a practitioner with statutory or professional responsibility to take the lead professional role.
>
> "For the framework to function effectively, those involved with a child or family will need to have access to information that helps them to make better decisions. A sound information base is essential if we are going to make sure that every child is safe and protected, enjoys the resources to take an active role in society, and understands and enjoys their human rights."

And again, the unanswered question: what kind of data will this Big Brother agency collect on the views, opinions and beliefs of parents, and how will it decide when the State should override the rights of parents?

> "THE CLEAR BENEFITS of sharing integrated information are that each and every social service provider has a clear picture of the child's experiences, strengths and needs, and can more effectively promote that child's rights, best interests and welfare."

Who determines what the child's rights, best interests and welfare are? Marxist sociologists whose ambitions of destroying the traditional family you read of earlier. In place of the traditional family, any number of permutations are being promoted by the state.

Now contrast that official draft policy of the New Zealand government, and compare it with this comment from Soviet writer A Slepkov in the late 1920s:[102]

"BOURGEOIS IDEOLOGISTS think that the family is an eternal, not a transitory organization, that sexual relations are at the basis of the family, that these sexual relations will exist as long as the two sexes, and since man and woman will both live under socialism just as under capitalism, that therefore the existence of the family is inevitable. That is completely incorrect.

"Sexual relations, of course, have existed, exist, and will exist. However, this is in no way connected with the indispensability of the existence of the family. The best historians of culture definitely have established that in primitive times the family did not exist ... together with the overcoming of earlier pre-socialist forms, the family will also die out.

"The family is already setting out on the road to a merging with Socialist Society, to a dissolution into it. An openly negative attitude toward the family under present conditions does not have sufficient grounding, because pre-socialist relationships still exist, the state is still weak, the new social forms (public dining rooms, state rearing of children, and so forth) are as yet little developed, and until then the family cannot be abolished completely.

"However, the coordination of this family with the general organization of Soviet life is the task of every communist, of every Komsomolite [member of Communist Youth League]. One must not shut oneself off in the family, but rather, grow out of the family shell into the new Socialist Society.

"The contemporary Soviet family is the springboard from which we must leap into the future. Always seeking to carry the entire family over into the public organizations, always a more decisive overcoming of the elements of bourgeois family living - that is the difficult, but important task which stands before us.[103]

As *Time* magazine wrote:[104] "In the 1920s the Soviet leadership talked of engaging in social engineering through education and propaganda to transform its feudal subjects into enlightened socialists -- a "Homo sovieticus" who would be compassionate and informed. Instead, these regimes found it easier to control their citizens by reinforcing their worst instincts."

Sounds like "Homo westernus" was "Plan B".

---

102   http://users.cyberone.com.au/myers/mount.html
103   Quoted in H. Kent Geiger, *The Family in Soviet Russia*, Cambridge, Mass., 1968, pp. 44-5
104   *Time* magazine 22/05/89, "Communism confronts its children"

13

You Sexy Thing
It Started With a Kiss

"Prosecutor Mark Rochford told the court Neal organised sex parties and orgies, which were called 'conversion parties', to thus facilitate the infection of people with HIV...to increase the number of men he could have unprotected sex with."
Melbourne Age, March 2007

Like the Marxists, Nazis, Jesuits and McDonalds, gay activists have recognized that getting kids onside through simple sloganeering and emotionally-loaded pitches, is 90% of the battle, and getting heterosexuals to accept lesbian and gay families as "normative" is a huge part of the current gay PR push, following those classic Jesuit teachings. If children can be exposed to these ideas when they're young, they won't resist them when they're older.

Lesbian activist and author Tammy Bruce, a former president of the National Organisation of Women in Los Angeles, pulls no punches in targeting what she calls "the agenda of the Radical Gay Elite." She argues that gay demands have moved way beyond basic "rights".

"For the gay establishment, the death of right and wrong began when gaining civil rights ceased to be enough. As the Gay Elite found Americans willing to tolerate and even accept their divergent lifestyle and point of view, they started exploiting that compassion.

"Thus began the furtherance of a campaign that, although promoted in the name of tolerance, understanding and compassion, has nothing to do with acceptance of homosexuals and everything to do with eliminating the lines of decency and morality across the board.

"Instead of being about tolerance and equal treatment under the law, today's gay movement, in the hands of extremists, now uses the language of rights to demand acceptance of the depraved, the damaged and the malignantly narcissistic."

Among the "depraved" sneaking in as Kirk and Madsen's "camel under the tent", Tammy Bruce counts transsexuals, sado-masochists, and gays seeking to lure children and teenagers into their web.[105]

"The idea of 'transgendered rights' dismays me the most," says Bruce. "I spoke up in many a meeting challenging the idea that those with so-called Gender Identity Disorders (GID) somehow belonged within a gay rights movement. My cautions about this issue were always met with the same dismissal as my warnings about the S&M crowd.

"In my opinion any man who thinks simply having his penis removed, having breast implants, and taking hormones turns him into a woman needs to be in a psychiatrist's office, not in a parade."

Bruce recounts being interviewed once by a transsexual named "Tina" for a radio show, and Tina's opening question was whether the lesbian Bruce would date a transsexual?

"In other words," writes Bruce, "would I, as a gay woman, date a man who had had his body surgically mutilated so he could pretend he was a woman. I was indeed Alice in Wonderland that day!...Nothing could disguise the fact...that Tina was 6 foot 4 and had wrists the size of mangoes. He was a man trapped in a man's body. Nothing a doctor could do to him would ever change that.

"If Tina had thought this up all by himself, I wouldn't bother to write about it here," says Bruce. "But the tragedy of transsexuals rests with the psychiatric and medical communities who participate in the charade by legitimizing 'gender identity' disorders. It also sits squarely with the Gay Elite for creating a cultural environment that makes serious discussion and analysis of psychological problems politically incorrect.

"As we've seen, these problems don't remain personal and private. The [publicity] drive, especially since this issue is associated with the world of 'gay rights', is to make sure your worldview reflects theirs.

"To counter this effort, we must demand that the medical and psychiatric community take off their PC blinders and treat these people responsibly. If we don't, the next thing you know, your child will be taking a 'tolerance' class explaining how 'transsexuality' is just another 'lifestyle choice'."

In 2003, when Tammy Bruce's book *The Death of Right and Wrong* was published, a transsexual doctor was pushing to lower the age of consent for sex changes down to the age of 16. But a news report in Britain's *Telegraph* in January 2007 reveals a German child began sex change treatment two years ago at the age of 12.[106]

Born as a Tim, the boy now goes under the name "Kim" and at 14 is two

---

105   Tammy Bruce, *The Death of Right & Wrong*, Prima, 2003
106   Telegraph.co.uk, "Sex-change child wants operation sooner", 31/01/07

years into hormone treatment cancelling puberty, pending "cosmetic surgery" to remove his genitals at the age of 16.

According to the official story being pushed by Tim and his parents to the psychiatrists who had to approve this, Tim self-identified as a girl at the age of two and played with Barbie dolls. He also enjoyed trying on girl's clothes. If that was the threshold for being castrated then the vast bulk of Gen-X males could be classified as transsexuals trapped in a man's body.

His father told journalists "[we] realized then [at two] it was not just a phase and that the problem was serious. After that, Tim went by 'Kim' at home. He played typical girl games with other girls, went to their birthday parties and even dressed up for the ballet."

Call me cynical, but my experience of two year old boys is that they find it hard to string two words together, let alone articulate a wish to become a transsexual. But according to Tim's liberal German parents they even gave him a piggy bank at the age of *five* so he could begin "saving for the operation".

Who the heck told a five year old boy there even *was* an "operation"?

But pre-pubescent children, whose sexual hormones have not started flowing, don't actually have a sexual identity in the way adults do. Whatever is happening in Tim is happening in his head, not his loins. By commencing hormone treatment to prevent testosterone flowing, his parents and medics are robbing him of the chance to be a fully functional member of society.

Yet the willingness of medics increasingly to consider sex changes for children is testimony, argues Tammy Bruce, of a transsexual "goal...to legitimize your own illness by forcing it onto everyone else, including children."

The idea that children are sexual beings is increasingly gaining momentum. New Zealand's left-wing Labour government toyed with the idea of lowering the age of sexual consent to 12 in certain circumstances, until a public outcry killed it off. Meanwhile in the Netherlands children are being recruited to join Amsterdam's 'Gay Pride' parade as young homosexuals, from the age of eleven![107]

CHILDREN HAVE BEEN the given the go-ahead to participate in Amsterdam's Gay Pride canal parade in the summer.

The gay children will have their own boat with room for 30 gay children, news service NIS reported on Friday.

Gay Pride involves groups of men and women going through the canals in countless boats, often scantily clad.

And with the support of gay rights organisation COC, a 14-year-old boy has taken the initiative to have a boat with homosexual children participate on 4 August.

107   http://www.expatica.com/actual/article.asp?subchannel_id=19&story_id=35686

The minimum age for children to join him is 11.

"From this age, there is already demand among young homo's to have contacts with their peers of the same proclivity," COC said.

Examine that last statement for a moment. By the age of 11, "there is *already* demand among young homo's to have contacts with their peers".

Not just in the Netherlands, either. Gay and Lesbian groups in the US and New Zealand are targeting schoolchildren. One American organization whose resources are used in New Zealand, the Gay, Lesbian and Straight Education Network (GLSEN), pledges in its mission statement to ensure that every primary and secondary school child is made to "accept all people, regardless of sexual orientation or gender identity/expression".

Brainwashing of the young? Got it in one.

It is very hard for Gay, Lesbian and Transgender groups to infiltrate your family by camping in your living room. On the other hand, by getting themselves employed under non-discrimination clauses in education departments and schools, they are perfectly placed to change the way your kids think, regardless of your views as a parent.

Take the early childhood education policy developed for two – four year olds in New Zealand, which pledges to teach toddlers how to "develop…the self confidence to stand up for themselves against biased ideas and discriminatory behaviour", while making "positive judgements on their own gender and the opposite gender" so they can learn "some early concepts of the value of appreciating diversity".

And you thought two year olds were just painting pictures and singing songs? It's more like shades of Children's Commissioner Cindy Kiro's Orwellian state.

Just whose "biased ideas" the children are being taught to recognise and reject is not made clear in the curriculum documents, but again, it raises questions about the levels of social engineering now being carried out by the New Zealand Government.

In the portion of the policy relating to infants (birth to around 18 months), childcare centres are required to ensure that story time for babies includes "picture books selected which show girls, boys, men and women in a range of roles."

Only a halfwit with no experience of real babies could think for a nanosecond that a six month old baby gives a monkey's about a picture of a man wearing an apron.

By the time they're three or four, the policy requires teachers to provide "successful, enjoyable experiences in non-traditional pursuits, for example boys in caring roles and girls with construction materials and in 'fixing' roles", and teachers are also required to ensure that "children see prejudice and negative attitudes being challenged by adults."

Regardless of whether one agrees or disagrees with the end goal, it should be remembered that some of the "prejudice and negative attitudes" expressed by young children probably reflect the values of their parents. Does the State have a right to undermine the family's values by implying to a toddler that his parents are wrong, or bad?

But that's what's happening.

In September 2006, the European Court of Human Rights (ECHR) upheld a German court ruling that the State's interest in "educating" children according to the State curriculum overrides any "interest" that parents might have.[108]

The case in point concerned a Christian family in Germany who had applied for the right to homeschool because of the increasingly secular humanist agenda in Germany's schools. Unlike the US or New Zealand, there is no homeschooling in Germany, and there hasn't been since it was outlawed by Hitler's Nazi party in 1938. Hitler, as we've seen, realized that compulsory school attendance was the best way of indoctrinating students into Nazi philosophy, and in case you don't recall the quote here it is again:[109]

> "WHEN AN OPPONENT declares, 'I will not come over to your side', I calmly say, 'Your child belongs to us already... What are you? You will pass on. Your descendants, however, now stand in the new camp. In a short time they will know nothing else but this new community.'"

The ECHR judgement declares that the State has a *primary* interest in promoting "pluralism in education, which is essential for the preservation of the 'democratic society'.

> "*IN VIEW OF THE POWER OF THE MODERN STATE, it is above all through State teaching that this aim must be realized...*respect is only due to convictions on the part of the parents which do not conflict with the right of the child to education." [emphasis added]

In other words, as long as parents agree with the State their views will be respected, but any disagreement will be determined in the State's favour. Germany's federal courts, said the ECHR, "stressed the general interest of society to avoid the emergence of parallel societies based on separate philosophical convictions."

---

108   http://www.hslda.org/parentalrights/courtreport22_6.asp
109   http://www.nizkor.org/hweb/imt/tgmwc/tgmwc-01/tgmwc-01-04-02.html

As you can see, such a position is a far cry from that outlined by President Thomas Jefferson when he decreed that a government had no legitimate business trying to change the opinions of a citizen. Today, the modern nation State believes it has every right to mould future voters according to its will. The tail, if you like, is wagging the dog. There can, in fact, be no true democracy if the State uses its power to brainwash people into voting a certain way.

"Education," ruled the ECHR, "by its very nature requires regulation by the State."

If you don't fight it, the claws stay hidden, but if you do fight it, it very quickly turns nasty. And again, the ECHR statement leaves a question hanging: *Why does Education require state regulation?* Some of the greatest minds the world has ever known got on famously in private schools with no state input ever. You know the real answer to the question, however.

Another homeschooling family in Germany hit the headlines[110] in early 2007 when a German police SWAT team raided their home and seized their 15 year old daughter because the girl had been homeschooled. A German judge then ordered that the teen be remanded to a *psychiatric* hospital for evaluation, and then held at a secure location unknown to her parents or lawyer. All this, only because the girl was homeschooled. In the eyes of the German secular humanist state, clearly that made her dangerous and mentally-ill.

In a letter smuggled out to international human rights lawyers in March, the 15 year old girl, Melissa Busekros, pleads for international help to reunite her with her family:

> "I WANT TO ASK YOU FOR HELP, to get my right to go back to my family, as I wish. I am not sick as the doctor said, and my family is the best place for me to live."

We live in an insane world where teenagers are imprisoned in psych wards because they are Christians being homeschooled, in a country still using Nazi education control laws.

These are not isolated cases. Throughout the world, left-wing activists in positions of power are flexing their muscles in the most coordinated attack on traditional families ever seen in history.

Take the case of a court battle[111] that's been raging in Massachusetts this year. Parent David Parker was outraged to discover in April 2005 that his six year old son Jacob was being "educated" about homosexuality and transgenderism

110   http://www.wnd.com/news/article.asp?ARTICLE_ID=54695
111   http://www.worldnetdaily.com/news/article.asp?ARTICLE_ID=54420

in the local public primary school. Again, the boy was *six*. Massachusetts has a state law that requires schools to notify parents in advance of classes on "human sexual relationships", so Parker naturally complained to the school and asked for prior warning so he could withdraw six year old Jacob from future classes on the topic. The school, Estabrook Elementary, refused. Parker arranged a meeting with school officials, but was arrested and charged with criminal trespassing when he refused to leave the scheduled meeting. He spent a night in jail as a result of the school pressing charges, but prosecutors later dropped the case amidst widespread publicity across America.

Parker and Estabrook School clashed again a year later in April 2006, however, when the teacher read a book by two Dutch writers to the class entitled "King and King", about two gay princes who decide to marry each other because they've "never cared much for princesses". This was to a class of six and seven year olds. Again, there was no prior notification to parents, as required by Massachusetts law.

So Parker and other parents at his son's school filed a lawsuit against the school alleging a breach of their parental rights. The lawsuit made headlines, and just a few days later a group of 8 to 10 children at the school took Parker's young son aside and gave him a beating.

At issue in the subsequent court battle, is that Massachusetts school officials claim homosexuality and homosexual relationships *don't* constitute 'human sexual relationships' under the terms of state law, therefore no prior warning to parents is needed.

Yeah, you heard right.

The school further argues that because Gay marriage is legal in Massachusetts, that public schools have a duty to teach children about the diversity of their state, and make sure the children are tolerant of it.

The schools lawyers argue that teachers have a "legitimate state interest" in teaching the homosexual lifestyle, and that parents should have no input into those decisions.

"The state must fight 'discrimination on the basis of sexual orientation' in ways that 'do not perpetuate stereotypes', argued school lawyers according to one news report. The only right that parents had, they said, was to send their child to a private school or homeschool them.

"Once I have elected to send my child to public school, my fundamental right does not allow me to direct what my child is exposed to in the public school," argued lawyers.

The school was joined in its defence of the lawsuit by a consortium of gay and lesbian activist groups, and the extreme liberal American Civil Liberties Union, the ACLU. In a brief filed by the gay-dominated Human Rights Campaign, the ACLU, the Massachusetts Teachers Association and Gay & Lesbian Advocates

And Defenders (GLAAD), the groups argued that parental rights:

> "[H]AVE NEVER MEANT that a parent can demand prior notice, and the right to opt a child out of mere exposure to ideas in public schools that a parent disapproves of.
>
> "The amici [friend of the Court] organizations urge this court to…dismiss, because *the scope of the rights of religious freedom and parental control over the upbringing of children, as asserted by the plaintiffs, would undermine teaching and learning in…public schools.*" [emphasis added]

One of the ACLU lawyers told the court it was actually "a tremendous bonus" if children could be exposed in school to information or ideas their parents did not approve of.

In New Zealand, such naked ambitions by the Gay elite are couched in less confrontational language, but they are still there and growing in dominance within the education curriculum.

The legal fights in the US generally and Massachusetts in particular provide a chilling warning of what is in store.

As part of their legal fight back, lawyers for the parents in the lawsuit argued that what the school describes as "diversity training" is better described as "indoctrination", because the school failed to cover opposing viewpoints in its teaching and only the pro-homosexual position was present in the classroom.

On the argument that if parents don't like it they can go somewhere else, the parents lawyers said the claim was offensive, and equivalent to telling blacks during the civil rights campaigns that if they didn't like racism they should go somewhere else.

Despite their arguments, a federal District Court judge in Massachusetts ruled late February 2007 that teaching homosexuality in public primary schools is virtually mandatory:[112]

> "UNDER THE CONSTITUTION public schools are entitled to teach anything that is reasonably related to the goals of preparing students to become engaged and productive citizens in our democracy," the judge wrote. "Diversity is a hallmark of our nation. It is increasingly evident that our diversity includes differences in sexual orientation."

"Diversity," said Judge Mark Wolf, requires students to be tolerant of

112   http://pacer.mad.uscourts.gov/dc/cgi-bin/recentops.pl?filename=wolf/pdf/parker%20opinion%20mlw.pdf

"differences in sexual orientation". The judge ruled parents would not be allowed to withdraw their children from tolerance classes:

> "AN EXODUS FROM CLASS when issues of homosexuality or same-sex marriage are to be discussed could send the message that gays, lesbians and the children of same-sex parents are inferior and, therefore, have a damaging effect on those students."

The case has now gone to appeal. Remember, we are talking here about sexual orientation indoctrination from the age of *five*. Even though the "born gay" myth has now been debunked by a long list of gay scientists and academics.

By the time they're in their teens, however, the messages are explicit. In 2004, the New Zealand AIDS Foundation, which is contracted to provide sex education lessons to schools, delivered a raunchy, no-holds barred talk to a group of 16 year olds at Auckland's Northcote College. They do them all the time, but this one became front page news.

The first the world knew of it was a call to Newstalk ZB's Leighton Smith show, from an angry father wanting to know why the Prime Minister "is trying to undermine me as a parent and through our high schools undermine parenthood? My daughter goes to Northcote College. She came home yesterday with a box of five condoms and strawberry-flavoured personal lubricant.

"Now, they had two – and I'll say they were gay because they were gay, they said to all the children that they were gay – two gay guys from the HIV clinic to give a talk. The first question they asked the kids was who in the last 24 hours has masturbated? I don't know what that has to do with them!"

The two men from the AIDS Foundation then handed out pamphlets, later obtained by the *New Zealand Herald*, which contained according to the paper "explicit titles".

"It had several types of condom attached, with advice on the best one to use for different types of sex. It referred to genitalia and also urged youngsters to practise with a condom by wearing one while masturbating. It included free sachets of lubricant, one a strawberry flavour, that 'will help make sex a lot more fun'."

Short of an actual physical demonstration of the sex act, it's hard to imagine how much more explicit the "sex education" class could have been. And is the purpose of it to encourage kids to abstain until they're old enough to understand the real consequences, or is the purpose to give kids the message that everybody's having sex so they should too?

But there are other and even more gruesome tales, and again Massachusetts features. In March 2000 a sex education course run by GLSEN, the Massachusetts Department of Education and the Governor's Commission hit the headlines[113] because of the messages it was teaching 14 to 21 year olds (although children as young as 12 actually attended). One workshop was entitled, "What They Didn't Tell You About Queer Sex & Sexuality In Health Class: A Workshop for Youth Only.

To put it in perspective, Massachusetts budgets more than US$1.5 million a year for the "Governor's Commission for Gay and Lesbian Youth" as part of the "safe schools" programme. More than 180 schools in the state run "clubs" under a wing of the programme called the "Gay/Straight Alliance", or GSA (whose resources are also promoted in New Zealand), which also gets federal money to promote relations between gays and heterosexuals. Events include screening R-rated gay porn for heterosexuals and gays to watch together, strangely enough.

But on this particular occasion, two lesbian women employed by the Department of Education, and a gay man employed by the Massachusetts Department of Public Health, ran the course.

After defining homosexual sex as "filling a bodily orifice with genitalia", and detailing the various "orifices" kids could use to experiment with, they quickly got down to business.

Young girls were taught how to engage in lesbian sex using dildos, and how to rub their clitorises together. Children were asked to "role play", and one tutor told children it wasn't too difficult because "when you are sexually aroused your clit gets bigger". Then they were invited to write questions which one of the tutors then pulled from a hat. The first question was, "What's fisting?" – a sex act which involves the insertion of a "fist and forearm" into an orifice of the partner.

Bet that got your attention. It got lesbian author Tammy Bruce's attention as well.

"If this was a question submitted by a child, then I'm Elizabeth Taylor!," remarked a cynical Bruce. "And even if it had been, the adults involved should have rejected it. But they did not, because it specifically suited their agenda."

Instead, the presenters showed the correct hand position involved, and described fisting this way:

> "FISTING OFTEN GETS A BAD RAP...[it's] an experience of letting somebody into your body that you want to be that close and intimate with...[and] to put you into an exploratory mode."

In a class discussion on oral sex, the gay employees of the Department of Education discussed the merits of "spit or swallow" while inviting kids to offer their own opinions on the practice. One 16 year old advised his classmates

113   www.massnews.com/past_issues/2000/5_May/maygsa.htm

they could avoid catching HIV by not "brushing your teeth or eating coarse food for four hours before you go down on a guy".

In another workshop – "Putting the 'Sex' Back Into Sexual Orientation" - specifically aimed at helping gay school teachers get more sex into the curriculum, the educators stated:

> "WE ALWAYS FEEL like we are fighting against people who deny publicly, who say privately, that being queer is not all about sex…We believe otherwise. We think that sex is central to every single one of us and particularly queer youth."

This is an important statement to bear in mind when you hear gay activists ridiculing claims that sexual addiction is a problem in the gay community.

It is worth noting that Heather Kramer, the Massachusetts primary school teacher who read the gay book *King and King* to a class of six year olds, had attended one of these GLSEN courses on how to promote homosexuality at school.

When another middle school lesbian teacher piped up at a GLSEN course saying she wanted more detail on how to get homosexuality into the general classroom, special education teacher Christine Hoyle told how she turned the Nazi Holocaust portion of her curriculum into "a gay affirming section".

Estabrook Elementary school's Kramer clearly followed that advice, because the gay propaganda book was not actually on the school curriculum, and the actual class she was teaching was about "Weddings", so she obviously used the occasion deliberately to bring in the gay material.

At the GLSEN briefing meanwhile, educator Hoyle also played a video done by her students, narrated by a Year 7 girl who told the audience that ancient Greeks "encouraged homosexuals; in fact, it was considered normal for an adolescent boy to have an older, wiser man as his lover."

The message left with these 12 year old students was that having sex with "older, wiser men" is a good thing. Hark! Is that the sound of the drooling NAMBLA apes shuffling up with stupid grins of anticipation on their faces?

Contrast Hoyle's subtle propaganda (sex with grownups is good) with the outraged denials on gay websites like hatecrime.org, the website exploiting Matthew Shepard's death.

Hatecrime.org has a list of what it calls false and hateful statements made about the gay community by Christians. Included on its list of 'false and hateful' comments of "extreme prejudice" are the following quotes:

1. "THERE IS A STRONG UNDERCURRENT of pedophilia in the

homosexual subculture. Homosexual activists want to promote the flouting of traditional sexual prohibitions at the earliest possible age....they want to encourage a promiscuous society - and the best place to start is with a young and credulous captive audience in the public schools." - Robert Knight, Family Research Council

2.   "Monogamy is not the norm for the average homosexual." – Family Research Council

"Prejudice" means to pre-judge something without evidence. These quotes are presented on the gay site as lies promoted by bigots. You can judge for yourself whether gay rights activists are trying to mislead gullible liberals about their real agenda.

As Tammy Bruce puts it in her book, "The death of right and wrong has so permeated our culture that the institutions we rely on to protect children now willingly participate in attempts to destroy them."

Another gay outreach programme to kids is a documentary for primary schools entitled "It's Elementary: Talking About Gay Issues In School, which features the usual propaganda as well as plenty of imagery of men kissing men. As Bruce points out, the credit music at the end of the documentary summarizes the attitude of the Left regarding children.

"Your children are not your children," intones the singer. "They come through you but are not from you, and though they are with you, they belong not to you."[114]

No, as we've already established, they apparently now belong to the NAMBLA freaks hiding in the bushes behind the Gay Pride guys.

Just in case you labour under the impression that New Zealand has escaped this nightmare, think again.

A sex education kit developed by the Christchurch College of Education and financed by the Health Funding Authority was trialed in 2000 at St Margaret's College for Girls, an exclusive private Anglican high school, among others.

This report[115] from the *New Zealand Herald* spells out the politically correct thinking behind it:

> SENIOR SCHOOL STUDENTS are being quizzed on how likely heterosexual teachers are to prey sexually on children. In a deliberately provocative teaching programme designed to expose anti-homosexual prejudices, pupils are asked questions including:

114   www.newsmax.com/commentarchive.shtml?a=1999/6/9/024710
115   *NZ Herald*, Dec 8, 2000, "School Quiz targets sex bias"

* "Ninety-nine per cent of reported rapists are heterosexual. Why are straights [heterosexuals] so sexually aggressive?"
* "The majority of child molesters are heterosexuals. Do you consider it safe to expose children to heterosexual teachers, Scout leaders, coaches etc?"
* "Forty per cent of married couples get divorced. Why is it so difficult for straights to stay in long-term relationships?"
Gillian Tasker, the principal health education lecturer who coordinated the resource's production,[116] said it contained ridiculous statements about heterosexuals that were often made about homosexuals, to get people to see how "crazy" such opinions were.

"Those statements are absurd - they are gross generalisations, they are based on faulty reasoning.

"The purpose is to get people to recognise that a lot of the myths and assumptions made about homosexuals are just as ridiculous."

Let's look at this insanity more closely. Sixteen and 17 year olds are being bombarded with a sex education course deliberately designed to break down "myths and assumptions" about gays. This is Kirk and Madsen's in-your-face, who-cares-about-the-facts? propaganda at work. The *Herald* story continues:

THE PROGRAMME HAS SEVEN sections - sexuality and gender; romantic love, sexual attraction and desire; sexuality and culture; sexuality and disability; HIV-AIDS; the sex industry; pornography.

Its introduction says that over recent decades many men and women have crossed the socially constructed boundaries of gender dominance in workplaces and the family.

"However, narrow, rigid constructs of masculinity, femininity and sexuality still predominate in many environments, sometimes causing harm to the wellbeing of individuals and restricting their life choices."

The aim is to make students think critically, and spark debate that encourages more acceptance of difference, social-justice values, respect for others' rights and care for themselves and others.

---

116   The resource was not fully original. Much had been copied from a US gay education presentation designed in 1993: http://www.temple.edu/theo/resources/OUTLINECONFERENCE. doc

And as an example of some of the specific questions, check how loaded these are:

* Is it possible that heterosexuality stems from a neurotic fear of others of the same sex?
* Considering the consequences of overpopulation, could the human race survive if everyone were heterosexual?
* How easy would it be for you if you wanted to change your sexual orientation, starting right now?
* What have been your reactions to answering these questions?

So what are kids supposed to take from this? Possibly that bisexuality is the default position for humans and heterosexuality is an overreaction. Alternatively the implication is that because people are born heterosexual, therefore gays must be "born" homosexual.

Do you notice the crafty linkage of heterosexuality with overpopulation? By playing on Gen XY's fears of global warming and the need to save the planet, it's almost as if being gay is heroic, because it'll keep the population down. Can't have those nasty little children around, can we?

And what about the earlier "ridiculous" statements? Most rapists are heterosexual because 99% of the population is heterosexual. What about child molestors? Once again, the majority of child molestors are indeed heterosexual, again because of simple population demographics. However, here is something the sex quiz didn't highlight: homosexuals *are* overrepresented in the child molestation statistics, meaning proportionately more homosexuals are paedophiles than heterosexuals are. But don't let that fact get in the way of student re-programming!

The sly dig at the heterosexual divorce rate is meant to suggest, "who are we to criticize gay relationships?", without – funnily enough – throwing in the huge instabilities and quirks of gay relationships. How would the schoolgirls have reacted if portions of Eric Rofes experiences in that San Francisco bathhouse had been read to them first?

Perhaps one could turn the first question around: Is it possible that male homosexuality stems from a neurotic fear of girls? Is homosexuality simply heterophobia manifesting itself in lashing out at all things heterosexual?

The course specifically mentions Scout leaders, so I ran a check of the *NZ Herald's* online database. Of the incidents of Scout leaders sexually violating children, all cases involved gay or bisexual scout leaders, which I'll elaborate on shortly. My curiousity piqued, I ran the word "paedophile" through the database as well. Of all the NZ cases listed by the *Herald* where the genders of the victims were specified, gays or bisexuals made up double the number of actual offenders compared with heterosexuals, even though there are 99 times more heterosexuals in the community than core gays. Admittedly, my study is unscientific, but the proportion of boys being abused by other men in studies generally is signficantly higher than expected. Not that the Gay activists are listening.

"The incorrect stereotype of the gay man as a pedophile is one that has been medically and scientifically debunked," argues New York's Glennda Testone, northern regional media manager for the Gay & Lesbian Alliance Against Defamation (GLAAD).

"Heterosexual men were responsible for 74 percent of assaults on male victims and 77 percent of assaults on female victims, according to an American Academy of Pediatrics study (July 1994)."[117]

Yeah. Sounds good, sounds authoritative. But the study was fatally flawed on two levels. Firstly, by definition, a "heterosexual" adult male is not attracted to other males – adult or child. While attributing many of the male assaults on young girls to heterosexuals is a correct analysis, describing male-boy sexual abuse as heterosexual is a contradiction in terms, a bit like describing something as "a square circle". The correct definition of the perpetrator is either gay or bisexual (some researchers call them "omnisexual". Secondly, the researchers in the study never actually interviewed either the victims, or the offenders, or their families. Instead, the "study" consisted only of reviewing the often-sparse case notes of child patients, where questions in regard to the sexual orientation of offenders were not generally asked, as it was a hospital ward, not the follow-up police inquiry.

In other words, as studies go it's not very good. But as Nazi Josef Goebbels kept saying: tell the lie often enough, eventually they will believe you. Gillian Tasker's controversial sex education kit for New Zealand schools proves the point.

Psychologist Judith Reisman, the woman whose investigations revealed sex researcher Alfred Kinsey and his team were involved in child rape as part of their famous sex surveys,[118] told journalists the gay community in the US seeks adolescent boys in foreign travel destinations.

"We looked at the leading gay travel guide," Reisman said of her research. "Forty-seven percent of the 139 nations they talked about, identified places to find boys. The average heterosexual travel guide is not concerned with finding children."[119]

But let's not get distracted by gay travelers trawling for illicit sex with boys, instead

117   http://pediatrics.aappublications.org/cgi/reprint/94/1/41.pdf
118   http://www.investigatemagazine.com/Kinsey.htm
119   Reisman's 1994 analysis of 139 nations described in a mainstream homosexual travel guide ("Spartacus: '92/'93--The Travel Guide For Gay Men," available in all "gay" bookstores) found 47% of 139 nations Spartacus recommended for "travel," included the legal age of consent for sex with boys as well as the best locations, parks, streets, plazas, where men might obtain young boys for random encounters.

let's return to the Boy Scout issue that the NZ sex education course touched on.

In 1998, a court case over the rights of gays to be Scout leaders hit the headlines in New Jersey, when that State's Supreme Court ruled that a ban on gays violated New Jersey's anti-discrimination laws. The ruling opened the way for gay men to join an organization that has been closed to them since it began a century ago.

In 2000, however, the US Supreme Court overturned the New Jersey ruling, saying that private organizations like the Scouts still had the right under the First Amendment to set their own moral code and viewpoint.

But the media continued to beat down the doors of Boy Scouts America with hate reportage against the "anti-gay" organization, in a publicity blitz that eventually lead to many of the major corporations that sponsored Boy Scouts severing ties with it. Even movie director and former Scout Steven Spielberg quit.

"[The] Democrats booed a Boy Scout color guard at their 2000 convention, because the Scouts said no to sending boys off into the woods with gay scoutmasters – which makes about as much sense as letting Bill Clinton sleep in a pup tent with cheerleaders," quipped *Frontpage* magazine's Don Feder in a column late 2006.

Nonetheless, reacting to the pressure from the liberal media and a former gay scout leader in New Zealand, the NZ Scouting organization was quoted in 2000 as "working on policies to ban discrimination on the grounds of sexual orientation, after a Scout leader said he was forced to resign because he was gay.

"The organisation's equal opportunities group has been briefed to produce anti-discrimination policies, but Scouting NZ said it would also take into consideration the concerns of members and parents opposed to gay leadership.

"The chairwoman of the working group, Lesley Anderson, said developing policies to stop gay members being discriminated against would be at the top of its meeting this month…"

That was in January 2000. Then the gay equivalent of al Qa'ida suicide bombers struck the NZ Scout movement.

- **August 2002: Former boy scout leader Stephen Thomas Roberts**, 55, was convicted of possessing 55,000 rape and sexual violation images involving boys aged from 6 to 16
- **September 2003: Gay Christchurch cub scout leader Ian Alexander Clark** was jailed for two years for sexually assaulting three youths, including Timothy Hueston, and supplying the boys with the gay sex drug isobutyl nitrite, known as 'Rush'. 17 year old victim Hueston later committed suicide. The court heard how Clark had even stalked

children while dressed in his scout leader's uniform, and been warned by police who found pornographic material in his possession at the time. The coroner at Hueston's inquest recommended that parents should be made aware of the histories of scout leaders like Clark, but Scouting NZ's CEO Geoff Knighton was reported as saying "privacy laws" prevented this.

• **October 2003: 35 year old Christchurch scout leader Roland Harding** killed himself rather than submit to police questioning about the sexual abuse of up to ten adolescent scouts in his troop. Although parents had complained to another Christchurch scout leader, nothing was done, allegedly because both scout leaders were "close".

• **December 2004: 32 year old Auckland scout leader Andrew Pybus** was convicted on ten charges of indecency and sexual violation of boys aged 11 to 13, including two representative charges that he photographed the abuse hundreds of times. Pybus was found in possession of 61,000 sexual abuse pictures on his computer.

• **December 2004: 48 year old Auckland scout leader Nigel Fenemore** became the second homosexual to be convicted in what the media were now calling a "paedophile ring". Although he had initially begun offending against adolescent boy scouts on his own, he later met fellow gay scout leader Andrew Pybus and the men began offending together with multiple victims. Fenemore's charge list included "sexual violation…anal sex…indecent assault" on boys under the age of 16. Both Pybus and Fenemore were given seven year jail terms. A third scout leader, aged 70, was charged with possessing objectionable material as part of the ring.

• **March 2005: 60 year old gay Christchurch scout leader John Henry Cootes** admitted eight charges of sexual assault, including sodomy, on four boys aged between 12 and 15. The court heard how Cootes had taken in one of the victims, a 14 year old, to live with him because of a deteriorating situation at the boy's home. "After a short period, Cootes started sexually abusing him," reported the *Herald*. "He told the boy that he was obviously gay and what they were doing 'was all right'. Cootes took the boy to parks where gay people congregated and encouraged him to have sex with other men. On three occasions the relationship developed to a stage where Cootes was sodomising the boys regularly." Cootes was jailed for seven and a half years, but the court was told he had already served a six year jail term for similar gay offending against teenage boys elsewhere.

And here's the twist. As more and more cases of gay scout leaders abusing adolescent boys hit the headlines, the same media outlets who'd criticized the "anti gay" position of the scouting movement turned around and called Scouting New Zealand "a nest of paedophiles". Talk about media hypocrisy. And whatever you do, don't mention the G-word.

The discerning reader has probably also noted a statistically significant appearance of Christchurch scout leaders in that list, which is ironic given that one of the schools to approve the use of the pro-gay sex education propaganda was St Margaret's College for Girls, an exclusive Anglican church school in the city.

What was it that the sex-ed kit said, again?

"The majority of child molesters are *heterosexuals*. Do you consider it safe to expose children to heterosexual teachers, Scout leaders, coaches etc?"

Kids who saw that phrase were supposed to see that if you replaced the word "heterosexual" with "homosexual", the sentence became homophobic. Yeah. Tell that to the boy victim who killed himself, and the others whose lives were destroyed according to victim impact reports.

You would think an exclusive private school for girls would be smart enough to know they were dishing up misleading gay propaganda, but apparently not.

"Senior schoolgirls taught the health curriculum from a kit containing deliberately absurd questions about sexuality gave it high praise, a teacher says," reported the *NZ Herald*.

"It was extremely well received", said Melissa Fenton, the head of health and life-skills education at St Margaret's College. She tried out the new kit with about 80 sixth formers…and intends continuing with it next year. Ms Fenton said [the] questions were quickly picked up by her pupils as assumptions commonly made about homosexuals, but twisted around to apply to heterosexuals."

I'm presuming that if you've made it this far through the book, you are beginning to see through the gay Goebbelsspeak, the slick sloganeering that is aimed at children and – through them – their parents. The campaign Kirk and Madsen envisaged back in the late 80's is in full swing: forget the facts, just keep tugging at the heartstrings.

Thus, the truth about the gay lifestyle, and even whether gays are born or made, is confined to scientific journals and gay niche media. The rest of the mainstream media are too scared to touch it – having been mentally conditioned to believe that anything challenging the "official" line is heresy. Even if the evidence is in a science journal and written by gay researchers. And because the mainstream media won't challenge it, the myths grow as they're copied and pasted into education textbooks and become virtually "Holy writ" for schoolchildren.

Author Tammy Bruce reflects on the clash between hard evidence, and what she calls "the slick gay-activist PR machine".

"Their mantra is: Gay men are not pedophiles. Technically, they're right, but it really is just a cynical spin of semantics. Pedophilia indicates attraction to those 12 years old and younger. In fact, the problem the Boy Scouts have avoided by excluding gay men as Scout leaders is ephebophilia, or an attraction to adolescents.

"What the gay establishment does not want you to think about is the fact that adult men being attracted to female adolescents is called 'heterosexuality', while adult men being attracted to male adolescents is called – surprise! – 'homosexuality'."

Tammy Bruce makes the point, as I did earlier but it is worth repeating, that all of this does not mean that most gay men are pedophiles (or ephebophiles, if you wish to make the distinction). But to allow school classes to be told effectively that *none* are is just a blatant, deliberate deception that does nothing to protect youths from predators – those older, wiser Greek men bearing gifts the lesbian educators in Massachusetts told us about.

Bruce cites numerous examples of Left wing writers and academics pushing for the normalization of sex with children. People like Judith Levine, in her book, *Harmful to Minors: The Perils Of Protecting Children From Sex*, argue that "Sex is not harmful to children. It is a vehicle to self-knowledge, love, healing, creativity, adventure, and intense feelings of aliveness. There are many ways even the smallest of children can partake of it."

As Wikipedia puts it:

> LEVINE IS BEST KNOWN for her 2002 *Harmful to Minors: The Perils of Protecting Children From Sex*, in which she suggests liberalization of age-of-consent laws in the United States and the conception of minors as sexual beings, which Levine argues is extant in Western Europe. Levine argues for weakening most United States laws governing possession of child pornography, the access of abortions to minors, and conduct classified as statutory rape. Conservative commentators have heavily criticized her work; its publication by the University of Minnesota Press caused controversy in the Minnesota state legislature. *The book was also widely praised by advocates of liberalization and educators.* It won the 2002 *Los Angeles Times Book Prize* and was named by SIECUS, the Sexuality Information and Education Council of the United States, as one of history's most influential books about sexuality. [emphasis added]

Did you notice in there how advocates of pedophilia and ephebophilia have "widely praised" Levine's book? Did you notice the next part: "and educators"? Did you notice the liberal Left love the book so much it won the *LA Times Book Prize?*

Here's another quote from high priestess of child sex Judith Levine:

"[Sex] is not ipso facto harmful to minors; and America's drive to protect kids from sex is protecting them from nothing. Instead, it is often harming them."

It was around the time this book was published that loopy liberals in New Zealand's Labour Government suggested they might look at lowering the age of consent between children from 16 to 12.

And Labour cabinet minister David Benson-Pope, the man in charge of Child, Youth and Family and also the Ministry of Social Development, is on record that a 12 year old girl who is sexually mature is "also a woman".[120]

Levine doesn't use the phrase "pedophilia" in her book. She calls it "child-adult sex".

Are you starting to see a pattern with the Left wing radicals yet, a pattern that began with Hitler's Nazis? By changing the language they bypass those deeply ingrained reactions linked to your conscience and gut instinct. How can you have a kneejerk reaction to a phrase you haven't heard before? "Intergenerational love" is another euphemism.

And just like Adolf Hitler, Judith Levine and the Left have their own message of hate, saved for the "conservative religious agenda that would deny minors all sexual information and sexual expression."

That's right, blame the Christians because they won't let their 11 year olds sleep with nice 'Uncle' Rupert from NAMBLA, or 'Aunty' Judith from the liberal left funny farm.

"They're the people," Levine continues,[121] "behind abstinence-only education, the child-pornography laws that get people arrested for taking pictures of their babies in the bathtub, or laws that make abortion risky and traumatic for young women. These so-called protections are more harmful to minors than sex itself."

Apparently, as the Left tells us, smacking a child is evil, but having sex with one is good. Levine displays just how disconnected from Planet Earth she is by then denying that sexual content or predators on the internet are harmful to children.

"In spite of sensationalist press coverage, there is little evidence that the Net is crawling with child molesters... We have moved beyond appropriate responses to serious offenses to hyperbolic responses to offenses with unproven harms, such as the assumed harm to a child of involuntarily glimpsing a penis, or reading sexy language online."

So there's "little evidence" that the Net is crawling with child molestors, claims this award-winning liberal? Tell that to two young sisters[122] whose lives almost ended after they met some pedophiles online:

---

120   Interviewed on New Zealand's National Radio, transcript repeated in Parliament, 9 Nov 2004 by Judith Collins during debate on the Care of Children Bill.
121   http://www.upress.umn.edu/HarmfultoMinorsQandA.html
122   http://www.timesonline.co.uk/tol/news/uk/crime/article1336929.ece

THEY NEVER MET IN PERSON, only in an internet chat room. But there three paedophiles plotted the abduction and rape of two teenage girls.

Alan Hedgcock, 42, identified two young sisters [aged 13 and 14] he wanted to abduct and rape. In one message to his co-plotters he wrote: "I want them done. I don't care what you do. I want them done in like Holly and Jess", a reference to the Soham murders of Holly Wells and Jessica Chapman.

Hedgcock and the two other men were left "drooling" over the possibility of turning their fantasies into reality, Southwark Crown Court was told. The case highlights growing concern about the use of chat rooms by paedophiles to arrange the abuse of children.

Hedgcock, who specialises in creating masks and special effects for horror films and worked on *Hellraiser II* and *28 Days Later*, planned to abduct the girls as they walked through a wood on their way to school.

A Google search of the words "murdered", "online", "chat", and "room" netted more than 1.3 *million* results, stories like this one:

AN OTTAWA COUNTY MAN is accused of having sex with a 13-year-old boy. Where do you think the man met the 13 year old boy? The boy told authorities he met him in November through an Internet **chat room**. This story was published on January 15 and they first started chatting in November. That's two whole months of chatting that somebody should have known about.

Or this one:

MAN CHARGED WITH INDUCING 14-year-old boy to have sex - Youngstown State student met youth in Internet chat room.

The man used the Internet to arrange sexual encounters twice last year with the boy, who is now 15, according to the FBI and Beaver County detectives. According to an FBI affidavit, the man and the boy met in a homosexual **chat room** in June and arranged a meeting. They didn't have sex that time, according to the boy, but they did in September after Murdoch picked him up at his home. The victim said they had sex again after another **online chat** in July. Again, they first started chatting in June and ended in September.

Or this one:

> OMAHA PROSECUTORS SAID they are charging a man after he used
> instant messaging and an Internet **chat room** to meet young boys.
> He is being charged in Douglas County with sexual assault. He
> also has sexual assault charges pending in Sarpy County and is on
> probation for an incident with a 9- and 11-year-old. He met both
> boys on the Internet, and then arranged to meet them in person.
> Again, they met on the Net, but the prosecutors said this
> relationship was sexual, and went on for months. They said
> Payne also had sexual pictures of himself and the boy on his
> computer.

No, the Net isn't crawling with molestors at all. Levine, the acclaimed Leftist
writer, also wants to change the language definitions surrounding AIDS.

"But sex does not cause AIDS…I heard Deb Roffman, the sex educator, say
that the expression "sexually transmitted disease" is like calling TB a "breathing-
transmitted disease." We don't blame breathing for "causing" tuberculosis."

No, of course not, let's take away any clue as to what causes AIDS, or how
it is usually transmitted.

On the subject of sex education, she wants that almost entirely in the hands
of the liberal State, telling parents to "support their children's sex education
by standing up for comprehensive programs at school, uncensored public
libraries and computers, and by encouraging them to form close relationships
with trustworthy adults other than their mothers and fathers."

Hmmm. People like 'Uncle' Rupert from NAMBLA? Or perhaps this man
whose story made the Associated Press in 2002:

> BRIDGEPORT, CONNECTICUT - CITY POLICE have accused a 75-
> year-old man of impregnating a 10-year-old girl he met at his
> senior centre. Jimmy Kave of Bridgeport admitted having sex
> with the girl several times, but claims she had enticed him,
> police said. He turned himself in Wednesday after learning
> there was a warrant for his arrest.
>
> The girl, now 11 and six months pregnant, has been removed
> from her home and taken into the custody by the state
> Department of Children and Families. The *Connecticut Post*
> reported that the girl apparently intends to have the baby. Her
> mother, who reported the assault to police, said her daughter
> met Kave through an "Adopt-a-Godfather" program at the
> Harborview Towers housing complex.

Classic, blame the 10-year-old hussy mentality. Or, as the New Zealand Labour Government's David Benson-Pope might say, "blame the 10-year-old woman!" It must have been consensual and on that basis we can only assume it was a positive experience, because Judith Levine tells us so.

Says Levine: "I think the teaching of "sexual morality" is a redundancy… Child or teen sex can be moral…if sexual expertise is expected of adults, the rudiments must be taught to children… Abstinence is not emphasized in European classrooms, if it's discussed at all."

Or perhaps the gay "elderly pensioner" referred to in this next story is one of those wise old Greeks we heard so much about:

PENSIONER IAN DOUGLAS GRIFFITHS was said to be a lonely, elderly man who was searching for friendship and intimacy. But he found it in young boys he preyed upon at Christchurch libraries and gaming parlours.

Griffiths, 75 and retired, was sentenced to five years and three months in prison last Friday after pleading guilty to one charge of sexual conduct with a person under 16 and one of sexual violation.

His victim – a 12-year-old boy from Aranui who he met through another child at the New Brighton Library.

From Ashburton, he drove to Christchurch on weekends to meet the boy.

This is the third time Griffiths has appeared in court for sex crimes against children.

He spent time in prison in 2002-03 for a similar offence [against an 11 year old boy]. His latest victim's mother said she was disappointed at Griffiths' sentence.

"I wanted him to die in jail," she said. "I'm grateful for any time he gets in jail, but think at 75 he should know what he is doing is wrong, everyone else in the world does."

Griffiths, single with no children, was introduced to the boy in January 2006 through one of the boy's friends, and unbeknown to his parents.

It was revealed that Griffiths had been travelling from his home Ashburton to Christchurch almost every weekend to meet the boy, sometimes at the New Brighton Library area, and other times picking him up from near his home.

He would park his car near the beach, where he would make the boy take his pants and underwear off and fondling him, often hugging him and kissing his cheek while he did so. On at least three occasions Griffiths also performed oral sex on the boy.

He would tell the boy not to say anything to anyone about what was happening and reward him for his involvement with money, toys, cigarettes and by letting the boy drive his car.

At his sentencing last week, Griffiths lawyer Raoul Neave described him as an isolated, elderly man, searching for friendship and intimacy.

Mr Neave told the court that Griffiths had been attending the STOP programme, a treatment programme for adult child sex offenders, in Christchurch and was meeting regularly with his probation officer, with whom he had a good relationship.

Judge Gary McAskill said he was concerned at Griffiths' reoffending, considering he had completed the Kia Marama sex offenders rehabilitation programme in prison.[123]

Of course, neither the lawyer nor the Judge noticed the elephant in the room: Griffiths was *gay*. And again, would Judith Levine write this off as harmless, consensual sex?

Do you want mentally-damaged hangovers from the sixties like Judith Levine teaching the educators who teach your kids? Heck no!

I would strongly urge parents everywhere to demand from their local schools a copy of the sex education curriculum, and I would urge parents to sit in on a class. Tammy Bruce goes further, she suggests parents simply vote with their feet.

"*Remove* your child from any school that allows a sexual message to be presented. It will most likely be presented under the guise of tolerance or preventing the spread of the disease. Don't be fooled. Realize that wanting to be your child's moral tutor does not make you a homophobe – and don't be silenced by bullies who try to exploit your compassionate nature."

A generation ago, people who advocated "child-adult sex" under the guise of love would have been locked up. These days Western civilization is so corrupt we fete them as heroes of emancipation from the dictates of the evil natural family.

The liberal steamroller suffered a slight roadbump when one of Levine's key sources for her book was arrested for pedophilia:[124]

A KEY SOURCE CONCERNING CHILD PORNOGRAPHY in Judith Levine's controversial book *Harmful to Minors* has been arrested and charged with possession of child pornography in Brazil.

Lawrence Stanley, 47, described by Levine as the author "of

123   14 Feb, 2007, http://www.starcanterbury.co.nz/localnews/storydisplay.cfm?storyid=3721 807&thesection=localnews&thesubsection=&thesecondsubsection=

124   http://www.cultureandfamily.org/articledisplay.asp?id=477&department=CFl&categoryi d=cfreport

the most thorough research of child pornography in the 1980s," is in jail awaiting trial. He was also convicted in absentia by a Dutch court in 1998 for sexual abuse of three 7—to 10-year-old girls, according to a July 24 article by Robert Stacy McCain in *The Washington Times*. Stanley faces a three-year prison sentence if he returns to the Netherlands.

Stanley is also wanted in Canada on charges of sexually assaulting a girl "under the age of 14," according to a wire services report in *The Miami Herald*.

In *Harmful to Minors: The Perils of Protecting Children from Sex* (University of Minnesota Press, 2002), author Levine quotes Stanley several times, mostly to make the case that the threat of child pornography has been exaggerated. Levine cites Stanley's article in the September 1988 *Playboy* magazine titled "The Child-Porn Myth." She also cites a more detailed article by the same name that was published in the Cardozo *Arts and Entertainment Law Journal* in 1989.

The book became controversial because it argues that sex does not harm children as long as the children consent, and contains numerous pedophile sources that are not identified as such.

But nonetheless I'm sure you'll be pleased to know Levine's book was given a glowing review in the *NZ Herald* by a lecturer at the University of Auckland's School of Education, one of New Zealand's main teacher training colleges.[125]

You'll not be surprised to know that Levine's book is also required reading at NAMBLA and at the International Pedophilia and Child Emancipation headquarters in Holland, where the age of sexual consent has already been lowered to 12 so the Dutch can go to hell in a handcart just a little bit quicker.

You will be seeing, also, a growing exposure to "positive" pedophilia models in the wider media as part of softening you up to accept the idea. Case in point? Well, a couple of them actually, movies recently released that put a positive spin on "adult-child sex".

The controversy over Nicole Kidman's 2005 film *Birth*, where she believes a 10 year old boy is her deceased husband and proceeds to get naked with him, is one. The other is Kevin Bacon's *The Woodsman*, produced by gay activist filmmaker Lee Daniels, who told a reporter for "Film Festival Today" that he wanted to "put a benign face on pedophilia". Once upon a time making a statement like that would get you booked into "Sunny Meadows" home for the pathologically insane. Nowadays it gets you and your movie screentime in

125   *NZ Herald* book review, 22 Sept. 2002

arthouse cinema circuits and *Sunday Theatre.*

Although gay organizations publicly distance themselves and decry the ideals of NAMBLA, many are nonetheless working to incrementally lower the age of sexual consent. Lithuania, for example, dropped its age of consent in 2004 to just 14, as a result of pressure from the International Lesbian and Gay Association (ILGA), which maintains a register on its website of the age of consent in every country around the world. And because of a big rise in prosecutions of men for underage sex in Sri Lanka, the government there passed a law dropping the age of consent from 16 to 13 in 2005.

The Dutch decision to lower the age of consent to 12, which I touched on a moment ago, is worth examining. Firstly, one of the biggest organizations lobbying for the right for adults to have sex with 12 year olds was the Dutch Association for the Integration of Homosexuality – the oldest existing gay rights organization in the world and one of the biggest in Europe, quaintly known by its Dutch acronym, "COC". The advantage of setting 12 as the age was that it includes children who may not yet have begun puberty.

As the *New York Times* reported on April 13, 2002, parents have virtually no say in the sexual activity of their children, and "can overrule their child's wishes only if they persuade the [State-run] Council for the Protection of Children that they are acting in the child's best interest."

Shades, again, of the kind of State-knows-best agency that NZ Children's Commissioner Cindy Kiro wants.

As long as a 12 year old "consents" to sex with NAMBLA's drooling 65 year old 'Uncle' Rupert, it is legal under Dutch law and parents are not allowed to intervene without first seeking approval from the State.

As the Dutch gay rights organization points out in a pamphlet for gay pedophiles, "nobody is allowed to interfere...as long as the situation is mutually agreeable."

Child sex priestess Judith Levine urges governments in the West to follow the Dutch lead and lower the age of consent to 12.

Spain did, also after lobbying from homosexual rights groups, although the Spanish have since raised it to 13. The Philippines' age of consent is listed as 12 on gay websites[126], while a number of other countries are now down to 13. And in many cases the International Lesbian and Gay Association has lobbied hard to get it lowered.

The problem for heterosexuals trying to debate these issues with homosexuals is that it's like trying to grab a blancmange. Usually the first thing thrown up is the false statement that there is no link between homosexuality and pedophilia. Once that denial fails, activists try and attack opponents by calling them "Christian fundamentalist bigots", as if the fact that they're Christian negates the truth of the studies they're quoting from. If that attack fails to get traction, the gay activists go back to denying there's any association between homosexuality and pedophilia. And so on it goes.

Yet the Dutch journal on pedophilia, *Paidika*, includes on its editorial board gay academic John De Cecco, who featured in a previous chapter on sexual orientation being chosen, not ingrained.

De Cecco's *Journal of Homosexuality* has itself published a special double-issue entitled, "Male Intergenerational Intimacy," which pushes the man-boy love line.

As *WorldNetDaily* reported,[127] "One article said parents should look upon the pedophile who loves their son 'not as a rival or competitor, not as a theft of their property, but as a partner in the boy's upbringing, someone to be welcomed into their home'."

The gay rights magazine *The Guide* has also sung that particular song, in 1995: "We can be proud that the gay movement has been home to the few voices who have had the courage to say out loud that children are naturally sexual [and]…deserve the right to sexual expression with whoever they choose.

"Instead of fearing being labeled pedophiles, we must proudly proclaim that sex is good, including children's sexuality … we must do it for the children's sake."

Veteran gay activist Larry Kramer, the founder of the group ACT-UP (the AIDS Coalition To Unleash Power) has written: "In those instances where children do have sex with their homosexual elders, be they teachers or anyone else, I submit that often, very often, the child desires the activity, and perhaps even solicits it."[128]

Yep, the old "the kid was begging for it" defence.

I could go on forever with quotes from mainstream gay media and academics celebrating the idea of child sex, whilst at the same time the general news media is told the opposite. I suspect however that if I haven't already presented enough evidence to de-programme the brainwashing you've suffered, I never will.

Suffice to leave it then, with one final example of the way the Left will play you for suckers on all this.

The National Gay and Lesbian Task Force in the US (NGLTF) is working with a group calling itself the Woodhull Freedom Foundation (WFF) to get lower consent laws passed[129] as well as wider legal recognition of sex in public places and "alternative sexualities" – the "camel's nose under the tent" that Kirk and Madsen wrote about in their propaganda epic, *After the Ball*.

The WFF is bankrolled by sex activists Richard Cunningham and Judy Guerin, who've worked on a "grassroots mission of advocacy for the SM-leather-fetish, swing and polyamory communities." Polyamory, by the way, is

---

127   http://www.worldnetdaily.com/news/article.asp?ARTICLE_ID=27431
128   Larry Kramer, "Report from the Holocaust: The Making of an AIDS Activist", as quoted at http://www.worldnetdaily.com/news/article.asp?ARTICLE_ID=27431
129   http://www.woodhullfoundation.org/about/projects.aspx

polygamy – another example of changing the language to avoid the baggage.

Guerin is described in promotional material[130] as "a highly visible political activist on freedom of gender and sexual expression, issues of youth sex education, and access to birth control. She is a widely published author, speaker and educator on these topics. Judy currently serves on the board of GenderPAC and is an advisor to the European Union Human Rights Commission on sexual freedom issues for gay, lesbian, bisexual, transgender and intersex individuals."[131]

In other words, she's a very, very, high level lobbyist. Cunningham is described as a long-time "social justice and sexual freedom advocate", also with national lobbying skills.

The WFF's executive director is a woman called Ricci Levy. In presenting Levy with the 2006 "Sexual Intelligence" award, sex activist and WFF board member Marty Klein said:

> "RICCI LEVY HAS BEEN A SEXUAL freedom activist for almost a decade, starting as the Director of Operations of the National Coalition for Sexual Freedom. In 2002, she helped found The Woodhull Freedom Foundation, and has been the Executive Director ever since. You ought to know about Woodhull--the non-profit organization working to affirm sexual freedom as a fundamental human right via research, advocacy, and professional and public education (www. woodhullfoundation.org).
>
> "Working tirelessly with dozens of organizations from the ACLU to NOW, Ricci has put "sexual rights as human rights" on the progressive and humanist agendas. She has helped educate many such groups and the national media about the importance of issues such as polyamory, age of consent, sexual minorities, sex worker discrimination, and sex-positive feminism. That's sexual intelligence in action."[132]

After all that fulsome praise, talking about their detailed "agendas" in coalition with the ACLU, NOW and 75 other national and international gay and sexual rights organizations for polyamory, lowering the age of consent with children, sado-masochism and the like, I just about fell off my chair laughing when I read an interview with Ricci Levy where she mocks the 'religious fundamentalist scare stories' about "the Gay agenda".

"[The Right] are obsessed with sex!" she added.

130   http://www.ncsfreedom.org/news/2003/0603sarfaty.htm
131   http://www.ambushmag.com/is504/sherwoods.htm
132   http://www.sexualintelligence.org/awards.html

Is it any wonder the Right are obsessed, when even more-obsessed liberals are roaming around lobbying to change every law in the book?

But all is not lost. As you are about to see, occasionally liberals fall off their perches trying to defend the indefensible.

14

The Rubber Hits The Road
The Myth of Safe Sex

"Twenty years into the AIDS epidemic among gays, the absence of such a self-sustaining heterosexual epidemic can no longer be explained by the fact that it hasn't had time to occur. It is not happening because, as we will see, the sexual [behaviour] of middle class western heterosexuals does not promote the efficient spread of HIV, and it will not occur unless there are major changes either in the biology of HIV or the behavior of heterosexuals or both."

Gabriel Rotello, gay activist, Sexual Ecology

As liberal mantras go, they don't get much bigger than the myth of "Safe Sex". You've heard it, and chances are you've bought into it. Back in the 80s, when condoms were found to cut the risk of heterosexual HIV transmission from, say, near zero down to near zero,[133] it was also assumed that the little slivers of latex would likewise work equally well against most of the other nasties that live down south.

Health services around the world quickly latched onto condoms and the "Safe Sex" message, figuring that rather than try and fight promiscuity as a way of combating AIDS, it was better to simply batten down the hatch and hope.

Massive advertising campaigns were launched to convince everyone, especially teenagers, to keep condoms with them at all times, "just in case".

So, given the hundreds of millions of dollars spent on sex education in the West since 1984, why is it that sexually transmitted disease (STD) rates are going through the roof?

Switzerland is just one case in point. The US National Institutes of Health reported in 1997 that "A national campaign in Switzerland to promote the use

---

133   The odds against an unprotected man catching vaginally-transmitted HIV from an infected woman, and then passing it on via unprotected vaginal sex to another woman, were calculated at 500 million to one in a study published in the *Journal of the American Medical Association* 259, no 16, 2428-32, in 1988

of condoms dramatically reduced risky sexual behavior... The results thus far have been impressive."

How impressive? Well, while large numbers of Swiss may have used condoms, when the rubbers hit the road it seems they left skid marks.

"Recent trends in western Europe," reported a medical journal in 2005,[134] "show an increase in sexually transmitted infections (STIs). Available surveillance data in Switzerland confirm this rising trend. Gonorrhoea rates more than doubled between 1996 and 2003, and for *Chlamydia* there was a 64% increase from 1999 to 2003. Notifications of syphilis cases almost doubled in the year 2002 and rose to 174% compared to the period of 1998-2001."

It's not rocket science. *More people use condoms, but more people are catching diseases. Something must be terribly wrong.*

All is not happy and healthy in New Zealand's bedrooms, either. While the number of AIDS cases is low, new HIV cases are on the rise, and the rates of many other infections are climbing strongly as well. While none are necessarily the death sentence that an HIV infection represents, they have potentially huge consequences, including cancer and infertility. Public health experts have seen a tremendous increase in cases of diseases like chlamydia and syphilis; in the Australian state of Victoria, the situation is so bad that the Chief Health Officer was compelled in March 2005 to issue a formal Health Alert to general practitioners telling them to watch out for the sudden uptick in syphilis cases. That sort of warning is not an everyday occurrence: the previous time the Chief Health Officer issued such a bulletin was in 2003, warning doctors to be on the lookout for SARS.

But if you think the Victorian warning is bad, Auckland's chlamydia epidemic is three times worse than Australia's, and in the far north of New Zealand as many as 25% of young people have the disease. Overall, the upper North Island's chlamydia rate is six times higher than the Australian average.

There are many factors behind the rise in various STDs, but one has gone all but unreported in a culture where, officially at least, condom use has taken on an almost sacramental nature: studies conducted over the past few years show that, far from being the be-all and end-all in sexual protection, condoms offer practically zero effective protection from most STDs apart from HIV, ironically.

In other words, when the emperor has no clothes on, a condom is of limited, if any, use in protecting him from a host of diseases.

Back in 2001, the United States' National Institutes of Health published a series of findings[135] that were shocking, both because they completely overturned long-held conventional wisdom on a very important topic, and also because they received virtually no media coverage. Indeed, the *Washington Post* at the time reported that "some health officials considered keeping the

134   http://content.karger.com/ProdukteDB/produkte.asp?Doi=82569
135   http://www3.niaid.nih.gov/research/topics/STI/pdf/condomreport.pdf

report private", adding that "some family planning advocates said they feared that the new report would be used to put pressure on the FDA to change condom labels to reflect the conclusions."

As one commentator puts it, "It's like hearing that Grandma died, and immediately asking if Grandma will be making brownies for the funeral. The reality of the loss just hasn't sunk in yet."

Among other things, the study found that when one partner is infected with herpes, using condoms cut the risk of transmission by only about forty percent. In other words, despite the condom, there's still a 60% risk of passing on the herpes virus, when compared with people who don't use condoms in the same situation. In plain language: if your partner has herpes and is infectious, you are still more likely than not to catch the disease through sexual contact, *regardless of whether you use a condom.*

Meanwhile, with regard to human papilloma virus, responsible for about 99% of cervical cancers, "the Panel concluded that there was no epidemiological evidence that condom use reduced the risk of … infection".

In non-medical speak, there's no evidence *at all* that condoms can prevent the spread of infection.

Follow-up studies in the past five years have only confirmed the worst fears of researchers – in the case of syphilis, for example, even consistent use of a condom may only give you 29% risk reduction against the venereal disease – you still have a 71% chance of catching the pox from an infected regular sexual partner, even if you use a condom, compared with the infections rates of those who don't use condoms.

I will, so there is no confusion however, just again spell out what these figures mean. What is being measured is the infection rate amongst condom users, compared with people in the same situations who don't use condoms. This is called "relative risk". Some STDs you are almost guaranteed to catch through just one exposure without a condom. Thus, a condom user who sleeps with that infected person twice might be pushing their luck, and in a longer term relationship they are virtually guaranteed to catch the STD regardless of condom use.

And this doesn't even begin to take into account the misuse, or irregular use, of condoms: according to just one study of Australian high school students, 68 percent of those surveyed who said they were sexually active admitted that they don't use condoms every time they have sex, despite the fact that virtually every kid in the state's schools is given lessons in how to use the things. And even among adults, condom usage can be irregular, or start too late in an encounter, to prevent the spread of many infections.

In the drive to simply get people to use condoms, it appears sex educators have dumbed-down the message so much that crucial information is missing.

Information that could change your life. Most people, you see, have been totally unaware the most sexually transmitted diseases can simply sneak around, or through, a condom.

Compare that reality, however, with the rubbish being spouted in school sex education classes and in New Zealand Ministry of Health info centres like the "Hubba" website, www.hubba.co.nz. The Ministry of Health website for 'Hubba' is so inaccurate that there are actually sufficient grounds to shut it down. After identifying a range of sexually transmitted infections, including "chlamydia, genital warts, herpes, or gonorrhoea", the website's FAQ section then asks:

> Q: How can I protect myself against STIs?
> A: Use condoms. Correctly used and used every time you have sex, condoms are the most effective protection against most STIs, including HIV/AIDs."

Now here's what the *most recent scientific studies have shown* about condom effectiveness for a number of the diseases listed on the Hubba site:

Chlamydia: *still a 60% relative risk* of catching it even if a condom is correctly used every time

Gonorrhea: *still a 60% relative risk* of catching it even if a condom is correctly used every time

Herpes: still a *60% relative risk* of catching it even if a condom is correctly used every time

Genital warts: *no published study has found condoms can protect against this at all.*

Either New Zealand Ministry of Health officials are woefully ignorant of the failings of condoms in new scientific data over the past five years, or the Ministry is deliberately ignoring the facts, knowing that hundreds of thousands of school students have been mislead about safe sex over that time, leading to now-record levels of sexually transmitted diseases in young people, at a cost of millions of dollars to taxpayers and the community.

The Hubba website doesn't care that its "information" for young people is dangerously incorrect, judging from its arrogant Q&A on condom 'safety':

> Q: Are condoms safe?
> A: Condoms do protect you. Some people say it isn't worth using condoms because they have holes big enough for viruses to get through, but that's not true. Bacteria and viruses…cannot pass through an undamaged condom."

Tell that to the international medical journals and research teams. In fact, one classification used in the NIH report from 2000 was, "Condom used, No break, No visibly detectable holes, but still passes virus."

I'm sorry, is the New Zealand Ministry of Health getting its public health "information" from the back of a cereal box?

For the Hubba website to claim that condoms are "the most effective protection" against sexually transmitted diseases is incredible, especially if the 40% STD protection failure rate in condoms is not being disclosed to young people.

Nor is New Zealand's influential Family Planning Association in the clear on this one. The Association's resource kits blatantly state: "Condoms are known to greatly reduce the risk of catching other STIs such as chlamydia and gonorrhoea."

In the course of researching the article, the revelations stunned many on the magazine's staff and in the wider community as we gathered interviews.

"I can't believe it," one woman told us. "There are women who go through their pregnancies terrified because they have a one in 600 risk of having a deformed child, and we're talking here about a one in two risk of contracting serious and in some cases incurable sexual diseases even if we use a condom. Why on earth hasn't anyone told us this before?"

While it is conceded that condoms can reduce your risk of catching an STD by around half, a one in two chance is still worse odds than a round of Russian Roulette, and hardly equates to "safe sex". And if teenagers are not being told the grim full story in their school sex education classes, thanks to a Ministry of Health cover-up or botch-up, is it possible that kids have increased their sexual activity in the mistaken belief that a condom will somehow protect them?

Is that the real reason for the massive increase in STDs?

Instead of telling teenagers the cold hard truth, they've been lulled into such a false sense of security that they've tripled or even quadrupled their "bonk-rate" over the past 20 years of "safe sex" campaigns, making the (at best) 50% effectiveness of condoms useless in practical terms. If you're having four times more sex because you think condoms make it safe, in real terms you've actually doubled your risk of catching an STD. Which is why national disease rates are climbing into the stratosphere.

And you won't read that in the "No Rubba, No Hubba" material. What you will read however is an HIV gay propaganda scare story. Under the heading "Unsafe Sex", the Hubba site says:

> IT IS VERY UNSAFE TO...[h]ave vaginal sex without a condom. If you have anal sex or vaginal sex without a condom, you run the risk of becoming infected by HIV.

Did you know (and I'll bet you didn't), that a study in the *Journal of the American Medical Association* determined the odds of a man catching HIV from an infected woman, and then passing it on to his wife through vaginal sex, were *500 million to one against?* The only reason for including this "you can catch HIV through vaginal sex" propaganda in the publicity was to take pressure off gay men. Gay activist and AIDS researcher Gabriel Rotello makes exactly the same point in his book *Sexual Ecology*:[136]

"SOMEONE HAS REMARKED that if you want to tell a really convincing lie, you have to believe it yourself. If so, AIDS activists must sound very convincing when we argue that "Sex does not cause AIDS, a virus does." Or when we say, "There are no risk groups, only risky behaviors." Or when we insist, "It's not who you have sex with or where you have it that counts, it's what you do." Fighting the soundbites of blame with our own soundbites of self defense has seemed essential to the goal of convincing ourselves of the absolute justice of our cause. And so we have thrown up a fog of half truths, and in the process we have blinded ourselves.

"In a cruel irony, the only public discussion likely to save gay men from further saturation with AIDS is the very public discussion we least want to have, one almost guaranteed to embarrass many of us.

"But I believe that there is little that a Jesse Helms or a Pat Robertson can do to gay men that approaches the damage wrought by the endless continuation of AIDS.

"The appearance of a multitude of epidemic disasters almost immediately after gay men had carved out zones of sexual freedom has opened up the grim, almost unthinkable possibility that for gay men, sexual freedom leads inexorably to disease.

"As time goes on and the epidemic continues to rage among gay men while largely sparing the rest of the population, that nightmare grows only more plausible. It was one thing to believe we were accidental victims who would soon be joined in our sorrow by everyone else. It is quite another to discover that we will not be joined, that we stand almost alone, consumed with disease."

Although you'll see references in the daily media to rising heterosexual HIV, if you actually check the figures you'll find genuine heterosexual transmission

---

136   http://www.gabrielrotello.com/sexual_ecology%20intro.htm

is infinitesimal, and the figures include people linked to intravenous drug users or bisexual males. Straight vaginal sex is incredibly safe. But the risk rises massively if you are into anal sex or any activity that draws blood, or if you already have existing STDs. That's one of the reasons Africa is suffering a big AIDS problem, because sexual behaviours in Africa are riskier, and the STD rates are very high. Rotello again:

> "IN FACT, HIV IS SPREADING in an extremely selective way in the wider world, causing disastrous epidemics in places where heterosexual ecology favors its spread, and causing no epidemic at all in places where heterosexual behavior is less conducive."

Sadly, creating public hysteria about the chances of catching HIV heterosexually has led to people worrying needlessly and sometimes even killing themselves because of their fears.[137]

By the same token however, we are seeing a huge rise in other STD infections in Western teenagers as their sexual behaviour becomes more varied, which makes Rotello's warning a salient one.

Anyway, naturally we asked New Zealand's Ministry of Health to justify the outrageously inaccurate data in the Hubba campaign.

"I've referred your question to one of our senior policy analysts," said Hubba director Sally Hughes, "and they tell me that the Ministry of Health is satisfied that condoms are effective. We rely on the World Health Organisation's *Bulletin*[138] of June 2004 which includes a study of condom effectiveness."

Again, naturally, our magazine *Investigate* checked up. Although the WHO *Bulletin* is bullish in its language and socially liberal in its conclusions by urging people not to panic and to stick with condoms as the only prevention mechanism available, even if dubious, the *Bulletin* nonetheless concedes through gritted teeth in the body of its report that every medical research study since 2001 has found condoms have only limited efficacy against venereal diseases:

> "A META-ANALYSIS OF 20 studies found *no evidence that condoms were effective* against genital HPV (warts or cervical cancer) infection."

So Strike One against condoms in the very report New Zealand's Ministry of Health is using to justify its fatally-flawed "safe sex" message. If just one New

137   "Fear of Acquired Immunodeficiency Syndrome and Fear of Other Illness in Suicide", Acta Psychiatrica Scandinavica 90 (1994): 65-69
138   http://www.who.int/bulletin/volumes/82/6/454.pdf

Zealand woman contracts cervical cancer because she relied on the 'No Rubba' campaign, does that make the Ministry of Health criminally negligent?

But there's more.

The WHO document also discloses that a study of teenagers in the US revealed that STD rates were virtually the same between those who always used condoms (a minority) and those who either used condoms intermittently or not at all.

Twenty one percent of those who always used condoms had caught STDs, compared with 23% of the "sometimes or never group".

"So why are you continuing to push this condoms = safe sex message," we asked a senior Ministry of Health official, "when clearly it's the biggest load of old codswallop that's ever been perpetrated in a PR campaign?"

"Well," pondered the official after a moment, "perhaps the studies didn't properly monitor whether people really did use condoms all the time."

"Well, this is the WHO *Bulletin* that your own Hubba team referred me to…" we responded.

The WHO document also acknowledged and quoted the same studies we quoted earlier, showing (at best) a 40% reduction in the chances of a herpes or chlamydia infection.

Yet despite confirming that condoms are less safe than a six shooter revolver with one bullet loaded, the WHO seems to regard any reduction in STD risk as a good reason to keep promoting condom use.

"Condoms are useful", maintains Anna McNulty, Director of the Sydney Sexual Heath Centre, when asked about diseases that spread despite the use of condoms. McNulty adds that the increase in the rates of infection various sexual diseases – chlamydia rates have trebled in her state alone in the last five years according to one estimate – could come from a variety of factors including, she claims, the lack of access to health care among young people.

The problem, says McNulty, is that "people use them some of the time but not all of the time", and admits that while a great way to prevent things like AIDS and unintended pregnancies, in terms of preventing herpes and the genital warts that can lead to cervical cancer, "they are not as effective."

An added challenge is that fact that many diseases such as chlamydia can be asymptomatic, especially in men. "It can be silent for a long time, but it can cause significant damage", says another doctor.

Despite this, many public health bodies are delivering a mixed message. While, for example, South Australia's Health Department's web site frankly states that "condoms will give you some protection from most sexually transmitted infections, but some, like herpes, crabs and genital warts, can spread through skin-to-skin contact", it is a message that often gets lost when it is boiled down to a catchy slogan – such as "Safe Sex, No Regrets", the message currently being pushed in an NSW Health ad campaign, or the aforementioned "No Rubba, No Hubba".

Featuring a variety of television and print ads, the "Safe Sex, No Regrets" campaign shows groups of healthy, happy, good-looking young people – straight and gay and of various ethnicities – in different social circumstances. The copy on the print ads says things like, "Tonight I'm picking up Chlamydia" or some other disease, with the name of the disease crossed out and the word "condoms" printed underneath it, the implication being that condoms are all one needs to have what the tag-line calls, "no regrets".

"No regrets" is a pretty broad statement that implies something close to 100 per cent reliability. Yet very little is ever 100 per cent when health and medicine are involved (and in the sense that condoms are used to prevent the spread of disease, they have a medical component), and if the maker of any other device with as many caveats as condoms have attached to them ever tried to advertise in a similar way, they would be shut down by the authorities sooner than the casual couples featured in NSW Health's campaign could wake up the following morning with a splitting headache and serious misgivings.

But while the campaign does not tell the whole truth about condoms, McNulty says that "you have to keep the message simple, and the 'Safe Sex, No Regrets' campaign did a good job as it targeted both young heterosexuals and gay men." She concedes, though, that even with 100% condom usage, people are not fully protected against skin-to-skin infections.

"Take the example of NSW's 'Safe Sex, No Regrets' campaign," *Investigate* put to Hubba director Sally Hughes. "That campaign features a poster on chlamydia."

"I've seen it, yes," she confirmed.

"Which, based on the scientific evidence now pouring in, is totally and utterly untrue!"

And yet the Hubba website makes pretty much the same claims online about using condoms to prevent chlamydia.

There is another aspect to consider. A generation ago, couples were getting married in their early 20s, entering stable relationships and generally avoiding promiscuity. As a result, STD rates were much lower in the seventies and eighties. But today, most people are not settling into long term relationships until their late 20s or early 30s. They now have multiple sexual partners before marriage, and a corresponding huge rise in sexual disease rates. By the time many women now get around to having children, age and their exposure to STDs have played havoc with their fertility. Just another price that Generation-X will have to pay for the safe-sex myth the liberal Baby Boom generation lumbered them with.

The problem is that sex is a much more complicated thing than people of all stripes care to acknowledge, which is why diluting information about condoms to a happy, easily-digestible slogan that inspires false confidence is an irresponsible position for public health authorities to take. Yet that is exactly what campaigns such as 'Safe Sex, No Regrets' and 'No Rubba, No Hubba' do.

The danger of "safe sex", or "safer sex" as a slogan is that it cons people into thinking there is either no risk, or minimal risk. Yet a 71% relative risk of catching syphilis through a condom is hardly "safe" or even "safer".

The resistance to telling the truth about condoms, however, is so thick you can cut it with a knife.

"What do you want us to do?" growled one sexual health campaigner spoken to by *Investigate's* Sydney office, "preach abstinence?"

It is as if the sex education lobby is so wedded to pushing the "free sex, no consequences" message that they regard the scientific facts as a mere inconvenience, and have no intention of changing their advertising campaigns.

Case in point? As the *Investigate* article was about to go to press, TV1's award-winning *Close Up* programme ran as lead story some Ministry of Health propaganda about a new survey that "...shows a lack of awareness among the young about the need to use condoms to prevent sexually transmitted infections," presenter Susan Wood intoned.

"What researchers say is noticeable in the survey is the way teenagers seem to think they're invulnerable when it comes to sexually transmitted infection. According to the stats, 74% of students agreed that it was likely young people their age would get some kind of sexually transmitted infection. But only 23% thought that it could happen to them. When students did use condoms the reasons were more likely to be a fear of pregnancy than of sexually transmitted diseases. That comes at a time when STDs nationally are showing an alarming increase. The latest national figures from the sexual health clinics show that chlamydia rates are up 28% and gonorrhea is up 44%.

"With the survey showing a cavalier attitude to condom use amongst teenagers, the concern is that sexually transmitted diseases will only continue to increase, despite the message: if you don't use a Rubba there'll be no hubba hubba."

That message, as we're now revealing, is a complete fraud. Nonetheless, both the *NZ Herald* and the *Christchurch Press* ran the propaganda as the front page lead story the next day.

In another fascinating aside, a study in the *British Medical Journal* measured the effectiveness of a condom promotion strategy, much like the Hubba and No Regrets campaigns, but targeted at gay men. The survey found that while the condom promotion resulted in fewer cases of unprotected sex, inexplicably the rate of sexually-transmitted diseases "significantly increased".

That's right: more men used condoms, and more men caught diseases as a result.

Perhaps, conned into thinking condoms were "safe", the men indulged in more sex and thus increased their overall risk of infection.

Before I move onto the meaty interview that shows just how shallow the "Safer Sex" campaigns are, pause for a moment to check these major medical studies on whether condoms work against STDs:

WHAT THE STUDIES SAY:

WORLD HEALTH ORGANISATION BULLETIN, June 04: "No published prospective study has found protection against genital human papillomavirus (cervical cancer/warts/HPV) infection".

JOURNAL OF SEXUALLY TRANSMITTED DISEASES, 2003; 30: 273-9: A study of 917 female sex workers in Lima, Peru, were re-examined monthly for STDs. Those women who consistently used condoms still had a chlamydia infection rate of 74% compared to the infection rate of women who didn't use condoms.

AMERICAN JOURNAL OF PUBLIC HEALTH, 2003; 93: 901-2: A study of 380 American girls aged 14 to 18 over six months revealed that 30% of the girls who did not use condoms had caught a sexually transmitted disease by the end of six months, as had 17.8% of the girls who always used condoms

AIDS, 2001; 15: 2171-9: A study of 17,264 adults in the town of Rakai, Uganda, over four years, measured STD infection rates in the population and the effectiveness of condoms. Only 4.4% (760 people) had always used condoms. Of those people, consistent condom use only resulted in a 29% reduction in syphilis infections, and a 50% reduction in chlamydia and gonorrhea. The prevalence of the STDs trichomoniasis and vaginosis "were not reduced". Even with HIV, the disease the condoms are most effective at preventing, the infection rate was still 37% of the rate of those who didn't use condoms.

JOURNAL OF SEXUALLY TRANSMITTED DISEASES, 2002; 29: 725-35: A meta-analysis of 20 studies "found no evidence that condoms were effective against genital HPV infection", warts or cervical cancer.

AMERICAN JOURNAL OF EPIDEMIOLOGY, 2003; 157: 218-26: A study of 444 female university students found "that consistently using condoms with a new partner was not associated with significant protection against HPV".

AMERICAN JOURNAL OF EPIDEMIOLOGY, 2004; 159: 242-51: A study of 4314 participants who visited STD clinics found consistent use of condoms still resulted in an infection rate of 82% compared against those who didn't use condoms.

JOURNAL OF INFECTIOUS DISEASES, 1999; 180: 1624-31: A study followed the progress of 484 adolescents at four STD clinics over six months, and found 21% of those who always used condoms had caught a sexually transmitted disease, compared with 23% of those who sometimes or never used a condom (a 91% risk of infection, group vs group).

JOURNAL OF SEXUALLY TRANSMITTED DISEASES, 1995; 22: 15-21: A study of 598 people attending an STD clinic in Baltimore found infection rates were almost the same, regardless of whether a condom was always used or not.

Armed with that information, you can easily see condoms are next to useless. What the bureaucrats at the WHO focus on is population infection levels, rather than individual levels. So when they see a 50% reduction in disease, they proclaim it as a good thing. And it is. But...they refuse to tell people that *there is more than a minor risk, there is a significant risk that they will catch an STD over a period of time, even if they use condoms.* We argue people have a right to be told the real risks so they can make informed decisions about their sexual behaviour, they same way they do over smoking. So join me as I go head to head with the Ministry of Health's Chief Advisor on Population Health, Dr Doug Lush:

WISHART: It would appear that the public health campaigns that have been going on have ignored the scientific data now pouring in that condoms will not protect against most STIs, and that the huge rise in STIs may be directly related to the promotion of condoms as a safe sex tool, when in fact they're not safe.

LUSH: I think that's wrong, that condoms are a very important part of protecting people from sexually transmitted diseases and have a growing importance in the prevention of STIs and HIV. I haven't seen the particular studies you refer to, however I do know there are problems in some studies in that the reported use and continued use of condoms cannot be verified or validated that these people are using them properly or consistently, and this can lead to the spread, so there are a lot of methodological problems

WISHART: Yeah, let's spread that the other way though, flip that coin, and you will never be able to prove condoms are effective. If you're going to say condoms are effective 'if they're used correctly' how on earth would you know?

LUSH: Have you heard of the Cochrane Collaboration? They did a very vigorous assessment of all the research in an area and they very strongly support the reduction of HIV incidence from condoms. Now HIV is somewhat different from other sexually transmitted infections but the work that's done on HIV shows that condoms are very useful in protecting people from transmission.

WISHART: I'm not going to disagree with you on HIV, I think all the medical studies are showing exactly what you're saying. What I will say to you is that it's the only sexually transmitted disease that condoms will protect you against. And I will tell you that categorically.

LUSH: Well I would say that that isn't the case. We know that gonorrhea can be protected also by the use of condoms, and there's good evidence of that. Other STIs like herpes, where it depends on where the herpes lesions are, there's variable protection from condoms. But syphilis, gonorrhea, chlamydia – there's good protection from condoms and I'm very comfortable with the approach we've used in New Zealand, "No Rubba No Hubba Hubba". We know that teenagers are sexually active and this is a way that they can protect themselves from STIs. It's not a foolproof way but it certainly does reduce the incidence of sexually transmitted diseases.

WISHART: What sort of level of protection would you expect a condom to give against chlamydia, gonorrhea or syphilis?

LUSH: If they're used consistently and regularly, then a very good rate of protection.

WISHART: How would you define that, percentage wise, allowing for the fact that three percent of condoms will result in pregnancy, so that's the ultimate sort of failure rate.

LUSH: I know studies have shown the failure rate is between two and eighteen percent in condom use. The physical characteristics of the condom suggest that we know the agents that cause STIs don't pass through the condom, so if a condom is used correctly there won't be any transmission.

WISHART: How would you feel if I told you the scientific evidence over the past five years is showing that, for example, that there may only be a reduction in chlamydia rates of 26% against those who don't use condoms at all. Those who are consistently and always using condoms according to the WHO's meta-analysis are still likely to suffer a 74% rate of infection. Would that surprise you?

LUSH: That would, and I'd be interested in looking at their methodology as to how they validated this.

WISHART: This was a study of 917 sex workers in Peru, published in the *Journal of Sexually Transmitted Diseases*. But even in the best studies the WHO's meta-analysis has pulled together, the chlamydia reduction rate is only 40%, so you're still talking worse odds than Russian Roulette.

LUSH: A 40% reduction is a useful reduction and I would see that as a worst case scenario [not the best case].

WISHART: It's useful in the sense of looking at the overall population demographic, it's not so useful if little Johnny or Mary goes out, reading the posters saying condoms are "safe sex", and that's the basic message. Up to 25% of young people in some Northland towns have chlamydia, so that's pretty good odds of catching it over time.

LUSH: It is a population approach, but it also is personal protection. And it is valid advice for someone who is sexually active that they should use a condom. The frequency of activity that prostitutes are involved in is very different from adolescents in NZ, as far as frequency of sexual contact. Although there may be some who are very sexually promiscuous, this isn't the norm and you can't really apply those studies to the type of protection you're going to get from condoms.

WISHART: I'll take you through some of these studies because they are fascinating, and they're the only evidence that the medical world actually has. A study of 380 American girls aged 14 to 18, revealed that 30% of the girls who didn't use condoms had caught a sexually transmitted disease by the end of six months, and 17.8% of girls who always used condoms also had caught STDs at the end of that period.

LUSH: This is reported condom use, and we see a very dramatic decrease.

WISHART: Well you do, and you don't. At a population level you see a decrease in the percentage, but at a personal level you've got a bunch of kids out there who are putting condoms on because the health authorities are telling them "safe sex – wear a condom", and the truth is they're not being told that "in actual fact you've still got a very high risk you're going to catch something".

LUSH: Our message to the youth of NZ, or sexually active people, is that if you want to avoid sexually transmitted infections, then the sure way is not to have sex. However...

WISHART: Where do you say that?!

LUSH: ... accepting the reality that young people do have sex and they want to protect themselves, using a condom is the best way.

WISHART: Well, are you telling young people though? Because I've looked across the Hubba site and I'll be frank – that site is grossly inaccurate. Even on the Q&A section, "Are condoms safe?", the site arrogantly is suggesting – it lists the STIs "Chlamydia, gonorrhea, herpes, genital warts" etc – and says "people say these things can get through, but they can't, it's safe". That's what they're saying, and it's a crock! There are something like 40 studies that the World Health Organisation has cited in its Bulletin, which ironically the Ministry of Health referred me to.

LUSH: Looking at the site, we have a question "Why aren't you promoting abstinence?" which is a question we are often asked. And I'll read out the response: "The campaign is about supporting choices made by teens, whether that is to have sex or wait. Those who are sexually active need protection to reduce the risk of STIs. Unfortunately many young people don't plan their first sexual experience, and this campaign aims to help young people think realistically and be ready to protect themselves."

WISHART: OK, if this campaign is about making young people think realistically, where is the evidence on your website that you are telling them there is still, for example, an 80% chance they're going to get syphilis?
LUSH: There isn't an 80% chance of getting syphilis from a single sexual encounter.

WISHART: Well how many kids are having single encounters and how do we know? This gets back to my question at the start which we don't have an answer to: You do query, and rightly so, that we don't know how well people are using the condoms, or whether they're really using them or whether they're just saying so to please the researcher. But the flip side of that coin is that the health authorities are making the point that a condom properly used will prevent this. But you've got no scientific evidence to back that up either, for exactly the same reason – because you can't get a control group that you can actually prove are doing it right.

LUSH: Fortunately we know the way a condom works. It is a direct barrier between the semen and the vagina.

WISHART: Yeah, it's great for preventing pregnancy, but according to the studies it's no good at protecting against most STIs.

LUSH: Problems occur both with the validity of reporting and the behavioural aspects. It is hard to conduct because the intimate nature of the activity you're investigating means you can't actually watch what's happening, so you just have to assume people are telling the truth.

WISHART: Exactly! But Doug, here's my point...

LUSH: The point of our campaign is that we go into a great lot of detail about the need for people to know how to use condoms properly, and even to practice using condoms, so for young men we would advise them to practice by themselves using condoms, so that when it comes to their first sexual experience they know how to do them, so its important not just to use them but to know how to use them.

WISHART: I'm going to come back to this question time and time again: how do you know that using a condom the way the Health Ministry recommends will actually achieve the result? I'll tell you why you don't know – there isn't one scientific study in the world that shows it, because there is no control group that you can monitor 24/7 to see whether they're doing it correctly or not. There has not been a study like that, therefore you cannot make the claim that "if you do it right it will protect you". You have no scientific basis for making that claim!

LUSH: We have extremely strong support for HIV from these meta-analyses that were done.

WISHART: Yeah, but as you've acknowledged, and I agree, HIV is contained within the semen, effectively, and is therefore trapped by the condom as part of the condom's design to prevent pregnancy. These other diseases are not constructed in such ways, and according to the WHO, according to the *Journal of the American Medical Association*, according to the *British Medical Journal*, and so on and so on and so on, these diseases are getting through. Yeah, sure, you can sit there and say "well, we don't know how well they're using the condoms or whether they're really reporting them", but the flip side of the coin is, you have no proof that using a condom correctly is going to work anyway, because that scientific study hasn't been done *either*.

LUSH: The studies that you've told me about that you say discredit the value of condoms still have significant differences between those who're using condoms and those who don't. So on that evidence alone it would be worthwhile to suggest using condoms and promoting condom usage.

WISHART: Well, let's take it through a little bit. I'll start with the World Health Organisation *Bulletin* of June 2004. Quote: "No published prospective study has found protection against genital human papilloma virus (ie, cervical cancer, warts, HPV) infection".

LUSH: Does it say that?

WISHART: It does say that.

LUSH: Is that what it reports?

WISHART: I will read you the exact quote: "No published prospective study has found protection against genital human papilloma virus HPV infection".

LUSH: And this is in?

WISHART: This is WHO's *Bulletin* June 04 [that you referred me to]. It's in the abstract. I've got a couple of others here. *AIDS Journal* 2001, a study of 17,264 adults in the town of Rakai, Uganda, over four years measured STD infection rates. Consistent condom use resulted in only a 29% reduction in syphilis infections as against the general population, and a 50% reduction in chlamydia and gonorrhea.

The *Journal of Sexually Transmitted Diseases*, 2002, a meta-analysis of 20 studies found, quote: "found no evidence that condoms were effective against genital HPV infection, warts or cervical cancer." Again, that contrasts directly with what's on the Hubba site.

LUSH: And the Hubba site is saying? I can't see the part where you say we mention the wart virus. I'm looking here and it says "condoms do work, used correctly and consistently". And they're the key points.

WISHART: Definition of STIs: "Chlamydia, genital warts, herpes or gonorrhea". Then you've got a question, "How can I protect myself against STIs?". Answer, "Use condoms. Correctly used, and used every time you have sex, condoms are the most effective protection against most STIs including HIV/AIDS". So you do mention genital warts in there.

LUSH: Well I do agree with that statement, that condoms are the most effective method of protection we know of. There aren't any other effective ways of doing this.

WISHART: I'm not suggesting that the Health Ministry simply throws up its hands in horror and says "OK, no sex", albeit that there are those who say it's a good idea. I appreciate that you're not going to get that message through to teenagers, but certainly fluffing around and ignoring the reality that condoms won't protect – I mean, let's get real! Condoms will *not* protect people against STIs. Parents out there are thinking the sex education methods are working. You've got the front page stories in the papers that are nothing but inaccurate propaganda. It's literally interwoven with all your publicity and has been for a long time. Is it not time that we admitted the Emperor has no clothes, and began investigating a different strategy for young people, because there's nothing on your website to suggest there's a risk at all?

LUSH: I think it [the website] implies that you need to be experienced and consistent in your use.

WISHART: I'll take you to another one. *American Journal of Epidemiology* 2003, a study of 444 female university students in the States found that "consistently using condoms with a new partner is not associated with significant protection against HPV".

LUSH: Yes, but that's not an area that we dwell on in the publicity, we're mainly talk about chlamydia.

WISHART: If you have got a partner who may have slept around, may have a disease, really, don't rely on a condom at all. Insist on a screening check because there is a very real chance that even if you use a condom, you're going to catch it. You're not saying that, but that's what you need to say. Is it time to say, "Condoms don't work except for pregnancy or HIV. Don't rely on them for any other protection". Isn't that a better way of giving kids the right choices to make?

LUSH: No I don't believe so at all!

WISHART: Why?

LUSH: Because condoms are effective.

WISHART: Against what!? With respect, what are they effective against?

LUSH: Syphilis.

WISHART: No they're not. The best study that the WHO meta-analysis found shows a reduction of 29% in syphilis rates, still a 71% chance of contracting syphilis, so you can throw that one out the window.

LUSH: But again, the methodology in a lot of these is...

WISHART: You still have *no* scientific evidence to make the claim that a condom, correctly used, will protect you, because as you point out no one has done the 24/7, hidden camera, monitored installation of people having sex. So you can't make that comment hand on heart, and your comment about the studies possibly not reflecting proper condom use is irrelevant, because if you don't know that condoms actually work – even in ideal conditions – then how can you criticize these studies? That's just fobbing it off.

LUSH: I will be a bit repetitive here. We do know that the viruses and bacteria that cause STIs do not pass through.

WISHART: You know from a lab test ...

LUSH: We know that if that physical barrier is in place these infections won't be passed from person to person. We know from the best studies which have been undertaken in people with HIV that there is an 80% reduction. So we know that condoms will also work for other sexually transmitted infections.

WISHART: Such as?

LUSH: We have some modest results from the literature, but the methodological problems with reporting and the competence in using condoms means we need to interpret these results carefully.

WISHART: Doug, you're not listening to me, with respect. You're repeating the same thing.

LUSH: I told you I'd repeat the same thing. That's my line and that's where we're at with this.

WISHART: But you cannot make this claim. You can't. You have no proof that a correctly-used condom, in the wild, will protect you. The results you have about viruses and bacteria not passing through the latex are lab tests in ideal conditions. But a human body is not an ideal condition. And you don't know, and I don't know, where in fact the bacteria from some of these things actually are on the person, or how easily transferable they are. That may be why the condoms are failing – not because people aren't using them correctly but just because condoms will not actually work in that situation. And you can't point to a [single] piece of research that shows I'm wrong on that.

LUSH: I'm not underestimating the complexity in the technique, but there are technical aspects to this.

WISHART: You don't have one single scientific study about using a condom correctly!

LUSH: We have extremely good studies.

WISHART: Name *one*. I have a suspicion after reading the WHO *Bulletin* that one has never been done.

LUSH: I'll refer you to the Cochrane Collaboration on condom use, which shows an 80% reduction in HIV incidence.

WISHART: But I agree with you on that. We've talked about HIV. You're not tackling the central issue. Before you can get up and slag off these studies by saying people may be misreporting their condom use, you have to be able to prove the claim that the Ministry of Health repeatedly makes, that a correctly used condom will protect you. Where's the proof?

LUSH: A lot of it comes through inference, and a lot of it comes through studies that do show a reduction in transmission.

WISHART: What studies? The ones I'm showing you are not showing a significant reduction in transmission. You've still got, at best, a one in two chance of catching something. That's worse odds than Russian Roulette, significantly worse odds.

LUSH: We'll stick with the Cochrane Collaboration and the results for HIV where there has been attention to the methodology. I'd venture to say the methodology on the other ones is problematic.

WISHART: Obviously we're going to be at loggerheads on this one. Is there any plan, on the basis of what I've revealed to you, to review the way the "safe sex" message is publicized in New Zealand, do you accept that the current publicity is flawed?

LUSH: No, I don't.

WISHART: Do you accept that it could be potentially flawed?

LUSH: I acknowledge that we need to watch what is in the literature and that abstinence is the most risk averse – for the most risk averse, abstinence is something that people might want to consider.

WISHART: What about on your websites and in all your literature, why are you not incorporating the studies that have been around for five years now – and these are the only studies you've got to work with because they're the only studies in the world – that are revealing significant – up to a 100% chance – risks of catching STIs regardless of using a condom. Why is this not on your website, why are teenagers not being told in school, and will you rectify that?

LUSH: Teenagers. The aim is to protect teenagers who are having their first, or infrequent, sexual encounters. We know that the people they're having sex with may well have an STI. There isn't good information on the protection per single episode, but we believe it would give a good level of protection for each single episode, and combined with reporting and treatment of STIs, this is a useful way to protect individuals and the population by reducing rates.

WISHART: Well I've quoted you two studies following teenagers over six months, and even those who consistently used condoms, and in some cases almost exactly the same number of condom-users caught sexually transmitted diseases as those who didn't use condoms. So we're going to be saying the "No Rubba, No Hubba" campaign is an absolute fraud. If you guys don't put this information in there, how can anyone trust what the Ministry of Health says?

LUSH: I don't have anything to reply to that, except to say that I'm certainly comfortable with Hubba.

WISHART: But how can you be comfortable with it, in the face of 40-odd studies quoted by the WHO? How can you look at those studies and tell me that there's nothing you have to do to Hubba and everything on your website is OK, when I've just proven scientifically that it's a crock.?

LUSH: I don't think you have proven that.

WISHART: We've had this discussion. You have no studies to back up your claim. You can make the claim for HIV and that's all you can make it for.

LUSH: You've raised a number of studies that show a low level of protection or no protection. There are problems, as we know, in the methodology of doing this. We know that what we see in HIV is generalisable. We know the physical characteristics of the condom.

WISHART: But that relates to pregnancy and semen. It doesn't relate to herpes or HPV, or syphilis, chlamydia and so forth. Those are different organisms. You are trying to extrapolate something which is specific to condom design – i.e., stopping semen from going through, and you're trying to extrapolate that out to venereal disease generally and you can't, there's not one study in the world that shows this.

LUSH: Still, on herpes, I did mention that herpes can occur when condoms are used.

WISHART: The studies show that at best there will be a 40% reduction in herpes infection rates if a condom is always and consistently used.

LUSH: That's a spectacular result.

WISHART: It's a spectacular result at a population level ...

LUSH: ... and at an individual level as well.

WISHART: *Not if the individual hasn't been told*. It's only spectacular if the individual knows before slapping a condom on that there's still a 60% chance they'll catch herpes if they sleep with someone who's affected over a period of time. And you're not telling them that.

LUSH: You shouldn't have sexual activity if you have lesions.

WISHART: But there's nothing on your website, nothing, that gives people any advice of the risks. I'll turn this around. You guys are going after the makers of vitamin supplements, for heaven's sake, and dietary supplements, and saying that because there is a slight risk that somebody may be mislead, that these things should all be tightly regulated, and here you are promoting the biggest load of old codswallop I've ever seen. It doesn't stack up against the scientific evidence. You're not prepared to make changes to your website or the way you do it. You are holding onto irrelevant studies to try and justify your position – if the Ministry was in private practice it'd be sued!

LUSH: I have no response to that.

WISHART: No, and with respect I'm not trying to get at you. But in general terms the Ministry of Health would be down on a private operator like a ton of bricks, as they are, and here's the MoH refusing, *refusing* to tell young people the real truth about condoms and the risks! Nowhere on your website or your material is that point raised, and you're saying "we're not going to change it", and I'm saying to you the best scientific evidence in the world says what you're saying is a crock. You've got no response to that apart from an HIV study that's irrelevant, and I think you guys are on dangerous ground. That's my personal opinion.

LUSH: Yep, I'm hearing you.

WISHART: So I'll ask the question again: Are you prepared to start giving much more information about the failures of condoms based on the scientific evidence to date, so that people can make informed decisions for themselves? You say abstinence doesn't work, but if people knew that every time they had sex there was a real 50% chance of their penis dropping off, do you think the abstinence rates would actually grow? I think they would. So abstinence can't be taken in isolation. Abstinence is relevant to the amount of information and risk that is out there. For the past 20 years we've been sold a safe sex message that says if you use a condom you're protected.

LUSH: I don't believe we've said that. We've said that if people are going to make a choice to be sexually active, then they can get a level of protection by using condoms. We've never said this is absolute, but we believe it is good protection they can get with consistent and proper use.

WISHART: Yeah, but your definition of good protection at the start of this interview was between two and 18% failure [a 98% - 82% protection], now there's not one study in the world that shows you'll get that level of protection from a condom with these diseases at all. Best case scenario, 50% protection, worst case zero protection.

LUSH: I'm talking about the condom failure rate. That is thought to be the way transmission can occur.

WISHART: Yes, but what I'm saying to you is that real tests in the real world are showing the transmission rate is much higher. There is a very good chance that our current sexual disease explosion is directly a result of the safe sex campaign, because people are not being told the full story about the risks and failures. And it seems you're not even aware of the failures in the Ministry.

I find it staggering. I don't know how many kids have got a disease now that's making them potentially infertile, and certainly giving them health issues, because we haven't faced up to this. And how many women die of cervical cancer, because of this?

LUSH: The Ministry is quite clear on screening policy for cervical cancer.

WISHART: Yes, but screening is after the fact. You're not giving people a choice before they endanger themselves. In fact the material on the Hubba site says condoms will protect you from genital warts. Your information is grossly inaccurate and possibly dangerous.

LUSH: I don't believe that any of the information is dangerous. I do agree with you that abstinence is something that needs to be considered and that is an option that young people may wish to explore. However there are sexually active people and the best way of protecting themselves is condoms. We're confident of that and we've had an expert group who have advised us on this.

WISHART: Well you'd better be going back to those experts and ask "why didn't you tell us this?". There is no study in the world that is giving people the confidence that you believe exists. And I can't believe that an NZ taxpayer-funded Ministry of Health, with the responsibilities that the Ministry has for public safety, can justify the stand that it is currently taking as if the iceberg is not in front of you. It's there all right.

LUSH: The iceberg is what?

WISHART: The iceberg is the cold hard reality that condoms don't work, and we've got a generation of kids now who've caught STDs because they believed the lie.

LUSH: I think the kids who've caught the STDs are ones who haven't used condoms or haven't used them in a way that's allowed them to protect themselves.

WISHART: Well, the international studies are showing that up to 100% of those using condoms correctly are still catching STDs. So again, you have no scientific basis for your anecdotal claim.

LUSH: That points to the problems they have in using them and using them consistently.

WISHART: And again, name me one scientific study that supports what you are claiming.

LUSH: I'll take you back to the Cochrane study on HIV.

WISHART: But you've got the WHO meta-analysis in front of you. It's telling you something you don't want to hear, and so you're ignoring it.

LUSH: We're going over the same territory now. We think condoms provide good protection from sexually transmitted diseases.

WISHART: How good is "good"?

LUSH: This is a difficult thing. Looking at what's happened in HIV, we'd say an 80% reduction in risk.

WISHART: So you'd say there's only a 20% risk when they use a condom with someone else who's infected, of catching it, and that's despite every single study I've taken you through today?

LUSH: I would have thought [the protection] was bigger than that. Obviously evidence in this area is difficult to come by.

WISHART: Doug Lush, Ministry of Health, appreciate your time.

Realising the NZ Ministry of Health had been soundly thrashed, caught with its pants down, hadn't done its homework, and all those other clichés,

Doug Lush sent a letter to *Investigate* to further clarify the Ministry's position. He urged the magazine to take cognizance of the fact that despite the bleak data in the studies, the World Health Organisation was still urging countries not to give up on condoms because they are effective at cutting population rates of STDs. The WHO also noted that more studies are needed on the subject. We responded as follows:

> WITH RESPECT TO THE WHO, rubbish! While one medical study could be treated as a rogue result, the medical journals are publishing study after study reaching the same conclusion. No study is showing any result backing up the fairy story that "a condom, properly used" will prevent STDs.
>
> While *Investigate* accepts that condoms certainly have a role in preventing HIV, and possibly other diseases at a population level, our major issue is one of informed consent. *Currently, there are no warnings in sex education publicity material that reflect the grave failings in regard to condoms and STDs.*
>
> It is only appropriate for condoms to continue being promoted if, and only if, the public is given the real facts about the disease transmission rates through condoms. If the public is not given the information from the dozens of medical studies published so far, then the Ministry is effectively conducting a new *Unfortunate Experiment*, only this time it affects hundreds of thousands of New Zealanders, their health, their fertility and possibly even their lives.
>
> As we said in the interview, people may change their sexual behaviours if they believe there is a real risk to themselves, despite the use of a condom. Of course, others won't change. But that should be the public's choice, based on their right to know, not secret information hidden away because the Ministry of Health and Family Planning Association don't want to upset their own publicity schemes.
>
> This is a national disgrace, and the Ministry of Health's continued denial of the only hard evidence in the world is an absolute scandal.
>
> **Ian Wishart, Editor**

The issue, as you probably saw in the interview with the New Zealand Ministry of Health's senior expert in the field, is actually quite simple. Just like the mythology surrounding homosexuality, so too have liberals built up a mythology surrounding condoms. The mythology is basically that a condom, used properly and always, will protect the user against STDs. And yet, no one in the entire world has done an in depth medical study actually testing whether a condom, "properly used", will deliver that protection, making the claim meaningless. The reason no study has been done is because it would require direct surveillance of couples having sex with and without condoms, whilst knowingly exposing one or both partners to a sexually transmitted disease as part of the study. *It has never been done and never will be!*

Repeat after me: "I will not be sucked in by liberals ever again. Liberals tell lies to brainwash the public. Condoms don't work."

Naturally, after we published our explosive interview, two things happened. Firstly, the story created barely a ripple because national media in New Zealand and Australia – despite giving frontpage coverage to the STD epidemics and the need for condoms – refused to cover the story. All, that is, except one, the radical liberal faction at Auckland University's student radio station 95BFM. Host Noelle McCarthy saw the magazine's cover story and thought she'd have a crack at *Investigate* by interviewing a woman from the Family Planning Association (the NZ affiliate of Planned Parenthood in the US) debunking our investigation. Instead Noelle, who whilst she may be liberal is no intellectual slug, twigged partway through her interview that *Investigate* was right, and she ended up getting Family Planning to admit as much. It struck Noelle, and her listeners, as odd that students were not being told the truth about condoms as part of informed consent.

The second development, however, was more expected – a backlash by Family Planning and the Ministry of Health as they tried to counter any impact the article might have, by continuing to repeat the existing lies in soothing tones to anyone who would listen, even us:

> LIKE THE ONGOING CRUSADE against condom use carried out in the US since the 1990s, *Investigate's* article on "safe sex" selectively cites findings to support its case while ignoring other findings that clearly support condom use and effectiveness. The WHO Public Health Review, used by *Investigate* to support its discussion, does highlight complexities and concerns in relation to condom use, but its conclusion is clear: Condom use "can substantially reduce the spread of STIs" including "reduced acquisition" of syphilis, chlamydia, gonorrhoea, trichomoniasis, urethral infections and of HIV. The Review states that: "Even partially effective interventions can have a major impact on controlling STIs".
>
> The US National Institutes of Health report findings, also cited by *Investigate*, clearly state that "beyond mutual lifelong

monogamy among uninfected couples, condom use is the only method for reducing the risk of HIV infections and STDs available to sexually active individuals".

It also states that condoms are "essentially impermeable" and "a highly effective barrier".

We do know that condoms do successfully reduce the transmission of most STIs, and the Family Planning Association (FPA) also agrees that their effectiveness depends largely on how correctly and consistently they are used and the type of STI. Rather than undermine confidence in the efficacy of condoms for diseases transmitted by semen or vaginal fluids, we need to assist sexually active people wishing to reduce the risk of infection, or unplanned pregnancy, to use condoms effectively.

There are many reasons for increased extramarital sexual activity around the world. In New Zealand these include a far later age for marriage than in the 1970s. To blame this increase in sexual activity on the successful promotion of condoms, when a range of research indicates well over 50% of sexually active New Zealanders do not use them, seems both simplistic and illogical.

FPA always speaks of 'safer sex' and places great emphasis on comprehensive sexuality education that includes the options of abstaining from sexual activity and delaying sex until it can be managed responsibly. Comprehensive sexuality education involves age appropriate programmes which contribute to building positive and healthy relationships, learning negotiation, communication and sex avoidance skills, while contributing to an understanding of the positive nature of sexuality, providing information on contraceptive options and information on how to access sexual and reproductive health services. Correct and consistent condom use is part of this.

"Just say no" abstinence-only messages in the US, and increasingly elsewhere, frequently ignore the complexity and diversity of young people's lives, rely on negative messages about condoms, encourage fear and guilt, and provide little information and understanding of the complexity of human sexuality. A body of research indicates that young people who have pledged abstinence develop STIs at rates at least equal to their non-pledged counterparts, and are more likely to have sex secretly and unsafely.

Regrettable though it may be for some, many New Zealanders will not choose to abstain from sex outside, or until, marriage.

One report indicated that only 3% intended to wait until their wedding night. Research indicates that internationally up to 30% of those who have HIV are unaware of this, while up to 70% of women and 50% of men are likely to be unaware that they have contracted chlamydia, the so-called 'hidden' disease.

Surely we must recognise such realities and give people the means, and motivation, to make positive, healthy decisions in order to avoid the transmission of STIs, and of unplanned pregnancies. This will require comprehensive strategies of which, in the words of the WHO, "condom promotion represents an important component".

Gill Greer, Executive Director
NZ Family Planning Association

Naturally, we were not going to let Family Planning get away with that load of old cobblers, especially as Greer is now the world head of Planned Parenthood International!

WISHART RESPONDS

Allow me to demolish this appalling piece of inaccurate spin, bit by bit. Your letter is peppered with rhetoric ('ongoing crusade') and hyperbole ('selectively cites'), but you don't actually deal with the dishonesty of your own Family Planning 'crusade'.

For example, you accuse us of 'ignoring' findings that 'clearly support condom use and effectiveness'. Go ahead, name *one* relevant study. The Ministry of Health couldn't and I very much doubt that you can.

You approvingly quote the WHO as saying condoms can 'substantially reduce' the spread of STIs, while ignoring the inconvenient fact that the WHO sees a mere 29% reduction in risk as 'substantial'. I, on the other hand, and I'm sure most sexually active people, would regard an infection rate of 71% among condom-users (compared to non-users) as still a majority risk. Perhaps Family Planning NZ wrote the WHO's conclusory paragraphs.

I note too that you conveniently don't mention herpes or genital warts, which condoms are useless against. Do you tell teenagers that when educating them about condoms?

You continue to quote empty rhetoric when you repeat the assertion that condoms are 'essentially impermeable' and 'a highly effective barrier'.

Against what? Fruit flies?

If condoms are what you say they are, why do a number of respected American medical journal studies show almost no reduction in STD rates between people who use condoms properly and those who don't?

That's what I mean Gill – between yourselves and the Ministry of Health the shallow rubbish you spout out to a gullible media is like *The Emperor Has No Clothes* meets *Groundhog Day*. It doesn't matter how many scientific holes get shot in the condom myth, both of your organisations pretend the scientific studies don't exist. You're like a healthcare Flat Earth Society.

You glibly state that condoms 'do successfully reduce' the transmission of most STDs. Name *one* relevant medical study that shows a condom used 'effectively' protects against STDs. Oh, that's right, there isn't one!

Once again, when the science blows holes in your family planning campaigns, you take the option of repeating the myths over and over again in the hope that you'll brainwash people into believing you.

You state: 'FPA always speaks of safer sex…' Yeah right. On FPA's own website are your own documents that use the phrase 'safe sex pamphlets' or 'Summer Safe Sex Campaign'. Nowhere in your 'comprehensive sexuality education' programmes are you disclosing that condoms are scientifically proven to be useless against herpes and warts, and near useless against chlamydia, syphilis, trichomoniasis and other nasties. Quite the contrary: Family Planning and the Ministry of Health lie like flatfish to teenagers, glossing over or avoiding the hard facts.

We are not saying don't use condoms. What we are saying is that young people have a right, under the principle of informed consent, to be told the real risks, as we now know them to exist, of condoms failing to offer significant protection against any STDs except HIV.

You bleat about the 'just say no' campaign effectiveness in the States, and yet the medical journal studies are saying condoms are equally useless . Family Planning is in a glasshouse on this one.

Here's a novel idea for Family Planning: be honest. Stop teaching social engineering propaganda and start giving young people real facts.

The disingenuousness of the NZ Ministry of Health and Family Planning over promoting "Safe Sex" was particularly galling. To see organizations like these prepared to blatantly lie to the media and the public was a frightening indicator of just how far the liberal poison has spread. It is almost as if the health "industry" wants a crisis, to keep them gainfully employed, whilst at the same time promoting promiscuity and a false sense of "safe". As we pointed out, "Safe Sex" is mentioned both in Family Planning documents we found, and also still on the Ministry's Hubba website as of March 2007, where it says:

> THERE ARE ALL KINDS **of ways to have safe sex**
> Here are some of the things that are safe:
> • Vaginal sex using a condom and water based lubricant
> • Anal sex using a condom and water based lubricant

The reaction from magazine readers to our story, meanwhile, was astounding. Most were stunned that they had clearly been sold a lie about condoms, a lie that might explain why kids were catching more STDs than ever before.

"I must tell you," wrote one mother, "that the message appears to have got through at the grass roots level. At the school my neighbour's daughter goes to, the health curriculum teachers had a meeting to discuss the implications of your article for the school, and they will now be clearly teaching that condoms will not protect against STIs."

Or this from another mother:

> FOUND YOUR ARTICLE on "Safe Sex" both timely and fascinating as it confirmed a concern that recently came to my attention.
>
> My 17 year old daughter had asked, while reading an historical novel, what the "French Pox" was. The description of the symptoms was mildly graphic, but graphic enough for her to look horrified when I replied the characters were discussing syphilis!
>
> During the discussion which followed, I was equally horrified when I discovered that the so called "Sex Education" our children are given at school does not include the vital information of what the symptoms of various STIs are. She promptly put down her book and checked out for herself the symptoms of every STI she could think of, on the net. She was quite rightly furious and outraged. In her words, "They are showing teenagers how to use a loaded gun, without telling them the consequences."
>
> She and her boyfriend read your article on "Safe Sex" – they are both pretty annoyed that the gun they were handed at school,

has an apparently faulty "safety catch". It is also a safe bet that this lack of information is the reason behind the increasing rate of infection in our young people.

Thank you for publishing this article – you have not only given me the opportunity to discuss this important subject with my daughter –you have given two teenagers the information they should have been given at school.

Pamela Travis, via email

Just in case you are still labouring under the impression this is just a scare story, consider reading the shocking new book *Unprotected*, written by an anonymous medical doctor serving on the campus of a major US university. Because of patient confidentiality issues and fears for her own job, she refused to author the book under her own name. In it, she recounts stories like that of "Stacey", a bright student with only a handful of sexual encounters where each time a condom had been used from whoa to go. After just a year of being sexually active, Stacey had an abnormal pap smear – she had HPV, the sexually transmitted disease that causes genital warts and cervical cancer. Four thousand women a year die of cervical cancer each year in the US, around the same number claimed by AIDS.

Writes her doctor:

> "EVEN IF STACEY WAS INFECTED with a 'low risk' [strain of HPV] it could still cause warts on her genitalia and cervix, and the treatment of these warts may be painful, cause scarring and be expensive. The virus could be with her for life, there is no cure. She could also transmit HPV to her newborn, causing respiratory disease. And being infected with one STD she may be more vulnerable to others."

Significantly, however, no one had ever bothered to mention that condoms offer no protection at all from the warts or cervical cancer virus. In fact, so useless are they that as far back as February 1999, years before "Hubba", the National Cancer Institute's director, Dr Richard Klausner, wrote in congressional testimony that the science on the uselessness of condoms was now so clear that "additional research efforts by NCI on the effectiveness of condoms in preventing HPV transmission are not warranted."[139]

While there have been some studies showing a slight improvement on useless, even the most positive results showed a large number of women consistently using condoms every time still managed to catch HPV within eight months.

139   *Unprotected*, by Anonymous, M.D., Penguin, 2006, Chapter 2, Footnote 10

One survey of students at a major university found 43% of them had caught HPV in the space of one year.[140]

Unlike other government disease prevention campaigns – such as quit smoking, fighting heart disease and obesity, or combating drink-driving and speeding – where the aim is to convince or shock people to cease risky behaviour, the author of *Unprotected* is highly critical of "Safer Sex" campaigns.

"Instead of the grim facts, women are fed oversimplified and whitewashed information. And when 'safer sex' fails, the consequences – both physical and emotional – are minimized.

"Why…when it comes to risky sexual behaviour, do they settle for risk reduction instead of risk elimination? Why do they tiptoe around and worry about judging? They wouldn't settle for merely cutting down on tobacco; they hound students about stopping altogether."

She cites an extract from one article advising doctors how to convince teenagers of the harms of smoking:

> ADVISE TOBACCO USERS TO STOP…Mention reduced athletic capability, cost, stained fingers and teeth, cigarette burns and odours on clothes…Share a few tobacco advertisements with the adolescent and point out how they make the habit seem fun and sophisticated but ignore all the unpleasant and harmful effects.

I had to stop reading the passage at that point, the tobacco ads sounded spookily like some of the sex promotion material on Hubba, emphasizing the glamour and fun of free sex while lying like flatfish to gullible teenagers about the risks. Who'd have thought Safe Sex campaigners would be copying the tricks of the tobacco barons?

Of course, as you've already seen, the argument from Condom-pushers is that if you can't beat them, join them. But *Unprotected's* author points out that a failure to achieve abstinence has never stopped health authorities in a relentless campaign against both cigarettes and alcohol. Indeed, one US government report urges campus health teams to keep their chins up, to have "treatment optimism" and keep repeating the age old messages of harm, even though levels of use "have changed little over the past 20 years on most campuses."[141]

The doctor who wrote *Unprotected* has called for an end to the 'condoms, bananas and strawberry lubricant' style of sex education so favoured by gay

---

140   *New England Journal of Medicine* 338, no 7 (1998): 423-28
141   "Clinical Protocols to Reduce High Risk Drinking in College Students", published by the National Institute on Alcohol Abuse and Alcoholism

activists and educators. Instead, she writes, tell kids the very simple truth that STDs will leave their genitalia covered in blisters and warts, with bad odours and the risk of infertility, other complications or even death.

She contrasts the messages praising abstinence in alcohol consumption – we call people who don't drink and drive "responsible". Yet there are no taxpayer funded safe sex pamphlets praising teenagers as "responsible" for choosing abstinence in sex. Instead, sex educators publicly laugh at them.

"The young people I know," the doctor writes, "are neither stupid nor enslaved to their urges. They are capable and motivated; many will respond to an ennobling message, reject the prurient messages of our culture, and learn new behaviours…But for this to happen, we must tell the whole story, warts and all.

"Tell them we're waging a war against these bugs, and the bugs are winning. Tell them 20 million people in [the US] have HPV, mostly women and minorities, and that doctors, drug companies and corporations are making billions. Tell them their behaviour and their friends' can make a difference. Tell them the truth!"

The doctor closes her chapter by reminding readers what a "delusion" is:

> A DELUSION IS 'A FALSE BELIEF that is resistant to reason or confrontation with actual fact'. I submit that 'safer sex' is a delusion, one that especially imperils young women on campus. We need to come clean and fully disclose to our youth the dreadful consequences of behaviours encouraged by our culture, so they can make fully informed decisions.
>
> The only people who are completely safe are those who, along with their spouses, waited for marriage and, once married, remained faithful. The ones who are 'safer' delay sexual behaviour, discriminate carefully in their choice, and understand the weight of their decisions. We don't hesitate, in other areas of health, to strive toward an ideal. Why, with Stacey and millions of others, do we settle for so much less?

Study it, and then compare it to the testimony of the Ministry of Health and Family Planning. On that test, I would say our interviews show both entities are delusional.

Look, I could go over scientific studies and statistics for Africa, but I don't think I need to. If your local school is providing sex education lessons promoting condoms as a protection against STDs, you may as well haul your child out of the class because it is based in fantasy, not fact. And here's something else worth considering: a survey of the circumstances leading up to each of New

Zealand's 18,500 abortions in 2004 found that nearly one third of them were using condoms when they became pregnant. How safe is safer sex? It isn't safe at all, and teenagers need to know so they can make informed decisions, not be treated as idiots by Family Planning or Planned Parenthood staff.

15

Population Control
The Rise of Eugenics

"If we accept that a mother can kill even her own child, how can we tell other people to not kill each other? Any country that accepts abortion is not teaching its people to love, but to use any violence to get what they want."
Mother Theresa

I f you had to think of one of the most bloodthirsty periods in world history, chances are you'd think of the Crusades. I tested this on a couple of people around the office, and hit paydirt every time. On Google, you'll find something like five and a half million search results on the word "Crusades". The word is continually thrown back at Christians as a justification for stripping churches of any authority, or to blame the Church for the current state of relations with Islam.

If you listen to talk radio on any given night you'll hear a liberal somewhere mention the "C-word" and perpetuate the myth.

So given all of that, prepare to have your eyes opened. According to tables published in Wikipedia,[142] the death toll from the Crusades was around one million people.

Now let's put that in perspective with figures they don't teach you in school.

The Crusades	1,000,000
Spanish Inquisition	350,000
Witch hunts	100,000

That's pretty gruesome, isn't it?

But what about these mass murders committed by Buddhist/Confucian/

Taoist regimes (note, none of the figures below includes battle deaths, they only measure civilian genocide):

Mongol Empire	29,927,000
Chinese purges (pre Mao)	33,519,000

Or these figures from Islamic regimes, prior to the 19th century:

Ottoman Empire	2,000,000
Persia (Iran)	2,000,000

Or these figures from the 20th century alone:

Marxist China	77,277,000
Soviet Russia	61,911,000
Nazi Germany	20,946,000

The question from all of this: why are we in the West conditioned to feel liberal guilt about the Crusades? You'll recall how students are compulsorily required to spend *ten weeks* on a Social Studies unit focusing on "racist" New Zealand treatment of Chinese immigrants in the 1860s, and Prime Minister Helen Clark's apology to China. Yet there is no mention in the curriculum of China's own racism to various cultural groups, or the more than 100 million killed as a result of genocide in China.

So why are we not all being taught about the much bloodthirstier regimes and religions? Answer, because Marxists are firmly entrenched in our universities and school systems and education policy units, and they would prefer attention is not drawn to it.

The ultimate grim irony is that by making your kids take out student loans, Marxists have figured out how to make young Westerners pay for their own cultural suicide.

You've already seen in previous chapters how Marxism and secular humanism have an unabashed agenda to smash Christianity as the foundation of Western culture. You've seen how the facts are not important in propaganda wars. The object is purely to discredit Western civilization and soften you up for a globalist Utopia ruled under some kind of UN arrangement. Surely, we owe it to our children to teach them the strengths of Western civilization, its greatest achievements, the truth that although we sometimes killed people, we killed far fewer than the other civilizations and political systems did. But we're not teaching them this truth. Instead, our kids are fed a diet of guilt – guilt over racism, guilt over sexism, guilt over religionism, guilt over colonialism, guilt over militarism. Slap me if I overlooked any!

Are we sending our kids to school to be educated, or indoctrinated? Are we sending our kids to school so the government can mess with their heads while both parents are forced to work for what in the old days was equivalent to one wage? Have we become the proletariat our grandparents warned us about at the height of the Cold War, and we just don't know it yet?

OK, let's cut to the chase. During the 20th century, an estimated 262 million people died in genocide and a further 40 million as battle deaths in war. More people were slaughtered last century than throughout the whole of human history combined. Forget the Crusades: the Nazis and Marxists – both essentially atheistic regimes – accounted for the most blood-filled period in world history.

Now, I'll grant you that history's single bloodiest battle in one day took place in Roman times when 80,000 men armed with swords, spears, arrows and pitchforks killed each other. But the 300 million genocide/war toll from last century averages out at 82,000 people dying every *single* day of last century, 365 days a year for 100 years.

But even that pales into insignificance next to the death toll resulting from the third dangerous philosophy we're exploring in this book – Eugenics. As you've seen, although Eugenics played a major role in the Holocaust, which is included in the Nazi genocide figures above, the philosophy that Man is the ultimate arbiter of life or death has played a direct role in a much bigger way than you suspect.

Over the past decade, nearly 500,000,000, that's *five hundred million*, children have been killed in the womb by abortion. In ten years, that's nearly double the combined death toll from genocide and war for the past 100 years! It equates to 137,000 children *a day*, or 95 children killed every minute, around the clock. Based on the best public estimates of abortion, the figure rises to around 800 million deaths over the past 20 years – nearly 20% of the current global population.

To put that horrific figure in context, *it equates to the entire human population of the world 200 years ago*. We have killed off in just 20 years the equivalent of the total planetary population in 1776.

A staggering one in three babies conceived in the West will be aborted, every year. As others have noted, who knows whether the next Einstein was among that tally?

While we march in the streets about the injustice of war in Iraq, where the death toll is measured in *thousands*, we have terminated – in the four years since Iraq was invaded – somewhere in the region of 200 *million* infants. *One hundred and thirty seven thousand a day.*

One cannot explore the link between abortion and eugenics, however, without a little history.

You'll recall back in Chapter 1 discovering how Charles Darwin's cousin,

Sir Francis Galton, pondered the Theory of Evolution long and hard. Galton believed that if Darwin was right, and humans really were just the animals at the top of the food chain, answerable to no god at all, then Man had a responsibility to take charge of his own genetic destiny.

Back in the early 20th century they didn't know much about genes, and nothing about DNA, but they did know about inheriting traits. Selective breeding had been used for centuries with livestock and crops to produce better animals and better yields.

It was Galton's belief that you could apply the same techniques to create a super-race of humans. This was called "positive eugenics". The other side of the coin was "negative eugenics", which involved actively suppressing the ability of rival races or social classes to breed.

The Nazis, for example, adopted both ideas. Men and women exhibiting the best physical and intellectual traits of Aryanism were ordered to breed as part of the project to create "uber-Nazis". At the same time, gypsies, Jews and other "sub-humans" were gassed.

The Nazi inspiration came direct from Galton's work, as you can see from this Galton quote:[143]

"I DO NOT SEE WHY ANY INSOLENCE of caste should prevent the gifted class, when they had the power, from treating their compatriots with all kindness, *so long as they maintained celibacy.* But if these continued to procreate children inferior in moral, intellectual and physical qualities, *it is easy to believe the time may come when such persons would be considered as enemies to the State, and to have forfeited all claims to kindness.*" [emphasis added]

One of Galton's disciples was American feminist Margaret Sanger, who set up America's first birth control clinic and created the organization Birth Control Federation of America. This organization later changed its name to the Planned Parenthood Federation, and under Sanger's influence set up branches around the world – New Zealand's Family Planning Association for example is part of Planned Parenthood and New Zealand's Dr Gill Greer now runs the international head office of the group in the same role that Sanger once held fifty years ago.

Have you ever wondered where the drive for birth control and sex education came from? You probably think it has a lot to do with genuine concern for girls who "get in trouble". In fact, Family Planning was effectively the eugenics division of the Ku Klux Klan, with a clear and documented agenda to prevent

143   *Fraser's Magazine* 7 [1873] quoted in *Aristotle to Zoos*, Peter and Jean Medawar, 1983 p87

Blacks and the poor from outbreeding whites and the middle classes.

"Those least fit to carry on the race are increasing most rapidly," complained Margaret Sanger in the 1920s. "Funds that should be used to raise the standard of our civilization are diverted to maintenance of those who should never have been born."

Sanger took her cues from both Darwin and Galton, but also from an 18th century cleric named Thomas Malthus who was convinced the "dirty classes" were breeding too fast and the world would be overpopulated.

Malthus wanted culling of already-born children:[144]

> "ALL CHILDREN BORN, beyond what would be required to keep up the population to a desired level, must necessarily perish, unless room is made for them by the deaths of grown persons. We should facilitate, instead of foolishly and vainly endeavoring to impede, the operations of nature in producing this mortality."

Malthus argued that the Christian response to third world or domestic poverty – charity, education and a helping hand – only encouraged more Blacks and white trash to breed. To give a New Zealand example of how Malthusian eugenics policy could have changed the course of history here, there would have been no Christian mission outreach to NZ's Maori community, and instead Malthus would have encouraged epidemic diseases to be spread to decimate the culturally "inferior" natives.

Family Planning's Margaret Sanger picked up on the anti-charity theme herself:

> "ORGANIZED CHARITY itself is the symptom of a malignant social disease. Those vast, complex, interrelated organizations aiming to control and to diminish the spread of misery and destitution and all the menacing evils that spring out of this sinisterly fertile soil, are the surest sign that our civilization has bred, is breeding and perpetuating constantly increasing numbers of defectives, delinquents and dependents.
>
> "We are failing to segregate morons who are increasing and multiplying . . . a dead weight of human waste . . .an ever-increasing spawning class of human beings who never should have been born at all.
>
> "To breed out of the race the scourges of transmissible disease, mental defect, poverty, lawlessness, crime … since these classes would be decreasing in number instead of breeding like weeds … such a plan would … reduce the birthrate among the diseased,

144   http://www.blackgenocide.org/negro.html

the sickly, the poverty stricken and anti-social classes, elements unable to provide for themselves, and the burden of which we are all forced to carry."

These, then, are the documented views, in her own books, of the woman hailed as the hero and founder of the Family Planning movement worldwide. And if you've ever wondered why Family Planning in NZ has been so active in promoting abortion, take one look at the attitude to children Sanger held:

"THE MOST MERCIFUL THING that a family does to one of its infant members is to kill it."

Although Sanger publicly professed that abortion should be a last resort, in practice it was something she and her organization worked hard to achieve, not for any altruistic purpose but purely because she didn't like poor people and coloured people, referring at times to "inferior races" and "human weeds".

If you think this was simply the view of one loon in the Family Planning movement, think again. British scientist Marie Stopes married a prominent eugenicist, then set up Birth Control Clinics in Britain, as one online biography recounts:[145]

DR MARIE STOPES and her fellow family planning pioneers around the globe played a major role in breaking down taboos about sex and increasing knowledge, pleasure and improved reproductive health. Marie Stopes was also a prominent campaigner for the implementation of policies inspired by eugenics.

In her *Radiant Motherhood* (1920) she called for the "sterilization of those totally unfit for parenthood (to) be made an immediate possibility, indeed made compulsory." Even more controversially, her *The Control of Parenthood* (1920) declared that "utopia could be reached in my life time had I the power to issue inviolable edicts... (I would legislate compulsory sterilization of the insane, feebleminded)... revolutionaries... half-castes."

Nice woman, and another fine example of how being a Darwinist (her main career was in paleobotany) wrecks your moral compass. Who needed Hitler's gas chambers when Stopes, Sanger and crew were pushing for a much larger genocide against people they didn't like, carefully cloaked in the name of "women's rights"? When Stopes died, incidentally, she left her fortune to the Eugenics Society.

---

145   http://marie.c.stopes.en.wikivx.biz/

Meanwhile, back across the pond in the US, Margaret Sanger's Family Planning organisation began publishing a regular journal, and many of the articles were written by eugenicists on the need to breed for racial and class superiority. One of her regular contributors was Dr Ernst Rudin, one of Adolf Hitler's key advisors, as Wikipedia reports:[146]

> RECOGNIZED AS ONE OF the fathers of Nazi ideology, his work was endorsed officially by the Nazi Party. He wrote the official commentary for the racial policy of Nazi Germany: "Law for the Prevention of Hereditarily Diseased Offspring"; and was awarded medals from the Nazis and Adolf Hitler personally.
>
> In 1933, Ernst Rüdin, Alfred Ploetz, and several other experts on racial hygiene were brought together to form the Expert Committee on Questions of Population and Racial Policy under Reich Interior Minister Wilhelm Frick. The committee's ideas were used as a scientific basis to justify the actions of the Nazi's racial policies. The "Law for the Prevention of Genetically Diseased Offspring" was passed by the German government on January 1, 1934.

Margaret Sanger's Birth Control Federation paid tribute to Adolf Hitler and his vision:[147]

> "WE, TOO, [LIKE HITLER'S REGIME] recognize the problem of race building, but our concern is with the quality of our people, not with their quantity alone ... "It is entirely fitting that 'Race Building in a Democracy' should have been chosen as the theme of the annual meeting of the Birth Control Federation of America."

Margaret Sanger also played an instrumental part in the Voyage of the Damned, a shipload of Jews fleeing Germany that arrived off the American coast. The incident was documented in William Tucker's book, *The Science and Politics of Racial Research*:

> THE AMERICAN EUGENICISTS even made their own modest contribution to the plight of Jews in the Reich. In the late 1930s there were last-ditch attempts to waive some of the restrictions in the 1924 Immigration Act in order to grant asylum to a few eventual victims of the Holocaust. These efforts were vigorously

---

146   http://en.wikipedia.org/wiki/Ernst_R%C3%BCdin
147   *Birth Control Review*, vol. XXIV, January 1940, quoted at http://www.all.org/abac/contents.txt

opposed by eugenicists...who submitted a new report, Immigration and Conquest, reiterating the biological warnings against the "human dross" that would produce a "breakdown in race purity of the ...superior stocks."

The Jews were sent back to Germany. You can guess the rest. The heavily racist ideology behind birth control led Sanger and other eugenicists to believe that different races were closer to apes in terms of social behaviour and intelligence:[148]

> IT IS SAID THAT A FISH as large as a man has a brain no larger than the kernel of an almond. In all fish and reptiles where there is no great brain development, there is also no conscious sexual control. The lower down in the scale of human development we go the less sexual control we find. *It is said that the aboriginal Australian, the lowest known species of the human family, just a step higher than the chimpanzee in brain development,* has so little sexual control that police authority alone prevents him from obtaining sexual satisfaction on the streets. [emphasis added]

One wonders how Sanger's supporters, who set up Family Planning in New Zealand in the 1920s, viewed Maori. In 1926, Margaret Sanger called for voluntary sterilization of the lower classes:

> "IT NOW REMAINS for the U.S. government to set a sensible example to the world by offering a bonus or yearly pension to all obviously unfit parents who allow themselves to be sterilized by harmless and scientific means. In this way the moron and the diseased would have no posterity to inherit their unhappy condition. The number of the feeble-minded would decrease and a heavy burden would be lifted from the shoulders of the fit."

One outcome of the eugenics PR campaign was that many US states adopted compulsory sterilisation of people deemed to be of mental defect or poor character. *Frontpage* magazine featured the case of one woman:[149]

> IN THE MID 1920'S, Carrie Buck, at the ripe old age of 17, fought the state of Virginia's mandatory sterilization statute. She was classified as a socially inferior woman, having borne a child out

---

148   http://en.wikipedia.org/wiki/Margaret_Sanger
149   http://frontpagemag.com/Articles/ReadArticle.asp?ID=10004

of wedlock and her foster parents stated that she was "a handful". Carrie's mother had also been incarcerated in a state institution as a 'promiscuous woman'. And at the age of 7 months, Carrie's child, Vivian, was 'certified' as being 'deficient,' based on the 'history' of Carrie and her mother.

Carrie lost her case at the state court level, and it wound up in front of the Supreme Court in 1927. The prominent Supreme Court jurist, Oliver Wendell Holmes, wrote the opinion in Buck v. Bell. The decision was 8-1, Justice Butler dissenting. Here's what the majority opinion boiled down to:

"In order to prevent our being swamped with incompetents... society can prevent those who are manifestly unfit from continuing their kind. The principle that sustains compulsory vaccination is broad enough to cover cutting the Fallopian tubes." ...

"It is better for all the world, if instead of waiting to execute degenerate offspring for crime, or to let them starve for their imbecility, society can prevent those who are manifestly unfit from continuing their kind…Three generations of imbeciles are enough." — Justice Oliver Wendell Holmes Jr. (Buck v. Bell, 1927)

Five months after this decision, Carrie was forcibly sterilized. It later came out that her promiscuity was nothing of the sort. She'd been raped by the nephew of her foster parents, himself a violent (unsterilized) little scumbag. And her daughter's school records show that Vivian was a B student, receiving an A in deportment (behavior), and she was on the honor roll. Genetic tests later showed that neither Carrie nor her daughter had any genetic defects.

In 1930, Sanger's magazine featured this suggestion from correspondent Norman Haire:[150]

"FOR THOSE WHO CANNOT be educated, sterilization or legalized abortion seems to be the only remedy, for we certainly do not want such stupid people to pollute the race with stupid offspring. The defective conditions of life call urgently for improvement."

In 1939, her Family Planning organization set up what it called "The Negro Project", with a view to dramatically cull the Black birth rates via birth control which, in many cases, led to *secret* sterilizations of African-American

150   *Birth Control Review*, July, 1930, as quoted at http://en.wikiquote.org/wiki/Abortion

women without their consent or knowledge. It is important to note that secret sterilizations were not a policy of Sanger's and she was unaware of them – however the culture that she created encouraged doctors to take the law into their own hands. Aiding her in the task of selling birth control to Blacks was Clarence Gamble, founder of the pure soap company Proctor and Gamble, who suggested that token Blacks, including a charismatic reverend, be paid to front the campaign so as not to arouse suspicions about the real Family Planning agenda. Sanger agreed:

> "WE DO NOT WANT the word to go out that we want to exterminate the Negro population, and the minister is the man who can straighten that idea out if it ever occurs to any of their more rebellious members."

While Family Planning successfully pitched birth control, it had the reverse effect to the one they intended, as *Citizen* magazine reports:[151]

> IN 1940, NONWHITE WOMEN aged 18 to 19 experienced 61 births per 1,000 unmarried women. In 1968, the corresponding figure was 112 per 1,000, a 100 percent jump. What other factor could account for the increased rate of sexual activity than wider access to birth control, with its promise of sex without tears and consequences?

This, of course, has been the outcome right throughout the Western world. Access to contraception heightened promiscuity, and if there was more sex taking place and people – being only human – failed to take proper precautions every time, then naturally the birthrates in the "inferior races" and among "human weeds" were going to rise.

In a bitter irony, however, that is directly relevant to the wider threat facing Europe and the West, the so-called "superior" races and classes took to contraception like ducks to water, and largely used it properly. As a consequence, birth rates in New Zealand, Britain, Canada, Japan and the whole of Europe have fallen well below population replacement, meaning our civilization is dying out. It was the last thing Sanger and Galton wanted to achieve, but a direct result of their policies.

African-Americans, likewise, are increasingly angry at the myth they were sold, with Black pro-lifer Clenard Howard Childress, Jr comparing it unfavourably to the worst excesses of the Ku Klux Klan:

"Between 1882 and 1968, 3,446 Blacks were lynched in the U.S. That

---

151   January 20, 1992 edition of *Citizen* magazine

number is surpassed in less than 3 days by abortion."[152]

Like all of these seductive and dangerous ideologies, at face value eugenics probably attracts some sympathy with many people as we look at crime, child abuse and poverty in our society. Yet eugenics assumes – like Marxism and Darwinism – that it has all the answers: if you stop the poor and the stupid from breeding eventually these problems will disappear. Additionally, eugenics takes a fatalistic view that an unwanted child can never achieve success or happiness.

But would the world be a better place without famous orphans like actress Ingrid Bergman, singer Faith Hill, writer James Michener, couturist CoCo Chanel, jazz musician Louis Armstrong, NZ Maori judge Mick Brown, opera singer Kiri te Kanawa, former All Black Grahame Thorne, actor Pierce Brosnan, actor Richard Burton, actor Charlie Chaplin, actor Ted Danson, James Dean, Nelson Mandela, or Bill Clinton?

Then there's the eugenics policy against large families, but Celine Dion was the 11th child in her family, and don't forget the Osmonds or the Jackson Five or even the Bee Gees from a family of five. There are thousands of other high achievers on the world stage who come from large families.

And what of those born into abject poverty? Again, the list could go forever, but a handful of names include Oprah Winfrey, Elvis Presley, Marilyn Monroe, Hilary Swank.

So again, does the stereotyping and generalization of eugenics justify the kind of population control they seek, or are their arguments simply hollow and racist?

We will return to the eugenics movement shortly when we explore what happened to eugenicists after World War 2 and where they are now, but in the meantime the story of Family Planning and its move into providing abortions sets the scene.

16

Child Abuse
Human Sacrifice, 20ᵀᴴ Century Style

"The essence of modernity is the death of the spiritual. A modernist is someone who is more concerned about air pollution than soul pollution. A modernist is someone who wants clean air so he can breathe dirty words. A modernist cares about big things, like whales, more than little things, like fetuses."
Peter Kreeft, Darkness at Noon

In the culture wars of the early 21st century, few battles are so loaded with implications and emotion as that surrounding abortion. Pro-life groups call abortionists "murderers", while pro-abortion advocates call their opponents "raving fundamentalists". Is abortion one of those issues where you can find a "happy" middle ground? No, it isn't. Abortion, because it involves killing a living entity, is a black and white subject. It is either entirely wrong, or entirely right, because you cannot "half-kill" the victim of an abortion.

According to the online encyclopedia, Wikipedia, the earliest specifically historically-recorded abortions took place in ancient China in the fifth century BC, when palace officials attempted to make royal concubines miscarry, so as to stem the chance of an illegitimate claimant to the throne. Legend suggests the practice in China predated that by centuries however. Techniques were varied: herbal combinations, or known poisonous substances like mercury, or sharp objects like needles or sticks which were used to penetrate the womb. The common factor in most of these cases was death, not just of the baby but of the woman trying her luck.

The Greeks and Romans, already awash in a range of civilization-destroying practices, included infanticide (the murder of children) and abortion in their cultural repertoire, with the blessing of Greek philosopher Aristotle (384-322 BC). Aristotle taught that a fetus at conception had a "vegetable" soul, which soon became an animal soul and later a human soul. It wasn't until this final evolution of the souls – which the philosopher calculated at 40 days' gestation in a boy child and 90 days for girls – that abortion became murder. Naturally, there were no ultrasound machines around back then so no one knew what sex a child was, making the distinction somewhat academic; Aristotle's doctrine, however, came to be known as "delayed ensoulment" and dominated Roman thought for some centuries to follow.

In Judeo-Christian tradition, the issue was much more clear-cut. The book of Exodus in the Bible, Ex. 21:22-23, records:

> 22 AND IF TWO MEN STRIVE and smite a woman with child, and her child be born imperfectly formed, he shall be forced to pay a penalty: as the woman's husband may lay upon him, he shall pay with a valuation. 23 But if it be perfectly formed, he shall give life for life.[153]

The clear implication is that the unborn are as alive and equally valued as the born. The book of Jeremiah, Jer. 1:5, records, "I knew you *before* I formed you in your mother's womb."

This goes even further than the Exodus passage. Here, Christians argue, God is saying he is responsible for forming the unborn child in the womb. Implicit in this, they say, is that anyone who deliberately kills a fetus is going head to head with God. The statement also implies that God knows someone before they are conceived. Some pro-abortionists have challenged this, suggesting it would mean personhood existed before conception, which is medically impossible. But given that God is credited with omniscience (knowing everything) and the ability to see into the future (including knowing the identities of yet-to-be-conceived people), the statement appears logical without suggesting personhood before conception.

Despite these passages however, the Catholic Church has not always been as strongly opposed to abortion as it is now. For the first four centuries of Christianity, it held to the orthodoxy above, but Catholic philosopher monk Augustine was rather enamoured of Aristotle's delayed ensoulment idea and pitched it as church policy. For centuries, the Catholic Church held that abortion was permissible up until the time of "quickening", when the baby's first movements are felt by the mother, but by the late Middle Ages the Church had swung back to the orthodox Christian view: human life begins at conception.

So that's the historical argument; now for the modern perspective.

Although backstreet abortions have taken place since time immemorial,

---

153   The verse is taken from the Greek version of the Old Testament, the LXX, which was the most common version used in synagogues at the time of Christ. http://ecmarsh.com/lxx/Exodus/index.htm

they have usually carried significant risk to the mother, as you've just seen. During the 20th century however, as higher standards were enforced in the medical profession, many doctors who'd been struck off for drunkenness or inappropriate behaviour used their newfound spare time to offer illegal abortions. I won't use the phrase "backstreet" because, as pro-abortion lobbyists themselves noted, these men were trained surgeons for the most part regardless of their character flaws and carried out their operations in a professional, albeit illegal, fashion. By the 1960s there were few fatalities in the US caused by illegal abortions.

In the early 1970s, however, pro-abortion lobbyists, including Family Planning, succeeded in pushing a test case, *Roe vs Wade*, all the way through to the US Supreme Court, that would open the way for abortion on demand as a "right".

In a split ruling, the Court decided to take the liberal view, and the abortion floodgates in the US were opened. New Zealand and other countries followed soon after. From an initial level of 6,000 abortions a year in 1977, it has more than tripled today.

The woman named as "Jane Roe" in the case, Norma McCorvey, has since testified she was duped as a young teenager into becoming a test case for the feminist movement, and asked to lie to the court by saying her pregnancy resulted from rape (it didn't), so as to make the case more emotional.

In New Zealand, while we (quite properly) agonize over half a dozen or so child abuse murders a *year*, we blissfully ignore the 71 or so abortions carried out each *day*, for a declared annual total of more than 18,500 (if you include patients sent to Australia for the procedure). Weigh it up: 6 deaths vs 18,500 deaths. One gets extensive TV and radio airtime. The other gets nothing. It is the issue we all refuse to talk about.

Regardless of where you stand on the abortion issue however, there is no denying that it is the single largest cause of death in the Western world.

I'm not saying this to moralize, because the purpose of this book is not to browbeat per se but to make you recognize the social conditioning surrounding you on a range of issues. Instead, what I'm asking you as readers to do is step back from everything you think you know, take a more objective look at the real factual matrix, and then see if it matches the conditioning.

So again I ask the question: *why* do we get so outraged at child abuse murders, yet not at killing in the womb? The answer, I suggest lies entirely in the conditioning. You can only believe that abortion is irrelevant to the debate if you adhere to one or more of the following:

- You believe the infant is not human
- You believe the infant is not really alive

- You believe there is nothing special about human life
- You believe that a woman's right to choose whether she has a child trumps the infant's right to live
- You don't feel you have a right to tell anyone else how to run their lives
- You believe that an adult life is worth more than a fetus'
- You believe only a wanted child should be brought into the world

There are variations on the theme, but the points above pretty much cover the spectrum of the main pro-abortion arguments. Again, without making a moral argument, I want to disconnect you from the emotion here and look at the cold, hard logic, or lack thereof, in the statements above.

The infant is not human:

This was an argument first raised centuries ago. In the modern abortion debate, this particular myth was reinforced by Darwinism and the biologist Ernst Haeckel, whose drawings – now admitted as a hoax[154] - of various animal and human embryos became a celebrated icon of evolution that you probably remember from your own school science classes. Haeckel believed the human embryo went through fish and animal stages before it eventually became human.

Lacking any ultrasound equipment to show them otherwise, and presented with Haeckel's fake embryo pictures, women seeking abortions during most of the 20th century were easily persuaded that the fetus was "just a clump of cells" and "not human yet".

Pro-abortion groups and Libertarian followers often still refer to the unborn child as "protoplasm" in a bid to depersonalize it. The argument has recently started to disintegrate rapidly, however, because most of us have now seen fetal ultrasound images of tiny humans with hands, faces, feet and personalities playing around in the womb. This is one of the prime reasons that abortion clinics are now seriously struggling to find doctors and nurses willing to carry out the procedures – the medics have seen for themselves.[155]

The infant is not alive/an adult life is more valuable than a fetus:

This is a variation on the theme above, but usually phrased in terms of the baby's ability to survive independent of the mother. In the US, where abortions can be performed right up to the date of delivery in some cases, this artificial distinction about life beginning at the time of first breath is just that – artificial. Here's why: if your test is the ability of a baby to live independent of the mother, then arguably you could include children up to the age of six

---

154   http://www.darwinismrefuted.com/embryology_04.html
155   http://www.life.org.nz/abortionmedicalkeyissuesabortionclinicstaff.htm

or seven as candidates for termination. After all, a fetus at 20 weeks is just as dependent for survival on its mother as a two year old child. Neither can survive without adult intervention at every moment.

This comment on an internet newsgroup shows how some people are indeed following the argument to its logical conclusion:[156]

> "NOT ONLY DO I THINK that there should be FAR more abortions performed, but I think that parents should have the option to euthanize their children before the age of 6 months. Life is cheap, food is expensive."

If you think that's a lone nutcase, think again. Here's another person displaying how well they've been brainwashed:

> "I HATE TO POINT THIS OUT to you, but: Infanticide is a perfectly REASONABLE choice in certain circumstances." - Christine Owens

Nor is it confined to uninformed members of the public. Australian born ethicist Peter Singer, now Professor of Bioethics at prestigious Princeton University in the US, argues that newborn babies should not be considered "human" until 30 days after birth, and that they can therefore be euthanized during that time. He also argues that disabled babies should simply be killed on the spot. Singer doesn't offer any real logical or scientific argument to support his beliefs, other than what academics call "functionalism", which is that humanity is defined by what you can or cannot do. Singer therefore sees the world through his own eyes as a functioning adult, and regards the disabled and babies as lesser beings because they are not as fully functional. In this sense, he is a reincarnation of the Nazi philosophers.

Critics, of course, argue that every single functioning adult on the planet began as a human embryo, and that artificially judging the worth of an embryo purely because it cannot yet drive a car, have sex or laugh is nothing more than clutching at straws to justify murder.

Taking a similar line is philosopher Michael Tooley who, in 1972, argued that a child "possess[es] a serious right to life only if it possesses the concept of a self as a continuing subject of experiences and other mental states, and believes that it is itself such a continuing entity." Naturally, anyone under the age of two need not apply.

Then there is ethicist and hypocrite Professor Jeffrey Reiman of American University, who contends that babies and toddlers do not "possess in their own right a property that makes it wrong to kill them." He further argues that infants have no particular "right to life" and that "there will be permissible exceptions to the rule against killing infants that will not apply to the rule against killing adults and children."

Why do I call him a hypocrite? Because in 1998 he co-authored the book, *The Death Penalty: For and Against* by Louis Pojman and Jeffrey Reiman, in which Reiman took the "against" position. Reiman argued that executions of murderers were unjust, sometimes painful, and discriminatory on the basis of race and economic status.

So here you have an ethics professor who would happily execute children without question, yet has a problem with executing murderers.

For some reason, this is a common problem on the Left. In New Zealand we've just witnessed the debate over making smacking a crime, yet those same liberal politicians who find the idea of physical discipline abhorrent are some of the strongest advocates of abortion. It is apparently more psychologically damaging to slap a child on the hand, than to rip it from a woman's womb and crush it to death. And, on balance, it is ethically better to kill a 6 month old baby whose parent(s) don't want it, than to execute a man who raped and killed two women. The two positions are logically irreconcilable, and don't lend credibility to any of the Left's arguments.

I think the argument that a pre-term baby or a newborn is "not alive" has been conclusively shown to be nothing more than a word game designed by the Left so they don't have to face the reality: abortion is the largest genocide ever undertaken on the planet.

There is nothing special about human life:

Here's where Darwinism and the Green movement collide. Darwin's Theory of Evolution claims Man is just another animal in the great tree of life. Although many Greens are neo-pagan in their spiritual beliefs, Darwin's theory is compatible from their point of view. It is Judeo-Christian tradition that teaches the supremacy of humanity, and the Greens don't like this for two reasons. Firstly, they reject Christianity. Secondly, they favour mass de-population and a return to simpler subsistence living that doesn't impact as much on the environment. Many Greens adhere to Gaia theory, the belief that Earth is in itself a kind of spiritual biosphere where everything must live in balance, and they add in a belief that humanity is evil and animals are innocent.

Ethicist Peter Singer, who describes himself as atheist, is also nicknamed "the Godfather of the animal liberation movement" as a result of his 1970s book *Animal Liberation*.

Singer argues that, *a la* Darwin, man is just one of millions of species and holds no special place. It follows, he says, that we should value animal life more highly than human life.

> "SURELY THERE WILL BE some nonhuman animals whose lives, *by any standards*, [emphasis added] are more valuable than the lives of some humans."

That's a pretty big call, to suggest that in a toss up between saving a panda bear or saving your five year old daughter, Singer would probably choose the bear. Singer says that if your daughter was disabled, there would be no toss-up at all, the child would be left to die. Are these the kind of "ethics" you want your kids to be brought up with? It reminds me of the line of a song that talks about being sung to sleep "by philosophies of save the trees / and kill the children".

Singer, and the other Greens, conveniently overlook that according to Darwin's theory it is survival of the fittest. If mankind is the fittest and animals die, tough luck – on Darwin's construction of the argument. Ascribing animals some kind of intrinsic worth higher than humans is getting dangerously close to animal worship.

The liberation group PETA, which looks to Singer for inspiration, illustrates the confusion and contradiction inherent in Green beliefs.

"There is no rational basis for saying that a human being has special rights. A rat is a pig is a dog is a boy. They're all mammals," claimed PETA president Ingrid Newkirk in a *Washington Times* interview.[157]

Then PETA's Alex Pacheco has said: "We feel that animals have the same rights as a retarded human child".[158]

So if animals are morally equivalent to a "retarded human child", that means we should treat them like Singer recommends we treat retarded children, right?:

"There are some circumstances, for example, where the newborn baby is severely disabled…when killing the newborn baby is not at all wrong," says Peter Singer.

Good one, Pete. Let's go kill all the animals then. "Severely disabled", by the way, means "haemophiliac", in Singer's book.[159]

This is the same Peter Singer who justified bestiality in a book review for sex website Nerve.com on the grounds that the only moral issue was whether the animal enjoyed it! Little wonder, perhaps, that some animal liberationists don't have pets, but "companion animals".

How sweet.

If you're an animal lover, chances are you have a cat or dog to keep you company. You may have some sympathy with the animal liberationists

---

157   *The Washington Times* August 29, 1999
158   *New York Times*, January 14, 1989
159   http://www.utilitarian.net/singer/by/1993----.htm

because, hey, they like animals too, right? What if you were to discover that these people – if they ever reach political power via the Greens – want to introduce laws banning the keeping of pets:

"It is time we demand an end to the misguided and abusive concept of animal ownership. The first step on this long, but just, road would be ending the concept of pet ownership," the appropriately-named Elliot Katz wrote in the Spring, 1997 issue of "In Defense of Animals".

The frightening thing is that some of these people have kids, people like the American Humane Society's then Vice President Michael W. Fox: "The life of an ant and the life of my child should be accorded equal respect."[160]

"Six million Jews died in concentration camps, but six billion broiler chickens will die this year in slaughter houses," PETA's Ingrid Newkirk told *The Washington Post*, in 1983. Apparently she failed to notice that the six billion chickens only existed in the first place by the grace of human farmers, or would she prefer that the world was overrun by chickens?

Apparently not, as the former National Director of Fund for Animals, Wayne Pacelle, pointed out: "We have no problems with the extinction of domestic animals. They are creations of human selective breeding."

So are we outraged that humans eat chickens, or would animal liberationists kill them anyway as symbols of oppression?

The idea that human life has no special value is used as a basis for justifying both abortion and euthanasia. However, it fails on its flawed logic. Its proponents cite Darwinism as the foundation for the claim "Man is just an animal" – but ignore the other element of Darwin's natural law: nature is red in tooth and claw, if Man makes animals extinct, that is simply nature taking its course.

Under Darwin's theory, mankind having risen to the top of the food chain is entitled to stay there. Killing our own young in favour of other species is decidedly unnatural, and little removed from human sacrifice to appease the gods.

Of course, if Darwin is wrong, as the evidence now suggests, then you can see how a century and a half of scientific stupidity has unleashed murder on a grand scale.

The variant heading on this section, that an adult is intrinsically more valuable than a child, still opens up the murder of toddlers, or anyone younger than you, as justifiable. The key point is, "says who?" Perhaps an innocent child still untainted by the bad decisions we have made as adults (including falling pregnant when we didn't want to) has a better claim to a chance at life than those who have tried and messed it up.

A woman's right to choose:

Says who? Where do we get the "right" to "choose" an innocent person's

---

160   *The Associated Press*, Jan. 15, 1989

death? If a woman doesn't like her boyfriend, does she have a right to choose to kill him? If she doesn't like her 12 year old son demanding food, shelter, time and money from her every day of her life, does she have the right to choose his death as well?

Do the parents who beat and neglect and murder their children have the right to "choose" such things? Sometimes, this argument is prefaced on the "it's my body" claim. But this logic could equally extend in that case to mothering in general. A mother must put up with the demands of either breastfeeding or having to hold a child to bottlefeed it. A mother must put up with having to drag her tired body upstairs in the middle of the night to change a baby's nappy. Surely if we're going to allow murder for what is an entirely natural and normal function (pregnancy) on the grounds of the impact on life or body, we can make the same allowance for killing toddlers or any other child who becomes inconvenient?

The "it's my body" claim also fails on the science. We now know that, right from the moment of conception, the embryo has its own unique DNA. It is entirely its own person. Yes, it is within the mother's body. But it is designed to be there, it has a natural right to be there as a consequence of having sex. Yes, it depends on the mother to stay alive, but so do older children.

When a child is born, society and the laws decree that parents have a responsibility to provide the "necessaries of life", that they must provide shelter, sustenance and nurture. This is a legal requirement, regardless of the pressures and complications in our lives. Yet what is so magical about the baby's status once born, in comparison with life in the womb? A parent's job lasts far longer than nine months, and involves far more work and dedication.

The truth is, that some of the strongest advocates of the "choice" option are women who, in former times, would have been assistants in Nazi death camps.

"I'd as soon weep over my taken tonsils or my absent appendix as snivel over those [five] abortions. I had a choice, and I chose life – mine," sneered British feminist and journalist, Julie Burchill, two years ago.[161]

Five abortions? Is the woman a career idiot? All those sex education classes and free strawberry-flavoured condoms were clearly wasted on her.

"Abortion is a failure of the feminist establishment," former feminist leader Tammy Bruce told Columbia University students. "With every kind of birth control available in the world, abortion is not something to be proud of. If you need an abortion, you've failed."[162]

If arguments do exist in favour of abortion, "a woman's choice" is not one of

---

161   "Abortion: still a dirty word", *The Guardian*, May 25, 2005, http://www.guardian.co.uk/Archive/Article/0,4273,4419718,00.html, also quoted at http://findarticles.com/p/articles/mi_qa3798/is_200210/ai_n9105415

162   Bruce, former member of NOW's national board of directors, to Columbia University students as quoted by Dan Healey in "Conservativism and Feminism Combined - Tammy Bruce, an Openly Gay, Pro-Choice, Pro-Clinton, Pro-Bush Conservative, Defies Labels", Columbia Spectator (April 6, 2005)

them. It is fatuously shallow, reducing the life of a child to a mere "inconvenience" that can be killed at whim. If the real test is that of "inconvenience", then there are many other people who we should be permitted to kill, by law, and Saddam Hussein should have been gone decades ago.

As US President Ronald Reagan wryly remarked in 1980: "I've noticed that everybody that is for abortion has already been born."[163]

We have no right to tell others how to live:

This is the argument from weakness. Logically, if this is true, then we have no right to intervene in the murder of a child by its parent on the street in front of you, and even less right to intervene in cases behind closed doors like the deaths of the Kahui twins. Nor can we tell a tribe of cannibals to cease their gruesome practice, or tell pedophiles to stop grooming children to the point where the kids "consent" to sex.

Logically, if this is true, then it also means we can pass virtually no laws, because that would require imposing society's will on someone. This is the default position of liberal guilt, and it has no credibility the moment you examine its implications.

Intriguingly, at least one Princeton ethicist seems to have his head screwed on, pointing out that our inhumane treatment of the unborn may be related to falling standards generally. "We should not be surprised at the epidemic of child abuse," comments Paul Ramsey.[164] "Obviously there is a connection between what we can do to a baby in the first nine months of life in the womb, and thereafter."

Only a wanted child should be brought into the world:

This is another argument that seems warm and fuzzy to start with, but is as bereft of balance as all the rest. It pre-supposes that the mother will be incapable of falling in love with her child – and most mothers do in fact love their kids regardless of whether they were "surprises" or not – and it frames the debate in terms of only the mother's "wants". What about the child's aspirations? There are plenty of children born in third world nations who, because of their religious faith, adapt happily despite the harsh hand in life they've been dealt. The pro-abortion argument presupposes that no child will ever find happiness, which clearly doesn't stack up with the facts.

And even if you can find the occasional case of a terminally-depressed child who wasn't wanted and has absolutely no joy whatsoever, does that justify knocking off thousands of other kids who might have been perfectly happy given the chance? If you remember the list of unwanted orphans from the previous

163   *New York Times,* 22 September 1980
164   http://en.wikiquote.org/wiki/User:Catamorphism/Abortion_temp

chapter, you'll note some very prominent names who've enjoyed their lives.

Sometimes people make bad choices, and see only negative options, because no one offers them an alternative of hope. Given the huge waiting lists for adoptions, and the few babies given up for adoption, there are certainly alternatives to the current killing fields.

In a recent *Time* magazine cover story,[165] staff at a North Carolina pregnancy crisis clinic explained how, rather than loudly protesting at abortion clinics, they simply offer distressed young women "kind, calm, nonjudgmental" support. Girls, they say, don't want babies because they don't think the support exists. The clinic shows them otherwise.

> THE PREGNANCY-CENTER CLINIC, with its new ultrasound machine, has been open only since December, but already the staff can count the women who came in considering an abortion and changed their minds: five women converted, six lives saved, they declare, since one was carrying twins. "They connected," nurse Joyce Wilson says, recalling the reaction of the women who saw the filmy image of their fetus onscreen. "They bonded. You could just see it. One girl got off the table and said, 'That's my baby.'"
>
> "Another got up," Deborah Wood says, "and said, 'This changes everything.'"

That's all it took to make them happy? Viewing an ultrasound and hearing some kind words? Why aren't they getting this at Family Planning or abortion clinics? Allegedly because clinic staff are not permitted to show girls ultrasound images, or offer them alternatives to abortion. And this conspiracy of silence is happening in New Zealand, as this letter from practice nurse educator Barbara Docherty discloses:[166]

> "PROFESSIONALLY, WE ARE OBLIGED to give accurate, current and factual information to our patients to assist them in making a fully informed decision. This is the basis of informed consent. Yet nurses are advised to avoid showing pictures which explain the development of the unborn child because it may make them feel guilty, even though it is often our patients who later question us as to why we did not give them more information."

Are you satisfied yet that you have been given the full truth about abortion,

---

165   http://www.time.com/time/magazine/article/0,9171,1590444,00.html
166   *New Zealand GP*, March 8, 2000

or that young women are getting frank and honest advice from government clinics?

You certainly are not getting it from the media. Some of you will recall a story that made world headlines last year, when the *New York Times* broke the story of an El Salvador woman named Carmen Climaco who'd been jailed for 30 years for murder after aborting her baby at 18 weeks. Liberals everywhere were outraged, but conservatives went digging, exposing the story as a fabrication and forcing an apology from the *New York Times* internal ombudsman, Byron Calame:

> "[FREELANCE CONTRIBUTOR Jack Hitt's] cover story on abortion in El Salvador in *The New York Times* Magazine on April 9 contained. . . a dramatic account of how Ms. Climaco received the [30-year jail] sentence [for homicide] after her pregnancy had been aborted after 18 weeks. It turns out, however, that trial testimony convinced a court in 2002 that Ms. Climaco's pregnancy had resulted in a full-term live birth, and that she had strangled the 'recently born'. . . One thing is clear to me, at this point, about the key example of Carmen Climaco. Accuracy and fairness were not pursued with the vigor *Times* readers have a right to expect."

As US blogger Michelle Malkin noted in early 2007, just after the apology was published, abortion is big business:[167]

> "TURNS OUT HITT'S MAIN SOURCES of info came from a pro-abortion group called IPAS. The group would profit from legalized abortion in El Salvador since it sells abortion vacuum aspirators."

Because, again, the debate surrounding abortion has been sanitized by liberals in the news media, and this book is about breaking through the brainwashing, allow me to briefly explain with a series of direct quotes what the process involves.

> " 'FORCEPS, PLEASE,' MR. SMITH slaps into his hand what look like oversized ice-cube tongs. Holtzman pushes it into the vagina and tugs. He pulls out something, which he slaps on the instrument table.
>
> 'There,' he says, 'A leg. You can always tell fetal size best by

167   http://michellemalkin.com/archives/006628.htm

the extremities. Fifteen weeks is right in this case.'

I turn to Mr. Smith. 'What did he say?'

'He pulled a leg off,' Mr. Smith says. 'Right here.' He points to the instrument table, where there is a perfectly formed, slightly bent leg, about three inches long. It consists of a ripped thigh, a knee, a lower leg, a foot, and five toes. I start to shake very badly, but otherwise I feel nothing. Total shock is painless.

'I have the rib cage now,' Holtzman says, as he slams down another piece of the fetus. 'That's one thing you don't want to leave behind because it acts like a ball valve and infects everything.... There, I've got the head now. Also a piece of the placenta.' I look at the instrument table where next to the leg, and next to a mess he calls the rib cage but that I cannot recognize, there lies a head. It is the smallest human head I have ever seen, but it is unmistakably part of a person."

That description was written by pro-abortion advocate Magda Denes, a clinical psychologist and psychoanalyst.[168] As you can see, she wasn't proud of what was taking place, but felt it important to shatter the "protoplasm" myth.

The strange thing is that ethicists like Peter Singer support the pain and trauma to a tiny human described above [no anaesthetic is administered], yet if you pulled a puppy apart by ripping its legs off, you would be jailed and Animal Liberationists would be burning down your house.

During debate on whether to legalise late term abortions – now known as "partial birth" because the baby has to be delivered naturally but killed before its head leaves the womb, an abortion nurse testified to the US Congress on the procedures at her clinic:

A MOTHER WAS SIX MONTHS PREGNANT. A doctor told her that the baby had Downs Syndrome and she decided to have an abortion. She came in the first two days to have the laminaria inserted and changed, and she cried the whole time. . . On the third day Dr. [Martin] Haskell brought the ultrasound in and hooked it up so that he could see the baby. . . On the ultrasound screen I could see the heart beating. . . Dr. Haskell went in with forceps and grabbed the baby's legs and pulled them down into the birth canal. Then he delivered the baby's body and the arms--everything but the head. The doctor kept the baby's head just inside the uterus. The baby's little fingers were clasping and unclasping, and his feet were kicking. Then the doctor stuck the scissors through the back of his head, and the baby's arms jerked out in a flinch, a startled reaction, like a baby does when he thinks that he might fall. The doctor opened up the scissors, stuck a high-powered suction tube into the opening and sucked the baby's brains out. Now the baby was completely limp. . . I was really completely unprepared for what I was seeing. I almost threw up as I watched the doctor do these things. . . After that, the doctor delivered the baby's head, cut his umbilical cord and threw him into a pan, along with the placenta and the instruments he had used. I saw the baby move in the pan. . . I asked another nurse and she said it was just 'reflexes.'. . . The woman wanted to see her baby, so they cleaned him up, put him in a blanket and handed him to her. . . She cried the whole time, and she kept saying, 'I'm so sorry, please forgive me!' "[169]

It is experiences like these that are increasingly driving medics away from performing abortions, and even pro-abortion groups can see their cause has been damaged by pretending abortion is not killing a baby. Ron Fitzsimmons, the National Coalition of Abortion Providers' executive director back in the 1990s, admitted "lying through my teeth" about the true numbers of late-term abortions being performed on spurious grounds, and confessed in 1997 that lying made him feel "physically ill":[170]

"YOU KNOW THEY'RE PRIMARILY DONE on healthy women and healthy fetuses, and it makes you feel like a dirty little abortionist with a dirty little secret. I think we should tell them the truth, let them vote and move on. In the vast majority of cases, the procedure is performed on a healthy mother with a healthy fetus that is 20 weeks or more along. The abortion-rights folks know it, the anti-abortion folks know it, and so, probably, does everyone else."

Although late term abortions are not officially provided in New Zealand, abortion clinics will refer patients overseas on subsidized trips.

Perhaps the last word on abortion, however, should go to pro-abortion researcher Professor David Fergusson, who is leading the world's largest tracking study, following the lives of 1265 children born in Christchurch,

169   Brenda Pratt Shafer, registered nurse for late-term abortion doctor Martin Haskell at Women's Medical Center in Dayton, Ohio, describing the procedure in sworn testimony to the U.S. House Judiciary Committee, 1995
170   "An Abortion Rights Advocate Says He Lied About Procedure", *New York Times* (February 26, 1997)

New Zealand, from 1977 onward. In a January 2006 update on the study, published in the *Journal of Child Psychiatry and Psychology*, Fergusson revealed that women who have abortions are significantly (up to double the rate) more likely to suffer mental illness, depression and suicidal thoughts in the years following, than those who don't.

"I remain pro-choice. I am not religious. I am an atheist and a rationalist," Fergusson told Australia's ABC network. "The findings did surprise me, but the results appear to be very robust because they persist across a series of disorders and a series of ages. . . . Abortion is a traumatic life event; that is, it involves loss, it involves grief, it involves difficulties. And the trauma may, in fact, predispose people to having mental illness."

It is a sign of everything I have warned you about in this book, about the hostile worldviews of those in positions of power, that Fergusson's groundbreaking study was rejected by a number of major medical journals who didn't like its conclusions.

"We went to four journals, which is very unusual for us – we normally get accepted the first time."

Even New Zealand's Abortion Supervisory Committee, charged by the Government with ensuring abortions are performed on the basis of the woman's "mental health", didn't want to know about the study and its finding that abortion actually *causes* mental health problems.

But if abortion is one of the byproducts of eugenics, it isn't the only one.

17

Commercialising Eugenics
The Ghost of Mengele

"The change is not merely that we are behaving like beasts, but that we are believing like beasts. Man has never obeyed the Tao very well, but he at least believed in it, and thus felt guilt. The new philosophy has removed guilt."
Peter Kreeft, Darkness At Noon

There are puddles of water in the gloomy corridors of Auckland University's School of Medicine, leftovers from a spring rainstorm and some bad building maintenance on this grey September afternoon. This nondescript urban edifice, now in the shadow of the new Auckland Hospital extensions, houses dark secrets. Or so I've been told.

"They're doing an undergraduate presentation next week in the Department of Optometry and Vision Science," a source in Auckland's optometry community confides in a cryptic email. "Thought you might be interested to investigate a research project involving tissue from aborted fetuses."

Optometry. Eye doctors. Hardly the first branch of medicine that springs to mind as the cutting edge of macabre experimentation. But inside the Cole Lecture Theatre, safely sheltered from the weather and the waterlogged corridor, fifty or so medical students have filled the room almost to capacity as teams of fourth-year undergrads present the results of this year's main research projects.

An American woman holds court, a scientific Mistress of Ceremonies taking clear pleasure in parading her protégés to their medical colleagues as they make audio-visual presentation after presentation. She is Dr Keely Bumsted O'Brien, and this is her baby, so to speak.

Across the road, in the big hospital's emergency rooms and oncology units, specialists, intensivists, nurses and registrars are working frantically to save the living. Here, in the School of Medicine, it turns out O'Brien's team has been dissecting the dead. And not just any dead.

"The title of the project," tipped our source, "is 'Photoreceptor-associated gene expression in human fetal and embryonic chicken retina'. As far as I am aware this project is unlikely to have received regional ethics approval from the Ministry of Health. The tissue has been obtained from elective abortions in the United States and was transported here for the experiments. This may be the first research of its kind in New Zealand and I am sure the public are quite unaware of it."

Just how did body parts from a group of aborted American infants end up in New Zealand for students to conduct experiments on? To find the answers, I began investigations in the United States, and a controversy that blew up there six years ago.

It was an interview that shocked America. An Insider, spilling the beans on massive malpractice to a reporter on ABC's 20/20. Only this time, it wasn't Big Tobacco in the gunsights, it was the US abortion industry, exposed as harvesting the organs from aborted babies. According to former abortion clinic technician Dean Alberty, clinics were harvesting eyes, brains, hearts, limbs, torsos and other body parts for sale to the scientific market: laboratories wanting to test new drugs or procedures, or researchers trying to find the causes of genetic disorders or discover new ways of treating disorders like Parkinsons.

To make matters doubly embarrassing for authorities, the trafficking was taking place inside abortion clinics run by Planned Parenthood, the US affiliate of New Zealand's Family Planning organization.

Alberty worked for a Maryland agency called the Anatomic Gift Foundation, which essentially acted as a brokerage between universities and researchers seeking body parts, and the abortion clinics providing the raw material. Alerted by the clinics about the races and gestations of babies due to be aborted each day, AGF technicians would match the offerings with parts orders on their client lists. Alberty and his colleagues would turn up at the abortions that offered the best donor prospects to begin dissecting and extracting what they needed before decay set in.

"We would have a contract with an abortion clinic that would allow us to go in…[to] procure fetal tissue for research. We would get a generated list each day to tell us what tissue researchers, pharmaceuticals and universities were looking for. Then we would go and look at the particular patient charts—we had to screen out anyone who had STDs or fetal anomalies. These had to be the most perfect specimens we could give these researchers for the best value that we could sell for.

"We were taking eyes, livers, brains, thymuses, and especially cardiac blood… even blood from the limbs that we would get from the veins" he said.

Alberty told of seeing babies wounded but alive after abortion procedures, and in one case a set of twins "still moving on the table" when clinicians from

AGF began dissecting the children to harvest their organs. The children, he said, were "cuddling each other" and "gasping for breath" when medics moved in for the kill.

Alberty had been asked by a pro-life group, Life Dynamics, to provide information about activities in the clinics, and the issue caused enough national scandal to see an episode of ABC's 20/20 devoted to it in March 2000.

On that programme, the imagery was highly sanitized so as not to upset sensitive viewers. The closest 20/20 got to screening images of trafficked human fetal tissue was a pea-sized fragment of unidentifiable tissue in a glass Petri dish.

Life Dynamics founder Mark Crutcher later told media:

"We are sympathetic to the explanation offered by the ABC producer who told us after the show that the network could not broadcast footage of dismembered babies, baggies full of tiny human eyes or any other accurate footage of the 'commodity' being sold by the baby parts merchants. But this should have been stated in the programme. Showing scientists poking at slivers of flesh in a Petri dish through a microscope was deceptive and it dehumanizes this debate."

In America, late-term abortions are permitted, even up to 30 weeks gestation. It's a three day procedure and involves forcing the mother to go into labour but killing the baby with a spike to the base of the skull before it leaves the birth canal. Even so, according to Alberty, it wasn't unusual out of the 30 or 40 late-term abortions each week to see several babies born alive on the operating table before clinicians could perform the procedure.

"They were coming out alive. The doctor would either break the neck or take a pair of tongs and basically beat the fetus until it was dead."

Alberty's testimony was verbal, and in many cases it was challenged by abortion providers who questioned his motives and accused him of "embellishing" the sordid details of the abortion industry. But Alberty the whistleblower wasn't alone. Another former clinic manager, Eric Harrah, gave a video interview disclosing live births as the abortion industry's "dirty secret":

"It was always very disturbing, so the doctor would try to conceal it from the rest of the staff."

One incident in particular haunts him. The clinic had begun inducing a woman 26 weeks pregnant, but sent her overnight to a nearby motel to await the full procedure in the morning. Instead, in the middle of the night she gave birth to a child and was brought back to the abortion clinic with the baby wrapped in a towel.

"I was in the scrub room when I saw the towel move," says Harrah. "A nurse said, 'Eric, you're just tired. It's three in the morning.' Then we both looked and a little baby's arm raised up out of the towel and was moving like a newborn baby. I screamed and ran out. The doctor came in and closed the door and when we went back in to process the baby out of the clinic into the lab, [the baby] had a puncture wound in his chest."

In the United States, trafficking in baby parts for profit is a criminal offence. But to get around the problem, universities and researchers pay a fee – not for the parts themselves but for the "cost of extraction". Thus, there are different fees depending on the amount of work involved. And shipping and handling is extra.

Harvesting fetal tissue is not yet illegal in the US. In fact, the programme at five major universities including the University of Washington is part funded by the US National Institutes of Health. It is the University of Washington that has been supplying Keely Bumsted O'Brien at the University of Auckland, with some of her eyeball retinas of aborted children.

The reality of the ethical boundaries wasn't lost on the stu-dents gathered in the Auckland School of Medicine lecture theatre when fourth year undergrads Tim Eagle and Kimberly Taylor wrapped up their presentation on genetic testing the eyeballs of chicken embryos and human fetuses. They told the audience they'd used tissue from a 10 week human embryo, a 12 week and a 16 week fetus. When Keely Bumsted O'Brien called for questions from the audience, the first was an ethical one, from a female student somewhere up the front of the crowded auditorium. Had Eagle and Taylor, she wondered, run their project past the Auckland University Ethics Committee?

"We have ethical approval under Keely as referee, which is obvious by itself. Her current ethical approval worked for what we were doing so we basically used hers, which was obtained as far as we're aware from America," Taylor responded.

When *Investigate* magazine rang O'Brien to clarify, she confirmed her teams were working on something big.

"There's a large ongoing project, and I don't think I need to tell you when and where I actually do specific things. Are you aware that importation of human tissue into New Zealand does not require any sort of permit?," she countered.

Apparently, she's right. Under current New Zealand law, you can import body parts to your heart's content as long as you do it in a biosafe manner. But what about seeking approval from the Ministry of Health's Northern Region Ethics Committee? Surely there must be laws governing the carrying out of experiments on aborted human infants in the name of science?

"No," says O'Brien emphatically, "because you're not required to, because it's tissue, not alive."

In other words, thanks to a loophole in New Zealand law, it is perfectly legal to conduct experiments on aborted human embryos. For all we know, there may be dozens of experiments being carried out on aborted children in research labs throughout New Zealand. The fetal eyes, O'Brien says, arrive in the country having been "snap frozen cryogenically" just minutes after death, then placed in formaldehyde.

So who supplies Auckland University with infant eyeball retinas? O'Brien repeatedly talks of the "organizations" that supply her, but names only one, the University of Washington.

"These organizations, like for example the University of Washington has a tissue programme. The UOW oversees the collection of tissue, they have their own ethics committee. So they have to be overseen by another committee. So to use fetal human tissue in NZ I have to go through the local ethics committee, and in addition the tissue that I'm gathering has to be gathered under a separate ethics protocol. That ethics protocol is overseen by the ethics committee that's on site."

When *Investigate* suggests that the body parts could be coming in without mothers even realizing their aborted baby had been harvested moments after death, O'Brien is outraged.

"Working with human fetal tissue is not taken lightly. You have to have respect for the donation of the tissue. Now the child obviously cannot give consent, it's the mother that's giving consent."

"Do you think they're asking these women, 'do you mind if we keep the baby for medical research?'," we ask.

"You absolutely have to! You absolutely positively have to! Do your homework man! You simply cannot take fetal tissue from an aborted fetus without informed consent from the mother. Oh my goodness, I'm shocked to hear you suggest that. I'm upset and shocked that you suggest that. Totally off base."

But is it really off base? O'Brien insists that women seeking abortions are asked to sign consent forms authorizing the use of their dead babies for medical research. It leads to a terse exchange with *Investigate*.

"There is an informed consent form that the mother signs. She is not coerced, she is not paid any money. She is informed of all of her options. That informed consent was part of my approval that was produced and shown to the ethics committee here [in Auckland]."

Great, we thought. So O'Brien actually knew the names of the mothers involved and had presented copies of their consent to her peers?

"Absolutely not! That is so unethical! All I know is that the tissue was donated by the mother, and the mother has signed an informed consent form."

But hang on, we asked, how do you know, if you don't have a signed form with a name on it?

"I don't keep those records on site."

No, but somebody must.

"Yes, they are kept by the organization that coordinates the donation."

So what, physically, does O'Brien have that proves there's been informed consent from the mother?

"You cannot collect the tissue without informed consent from the mother. It is unethical for the organization that coordinates the collection of the tissue to provide me with any sort of information that might link it back to the mother."

In other words, there's no signed paperwork for O'Brien or the ethics committee to see. It's done on trust. To *Investigate's* knowledge, O'Brien has never seen a signed informed consent form.

So for all you know, we pushed her, it could be somebody in an office somewhere chucking out these forms on a word processor saying 'yeah, we do all this' and of course they don't. "If you've never seen a signed copy, how do you know?"

And when *Investigate* went searching, those are exactly the kind of discrepancies we began to find. Like this extract from the *Seattle Post Intelligencer* newspaper in the wake of a congressional visit to the University of Washington lab:

"Women who agree to the use of their aborted babies for research sign a simple "informed consent" document at the abortion clinic, which includes no information on where the particular "donation" will be sent or how it will be used. This oversight is inconsistent with the regulation requiring "informed" consent, according to a physician familiar with research protocols, and could be problematic for the University of Washington laboratory."

The newspaper also discovered other discrepancies in the University of Washington paperwork, such as the University letting outside labs fill in forms instead of doing the paperwork themselves. Nor was the University of Washington doing the actual organ harvesting at the abortion clinics, so the University itself was one step removed from the informed consent process in terms of verifying whether the consent was genuine. In other words, the University of Washington's ethical oversight could not have included whether the tissue was harvested 'ethically', because the University has never been in a position to know.

The congressmen went away sufficiently concerned that six separate pieces of legislation were drafted to combat the harvesting of tissues. But with a change in administration, those bills went onto the backburner.

Then there's the issue of the other 'organisation' O'Brien refers to but doesn't name. *Investigate* traced two scientific papers published by O'Brien in the past 24 months. One, "Expression of photoreceptor-associated molecules during human fetal eye development",[171] was published in the journal *Molecular Vision* in 2003 and can be found on the internet through a Google search. In the paper, O'Brien discloses she used body parts supplied by the University

171   http://www.molvis.org/molvis/v9/a52/

of Washington, but also by a private broking firm like the controversial Anatomic Gift Foundation referred to earlier; this one is named Advanced Bioscience Resources, or ABR, and is based in California. After Anatomic Gift Foundation was sprung thanks to the testimony of insider Dean Alberty, Advanced Bioscience Resources moved to fill the fetal tissue power vacuum. In an industry now estimated to be worth around $2 billion globally, ABR is believed to be a major player, particularly as it's prepared to supply organs harvested from second trimester late-term abortions, which the University of Washington refuses to do.

Investigate has confirmed that an early second trimester baby was dissected for the Auckland University study, making ABR the likely supplier to O'Brien. And O'Brien has used babies up to the fetal age of 22 weeks, according to her published studies.

Her *Molecular Vision* paper describes how experiments were "prepared from snap frozen intact human fetal eyes ranging from fetal week 9 to fetal week 19…labeling was performed in a large number of eyes within an age group."

There is no disclosure in the internet version of the paper how many eyes were harvested for the experiments. At least ten babies from fetal weeks 9 to 22 are known to have been harvested for O'Brien's second scientific paper we found, published in *Investigative Ophthalmology and Visual Science* in August 2004.[172] Again, suppliers were both ABR and the University of Washington. One paper on eyes supplied by ABR describes how the baby's eyes are "enucleated" from the skull – medical talk for being scooped out with a knife.

Although she was working at the University of Auckland at the time, O'Brien has told *Investigate* the experiments detailed in her published papers were carried out "elsewhere".

And what do we know of Advanced Bioscience Resources? According to O'Brien, her suppliers operate with transparent ethical rules and committees. But Advanced Bioscience Resources appears far from transparent. At least one American news report says the company has refused to comment on its body parts trade, making it impossible to ask whether ABR's practices comply with federal US law.

"We're a biotechnology firm, we don't talk to the press," a company spokeswoman is quoted as saying on another occasion.

Investigate has confirmed that ABR supplied aborted baby brains to be injected into mice, as part of experiments creating a part human/part mouse chimera. The genetically-engineered mice have been given – all courtesy of aborted fetuses from ABR – a human immune system, a human fetal thymus, liver and lymph node. The mice are then infected with HIV as part of AIDS research.

The US National Institutes of Health, which funded the grisly harvesting and experiment, has refused to provide any written proof that ABR holds informed consent forms, nor has the NIH confirmed that mothers were told by ABR that organs from their dead babies would be transplanted into genetically-engineered mice.

ABR has also supplied human baby hearts for transplantation into pigs, and fetal stem cells.

I asked O'Brien whether she felt modern scientists were stepping into a dark pedigree. "Do you see a correlation between the boundaries of science and experimentation on humans in this area, and the dreams of Nazi Josef Mengele and others back in World War 2 and the kind of experiments they were conducting?"

"No."

Mengele had taken particular interest in dissecting live infants for medical experiments.

"You see no correlation?"

There was a pause as O'Brien drew in her breath. "What you're trying to get me to say is that research on human fetal tissue is morally and ethically wrong, and I'm not going to say that. Because obviously I'm working on the tissue. I think the information to be gained is extremely valuable and it's not something taken in lightly. I don't think the information I use can be interpreted and used for eugenics. The reason that we have ethics committees is so we don't have a scientific free for all."

Other ethicists, like Princeton's Paul Ramsey in the US, disagree however.

"Far from abortion settling the question of fetal research, it could be that sober reflection on the use of the human fetus in research could unsettle the abortion issue."[173]

Are human children, ask ethicists, any less-deserving of protection from medical experiments and execution than animals?

Pittsburgh-based researcher Suzanne Rini, who interviewed Ramsey and whose 1995 book *Beyond Abortion: A Chronicle of Fetal Experimentation* brought to light a body parts trade that's existed since the 1950s, believes the very fact that scientists need the elixir of youth from fetuses may be the ethical catch-22 that kills the abortion industry. On the one hand, she says, medical researchers try to argue the fetus is not a live person. On the other, whether it's a cure for Parkinson's, diabetes, Huntington's, MS or a range of other disorders, medical researchers claim the *life* in fetuses is the only thing that can save adults. But only if you kill the fetus first.

University of Auckland's Deputy Vice Chancellor, Research – Tom Barnes – says it is ethical under current NZ law to harvest organs from fetuses for the sake of improving the lives of adults.

---

173   http://www.interlife.org/secrets.html

"As you know [Keely's] research is looking at eyes. She's trying to solve the problem of macular degeneration which is a disease that affects 60% of more of people who are 70 years old or over. She's also trying to solve some problems to do with eye disease in younger people as well."

It is a modern, relativistic idea that you can sacrifice the few for the good of the many. Indeed, this was one of the justifications Hitler used in whipping up hatred against Jewish, Gypsy and gay minorities. In 21st century form, the argument is more subtle: that if a cure for crippling diseases can be found by harvesting fetal organs from abortions, or growing human embryos in the laboratory for stem cell harvesting, then the deaths of those infants are justifiable because of the perceived greater good to the community at large.

Indeed, O'Brien makes a similar appeal when we ask what the ultimate benefit of dissecting children's eyeballs is:

"You achieve knowledge, so that you can start to try and find therapies to help people regain their vision, or intervention so that you can help people who have congenital abnormalities that we might be able to fix them.

"Obviously I don't think there should be a blanket ban on the use of human fetal tissue because I think the information that you get out of the use of human tissue is very valuable in trying to help people."

But is that a valid line of reasoning that justifies made-to-order abortions?

At the Nuremberg War Crimes trials, evidence was presented of horrific scientific experiments being performed on captives in the concentration camps. The Nazi medics on trial attempted to justify it by saying the test subjects were due to die anyway and the knowledge gained would benefit the rest of humanity.

Needless to say, the Nazis were shot down in the courtroom (and later simply shot outside it) and Nuremberg issued a declaration condemning the role of the medical profession in experimentation and slaughter of innocents.

University of Auckland's Keely Bumsted O'Brien resents modern scientists being likened to Hitler's gruesome genetic engineers, and points out that when Germany's Max Planck Institute for Brain Research recently discovered it possessed the brains of many Down's Syndrome people slaughtered by the Nazis, the Institute did the decent thing.

"Rather than use [the brains for research], it was the decision of the Director to give those brains a decent burial. Which one could argue might be the ethical way to do it, if they were gathered by the Nazis in an unethical way dealing with eugenics. Now I don't compare what I do to eugenics."

But *Investigate* challenged O'Brien on her example.

"There is an arguable case that in 50 or a hundred years time society will look back and say the current Western practice of mass abortion was a similar sort of thing to what the Nazis did and they'll look at it the same way, what's your response to that?"

"I don't think they will," exclaims O'Brien. "And I think we take much more care in how we carry out the research than the Nazis did."

It is clear to *Investigate* after an hour long interview with O'Brien that she is sincere in her beliefs, and she makes special mention of the fact that she respects the humanity of the tissue. She also attends an annual memorial service, she says, that the medical school has for the cadavers and tissue used during the year. Nonetheless, our inquiries into the baby parts business gives no reason to think that the harvesting of organs in America from dead or dying infants is done more humanely than the Nazis did.

For a start, the death toll alone from abortion far eclipses anything Hitler was able to achieve. For the record, international studies like a 1999 paper from International Family Planning perspectives suggest 46 million lives a year are taken throughout the world.

At the Mayfair Women's Clinic in Aurora, Colorado, staff admitted under cross examination in court that they had so many aborted babies to get rid of that clinician Dr James Parks used to put the bodies of larger babies (up to week 22) into meatgrinders so the remains could be reduced to the consistency of toothpaste and flushed down sinks.

Leaked documents from inside abortion clinics have hit the headlines across the US, and they make dark reading. They're order forms from scientists to agencies like Advanced Bioscience Resources, instructing what parts they need and how to get them.

"Dissect fetal liver and thymus and occasional lymph node from fetal cadaver within 10 (minutes of death)." "Arms and legs need not be intact." "Intact brains preferred, but large pieces of brain may be usable."

Or this, from a scientist studying the "Biochemical Characterization of human type X Collagen," who requests "Whole intact leg, include entire hip joint, 22-24 weeks gest."

The harvesting technician is asked to "dissect by cutting through symphasis pubis and include whole Illium [hip joint]. To be removed from fetal cadaver within 10 minutes."

Another, from University of Colorado's Gary J. Miller, a professor of pathology, seeks the prostate glands of 24 fetuses from the first and second trimesters. The glands, he says in his request to Anatomic Gift Foundation on November 10, 1998, are "To be removed and prepared within 5 minutes ... after circulation has stopped."

According to *World* magazine in the US, which broke the story, other specifications state that they are to be "preserved on wet ice," "picked up immediately by applicant," have "low risk no IV drug abuse or known sexually transmitted diseases," and no prescription medications used by "donor" mother. The contract is signed both by Dr. Miller and, for the Regents of the

University of Colorado, by "Sharon Frazier, Director of Purchasing."
O'Brien refuses to believe there is anything dodgy about the fetal tissue harvesting operations in the US.

"I have to put my faith in the fact that the organizations that I'm obtaining tissue from are obtaining it in an ethical manner."

But let's look at that more closely. The American Society For Cell Biology, an association of cell biologists, lobbied hard against regulating the fetal tissue harvesting industry, including a suggestion that researchers should have to "verify that the tissue was obtained properly". This condition, and others, were regarded as too onerous for the scientists to accept.

None of the many articles and papers *Investigate* has read on the issue suggest that the abortion clinics or tissue harvesting organizations are subject to ethical oversight committees. In fact, the Anatomic Gift Foundation, which is similar to ABR, openly puts the onus on its clients – the researchers – to get ethical approval before they make an organ purchase application. *Investigate* has found no evidence that AGF or ABR are themselves audited by anyone.

And how ethical is the behaviour of another big fetal tissue provider (until it was sprung in the ABC 20/20 programme), Opening Lines?

A division of Missouri and Illinois-based Consultative and Diagnostic Pathology Inc, Opening Lines made no bones about the fact it was in business to make money. A 20/20 producer, posing as a potential investor in the 11 year old company, visited its founder, pathologist Dr Miles Jones.

Jones, unaware he was being recorded on a hidden video camera, explained how his company obtained fetal parts from clinics across America for shipment to research labs. "It's market force," Dr. Jones told the producer about how he sets his prices. "It's what you can sell it for." He said he was looking to set up an abortion clinic in Mexico in order to get more fetal tissue by luring women in with cut-price abortions.

"If you control the flow — it's probably the equivalent of the invention of the assembly line."

As to the financial benefits of his business, Jones was brutal about the demand from researchers: "If you have a guy that's desperate for, let's say, a heart, then he'll pay you whatever you ask," he said.

"That's trading in body parts. There's no doubt about it," Arthur Caplan, director of the University of Pennsylvania's Center for Bioethics, told the *Alberta Report* newspaper after reviewing Jones' statements.

The Opening Lines corporate brochure reads more like a supermarket advertisement than an ethical, dignified approach to the death of a baby.

"The freshest tissue prepared to your specifications and delivered in the quantities you need it."

Despite compiling a baby parts price list and charging fees, an FBI investigation concluded that Opening Lines had broken no laws in what it had done and how it had done it. So if the American ethical rules are tough, there's been no evidence of it to date.

Then there's the question of whether the University of Auckland Human Ethics Committee is tough enough in demanding proof of informed consent in cases like O'Brien's. You'll remember O'Brien is insistent that she could not provide the University of Auckland with copies of the informed consent because it would be unethical for her to know the identities of the mothers who'd signed them.

"It is unethical for the organization that coordinates the collection of the tissue to provide me with any sort of information that might link it back to the mother."

Contrast O'Brien's statement with this extract from the ethical guidelines imposed on fetal tissue research by the University of Texas at Houston:

"An investigator proposing to use fetal tissue must complete an application form for full [Ethics Committee] review and approval. The application must include a copy of the consent form used to obtain consent for donating the tissue. [Ethics Committee] must be assured that the woman donating tissue has been given an opportunity to understand the procedures, any possible risks to her privacy and well-being, and to assure that she has an opportunity to give free and informed consent to the donation." [emphasis added]

Additionally, the University of Texas requires that the consent form cannot be generic, and must relate to the actual research project that is planned, with "a short description of the reasons for the research."

While O'Brien claims it would be unethical for her to know the donor or talk to them, the University of Texas requires its researchers to include on the woman's copy of the consent form "the name and telephone number" of the researcher, so that the donor can make contact, ask further questions, and even withdraw their consent.

Implicit in this is that the researcher must take ethical responsibility for the collection of the tissue, and should know who the donor is. Both of these aspects corroborate the comments made about the flawed informed consent procedures of the University of Washington earlier in this report.

It is clear from O'Brien's interview with *Investigate* that none of the women donating their dead babies' eyeballs would have been able to reach her to withdraw their consent or ask questions.

But *Investigate* didn't leave the issue there. Despite the fact that Advanced Bioscience Resources refuses to give media interviews, we obtained the cellphone number of its President, Linda Tracy, and we rang it. What we obtained is a world exclusive:

"We're just doing a story on fetal tissue use over here in NZ, and one of the suppliers is ABR, and people tell us you guys are subject to ethical committee oversight, would that be right?"

"Who are you with again?"

"*Investigate* magazine."

"OK, I don't give any information to magazines or interviews to anyone."

But just as Tracy was about to do what she'd done so many times before to American journalists – hang up – we reminded her that negative publicity could affect her business, and she had a responsibility to put her side of the story.

"In this particular case, the researcher says that the suppliers such as yourself are subject to ethical committee oversight. I'm trying to find out who is responsible for ethical oversight in terms of ABR, would it be you or is it the researcher who must seek approval?"

"Both."

"What committee do you people report to, how does it work?"

"Well, we are overseen by the IRS, the Internal Revenue Service. As a non-profit organization we have guidelines to abide by, but that's about the only regulatory committee that we are subject to."

So much for ethical oversight. Is there, we asked, an external ethical committee that Advanced Bioscience Resources reports to or which oversees its baby harvesting operation?

"No."

What about the actual extraction of eyeballs and other fetal tissue, who carries that out?

"It is our responsibility to collect the tissue," confirms Linda Tracy.

"So you're in control of the process all the way through?"

"No."

This 'ethical oversight' is getting more fascinating by the minute. Which part of the process, we asked, was outside ABR's control?

"The [abortion] clinic consents the patient."

"And then the clinic provides you with the consent?"

"Yes."

"Is there any possibility that the clinic may not properly consent the patient, the clinic may take the view 'we're never going to see the patient back through here, they're never going to know', and they'll just write out the forms. How do you know the clinic is doing the informed consent properly?"

"We just have to trust them," says ABR's Linda Tracy.

Don't forget, the abortion clinic gets paid money for providing 'office space' to the harvesters, and has a financial interest in the success of harvesting as an industry.

Keely Bumsted O'Brien may have expressed "shock" and outrage when *Investigate* suggested the harvesting programmes could be ethically shonky, but the evidence now appears pretty damning.

Not only is there no ethical oversight of the abortion clinics, there is none on the companies doing the fetal tissue harvesting either. All the way through, the process appears to be done purely on "trust".

And just how good is the actual informed consent process that the ethics committees rely on? According to the University of Texas, informed consent forms had to spell out what kind of research was specifically planned.

We asked ABR whether, for example, donating 'mothers' would be told their child's organs would be used for eye studies, or for transplantation into animals for experiments?

"The law requires that we always state that it is possible that it may be used for important stem cell research, and if the patient asks specifically what it might be used for then that is explained to her verbally. The consent itself is somewhat generic except for the pluripotent stem cell use."

Based on Linda Tracy's interview with *Investigate*, it now appears certain that no donating mother gave informed consent for her baby's body parts to be transplanted into human/mouse hybrids, or injected into the veins of rats. Little wonder the US Government National Institutes of Health refused to release informed consent forms from ABR regarding those projects.

There was another aspect we wanted to clarify: O'Brien's insistence that it would be unethical for her to see a donating mother's consent form.

"Are those forms available to researchers if they need them for ethical approval?", we asked Tracy.

"Yes."

Naturally, all these discoveries raised more questions than answers. We went back to the University of Auckland's Tom Barnes, the man the university's ethics committee reports to.

"Keely does have ethical approval from the University of Washington to do this and that ethical approval is current and has gone through their prescribed procedures."

Barnes explained that the project is a collaboration with the University of Washington's Anita Hendrickson, who was apparently the principal point of contact with tissue harvesters.

But Barnes was not aware that University of Washington's ethical procedures were found wanting, as referred to earlier in the *Seattle Post-Intelligencer* report.

"I'm sorry, I can't comment on that," reflected Barnes. "I'd have to know exactly what the situation is before I comment.

"In terms of what this university knows, we have the ethical approval from Washington, and also the proposal has been examined by our ethics committee de novo [as if for the first time] as well."

When we pointed out that neither University of Washington nor ABR had directly sought informed consent from women and instead relied on abortion clinics to get it, Barnes said the University of Auckland had to trust the paperwork in front of it.

"As I say, I understand the ethical approvals were granted over there and we have paperwork that backs that up. Whatever happened over there I can't comment on."

We explained to Barnes the stringent ethical conditions imposed on informed consent forms by the University of Texas, and asked whether he was satisfied that the University of Auckland's ethical rigours were tough enough.

"Let me say that our ethics committee operates under guidelines that are set nationally, and those guidelines are approved by the HRC. I believe we have an ethics committee that is absolutely committed to research being done in the correct way and I believe they do an excellent job of that."

Having said that, says Barnes, the University of Auckland will ponder *Investigate's* allegations that the US ethical process is flawed.

And what about the overall ethical issue of whether human infants should be experimented on at all? Barnes says it is legal under current New Zealand law, and proposed new rules to control it have not yet come into effect. When we again raise the comparison with Auschwitz, Barnes rejects the analogy.

"I think that's entirely inappropriate."

"How?"

"Well it's a totally different situation."

"How?"

"If you accuse, by default, Keely of behaving like somebody in a Nazi death camp, I do think that's unfair. If the issues you've raised about ethical approval in America are resolved satisfactorily, if the mothers are in fact giving informed consent for the use of their tissue, that's really quite different to somebody who's in a Nazi death camp being experimented on," says Barnes.

But doesn't the answer, we pointed out, really turn on whether the fetus is the 'mother's tissue' to dispose of in the first place?"

"We make sure we fall within the ethical guidelines as they are laid down," says Barnes. "Whether those guidelines are flawed or not or whether they'll change or not is a matter for the future, and in the meantime we have to operate within those constraints.

"To be honest with you, I think that that [whether a fetus is an individual human life or just part of the mother] is a broader debate which would have to take place in the country at large."

It's a good point. Researchers talk of the baby simply being "the mother's tissue", but advances in DNA mean we now know the fetus has its own unique DNA and tissue, and is not merely an extra piece of maternal flesh. The mother, in real scientific terms, can no more "own" the fetus on such grounds than she can "own" her older children and consent to their execution and vivisection. Is it time for renewed public debate?

It's an argument that the University of Auckland is sympathetic to.

"You have to sort of balance the tremendous potential of this research to solve some absolutely debilitating problems – people being blind for years and so on. So we do the best we can at balancing all these factors within the guidelines and the law as it stands, and we contribute to and take part in that ethical debate and we will abide by what comes out of that ethical debate. We're not trying to cover anything up.

"If the result of that debate that you're referring to is that it's unethical to work with this kind of tissue, then we wouldn't do. No question."

Another who shares that view is Steven Bamforth, a Canadian geneticist harvesting fetal tissue at the University of Alberta for his research colleagues. Every day, his job entails sifting through aborted remains, searching for recognizable eyes, hearts, livers and other organs sought after by universities.

"The humanity is always before us," Dr. Bamforth told *Alberta Report* magazine recently. "If society said this research is not acceptable, of course, we would immediately desist. It's not something that I do happily."

Nor does the "helping older people with their health" excuse carry water with Christopher Hook, of Illinois' Centre for Bioethics and Human Dignity.

He told *World* magazine the exploitation of pre-born children was "too high a price regardless of the supposed benefit. We can never feel comfortable with identifying a group of our brothers and sisters who can be exploited for the good of the whole. Once we have crossed that line, we have betrayed our covenant with one another as a society, and certainly the covenant of medicine."

Despite her denials, the work of Keely Bumsted-O'Brien and others is entirely in keeping with eugenics, at least in its modern form. As you'll see in the next chapter, we return to eugenics and its role in the final frontiers of science.

PRICE LIST FOR BODY PARTS (US$)

Opening Lines Fee for Services Schedule
> age greater than
< age same or less than

Unprocessed Specimen (> 8 weeks) $ 70
Unprocessed Specimen (< 8 weeks) $ 50
Livers (< 8 weeks) 30% discount if significantly fragmented $150
Livers (> 8 weeks) 30% discount if significantly fragmented $125
Spleens (< 8 weeks) $ 75
Spleens (> 8 weeks) $ 50
Pancreas (< 8 weeks) $100
Pancreas (> 8 weeks) $ 75
Thymus (< 8 weeks) $100
Thymus (> 8 weeks) $ 75
Intestines & Mesentery $ 50
Mesentery (< 8 weeks) $125
Mesentery (> 8 weeks) $100
Kidney-with/without adrenal (< 8 weeks) $125
Kidney-with/without adrenal (> 8 weeks) $100
Limbs (at least 2) $150
Brain (< 8 weeks) 30% discount if significantly fragmented $999
Brain (> 8 weeks) 30% discount if significantly fragmented $150
Pituitary Gland (> 8 weeks) $300
Bone Marrow (< 8 weeks) $350
Bone Marrow (> 8 weeks) $250
Ears (< 8 weeks) $ 75
Ears (> 8 weeks) $ 50
Eyes (< 8 weeks) 40% discount for single eye $ 75
Eyes (> 8 weeks) 40% discount for single eye $ 50
Skin (> 12 weeks) $100
Lungs & Heart Block $150
Intact Embryonic Cadaver (< 8 weeks) $400
Intact Embryonic Cadaver (> 8 weeks) $600
Intact Calvarium $125
Intact Trunk (with/without limbs) $500
Gonads $550
Cord Blood (Snap Frozen LN2) $125
Spinal Column $150
Spinal Cord $325

18

The Fourth Reich
The Return of 'Futuregenics'

"The philosopher who finds no meaning in the world is not concerned exclusively with a problem in pure metaphysics, he is also concerned to prove that there is no valid reason why he personally should not do as he wants to do, or why his friends should not seize political power and govern in the way that they find most advantageous to themselves. For myself, the philosophy of meaninglessness was essentially an instrument of liberation, sexual and political."
Aldous Huxley, atheist philosopher

So what happened to the Eugenics movement in the wake of World War Two and the Holocaust revelations? As you've seen from the last chapter, eugenics work of the kind pioneered by the Nazis continues unabated at major research institutions in the West, albeit under a different name. Your children, or your friends, or perhaps even you yourself, may be studying a eugenics subject at high school or university.

Although there is very little publicity, eugenics programmes almost parallel to the Nazi ones were being considered in the US and other countries up to and during WW2.

Germany had implemented a euthanasia campaign against the disabled and mentally ill in the 1930s, that many American psychiatrists felt was a good idea to replicate. Testimony to a Canadian senate hearing on euthanasia in 1994 touched on just how close it came:[174]

"FINALLY, I WANT TO SPEAK as a parent. On September 10 this year, we held our son David's birthday party. We had pizza; there was music; everybody had a good time. It was particularly meaningful to me because of what I have learned about the

---

relationship between the German euthanasia program and what has happened in North America.

"It was only because of the vilification of the Nazi euthanasia program that we got sidetracked from a powerful euthanasia movement in North America in the 1940s. This is one of the things I thought about on my son's fourth birthday. The plan which was proposed for many people in North America was published as an editorial in the *Journal of the American Psychiatric Association*. It was a much more humane plan since we were not evil like the Nazis. It suggested that severely-handicapped children, like my four-year-old, should be killed but not until their fourth birthday. The suggestion was made for humanitarian reasons because they did not want to make any mistakes. They thought that, if they killed children as soon as they were born, they might accidentally kill some who were not severely handicapped. They would give the kids until their fourth birthday to kind of shape up.

"However, in suggesting that, they thought of a potential complication. If these kids hung around for four years, their parents might actually get to like them. The humanitarian solution was to refer to the attachment of parents to their disabled children as "morbid obsessions". The article suggested it was the duty of every physician to do everything in their power to stop that morbid obsession because to do so, in their words, could only be good mental hygiene practice."

Euthanasia, as it is still advocated today, is essentially Nazi in its ideology. In Holland, where voluntary euthanasia was introduced several years ago, there has been a growing number of elderly couples euthanizing themselves because popular culture deems the elderly are a burden to society, and the Dutch government, following the traditional "slippery slope" course, is now proposing the involuntary euthanasia of disabled children.

If you want to see where the "Death with dignity" brigade are going, take a look at this report out of Switzerland earlier this year, from Britain's *Daily Mail*. Fifty-nine year old motor neurone disease sufferer Maxine Coombes had been convinced by Death with dignity advocates that an assisted suicide in Switzerland, where the procedure is now legal, would be a beautiful way to "meet a peaceful end surrounded by music, candles, flowers and compassionate staff."

Selling her car and saving money from her invalid's benefit, she travelled to the Dignitas clinic in Zurich which, as the *Daily Mail* notes, has the motto

'Live with dignity, die with dignity'. But compare the perception to the reality of commercial eugenics - Coombes was accompanied by her twin sister and her son, Paul Clifford, who were there to hold her hand and say goodbye:[175]

> MR CLIFFORD, WHO IS BACK home in Bermondsey, South London, following his mother's death on January 10, said: 'When we arrived at the place it was a block of flats, with a buzzer marked Dignitas but there was no answer.
>
> 'We were standing there for about three-quarters of an hour until a man arrived wearing a leather jacket with a sports bag over his shoulder, a dirty blue T-shirt, jeans with the knees cut out and smoking a roll-up. There was paint and graffiti on the walls outside, and the same on the door to the apartment.
>
> 'Inside there was a coffee table, four chairs around it, a bench, and a little washbasin.
>
> He said he had to make a video and asked my mother, "You know what you are doing, don't you? Nobody's pressuring you to drink this drink, are they? You know if you drink this drink you are going to die?'
>
> Mr Clifford said his mother, a former court usher, took a lethal dose of barbiturates just 15 minutes after entering the room. He and Mrs Coombes's sister, Dawn Davis, were told she would be conscious for another 45 minutes, but just 40 seconds later, they watched her head slump to her chest.
>
> The Swiss member of staff, who had introduced himself as Arthur, then announced: 'Let's make sure we get our stories straight.'
>
> When they were let back in to spend a few minutes with his mother's corpse, they found her on a bench 'going blue', covered in a 'dirty blanket like half a curtain', with 'her clothes chucked on the floor'.
>
> After they returned to UK, Mrs Coombes's ashes were posted back to the family in a cheap clay pot in a polystyrene tub, to which was taped her death certificate and an invoice for postage costs.

Before her death, Maxine Coombes had mentioned to the Dignitas staff member that her son often suffered from depression. The entire family were stunned when the man responded that her son could also "die at a 'cut price' rate" if he wanted!

---

175   http://www.alertuk.org/node/83

As with so many bad ideas in the West, they begin with a camel's nose under the tent flap. London's *Weekly Standard* newspaper provides a very effective snapshot of how "compassionate" euthanasia incrementally led to Auschwitz in Germany, by altering the public's perceptions and lowering resistance over a period of years:[176]

THE SEEDS OF GERMAN EUTHANASIA were planted in 1920 in the book *Permission to Destroy Life Unworthy of Life (Die Freigabe der Vernichtung lebensunwerten Leben)*. Its authors were two of the most respected academics in their respective fields: Karl Binding was a renowned law professor, and Alfred Hoche a physician and humanitarian.

The authors accepted wholeheartedly that people with terminal illnesses, the mentally ill or retarded, and deformed people could be euthanized as "life unworthy of life." More than that, the authors professionalized and medicalized the concept and, according to Robert Jay Lifton in *The Nazi Doctors*, promoted euthanasia in these circumstances as "purely a healing treatment" and a "healing work"--justified as a splendid way to relieve suffering while saving money spent on caring for the disabled.

Over the years Binding and Hoche's attitudes percolated throughout German society and became accepted widely. These attitudes were stoked enthusiastically by the Nazis so that by 1938 the German government received an outpouring of requests from the relatives of severely disabled infants and young children seeking permission to end their lives.

Those deemed killable were usually dispatched via an overdose of a drug, most typically a sedative called Luminal. The euphemism of choice for this murder was "treatment." Most, but not all, of this killing was done in secret.

It is important to note that throughout the years in which euthanasia was performed in Germany, whether as part of the officially sanctioned government program or otherwise, the government did not force doctors to kill. Participating doctors had become true believers, convinced they were performing a valuable medical service for their "patients" and their country.

It is often the way. People tend to justify their actions because it is far easier

176   http://www.weeklystandard.com/Content/Public/Articles/000/000/012/003dncoj. asp?pg=1

to believe you are doing something for the right reasons, than to believe your own morality is evil.

Despite the bad publicity that Auschwitz gave them, the leading lights in Western eugenics clung to the name for at least a couple of decades. The first organizations to ditch the word "eugenics" were the research journals of the various societies. In 1968, *Eugenics Quarterly* in the US changed its name to *Social Biology*, while across the Atlantic England's *Eugenics Review* became the *Journal of Biosocial Science*. Five years later, the American Eugenics Society morphed into the Society for the Study of Social Biology, and in the late 80's the British Eugenics Society renamed itself the Galton Institute.

One eugenicist who wasn't happy with the name change was American Carl Bajema, who lamented in a 1983 interview the lack of courage, suggested adopting the name "Futuregenics", and urged continuing engagement by eugenics in popular culture:[177]

> "THERE ARE POLITICAL CONTROVERSIES we need to get involved in, because in some cases, the side eugenics is on is losing. I'll give you some examples: *First, it's very important for anyone who supports eugenics to also support Planned Parenthood and various abortion rights groups. Second, it is crucial to support sex education and contraceptive education in the schools. Third, we need to counter the fundamentalists' attack on the teaching of evolution. And fourth, there's the controversy going on with respect to the teaching of values which concerns us.* What is called "values clarification" [called "Values Exploration" in the NZ school curriculum, and a core subject] helps students learn about different ways of viewing an act in terms of both personal consequences and social consequences. An extreme right wing faction wants to force this out of the schools. [emphasis added]

As you can see, it's a re-statement of all the core eugenics principles, including their growing foothold in schools, indoctrinating kids in eugenics "values".

The reason eugenics has made these inroads, however, is precisely because its name change to "Social Biology" has opened doors in educational circles. After all, most eugenicists are highly qualified psychologists and sociologists. People like Emeritus professor of Psychology at the University of Ulster, Richard Lynn.

In a review[178] of another eugenics book, Lynn quotes approvingly some of the book's main points, which include that America is going down the gurgler because coloured people are not smart enough:

177   http://www.eugenics.net/papers/eb5.html
178   http://www.eugenics.net/papers/RLSPECREV.htm

"LOW INTELLIGENCE IS A SIGNIFICANT determinant of a variety of social pathologies including poor educational attainment, chronic unemployment, long term welfare dependency, crime, single motherhood and poverty;

"These social evils would be reduced if the intelligence of the population could be increased and it would be desirable if this could be accomplished;

"There is little chance of being able to do this because the things that have been tried such as improving education and headstart programs have little or no impact on intelligence;

"The situation is getting worse because the genetic component of intelligence is deteriorating through the process of dysgenesis [meaning "bad breeding" and falling IQs, the opposite of eugenics, or "good breeding"] or dysgenics resulting from the tendency of the intelligent to have fewer children than the unintelligent, for the generation length to be shorter for the less intelligent, and through the large scale immigration of those with low intelligence;

"Blacks have on average lower intelligence than whites and Asians and this contributes to the over-representation of blacks in respect of the social pathologies of poor educational attainment, single motherhood, crime, etc.; the low average IQ of blacks probably has some genetic basis; the social condition of blacks is likely to deteriorate in the future because dysgenics is greater among blacks than among whites and this will lead to a widening of the intelligence gap between blacks and whites;

"Nothing much can be done about any of this; the United States will become increasingly like South America, with high IQ whites and Asians living in fortified enclaves protected by high fences and armed guards from 'the menace of the slums below' (p. 518);

"The future is consequently pretty bleak and the best that can be done is to try to return to a simpler small town America of yore in which the unintelligent could be usefully employed doing cognitively undemanding jobs and the local cognitive elite could exercise stronger social controls over those who step out of line by punishing them more swiftly and effectively than is done in the megalopises of the contemporary world."

Now where have we heard that line before?
You may have noticed in there some blatant references to the fact that Black

people have what eugenicists call significantly lower intelligence than white people or Asians. Let's assume for the sake of their argument that their science is correct (and from the independent studies they quote there may be a differential, but its truth or falsity is not relevant to the point I'm about to make):

The eugenics movement, or social biologists as they now prefer to be called, are taking broad brush studies at a race level, and arguably trying to make social policy from those studies. So what if, on average, Blacks have a slightly lower IQ than whites? Does that mean we automatically treat Blacks as second class citizens all over again or restrict their activities?

The biggest problem with the eugenics movement, and the modern biotechnology sciences that are hugely tainted with it, is that they misuse data.

A good analogy is an insurance company. An insurance company knows, from the total number of claims it faces each year, and the total level of premiums it takes in, and the total number of heart attacks it covers, pretty much everything it needs to offer an average insurance package. But along comes a bright spark eugenicist who crunches some numbers, looks at some genetic tests, and says all males over 50 are a higher risk for cardiac problems, so let's hit them harder in premiums.

Then the eugenicist repeats the task for every single sub-group of insured people he can find, looking for obscure genes and diseases that *theoretically* might increase the risk to the insurance company in that sub-group.

Pretty soon, the whole customer base is facing higher premiums, all of it justified by the eugenicist based on weighted risks, yet there has been no overall increase in risk for the insurance company at all: they still have the same customer base as last year, and they're likely to get the same spread of claims. But the customers are paying more.

What I'm saying is, we don't need to know that Blacks are less intelligent than whites or that Asians are smarter than all of us. How does that change anything we do, unless we're introducing policies aimed at races generally instead of behaviours?

What the data does do is reinforce racist beliefs, but for what and whose benefit?

The other aspect, often missed because of the way the debate is framed, is whether IQ is the proper measure of intelligence across all cultures and races, or whether life skills, emotional intelligence or some other measure is better. The whole argument swings on this.

And if you think eugenics is confined to America and Britain, think again, our own society is increasing becoming exposed to its subtle, cloaked-in-science philosophies. Take the alleged discovery last year of a Maori "warrior gene" that supposedly makes Maori more violent. No matter how you couch it, and despite the serious scientific doubts that genes play any major part in behaviour at all – the search for a genetic cause of behaviour is pure eugenics, and from that comes the science of solution – genetic modification, fetal embryo screening, insurance company testing, your employer knowing your entire family's genetic "weaknesses", the works.

In a review of Richard Lynn's latest book, *Eugenics – A Reassessment,* it is argued that the original aims of eugenics remain worthy:[179]

> "THE EUGENIC OBJECTIVES of eliminating genetic diseases, increasing intelligence, and reducing personality disorders he argues, remain desirable and are achievable by human biotechnology...The new eugenics of human biotechnology--prenatal diagnosis of embryos with genetic diseases, embryo selection, and cloning-- may be more likely than classic eugenics to evolve spontaneously in western democracies. Lynn looks at the ethical issues of human biotechnologies and how they may be used by authoritarian states to promote state power. He predicts how eugenic policies and dysgenic processes are likely to affect geopolitics and the balance of power in the 21st century. Lynn offers a provocative analysis that will be of particular interest to psychologists, sociologists, demographers, and biologists concerned with issues of population change and intelligence."

As British paediatrician Dr Tony Cole counters, however, the whole idea of altering the human genome to get rid of "weaknesses" is fraught with danger.

"If you are going to manipulate the genetic composition of an individual, you are changing not only that individual but perhaps a thousand descendants of that individual," Cole told the BBC.[180]

Not only that, scientists are starting to discover that some "weaknesses" help protect the population from worse complaints, and that correcting the "weakness" might in fact open an entirely new Pandora's Box. In other words, eugenics is as close as we get to mad science.

Perhaps the only difference between modern eugenicists and their predecessors in Family Planning is that they've now realized the contraception and sex education messages of the 20th century backfired big time, as Marian van Court argues in her essay favouring eugenics:[181]

> "CONDOMS AND DIAPHRAGMS became available, and the birth rate of the middle and upper classes declined. By the middle of the century it had become apparent that educated people were having fewer children than the uneducated."

179   http://www.greenwood.com/catalog/C5822.aspx
180   http://news.bbc.co.uk/2/hi/health/1952449.stm
181   http://www.eugenics.net/papers/caseforeugenics.html

But it gets worse. The latest studies, according to the social biologists, confirm that the West has lost roughly 4.4 IQ points in the past 125 years, because of unequal breeding caused by birth control and sex education. In real terms, says eugenicist van Court, "a loss of this magnitude would approximately halve those with IQs over 130, and double those with IQs below 70."

I guess that means we *did* abort a few Einsteins last century after all. But as you've seen, this is a mess entirely of the eugenics and Family Planning movement's own making.

The drop in IQ could be even greater, according to other studies. One of Britain's more prominent educationists, Professor Philip Adey at Kings College in London, compared the exam results of 25,000 eleven year olds in 2004, the 1990s and the 1970s, in a specific intelligence test that's used exactly the same questions for thirty years.

They found that in that time, the average 11 year old is now performing academically at an 8 year old's level – a loss of three years' worth of intelligence under modern schooling methods, as this extract from the *Times* of London shows:[182]

> IN THEIR PAINSTAKING RESEARCH project Adey and his colleague, psychology professor Michael Shayer, compared the results of today's children with those of children who took exactly the same test in the mid-1990s and also 30 years ago. While most exams have changed (been made easier, if you listen to the critics) this one is the same as it was in 1976 when pupils first chewed their pencils over the problems.
>
> In the easiest question, children are asked to watch as water is poured up to the brim of a tall, thin container. From there the water is tipped into a small fat glass. The tall vessel is refilled. Do both beakers now hold the same amount of water? "It's frightening how many children now get this simple question wrong," says scientist Denise Ginsburg, Shayer's wife and another of the research team.
>
> Another question involves two blocks of a similar size — one of brass, the other of plasticine. Which would displace the most water when dropped into a beaker? children are asked. Two years ago fewer than a fifth came up with the right answer.
>
> In 1976 a third of boys and a quarter of girls scored highly in the tests overall; by 2004, the figures had plummeted to just 6% of boys and 5% of girls. These children were on average two to three years behind those who were tested in the mid-1990s.

182   http://www.timesonline.co.uk/tol/news/article721863.ece

"It is shocking," says Adey. "The general cognitive foundation of 11 and 12-year-olds has taken a big dip. There has been a continuous decline in the last 30 years and it is carrying on now."

But what exactly is being lost? Is it really general intelligence or simply a specific understanding of scientific concepts such as volume and density? Both, say the researchers. The tests reveal both general intelligence — "higher level brain functions" — and a knowledge that is "the bedrock of science and maths" says Ginsburg. In fact it's nothing less than the ability of children to handle new, difficult ideas. Doing well at these tests has been linked with getting higher grades generally at GCSE.

Naturally, there's dispute among educationists as to the cause. Adey reckons it is too much concentration on reading and writing and not enough on experimentation and lateral thinking. One however could possibly also point the finger at the excessive time spent on social engineering subjects in schools. Rather than slacken off on the 3-Rs, throw out women's studies and Confucianism.

Eugenicists, on the other hand, would see it as proof of bad breeding creating generations that are each dumber than the last.

Marian van Court has one happy piece of news. In a survey of IQ and dysgenic breeding in 185 countries around the world, "the only place dysgenic fertility [dropping IQs] is not found is sub-Saharan Africa, where birth control is not used."

So Black Africans are having the last laugh after all, their IQs are still trending up because they're not using birth control, while the West's spiral downwards.

Can you now see how the line, "fools rush in where angels fear to tread" applies to the bright ideas of Darwinism and Eugenics? Can you see how meddling with the structure of human society on the basis of a dedication to atheism and science has created unexpected problems?

"As the reader may have begun to suspect," writes van Court, "the main reason for dysgenic fertility is that intelligent women use birth control more successfully than unintelligent women do. This seems to be the case regardless of which method is used.

"A second factor is that very intelligent and successful women (doctors, lawyers, professors, engineers, and women working at high levels in business) often end up having far fewer children than they would like to have. A recent study found that 33% of high achieving women are childless by age 40, and only 14% *of this group* are childless by choice."

According to van Court, the writing on the wall of the damage caused by birth control is that Western civilization is going down, and she comes up with a neat example:

"THE CONCEPT OF CIVILIZATION is abstract, but here's one way to conceptualise what, precisely, it means when 'civilization declines': North Americans, Europeans, and Japanese can simply imagine living their entire lives in [current] Mexico. Mexicans can imagine living their entire lives in Africa. That's what a decline in civilization means, and few would attempt to argue that it's a good thing."

At least we won't have to travel far to reach a banana republic, we'll be living in one. Van Court repeats a warning first raised in the 1994 eugenics book, *The Bell Curve*. In it, she says, the authors found that all social problems got worse when they moved the average IQ down just three points in their sample, from 100 to 97:

"THE NUMBER OF WOMEN chronically dependent on welfare increased by almost 15%, illegitimacy increased by 8%, men who were incarcerated increased by 13%, and [the] number of permanent high school dropouts increased by 15%.

"With an actual 3-point drop, these percentages would represent the unhappy lives of millions of real people, plus a major tax burden for millions more.

"There's also the top end of the IQ distribution to consider – all the scientists, statesmen, entrepreneurs, inventors and free-lance geniuses who were never born, and whose positive contributions were never made."

And the Science Experiment Award for Shooting Yourself In The Foot goes to…Francis Galton, Margaret Sanger, Marie Stopes and Family Planning, with the assistance of a now-chastened eugenics movement in Best Supporting Role in a Major Drama.

Halfwits.

"We often feel a smug, self-satisfied superiority when we read about the follies of the past," continues van Court, "such as the Salem witch trials, the Inquisition, bizarre medical practices, such as bloodletting or applying leeches to cure disease. Old films of man's early attempts at flight are guaranteed to get a laugh. But how do we know that we ourselves are not, at this very moment, in the grips of one staggeringly-stupid delusion which will make us look like fools to people in the future?"

Indeed.

If Darwinism treads a middle line, politically, and Marxism takes a left-wing, egalitarian line, Eugenics is on the political right of the equation, albeit with some common overlap into the other ideologies, such as its previous support for birth control, sex education and abortions.

The problem with all three ideologies is that they each profess mankind has become "God", and that the leaders of each ideology are those best placed to lead us into Huxley's Brave New World. But we have seen how each of those ideologies, stripped of accountability to a higher power, quickly generates megalomania.

Take this 1999 suggestion from the late American eugenicist Glayde Whitney in a paper for the Galton Institute,[183] where he hails the possibility of using cloning to isolate geniuses, and create a highly intelligent new racial strain:

> "INSTEAD OF PLAYING NATURE'S ROULETTE, the blind chance and dumb luck of sexual reproduction can be eliminated…As David Lykken (Lykken et al, 1992) has emphasized, some genetic characteristics are not normally transmitted from parent to offspring…but can be retained by cloning. He refers to such traits as 'emergenic', extremes of genetic characteristics that are often not familial, but rather emerge as a consequence of a unique combination of genes in a unique genotype.
>
> "Geniuses are perhaps one class of emergenic individuals… the truly extreme genius often crops up in an otherwise undistinguished family and often leaves undistinguished progeny…such emergenic individuals…will have a chance at recreation through nuclear substitution [cloning]."

The idea of creating some kind of genetic master race – and I remind you that some of these guys are leading scientists – is fraught with bogeymen that apparently they cannot see. And the reason they cannot see it is because in following Darwin's theory they have divorced themselves from the constraints of morality. To them, it hasn't occurred as to whether they create evil genius or good genius – creating any kind of genius is the main goal. Their Darwinian blinkers make them *assume* that a genius race would want good for mankind, because they're so smart. The rest of us know, however, that mankind left to its own devices is corrupt. As noted jurist Lord Acton famously said, "power corrupts, and absolute power corrupts absolutely".

Man, set adrift from an external moral code, becomes a law unto himself, and survival of the fittest becomes the mantra. As a further extension of his idea, Whitney then advocates digging up the bones of the founder of eugenics,

183   www.eugenics.net/papers/gw002.html

Charles Darwin's cousin Sir Francis Galton, and cloning their high priest:

> "MANY AUTHORS HAVE COMMENTED on the irony that Sir Francis Galton himself passed without progeny. With improvement of techniques for recovery of DNA from tissue samples, and nuclear substitution, I expect that Sir Francis' unique genotype will be reborn in the new millennium."

Cue majestic pipe organ, and the maniacal laughter of *Dr Phibes*. But Whitney doesn't stop there.

> "THE FIRST CENTURY OR TWO of the new millennium will almost certainly be a golden age for eugenics. Through application of new genetic knowledge and reproductive technologies the Galtonian Revolution will come to fruition.
>
> "This new revolution…will be more momentous for the future of mankind than was the Copernican Revolution or the Darwinian Revolution. For with the Galtonian Revolution, for the first time, the major changes will not be to ideas along, but rather the major change will be to mankind itself."

Genetically-modified humans. A master race of genius overlords who guide the planet toward tranquility, and black servants for every household. Marian van Court adds her own voice to this to remind us that Darwin's cousin wanted eugenics to become a spiritual movement:[184]

> "ONE CAN IMMEDIATELY GRASP the potential of eugenics for evolving ourselves into better people, more fully in the image of God. Francis Galton envisioned eugenics as a large-scale humanitarian endeavor, firmly grounded in science, which also contained the seed of a new religion."

There are many levels to eugenics. If you are a person who believes in choosing the traits of your baby through genetic testing, you are buying into grassroots eugenics. If you read newspaper reports about ~~high priests~~, sorry, scientists, demanding to do stem cell experiments, you are seeing the cutting edge of modern eugenics, even in frontierlands like New Zealand.

Professor Glayde Whitney, for example, advocates a range of experiments on human embryos, some involving transplanting animal DNA into a baby:

---

184   http://www.eugenics.net/papers/crown.html

"MONKEYS ARE BEING DEVELOPED that have bioluminescence from Jellyfish (Lau, 1999). Personally I have no interest in having my private parts glow in the dark; however it would be interesting to be able to navigate like a homing pigeon."

I hesitate to suggest that Whitney might not have found the idea quite so appealing if it also left him attracted to scraps of bread on the pavement and perching on high ledges. Yeah, you could keep doing the experiments to see if there were any unintended side effects, but each one of those seemingly innocuous 'experiments' they talk of on the TV news involves the creation and destruction of a human life purely so a mad scientist can test a theory.

As eugenicists get more concerned about the errors of past policy, they're also getting increasingly angry at the negative press they attract and the assumption that we shouldn't discuss racial differences. Ironically, they blame Marxists in the media and educational institutions, as Marian van Court writes:

"THIS MASSIVE DISINFORMATION campaign about IQ, genetics and race has been waged by liberal journalists and Marxist academics against the Western world since the 1950s. Like an octopus with far reaching tentacles, it's wreaked havoc in a multitude of ways, not the least of which is that it's made it impossible even to have a serious public debate about eugenics, an obvious prerequisite to implementing a eugenics programme."

Again, one could argue these are self-inflicted wounds, given the dangerous propaganda the eugenics movement was heavily involved in before World War 2 and its continuing extremes, but I'll permit van Court to continue because she seems to have twigged to some of the bigger vultures now circling the carcass of the West:

"SUCH WHOLESALE DISHONESTY might be expected under a Communist regime, but for this to take place in democratic societies cries out for an explanation.

"To fully understand why egalitarianism (everyone is equal) reigns supreme and eugenics has been made into a taboo subject, this topic must be viewed as part of the larger *Zeitgeist* which also includes obeisance to 'diversity' and 'multiculturalism', reverse discrimination, attacks on Christianity, support for ruinous immigration policies, promotion of promiscuity and homosexuality, advocacy of miscegenation (racial interbreeding) and moral relativism, much of which can be subsumed under the rubric of Political Correctness.

"Did this pervasive belief system just 'happen', like the weather, or did people make it happen? If the latter, who and why?"

I do hope Marian van Court gets a chance to read this book. You can see in her list of complaints that *little* reference to "miscegenation", which I guess still underpins the worldview of eugenicists: that desire for racial purity that makes the prickles on the back of the neck rise as we remember the horrors of the various genocides last century. On everything else in the passage just quoted, there'd be a lot of people in agreement. But it is just as I warned much earlier in this book: you probably cannot categorise any secular ideology as fully evil or fully good. Hitler, after all, recognised the evils of communism, while communists recognised the evils of Hitler, but neither extreme was right in themselves.

Prominent eugenicists, or advocates of eugenic science and theories, include British evolutionary author Richard Dawkins who argues, "if you can breed cattle for milk yield, horses for running speed, and dogs for herding skill, why on Earth should it be impossible to breed humans for mathematical, musical or athletic ability?"

Dawkins also relies extensively on the arguments of eugenicists Peter and Jean Medawar for his arguments in favour of abortion, in *The God Delusion*.

He talks approvingly in *Delusion* of the major eugenics policies of euthanasia, stem-cell embryo harvesting or, in the quote below, abortion:

"IT [THE BABY BEING ABORTED]…surely suffers less than, say, an adult cow in a slaughterhouse."

Yeah, I guess if an adult cow had each of its limbs torn off with heavy duty vicegrips, followed by its head, all without the benefit of being anaesthetized or stunned – which is required by law – an adult cow might suffer more. I know of no documented case of such a cow-slaughtering however.

As well as Dawkins, and half the Darwin family, other promoters and sympathizers include the co-discoverer of DNA, Sir James Watson; the editor of *Skeptic* magazine, Frank Miele; Harvard biologist E.O. Wilson; Berkeley psychologist Arthur Jensen; and the late Nobel physicist (and inventor of the transistor) William Shockley.

Princeton's rogue Professor of Bioethics, Peter Singer, also quoted favourably by Richard Dawkins, is a prominent eugenicist, as are many members of the International Association of Bioethics, which Singer founded. Isn't it ironic that the supposed gatekeepers of ethics in the modern world – the men and women who advise governments and the media – are little more than the stormtroopers for The Fourth Reich?

The website EugenicsWatch makes the same point:[185]

THE HUGE GULF between bioethicists and the rest of the world may be easiest to describe by looking at a recently published book that was available at the conference, written by Daniel Wikler and others. Wikler helped Singer form the IAB, and succeeded him as president of the organization.

The new book, *From Chance to Choice: Genetics and Justice*, is a forthright defense of eugenics, by name. A key chapter in the book, written by Wikler, is an "ethical autopsy" of the eugenics movement that culminated in the Holocaust; it is supposed to show that the authors learned the lessons of the past. But it is not honest history; it is transparent propaganda.

For example, many (most? all?) historians of the eugenics movement point to a specific book published in Germany in the 1920s as an immensely significant event. That book was *The Release of the Destruction of Life Not Worth Living*. At the Nuremberg trials after the war, at least one of the judges stated his conviction that there was a straight and direct line from that book to the gas chambers. The book argued in medical and legal terms that some lives are not worth living, and should be destroyed.

Wikler does not mention the murderous book. And in fact, he and his coauthors use the same phrase (p. 239, "a life not worth living") without apology, although they prefer to speak of conditions that are "incompatible with a worthwhile life." They have no problem with aborting children whose lives would not be "worthwhile," in their opinion. They do not advocate eugenics infanticide, but they do not oppose it either, nor attempt to draw a sharp line between abortion and infanticide. And yet, even as they go down the same path with the same ideology and language, they claim that they see how society can embark on a full-scale eugenics program again without making the same mistakes as last time.

One of the most bizarre aspects of the book is its complete reliance on the ostrich posture for dealing with population control. Wikler asserts that modern eugenics is not like Nazi eugenics, but then compares modern genetics to Nazi evils. Modern eugenics includes abuses of genetics, but also includes a very determined effort to drive down the birthrate of nonwhite populations. *From Chance to Choice* does not have a word about population control. It is simply dishonest to overlook this and claim to be a scholar.

It is disheartening that Wikler and his coauthors would perpetrate this fraud. But worse – and revealing of the state of bioethics today – the book was written with a grant from the American government, through a program designed to explore the ethical problems in the human genome project. Those funds were supposed to assure the public that there would be some scrutiny of the moral problems, but (in this case at least) the funds went to an extended and pompous whitewash.

So much for professors of bioethics. The International Association of Bioethics, and its Pacific Rim affiliate Eu-bios (do Eu get the connection?) which covers New Zealand, Australia and Japan, work closely to push the bioethics line in schools around the world with the United Nations and its UNESCO project. The Eu-bios website, for example, has a page on "bioethics in education":[186]

> "BIOETHICS HAS ALSO EMERGED as a topic in social studies and moral education. In fact it is not limited to any subject, and in the results presented here we see it being considered in a range of classes across the school curriculum. We have also found teachers from all subjects have been interested in the teaching materials prepared. Another question is where should bioethics education be best taught - in biology or social studies or both classes, and/or other classes within the school curriculum?"

The website then reports on a survey of several hundred schools in NZ, Japan and Australia, with a significant section on animal rights (Peter Singer's pet project), before concluding at the end:

> "SCIENCE TEACHERS SHOULD also be encouraged to include the teaching of these issues in science courses, especially in some subjects, such as human gene therapy, biotechnology and genetic engineering."

There are many others promoting eugenics, but you'll notice most are heavyweights in either Darwinism or Social Darwinism. Virtually all are

186   http://www.csu.edu.au/learning/eubios/BHS.html

atheist or close to it. Some would deny association with the word "eugenics", but if you study their ideas you see they are infused with it. Eugenics is, after all, the logical outcome of Darwinism.

The irony is, especially with people like Dawkins carefully stirring the pot, is that eugenics is really Darwin's answer to Intelligent Design, transposing man instead of God as the designer.

Eugenicists raise a number of arguable points, but their solutions have failed the world once, they're still asking for chances and some of their fantasies, like cloning a genius master race, are positively terrifying. Likewise Marxism has some valid concerns, but its methodology is inherently evil and its concentration on reducing everyone to the lowest common denominator because of political correctness is, as the eugenicists point out, insane and part of the dumbing down of the West. Darwin had good intentions but his theory is out of date and his ideas ultimately caused some of the greatest bloodshed in world history.

The extremes of western Marxism don't make the extremes of scientific eugenics the answer, and vice versa. If the West is going to survive as a civilization, it has to reconnect with the core beliefs it once held, and reject the extremists of social or scientific engineering who were let loose post-Darwin.

In truth, despite the plaintive pleas of van Court - now that she and other social biologists are starting to realize the damage they have been a party to – it is too late to turn the Titanic around. As Mark Steyn points out, there's an iceberg dead ahead and a serious shortage of lifeboats.

19

A Book Of Revelation
The Clear & Present Danger

"Fight and slay the pagans wherever you find them, and seize them,
beleaguer them and lie in wait for them in every stratagem."
Surah 9:5, The Qu'ran

A s if all of the preceding was not enough, there is an approaching flood
tide in the affairs of Men which, like it or lump it, you and your children
will be swept up by in the not too distant future.

Forget the deluded rantings of Richard Dawkins, Karl Marx or their
ilk. Concentrate now on that which approaches.

For nearly 1,300 of the past 1,400 years, two vast empires have been at
war. Long before there were Marxists, long before there were Darwinists, and
long before there were eugenicists, a civilization calling itself Islam, meaning
submission to the religion of Allah, sprang up out of an obscure dusty village
in ancient Arabia in 611 AD.

Muhammad, in a letter signing himself "Apostle of Allah", invited the kings
of neighbouring empires to become Muslim. The King of Persia greeted the
invitation with contempt, tearing up the letter in front of Muhammad's
emissary and ridiculing the Muslim. The Christian King of Constantinople,
Jerusalem and Damascus, Heraclius, however, "treated this letter with grudging
respect," writes Muslim journalist and author M K Akbar in his bestselling
book, *The Shade of Swords*.

"He made enquiries about this man who claimed to be another messiah."
As it happened, one of Muhammad's lieutenants was nearby with a trade
caravan and was able to hold a "respectful" discussion with Heraclius about
the prophet's offer, which he kindly declined.

Despite the respect, however, Muhammad brooded over the possibility
of waging war against the Christians who, at that stage, had made no move
against Arabian Islam.

Within just 25 years of its origins, Islam was powerful enough to launch a surprise attack on Christian Syria and its capital, Damascus.

"One of the cheerleaders on that day, incidentally, was the indefatigable Hind [the wife of one of Islam's leaders]," writes Akbar, "urging her sons to cut off the limbs of the uncircumcised Christians."

You can see how that would go down well with the churchgoers; there was apparently a huge rise in circumcisions that week. The sleeping and largely peaceable giant, Christianity, was thus awakened by fundamentalist Islam in 636 AD. The following year, with Muhammad and his first successor Abu Bakr now dead, Islam continued its bloody path to conquering the world by attacking and invading the Christian and Jewish holy city of Jerusalem.

All of this, by the way, was unprovoked. You are learning here a historical lesson about the "Religion of Peace" in action. I'll deal, incidentally, with this "Peace" moniker here and now.

"Both sides should acknowledge candidly," said Muslim professor Bassam Tibi of Germany's Göttingen University in 2002, "that although they might use identical terms these mean different things to each of them. The word 'peace', for example, implies to a Muslim the extension of the Dar al-Islam - or 'House of Islam' - to the entire world. This is completely different from the Enlightenment concept of eternal peace that dominates Western thought."

Muhammad, by the way, had already written the Qu'ran with its verses about there being no compulsion in religion, followed later by "slay the infidels where you find them". Islam is a religion of ridiculous contradictions, and a religion of war. As you shall see.

Fresh from victory in Jerusalem, the Religion of Peace "aimed immediately for the heart of Christian power, Constantinople," writes M J Akbar.

Troops from the Religion of Peace tried their luck in:

653 AD	664 AD	668 AD	670AD
671 AD	672 AD	673 AD	674 AD
675 AD	676 AD	677 AD	678 AD

Are you getting the picture? After a 40 year truce, the Muslims broke the "peace" treaty in 717 AD when a force of 180,000 Arabs launched a naval and land assault on the Christian capital. Despite the incredible ferocity, the Christians used "Greek fire", a type of early napalm, to savage the marauding Religion of Peaceniks, who eventually retreated to lick their wounds after suffering heavy casualties.

Rather than taking the Christians head on, the Arabs' next push was to capture Cyprus, Rhodes, Sicily and the island of Majorca, in preparation for an invasion of Spain.

When Muslims, antiwar activists and high school teachers talk about the Crusades, the 400 year lead-up is usually conveniently left out.

Incidentally, it was the founder of the Wisharts, Robert Guischard, who finally reclaimed Sicily by attacking and defeating the Islamic armies there in the mid 11th century, but that's another story.[187]

By the year 732, however, on the 100th anniversary of the prophet Muhammad's death, the 121 year old Religion of Peace was poised on the banks of France's Loire River, ready to capture France and from there, all Europe.

The army of the Peaceniks, heavily armed with strong cavalry, outnumbered the Christian defenders at Tours by 2-1, but the Christian commander, Charles Martel, had chosen his defensive position well, backed up by woodland and a steep rise.

These battles were fought, of course, without gunpowder and guns. You couldn't sit happily behind a bunker or in a LAV3 Stryker and take comfortable pot-shots from a distance. Instead, this was hand-to-hand combat, and I find it difficult to envision the following account from Wikipedia ever being matched in terms of courage by ordinary Westerners today:

> MARTEL HAD BEEN PREPARING for this confrontation since Toulouse a decade before. He was well aware that if he failed, no other Christian force remained able to defend western Christianity. But Gibbon believes, as do most pre and modern historians, that Martel had made the best of a bad situation. Though outnumbered and depending on infantry, without stirrups in wide use, Martel had a tough, battle-hardened heavy infantry who believed in him implicitly. Martel had the element of surprise, and had been allowed to pick the ground.
>
> The Franks in their wolf and bear pelts were well dressed for the cold, and had the terrain advantage. The Arabs were not as prepared for the intense cold of an oncoming northern European winter, despite having tents, which the Franks did not, but did not want to attack a Frankish army they believed may have been numerically superior. Essentially, the Umayyads wanted the Franks to come out in the open, while the Franks, formed in a tightly packed defensive formation, wanted them to come uphill, into the trees, diminishing at once the advantages of their cavalry. It was a waiting game which Martel won: The fight began on the seventh day, as Abd al Rahman did not want to postpone the battle indefinitely with winter approaching.
>
> 'Abd-al-Rahman trusted the tactical superiority of his cavalry,

187   http://en.wikipedia.org/wiki/Robert_Guiscard

and had them charge repeatedly. This time the faith the Umayyads had in their cavalry, armed with their long lances and swords which had brought them victory in previous battles, was not justified. The Franks, without stirrups in wide use, had to depend on unarmoured foot soldiers.

In one of the instances where medieval infantry stood up against cavalry charges, the disciplined Frankish soldiers withstood the assaults, though according to Arab sources, the Arab cavalry several times broke into the interior of the Frankish square. "The Muslim horsemen dashed fierce and frequent forward against the battalions of the Franks, who resisted manfully, and many fell dead on either side."

Despite this, the Franks did not break. It appears that the years of year-round training that Charles had bought with Church funds, paid off. His hard-trained soldiery accomplished what was not thought possible at that time: unarmoured infantry withstood the fierce Umayyad heavy cavalry. The Mozarabic Chronicle of 754 says: "And in the shock of the battle the men of the North seemed like a sea that cannot be moved. Firmly they stood, one close to another, forming as it were a bulwark of ice; and with great blows of their swords they hewed down the Arabs. Drawn up in a band around their chief, the people of the Austrasians carried all before them. Their tireless hands drove their swords down to the breasts of the foe."

Naturally, hand-wringing liberals now take a different view of the Battle of Tours, one of them, quoted by military historian Victor Davis Hanson, goes so far as to suggest "a Muslim victory might have been preferable to continued Frankish dominance."

Ah, yes, well he may not have long to wait. I'm not sure what it is about the intellectual pixies of the Left, but they almost seem to delight in taking a contrarian approach to anything Western, just for the sheer hell of it. And of course, Frankish "dominance" in France would be unthinkable.

Atheists like Richard Dawkins, who constantly slam "The Church" for its various perceived crimes during the Middle Ages, owe their very existence to that "Church" and some of the violence it was involved in. Had the Arabs won that day at Tours, the world today would be a very different place, Dawkins wouldn't exist and neither would anyone reading this book. More significantly, the option of atheism or secular humanism would not be available to anyone living under Islamic law.

The thought that Islam might not appreciate the liberal approach to life clearly has not occurred to its apologists in the West. They also forget recent history. Despite its losses, Islam did eventually capture Constantinople, beat off the Crusaders who – quite frankly – were only pushing back into their original territory, and ensconced themselves at the head of an empire stretching all the way from India in the East to Spain in the West.

Perhaps it is a case of generational collective amnesia. The last Europeans to remember Muslim armies storming their barricades – the war with Russia in Crimea in 1859 which eventually drew in England and France as well - died less than 60 years ago, outlasting the final Muslim Caliph who was deposed soon after the Ottoman empire was crushed at the end of World War I.

With the Muslim 'peril' beaten for the first time in 1,400 years, the world hardly had time to breathe a sigh of relief before a new threat in the form of Nazi fascism was on the rise, heralding yet another massive war.

From those wars, and the smaller conflicts that followed, a shell-shocked civilian populace in the West begged for peace. When Communism collapsed in the 1980s, it seemed as if the world was finally, after a century of conflict, about to witness calm. But they had forgotten the ambitions of the remains of Empire, Islam's nascent priesthood who nursed fantasies of their own.

"Perhaps," writes M J Akbar in *The Shade Of Swords*, "the West became too complacent, and too certain that Arab regimes that owed their survival to Western patronage had ended their last jihad against Israel in 1973.

"They underestimated the Muslim will to martyrdom. They did not recognise the child who would walk with complete calm under the shade of swords."

The phrase, and title of the book, is an allusion to a reputed saying of Muhammad recorded in the Hadith – a collection of alleged quotes and anecdotes that together with the Qu'ran form the backbone of Islamic literature:

"Know that Paradise is under the shade of swords."

At the height of its conflict with Christendom, the Muslim population in Europe was tiny. Today, thanks to immigration and very high birthrates, more than 22 million Muslims call Europe home. And as commentator Mark Steyn notes in his compelling new bestseller, *America Alone*, those birthrates are pushing the next generation of Muslims into a commanding position:

> EXPERTS TALK ABOUT ROOT CAUSES, but demography is the most basic root of all. Many of the developed world's citizens gave no conscious thought to Islam before September 11. Now we switch on the news every evening and, though there are many troublespots around the world, as a general rule it is easy to make an educated guess at one of the participants: Muslims vs Jews in 'Palestine', Muslims vs Hindus in Kashmir, Muslims vs Christians in Africa, Muslims vs Buddhists in Thailand,

Muslims vs Russians in the Caucasus, Muslims vs backpacking tourists in Bali, Muslims vs Danish cartoonists in Scandinavia.

The environmentalists may claim to think globally but act locally, but these guys live it. They open up a new front somewhere on the planet with nary a thought. Why? Because they've got the manpower. Because in the seventies and eighties, Muslims had children (those self-detonating Islamists in London and Gaza are a literal baby boom) while Westerners took all those silly doomsday tomes about "overpopulation" [a eugenics scare story] seriously.

A people that won't multiply can't go forth or go anywhere. Those who do will shape the age we live in. Because, when history comes a-calling, it starts with the most basic question of all:

Knock-knock.

Who's there?

Mark Steyn is not the only one to have crunched the numbers.

Philip Jenkins is the Distinguished Professor of History and Religious Studies at Penn State University. His 2002 book, *The Next Christendom: The Coming of Global Christianity*, was among the first to sound the warning about dramatically falling birthrates in the West, where populations in Europe and Japan are effectively halving with each generation, while populations in the Middle East, Africa, Asia and South America are growing strongly. A woman in France is likely to have only one child. A woman in many parts of the Arab world will have 6 or 7 children. The median age on the Gaza strip is 15.8 years old. The median age in Europe is 40.

Saudi Arabia, Afghanistan, Yemen and Iraq are, on current birthrates, expected to double their populations by 2025. The proportion of the population aged under 14 is normally 16 to 20% in European countries, but in Muslim countries it lies between 33 and 50%.

To give you some perspective, Jenkins outlines the 1975 populations of Yemen, Iran, Saudi Arabia, Sudan, Egypt. Together, they totaled 100 million people in 1975. By 2025, those countries will have grown to 332 million. By 2050, they will total 460 million people.

"By the end of the present century," writes Jenkins, "fourteen states could each have 200 million people or more, and of these, only the United States will represent what is presently the advanced Western world."

Vietnam, for example, is on track to overtake Russia by 2050, and tiny Yemen may as well.

What will this mean on the geopolitical scene? It means, based on last century as an example, that the world our children are inheriting will be the most dangerous in human history, and none of our politically-correct, "make love, not war", "ban guns now!" social engineering education slogans will have prepared them for what they are going to face. The 21st century will see battles over diminishing resource, and battles over ideology. And if you don't have any ideology worth living for you won't fight very hard to save it. Advanced nations sitting on wealth and resource but with few people will become exceedingly attractive in the next few decades. Russia may be the first Western nation to fall, but it certainly won't be the last.

Steyn poses the problem this way:

> DEMOGRAPHY IS AN EXISTENTIAL CRISIS for the developed world, because the twentieth century social-democratic state was built on a careless model that requires a constantly growing population to sustain it.

But guess what? We in the West aborted our growing populations. In much the same way New Zealand's anti-nuclear stance in 1985 was supposed to be a symbolic gesture to the world, and paying a carbon tax to the government in Wellington is supposed to save yak herders on the steppes of Mongolia from global warming, we in the West are big on symbolism and short on intelligence. Which, as you saw earlier, is trending down, again because we're killing off the bright kids.

Unfortunately, the third world took one look at the West's symbolic gesture of population control to "save the trees", and just laughed at us, responding with a symbolic gesture of their own.

There is little point paying hard-earned tax dollars into compulsory superannuation plans in Australia, New Zealand or elsewhere, which is the message currently being pitched at Gen-Xers born post 1964, because there's not a snowball's chance in hell that your money will still be there 20 to 40 years from now. Not in this particular century.

Continues Steyn:

> YOU MIGHT FORMULATE it like this:
> Age + Welfare = Disaster for you
> Youth + Will = Disaster for whoever gets in your way
>   By "will", I mean the metaphorical spine of a culture. Africa, to take another example, also has plenty of young people but it's riddled with AIDS and, for the most part, Africans don't think of themselves as Africans; as we saw in Rwanda, their primary identity is tribal, and most tribes have no global ambitions.

Islam, however, has serious global ambitions and it forms the primal, core identity of most of its adherents in the Middle East, South Asia, and elsewhere. Islam has youth and will. Europe has age and welfare.

Europe has only itself to blame. Once the home of Christendom, its leaders fought very hard to stop Islam from extinguishing the light of western civilization. But when Marxism took hold in the cafes and universities post the 1917 Bolshevik revolution, that poison permeated through the entire European political and education system.

Europeans were the first Westerners to lose their religious faith, abandoning it in droves. There are so few European priests in the Catholic church now that some churches are being pastored by Catholic priests from Africa – a sign of what Philip Jenkins calls the coming global Christianity. In our Western arrogance, he says, we thought it would be centred on us, but Christianity is now the fastest growing religion in the third world, while European cathedrals sit empty.

Europeans bought the political lines about multiculturalism and a "United Europe", and they initially welcomed immigration. They loved the idea of the United Nations as some kind of global governing body. Countries like Sweden, the Netherlands and Germany pioneered sexual liberalization, even amongst and with children. They saw themselves as "enlightened" and, briefly during the sixties and seventies, they even enjoyed themselves. Now, the joy has gone.

They don't tell you in the travel brochures, but in many of Europe's major cities, large suburbs have become no-go areas where police can only enter with the permission of Islamic leaders.

Paul Belien, over at *The Brussels Journal*, has compiled comments from various cities:[188]

> SWEDEN "'If we park our car it will be damaged – so we have to go very often in two vehicles, one just to protect the other vehicle,' said Rolf Landgren, a Malmo police officer. Fear of violence has changed the way police, firemen and emergency workers do their jobs. There are some neighborhoods Swedish ambulance drivers will not go to without a police escort. Angry crowds have threatened them, telling them which patient to take and which ones to leave behind."

> BELGIUM: "The police have been told [by the Mayor] that it is 'not expedient' to patrol [in the Brussels suburb of Molenbeek]

and officers are not allowed to drink coffee or eat a sandwich in the street during ramadan."

Then there's this example:

> YES, IT'S LOVELY HERE IN BRUSSELS. In the centre on Monday night a friend was attacked and robbed by what are jovially termed "Southern Europeans". He reported it to the "police" who told him they were too busy to deal with it; and where it happened was about 50 metres from the central Brussels police station. The police do as little as possible about the attacks, the muggings, the robberies, the murders and attempted murders. In the centre, about 150 metres from the Grande Place, they will not patrol on foot at night because it's too dangerous for them. They prefer to hear nothing, see nothing and do nothing. Some Brussels communes like Molenbeek are almost totally Arab-controlled; in effect no-go areas. It goes mostly unreported lest people are accused of racism. For a woman like me, it's frightening and the Arabs call you "putain" (whore) if you don't respond to their overtures. Belgium is blind to its inevitable fate.

Meanwhile, one French blogger filed his own report on the state of Europe in late 2006:[189]

> AN INCREASINGLY COMMONLY thing in European cities is the no-go zone. These are places where the police, medical rescue crews, and other government agents will not venture into. The areas are viewed as just too violent and/or risky to enforce rules. Following the rules of ungoverned spaces, anarchy does not reign for long. A group will enforce their own rule set and the no-go zone will become a microstate.
>
> In France no-go zones are referred to as Zones Urbaines Sensibles (Sensitive Urban Zones). Approximately 12 percent of all French in France live in a Sensitive Urban Zone (5 million out of approximately 60 million French)! Some of the zones are governed under Islamic Sharia law. From these no-go zones Islamic militants are waging guerrilla warfare against French police. The police are now taking to the streets in protest against the violence targeted at them in Lyons with police unions claiming there is a civil war against them.

---

189   http://catholicgauze.blogspot.com/2006/11/no-go-areas-of-france-and-rest-of.html

Microstates in France are growing. [Government] Maps and location of all 751 no-go areas in France can be viewed here[190].

The rest of Europe is going down a similar path. The United Kingdom is wondering if different groups should be under separate laws. If this were to happen with official approval it would only be a matter of time that political unity would be called into question. Europe, with a dying population and hostile minority groups, faces a bleak future.

As if illustrating the point, France's *Le Figaro* daily reported on November 2, last year, that police in Roubaix, a northern French town, had been ordered not to search the house of a suspected drug trafficker because he lived in a no-go part of town. Police officers reported in an official but confidential document that "the Prefect [the Governor] of the Nord Department [Province] currently does not authorize police actions in that sector for reasons concerning public order."[191]

Quite.

Over on the JihadWatch website, one essay from the middle of last year paints an even grimmer picture about the transfer of power and its causes:[192]

THE *JERUSALEM POST* NOTED that some Muslim leaders explained that what they wanted was autonomy in their ghettos: "They seek to receive extraterritorial status from the French government, meaning that they will set their own rules based, one can assume, on Sharia law. If the French government accepts the notion of communal autonomy, France will cease to be a functioning state."

Following three weeks of unrest, the police said 98 vehicles torched in one day marked a "return to a normal situation everywhere in France." Some of the rioters left boasting messages on various Internet forums. "We aren't going to let up. The French won't do anything and soon, we will be in the majority here" One observer stated: "In France, the majority of young Muslims believe that French society is dying, committing suicide. More like 10 percent to 20 percent of them believe that they are in the process of replacing European civilization with an Islamic one." In the southern city of Marseille, Muslims make up at least a quarter of the population, and rising fast.

---

190   http://i.ville.gouv.fr/divbib/doc/chercherZUS.htm
191   http://coloradoright.wordpress.com/2006/11/02/police-no-go-areas-in-france/
192   http://www.jihadwatch.org/dhimmiwatch/archives/2006/07/012204print.html

In the Netherlands, Muslims will soon make up the majority in all major cities. "Today, we have 1 million Muslims out of 16 million Dutch," according to Frits Bolkestein, Dutch politician. "Within 10 years, they will have an absolute majority in both Amsterdam and Rotterdam. We are staring into the face of a shortly to be divided community.

And the cause? Like me, the essay's author picks a lack of soul in the West:

WE ARE WITNESSING A DRAMATIC change in Europe, which men like Bolkestein see as underlined by a drop in national confidence in European countries over the entirety of the last century. The immigration problem, he said, "has to do with the loss of confidence in one's own civilization. It started with World War II, which was really a mass European suicide. Then, the rise of fascism, the Holocaust and the 1968 student cultural revolutions across Europe. There is no clear European identity today. This has a real impact on foreign policy."

Douglas Murray attended a conference in memory of the murdered Islam critic Pim Fortuyn in 2006, and noted with concern the strict security measures and what he saw as a nation under siege. "All across Europe, debate on Islam is being stopped. Italy's greatest living writer, Oriana Fallaci, soon comes up for trial in her home country, and in Britain the government seems intent on pushing through laws that would make truths about Islam and the conduct of its followers impossible to voice. Europe is shuffling into darkness. It is proving incapable of standing up to its enemies, and in an effort to accommodate the peripheral rights of a minority is failing to protect the most basic rights of its own people."

Picking up on this, and other recent developments, a group of ex-Muslims have recently established a website, www.islam-watch.org, to highlight the dangers of what is coming.

AS ISLAMIC TERRORISM OVERWHELMS the world, we also felt it incumbent upon us to let the civilized world recognize the reality about Islam and take timely precautionary measures against this religion of terror, hate and mayhem.

We want to tell the world that the current Islamic terrorism is not an aberration of the so-called 'peaceful Islam', rather it is the real Islam preached and practiced by the alleged Prophet Muhammad. This can be confirmed from a thorough study of the Qur'an and Hadis. We, therefore, have launched this website to expose the real Islam - the Islam that is determined to replace the current civilization with the 7th century Arab Bedouin barbarism, which is peddled as the Islamic Civilization. Let the world watch Islam through www.islam-watch.org and be warned.

Islam-Watch describes a process of Islamification that begins with routine immigration:

> THE ISLAMIC TAKEOVER of a country or a region of the country – is dependant on the relative proportion of Muslims compared with non-Muslims, and/or the influence of militant Muslims among the Muslim population. A higher proportion of Muslims among the population - or the growth of the number of militants among Muslims (even though Muslims constitute a smaller part of the population) – drive the political development along a certain path. A successful assimilation process may change that path but there seems to be no definite examples yet of such a process.

One of the significant aspects, hinted at in the passage above, is the political clout of the Islamic community. With proportional representation in most European countries, the magic 5% threshold appears to be the point of no return in terms of Islamic muscle-flexing:

> AN UNDERLYING ASSUMPTION is that a growing Muslim minority allows radical Islamists to influence a growing part of the population in the country.
>
> The contents of the traditional Islamic doctrine which is recognized by all four schools of Islam to be the valid one (various interpretations differ - of course - between them), seems to support the interpretations of the radical Islamists regarding many matters. That is probably a main reason for the passivity and silence of the so called "moderate" Muslims who don't have a comprehensive theoretical doctrine to lean upon.
>
> Another reason may be that many, or most, "moderates" share the same goals as the radical Islamists but just oppose some of their methods. Fear of reprisals can also be a cause of their

passivity. The radicals also have strong international support, including the financial support.

On the basis of our empirical knowledge about the political development in Muslim countries, the attitudes regarding many matters of Muslims in Europe and other pieces of information e g their reactions during the first five years of the war on terror, a good prognosis can be made. During the coming decades, numerous examples from Europe will illuminate the different phases and their contents.

Among warning signs, the former Muslims say, are attacks on Western women, such as those in Australia and Europe, and increasing calls for tolerance of Islamic religious symbols and holidays:

INFREQUENT PROPOSALS AIMING at establishing sharia regarding various matters, acknowledging Muslim holidays and so on are presented. Another characteristic is increasing levels of crime motivated by attitudes often connected to jihad e.g. an increasing level of rapes of non-Muslim women.

The incidence of rapes carried out by Muslim men in Norway against non-Muslim women is many times higher than rapes by non-Muslim men. The rape frequency in e.g. Oslo per capita is said to be more than five times higher than in New York City. And two thirds of these rapes are committed by immigrants even though they still constitute a rather small part of society. This does not only reflect the dysfunctional relations between sexes in the Muslim part of society but is also a sign of an early "light-version" example of the influence of jihad thinking in the country. Charities, property crimes including credit card crimes are used to collect money for global jihad.

At the current time, warns Islam-Watch, these events are happening in the US, Sweden, Norway and Denmark. But the next phase is worse:

PREPARATIONS FOR JIHAD: Beginning of geographic no-go areas for the police and public administration officials. Frequent physical attacks and even single infrequent murders of policemen or persons opposing political Islam. Death threats against adversaries are common. An increasing physical destruction of property by groups, influenced by the radical imams and the jihadists.

Besides frequent proposals to introduce sharia laws, we find established "private" sharia courts in certain areas judging matters of special interest to Muslims. Property crimes of various types in order to finance the beginning of a domestic jihad movement.

Current examples: France; beginning in England, Holland.

Under phase four, which the group warns has just begun in France:

START OF JIHAD: Murders of individual policemen or active anti-Muslims with a certain frequency, which murders carry an evident political message. An organized countrywide Islamist movement appears, and some mosques start to retreat from liberal versions of Islam used as a deception during the initial stages (1-3). Establishment of definite no-go areas where militants put taxes on corporations and individuals. Extortion of individuals outside these areas.

Frequent use of unofficial (or now maybe even official) sharia courts as a substitute for ordinary courts, in the "liberated" areas. Militias start to form among non-Muslim groups in society. Nationalistic non-jihad parties grow rapidly in importance in the political life. The emigration of European citizens from the country increases significantly.

Current examples: Beginning in France.

Shari'a law is already in force in parts of England, according to the *Daily Telegraph*, with the acquiescence of British authorities who feel they have little option, given the Islamic community size at 1.7 million.

Another leading thinker to address the problem is British philosopher Roger Scruton, who argues that the global political agenda to strip the nation-state of its authority by ridiculing nationalistic loyalties (except in sport), is leaving a power vacuum.[193]

"DEMOCRACIES OWE THEIR EXISTENCE to national loyalties – the loyalties that are supposedly shared by government and opposition, by all political parties, and by the electorate as a whole. Yet everywhere the idea of the nation is under attack – either despised as an atavistic form of social unity, or even condemned as a cause of war and conflict, to be broken down

---

193   The West and the Rest: Globalization and the Terrorist Threat, quoted online at http:// www.brusselsjournal.com/node/1101

and replaced by more enlightened and more universal forms of jurisdiction. But what, exactly, is supposed to replace the nation and the nation state?"

The move to a "united" Europe, for example, means a "process has been set in motion that would expropriate the remaining sovereignty of our parliaments", yet the replacement system has no credibility with the public. It is, in effect, an edict from on high, something we are seeing far more of in politics as each retreating nation-state defers to the United Nations or some other globalist body.

Says Scruton:

> "WE HAVE REACHED the stage where our national jurisdiction is bombarded by laws from outside [via international treaty obligations and UN conventions] even though many of them originate in despotic or criminal governments, and even though hardly any of them are concerned with the maintenance of peace. Even so we, the citizens, are powerless to reject these laws, and they, the legislators, are entirely unanswerable to us, who must obey them [...]
>
> "The despotism is coming slowly: the anarchy will happen quickly in its wake, when law is finally detached from the experience of membership, becomes 'theirs' but not 'ours' and so loses all authority in the hearts of those whom it presumes to discipline."

In mid-March 2007, New Zealand's Prime Minister Helen Clark confirmed on Newstalk ZB that NZ's anti-smacking legislation would have to be passed because it was an edict from the United Nations under the UNCROC convention. This, despite overwhelming public opposition to the legislation.

The "we know best" attitude from social engineers will destroy both them and the West, warns an essayist quoting Scruton in *The Brussels Journal*, because globalised Islam is waiting in the wings:

> THE IRONY OF THIS is that "Western civilization depends on an idea of citizenship that is not global at all, but rooted in territorial jurisdiction and national loyalty." By contrast, Islam, which has been until recently remote from the Western world, is founded on an ideal "which is entirely global in its significance." Globalization, therefore, "offers militant Islam the opportunity that it has lacked since the Ottoman retreat from central

Europe." It has brought into existence "a true Islamic umma, which identifies itself across borders in terms of a global form of legitimacy, and which attaches itself like a parasite to global institutions and techniques that are the by-products of Western democracy."

The contrast, then, goes three ways. Westerners instinctively feel loyalty to their nation-state, but their state education systems and political leaders are increasingly telling them to embrace global authority instead. Islamists are actively using global principles and Western human rights laws to put in place their own global empire. Western leaders, meanwhile, conditioned to believe the global ideal will work, cannot understand what they're doing wrong.

Scruton and others argue that the lack of a nation-state concept in Islam is what Western multiculturalists overlooked when the immigration floodgates were opened. Instead of welcoming those seeking liberty, they found an influx of Muslims who saw it as an Allah-given opportunity to establish footholds and declare each host country an extension of Islamic territory. In short, we have brought in immigrants who don't recognise the nation-state.

This is also, says the *Brussels Journal*, a crucial reason why Muslims feel such a hatred for Israel, "an outreach of the West in the dar al-Islam. The Islamic militants can therefore be satisfied with nothing short of the total destruction of Israel. For Israel is a nation-state established where no nation-state should be – a place where the only law should be the sharia, and the only loyalty that of Islam."

Instead of criticising Israel, the West should be defending it. The problem is, how does a society conditioned in political correctness claw its way back out of the hole it dug for itself?

On the extreme scientific right you have the Fourth Reich eugenicists arguing racial supremacy and other rubbish, while on the extreme Left you have exactly what caused the problem in the first place: Marxist globalization theory and the eradication of national borders.

The key for the West is not to define the problem in racial terms, which it isn't, but in cultural and socio-political terms, which it is.

The one difference between Islam and any other major religion on the planet is that Islam is a political system. They forgot to teach kids that in tolerance classes, which is why we have all been urged to tolerate what is in effect an absolutely hostile rival to democracy. While it was seen as legitimate to ban the Nazi party and Communist party in many western nations, because of the clear and overt threat they posed, we balk at dealing with the Islamic party, because it cloaks itself in religion, and we've all been brainwashed to tolerate religion (unless it is Christianity).

The discovery by *Investigate* magazine, hot on the heels of Britain's Channel 4 documentary in January 07, that leading extremist Islamic clerics linked to terror organizations have been running youth camps and training seminars in far away New Zealand[194] and that local Islamic groups are setting up suburban Shari'a systems is an illustration of just how high-stakes the situation is getting.

Many in the liberal Western media, however, are choosing to ignore the growing pile of dead canaries being thrown back out of the mineshaft. Instead, the liberal doomsday theory of choice is "Global Warming".

But as Mark Steyn points out, by the time the sea levels rise high enough to cause a problem, it'll be Islam's problem, not ours. What's the point in worrying about the planet's fate 100 years away if you can't guarantee your civilization will even exist by then?

It is typical of the politically-correct West that we have these meaningless, academic, feel-good discussions about environmental issues at a time when the barbarians are storming through the gates.

There is still a chance to save the West, but not if we continue to twitter away about the weather and other meaningless issues. Even liberal climate change scientists have been forced to concede that the full adoption of Kyoto would only alter world temperatures by 0.05 degrees by 2050.[195]

And with growing evidence that climate change is being caused by solar changes affecting not just earth but the entire solar system, it seems unlikely that all Al Gore's handwringing is going to make a blind bit of difference to whatever the sun chooses to do.

So what is the likely upshot of all of this? If hope is to be found, where is it?

I turn again to a liberal academic, but one honest enough to see the writing on the wall and acknowledge it. Philip Jenkins, the religious studies professor at Penn State, believes the Western world has ignored Christianity in recent decades at its peril, but not in the way you might think.[196]

Trapped by a Euro-centric perception of "The Church", Westerners have celebrated "the death of God" whilst failing to see the image was a reflection of the West's own fate. God may be dead in Europe, but he's alive and kicking in Africa, Asia and the Americas. While affluent Europeans sneer cynically at the gospels or the apocalyptic book of Revelations, hundreds of millions of Christians in the Southern hemisphere are living it, writes Jenkins:

> "FOR THE AVERAGE WESTERN audience, New Testament passages about standing firm in the face of pagan persecution have little

---

194   http://www.thebriefingroom.com/archives/islamofascism/index.html

195   Fred Singer, atmospheric physicist and Emeritus professor of Environmental Sciences at the University of Virginia, in a letter to the Wall St Journal, 9/10/01

196   *The Next Christendom: The Coming of Global Christianity*, by Philip Jenkins

immediate relevance...[but] Millions of Christians around the world do in fact live in constant danger of persecution or forced conversion, from either governments or local vigilantes. For modern Christians in Nigeria, Egypt, the Sudan or Indonesia, it is quite conceivable that they might someday find themselves before a tribunal that would demand that they renounce their faith on pain of death...

"The church in Sudan, the victim of perhaps the most savage religious repression anywhere in the world, has integrated its sufferings into its liturgy...and produced some moving literature in the process ('Death has come to reveal the faith/It has begun with us and it will end with us').

"Churches everywhere preach death and resurrection, but nowhere else are these realities such an immediate prospect...

"In this context, the book of *Revelation* looks like true prophecy on an epic scale, however unpopular or discredited it may be for most Americans or Europeans. In the [Southern hemisphere], *Revelation* simply makes sense in its description of a world ruled by monstrous demonic powers.

"To quote one Latin American liberation theologian, Néstor Míguez, 'The repulsive spirits of violence, racial hatred, mutilation and exploitation roam the streets of our Babylons in Latin America (and the globe); their presence is clear once one looks behind the glimmering lights of the neon signs'.

"Making the biblical text sound even more relevant to modern Third World Christians, the evils described in *Revelation* are distinctively urban. Then, as now, evil sets up its throne in cities. Brazilian scholar Gilberto da Silva Gorgulho remarks that '*The Book of Revelation* is the favourite book of our popular communities. Here they find the encouragement they need in their struggle, and a criterion for the interpretation of official persecution in our society...The meaning of the church in history is rooted in the witness of the gospel before the state imperialism that destroys the people's life, looming as an idol and caricature of the Holy Trinity'.

"To a Christian living in a Third World dictatorship, the image of the government as Antichrist is not a bizarre religious fantasy, but a convincing piece of political analysis.

"Looking at Christianity as a planetary phenomenon, not merely a Western one, makes it impossible to read the New Testament in quite the same way ever again. The Christianity we see through this exercise looks like a very exotic beast indeed, intriguing, exciting, and a little frightening."

And looking at *Eve's Bite*, you could equally recognise an unholy trinity in Darwinism – the father figure replacing God; Eugenics – the ill-begotten son of Darwinism; and Marxism – the crushing spirit of darkness and destruction of freedom.

In one of the most powerful and dramatic verses of the Bible, in John 14:6, Christ is seen throwing down a gauntlet to a world that figured Man could do things better himself. And it is interesting to measure our unholy trinity against that verse: they've lost their way, abandoned truth, and have spent the last century killing more human life than in all previous centuries combined, motivated not by an honest pursuit of science but, as Harvard's Ernst Mayr admitted, united by an overwhelming desire to proclaim the death of God.

All three are hostile to Western civilization and religious belief. Perhaps we in the West are about to join our colleagues in the third world, and find out what this century really has in store for us, for our children, for our very nations, and for our souls.

The End
A Wake-up Call

"It is proof of a base and low mind for one to wish to think with the masses or majority, merely because the majority is the majority. Truth does not change because it is, or is not, believed by a majority of the people."
Giordano Bruno, 16th century Italian philosopher

Why did I write this? "Are you scared of reds under the bed?" quipped Newstalk ZB Christchurch host, Alison Jones. To be fair, Alison had not read the book at that point. So let me put it another way: One in three people in the West is falling for the 9/11 conspiracy theory that says airliners didn't hit the twin towers, even though the whole event was caught on video - even moments after the first crash when a TV news crew doing a drainage story whipped their camera skyward.

Another sizeable group have fallen for the conspiracy theory that astronauts never landed on the Moon.

Another sizeable chunk believe the AIDS virus is man-made, overlooking the rather salient point that scientists have been unable to create anything faintly resembling life despite decades of trying.

Yet these same people cannot comprehend that some of the most pervasive ideologies on the planet are affecting their lives.

I have laid out in this book, chapter and verse that illustrates a clear intellectual agenda to dominate the halls of power in the West. Is that such a hard concept to get your head around? Is it really that hard to believe, as human history teaches over, and over and over again, that the lust for power over our fellow humans is a prime driving force in the world? Or have we all bought the lie - *Matrix*-style - that we've suddenly become more enlightened, that we really can trust Big Brother/Big Sister, and if we just keep taking our medicine we'll be OK?

Population control requires big budgets (taxes) to staff big bureaucracies (cushy jobs for the intelligentsia as they oversee millions of 'proles' on the public payroll), and a set of policies that convince the public they will be better off in the State's care.

If you think a Marxist-based West is capable of dealing with the existential crisis that faces us, then fine. But the experience of Marxist-based Europe should be a canary down the mineshaft for all of us.

When we joke about "reds under the bed", and Lord knows I've sniggered about it in the past, the image usually conjured up is one of military takeover, domino theory, and KGB agents hiding in the bushes. But I venture the reason these stereotypes persist is because our education systems have deliberately avoided teaching kids the obvious - that Marxism is alive and well and has been controlling education for decades.

To break free of the mental conditioning takes some doing, but with books like this and others it can be done.

We can only have an honest debate about the future if we are not afraid to debate facts. It is for this reason that I have highlighted sexual ecology, as gay academic Gabriel Rotello calls it. Personally, I have no interest in what people do in their own homes. Provided no one else is being harmed and no public funding or issues are involved, then what we do in our private lives should remain between ourselves and our maker.

But when people following a particular lifestyle demand taxpayer funded privileges, positive discrimination, or access to other people, such as children, then I believe the debate moves beyond the realm of "private choice" to "public issue". If you are gay and want to adopt children, then society has a right to debate that. Many gay websites crawl with hatespeech against conservatives, yet conservatives are treated as "bigots" when they want to engage in rational debate.

Which is not to say that nutjobs don't exist on the right. Of course they do, and their actions should also be condemned. But it cuts both ways.

I am not arguing in this book for a return to repression. Let's make this very clear. Gay people are, first and foremost, people. The "gay" bit is a manifestation of their beliefs, just the same way the "Christian" bit is a manifestation of mine, or the "Socialist" bit is a manifestation of left-wing politicians. Gay people should not be discriminated against in all the usual humdrum things of life or relationships, except to the extent where so-called "gay rights" overlap the "rights" of others. If the "gay elite", as lesbian author Tammy Bruce calls them, want to go head to head with society, then citizens should not feel intimidated into silence by political correctness. There *are* major issues to discuss, there *are* other people to consider, and anybody who tries to shut down debate by shouting and bullying opponents rather than tackling the issues generally has something to hide.

I have happily worked for gay bosses, alongside gay colleagues, and lived in a house with gay men. Do not lecture me about homophobia. Instead, deal with the issues raised in this book.

People will attack *Eve's Bite* because it demolishes a number of sacred cow myths permeating the West. They will attack me, as well. I would hope that in this book my arguments against named individuals are based on what they have actually said and what they have actually done. It is not good enough to ridicule Hitler, just for being Hitler. It is the ideas and actions of Hitler that make him a legitimate target.

There is a rule on the internet called "Godwin's Law", which basically says that if a debate continues long enough eventually someone will be compared to Hitler and the Nazis. In this book, there is a very good reason for comparison to the Nazis: because Nazi techniques are being aped in some of these propaganda campaigns and because the Nazis were very, very good at social control.

Eugenics is not evil, for example, simply because Hitler supported it. But Hitler is evil for supporting eugenics. And so are modern eugenicists.

Am I arguing against multiculturalism? Only to the extent that if a culture brings its politics with it, which Islam does by definition, it requires much better planning than the West has shown to date. Hindus, Buddhists, whatever, none of those religions are political. Islam is. You cannot tolerate "Islam" in the same way you do other religions, unless the ground rules are made very, very clear.

My biggest wish for this book is that you will realize how you have been played like a fiddle by social engineers, and allow yourself to see the world as a fast-growing number of others in the West are seeing it: as if waking up from a deep, deep darkness.

If you enjoyed this book, I recommend:

ON CULTURE: *America Alone* by Mark Steyn; *The Death of Right & Wrong* by Tammy Bruce; *Godless* by Ann Coulter; *The Marketing of Evil* by David Kupelian; *Shut Up & Sing* by Laura Ingraham; *Bias* by Bernard Goldberg; *Persecution* by David Limbaugh; *The Politically Incorrect Guide to Islam (and the Crusades)* by Robert Spencer; *The Enemy Within* by Michael Savage

ON DARWINISM: *The Privileged Planet* by Guillermo Gonzalez and Jay Richards; *Not by Chance* by Lee Spetner; *Darwin's Black Box* by Michael Behe; *The Creator & The Cosmos* by Hugh Ross; *Darwin on Trial* by Phillip Johnson; *Icons of Evolution* by Jonathan Wells; *Signs of Intelligence* edited by William Dembski and James Kushiner

ON THE EVIDENCE FOR CHRISTIANITY: *The Case For Christ* by Lee Strobel; *The Case For Faith* by Lee Strobel; *New Evidence That Demands A Verdict* by Josh McDowell; *Fabricating Jesus* by Craig Evans; *Reinventing Jesus* by Komoszewski, Sawyer & Wallace

If you need to purchase a digital version of this book for instant text searching and active hyperlinks, or you would like to purchase another hard copy, please visit www.evesbite.com